Western Fictions, Black Realities

Western Fictions, Black Realities

MEANINGS OF BLACKNESS AND MODERNITIES

EDITED BY
Isabel Soto
Violet Showers Johnson

MICHIGAN STATE UNIVERSITY PRESS | *East Lansing* ■ LIT VERLAG | *Münster*

Copyright © 2012 by LIT Verlag

♾ The paper used in this publication meets the minimum requirements of ANSI/NISO Z39.48-1992 (R 1997) (Permanence of Paper).

LIT Verlag
Münster

Michigan State University Press
East Lansing, Michigan 48823-5245

Printed and bound in the United States of America.

18 17 16 15 14 13 12   1 2 3 4 5 6 7 8 9 10

LIBRARY OF CONGRESS CATALOGING-IN-PUBLICATION DATA
Western fictions, black realities : meanings of blackness and modernities / edited by Isabel Soto and Violet Showers Johnson.
  p. cm.
Includes bibliographical references.
ISBN 978-1-61186-044-3 (pbk. : alk. paper) 1. African Americans—Race identity. 2. African Americans—Intellectual life. 3. United States—Civilization—African American influences. 4. United States—Race relations. I. Soto, Isabel. II. Johnson, Violet Showers.
E185.625.W43 2012
305.896'073—dc23
                           2011042100

Cover design by Sharp Des!gns, Inc.
Cover art is *A Black World in Motion* by Percy A. Johnson Jr. © 2011

g green press initiative Michigan State University Press is a member of the Green Press Initiative and is committed to developing and encouraging ecologically responsible publishing practices. For more information about the Green Press Initiative and the use of recycled paper in book publishing, please visit *www.greenpressinitiative.org*.

■ Visit Michigan State University Press at *www.msupress.org*

Contents

Acknowledgements   vii

Isabel Soto and Violet Showers Johnson
Introduction
Blackness and Modernities: Varieties and Re-Examinations   1

I.   Literary and Cultural Perspectives

Clarence Sholé Johnson
Resistance to Modernity: Two Contesting Viewpoints   23

María M. García Lorenzo
The Unwhitening of Discourse: The Gothic in African-American Literature   47

Christopher Mulvey
The Modernity of James Weldon Johnson and the African American Twentieth Century   61

Claude Julien
Wolf Whistle and *A Killing in this Town*: Two Ways to Exorcise Racial Hatred   77

Alexander Beissenhirtz
Theorizing the Vernacular Modernism of Jazz: The *New Jazz Studies*   95

II.   Race, Diasporas and Modern Encounters

David Abulafia
The First Atlantic Slaves, 1350-1520: Conquest, Slavery and the Opening of the Atlantic   107

Paul Delaney
From Tourist to Bureau Chief: Witnessing Spain's Racial Emergence   129

Mar Gallego-Durán
African American Women Travelers: Claiming Voice and Transgressing Boundaries   137

Ime A. S. Kerlee
Somos una Mezcla?: Re-Constructing Race in *Dominicanidad*   153

III. HARLEM RENAISSANCE: LEGACIES OF AN AFRICAN AMERICAN EPOCH

Simon Dickel
Modernism, the Harlem Renaissance, and Negotiations of Black Gay
Identity in the 1980s ... 183

Alison D. Goeller
Zora on the Mountain: Zora Neal Hurston's Artistic Exodus in
Moses, Man of the Mountain ... 199

Małgorzata Ziółek-Sowińska
African American Modernism and the Music of Duke Ellington ... 211

Emil Sîrbulescu
Louis Armstrong's Unknown Addiction, or the (Un)Willing
Autobiographer ... 229

IV. RACIALIZED BODIES, ACTIVIST MINDS

Simone A. James Alexander
Embodied Subjects: Policing and Politicking the Black Female Body ... 251

Georg Bauer
Challenging the Great White Hopes: Black Boxers in Film ... 269

Yvonne Gutenberger
I am Remembered as a Hairdo: Angela Davis's *Autobiography* as a
Revision of the Public Persona and Self-Reconstruction as Political
Activist ... 297

Notes on the Contributors ... 317

Acknowledgements
This project has been some time in the making, having had to negotiate all the obstacles, distractions, and other complications that are the lot of a working academic. "Life. Always life" (as Raymond Carver put it) has interrupted and driven this volume in equal measures.

And finish it we did. Initial thanks for persuading us to edit the present volume must go to FORECAAST General Editors Maria Diedrich and Sabine Broeck, not just for the trust they placed in us but also for sensing something that emerged only as the project unfolded, namely, the editorial and personal rapport that has helped this volume to see the light of day.

Of course, the volume exists in the first instance as a result of the 2007 CAAR Madrid conference and the people involved. This includes the conference committee comprising the then CAAR President, Chris Mulvey, Hanna Wallinger (Secretary), Mar Gallego (Treasurer), and Isabel Soto (local conference secretary). It goes without saying that none of us on the committee would have made it past first base without the dedicated support of the legions of student helpers, department and faculty members, and employees of the host institution, Spain's Universidad Nacional de Educación a Distancia (UNED), who quite literally made the whole thing happen. The UNED provided logistical and financial backing through the Departamento de Filologías Extranjeras y sus Lingüísticas, the Facultad de Filología, and the Vicerrectorado de Coordinación y Extensión Universitaria. The Ministerio de Educación y Ciencia also gave substantial funding and the Ministerio de Cultura kindly allowed the premises of the Museo de América to host a number of events, as well as giving permission to reproduce a fragment of a *casta* painting for the conference poster – all free of charge! La Fundación General de la UNED provided the organizational framework, as well as designing the conference web-page.

Our deepest thanks to the contributors who have remained committed to the project and been willing to share their work. That this volume exists at all is testimony to their patience, professionalism, and generosity. Our gratitude also to the anonymous readers who contributed to the final outcome with their time and unfailingly valuable feedback, and to Jesper Reddig, Universität Münster, for his meticulous formatting and copy-editing.

Life, ultimately, includes those with whom we are blessed to share it on a daily basis, our families. The time we have devoted to this project has been their time also. In the case of Percy Johnson Jr. (PJ), that precious gift has yielded palpable consequences. To him we owe and gratefully acknowledge the design of our book cover.

The Editors
June 2011

Isabel Soto and Violet Showers Johnson

Introduction
Blackness and Modernities: Varieties and Re-Examinations

Very often, the most used words, terms, and concepts are the most problematic. Modernity/Modernities and Blackness are such concepts, as undisputedly confirmed by the plethora of heated debates and discourses they have elicited in the social sciences, especially, but also in the humanities and other disciplines. The title of this book contains these two complex concepts. Therefore, a necessary prelude, which we undertake in this introduction, is to take the bull by the horn from the outset and comment on these premises within which this volume is couched. We do not intend to present a loaded, coded critique accessible only to intellectuals and academics who craft and interrogate the many narratives on the subject. Rather, we hope to provide a relevant backdrop for the diverse essays in this work.

Modernity, Modernities
As a marker of epochs, the idea of modernity is centuries-old. By the late twentieth century, it demarcated pre-modern, modern, and post-modern. Since its introduction as a phenomenon that denoted development and advancement, distinguishing the old from the new or traditional from contemporary, modernity for the most part has been posited as universal, uniform, predictable, and inevitable world-altering processes. One of the foremost twentieth-century exemplars of this depiction is American economist Walt Whitman Rostow's *Stages of Economic Growth*. In this classic, published in 1960, Rostow outlines the five stages through which societies must pass in their progression from traditional to modern, industrialized, technological, consumer-based entities. Rostow's *Stages* is illustrative of the emphasis on a singular modernity premised on Western/European/Euro-American cultures and societies. This notion of a universal, Western modernity has been subjected to hard-hitting criticisms, even before Rostow; to quote from Leszek Kolakowski's book title, "modernity has been on endless trial." The interrogations became acutely pronounced since the second

half of the twentieth century. The complex array of post-World War II developments – the rise and fall of communism; nationalist and independence movements in Asia, Africa, and the Caribbean; liberation struggles in Latin America; the Civil Rights and Black Power Movements; the economic ascendency of certain Asian nations and the emergence of the Asian Tigers; transnationalism and globalism – exposed more than ever the flaws in how modernity had been defined, interpreted, and applied. By the first decade of the twenty-first century reexaminations of existing modernity theories challenged the hegemony of the West in the master narrative. Scholars revisited questions about what constitutes "modern" and how modernity is achieved. Fuller, more objective attention to non-Western societies and movements furiously questioned Western domination (or even monopoly) of modernity. It was in this tradition, for example, that a 2003 anthology used cases like the Iranian Revolution, the struggle against Apartheid in South Africa, and the impact of colonial policies and neo-colonial Structural Adjustment Programs in sub-Saharan Africa to show that historical forces that shape the contemporary world or modernity are disparate in their origins and outcomes, while remaining legitimately modern (Kaiwar and Mazumdar).

By bringing non-Western societies into the core of the discourse on modernity the revisionists emphasized that modernity and Westernization are not synonymous. As Charles Taylor and Benjamin Lee explain:

> Transitions to what we might recognize as modernity, taking place in different civilizations, will produce different results, reflecting their divergent starting points. Their understandings of the person, social relations, states of mind, goods and bads, virtues and vices, sacred and profane, are likely to be distinct. The future of the world will be one in which societies will undergo change in institutions and outlook, and for some these changes will be parallel, but it will not converge, because new differences will emerge from the old. Thus, instead of speaking of "modernity" in the singular, we should speak of "multiple modernities."

Thus, a replacement narrative emerged to rectify the deficiencies of a singular, hegemonic outlook on modernity. The first decade of the twenty-first century saw a burgeoning in the literature on multiple modernities. The whole 2000 Winter volume of *Daedalus* was devoted to the subject. The main objective of this journal collection and the other studies was to demonstrate the multiplicity and diversity of modernity. As Shmuel Noah Eisenstadt, one of the foremost proponents of this approach, points out, "Western patterns of modernity are not the only 'authentic' modernities, though they enjoy historical precedence and continue to be a basic reference point for others" (*Multiple Modernities*, 8). Diverse scholars, social scientists in particular, researched and discussed how multiple modernities allowed for a more meaningful depiction of modern realities (Eisenstadt "Multiple Modernities," *Multiple Modernities*, and *Comparative Civilizations*; Wagner; Kamali; Roniger and Waisman). Multiple modernities accommodated the study of a variety of distinct modernities, from Swahili modernities (Caplan and Topan) to Chinese modernities (Martin and Heinrich) and Indian modernities (Sivaramakrishnan and Agrawal).

While multiple modernities provided alternative ways of studying modernity, the new approach did not end scholarly re-examinations, for multiple modernities itself is also under endless scrutiny. Some critics have called for a complete return to singular modernity, while others have appealed for a revised singular modernity which reflects the multiplicity within it. Sociologist Volker Schmidt is in the forefront in calling for a return to a singular but complex modernity in order to ferret out not a host of different modernities, instead to recognize and discuss the varieties contained within the one modernity. Eisenstadt recognizes, despite his path-breaking contributions to the discourse, that he will not have the last word. He points out:

> in all societies these attempts at interpreting modernity are continually changing under the impact of changing historical forces, giving rise to new movements that will come, in time, to reinterpret yet again the meaning of modernity. ("Multiple Modernities" 24)

He alludes to the inevitable futility that awaits every re-examination: "whatever else they may be, modernities in all their variety are precisely those responses that leave the problematic intact" (*Multiple Modernities* 4).

One aspect of this problematic is marginalization within modern entities. Much has been said and written about non-Western societies drawn into the modern world of the West but grappling with tensions arising from being part of that world. While attention to Western versus non-Western is important, focus on tensions and awkwardness within the Western world is also crucial. Singular modernity is not only Western, it is also white. As James Perkinson, examining modern theology, discovers, modernity privileges whiteness as much as it does Western. How, then, should African American experiences within the "modern,

Western" world of the United States of America and other Western societies be studied? Do African Americans feel similar tensions from at once belonging to and alienated from America's modernity? What are the specific modernities of people of African descent in societies persistently projected as of the West and that both subtly and overtly are white? Are these modernities shaped and sustained by blackness?

Blackness in Modernities
Whether acknowledged, ignored, or denied, Blackness, in its many forms, is central in singular and multiple modernities. Famous collector and promoter of modern art Paul Guillame remarked in France in 1930: "The spirit of modern man – or modern woman – needs to be nourished by the civilization of the Negro" (cited in Ikonné 4). Acknowledgements like Guillame's were rare. Instead, more typical was the relegation of the Negro, defined by his/her blackness, to the margins. This marginalization (or in some cases complete obscurity) never went unchallenged, as the black contributors themselves were always cognizant of their vitality in projects of modernism. Invoking this centuries-old reinterpretation from the margins, prominent African American scholar Henry Louis Gates Jr. declared:

> Only a black person alienated from black language-use could fail to understand that we have been deconstructing white people's languages and discourses since that dreadful day in 1619 when we were marched off the boat in Virginia. Derrida did not invent deconstruction, we did! (34)

Around the same time that Guillame was invoking the vitality of the Negro, across the Atlantic scholars and artists, pointing to cultural production, that indispensable component of modernity, were also deconstructing Western fictions in their attempts to present the realities. Alain Locke noted, in his commentary on the contributions of blacks to American art and literature: "it is a fallacy that the overlord influences the peasant and remains uninfluenced by him" (234).

By the end of the twentieth century, the critics of Western/white, Euro/American-centric interpretations of modernity could benefit from the earlier generations. Building on the foundations, this new crop of intellectuals took the discourse further, problematizing the very notion of blackness and arguing beyond varieties of Western/white modernities, advancing instead alternative modernities that speak more specifically to the black experience across nations and regions. The burgeoning field of black cultural studies, represented by scholars like Manthia Diawara, Stuart Hall, and Paul Gilroy, set out to illustrate how African diasporic cultural production confuses the simple definitions, periodization and application of modernity and post-modernity. Paul Gilroy in his seminal work *The Black Atlantic: Modernity and Double Consciousness* (1993), more than any other scholar, simultaneously showed the viability and validity of alternative black diaspora modernities and their shortcomings. Whether criticized for privileging an Anglo black Atlantic (Zeleza) or unconvincingly deconstructing race and nation (Hlongwane), Gilroy's "counterculture" of modernity will not be the last work on the re-examinations of black realities in modernities.

Whatever the issues raised in the debates around black modernities, the crux was (and is) deciphering the realities of black roles and experiences in the complex arena of modernism. Much of the polemics derive from the malleability of blackness itself. Thinkers and re-thinkers have grappled with the various manifestations of blackness and what they denote or connote. Even after all the path-breaking reassessments pioneered by black cultural studies of the 1980s and 1990s, conceptualization of blackness is still an unfinished business. Attending to the loose ends, Cecil Foster in his much talked about recent work *Blackness and Modernity: The Colour of Humanity and the Quest for Freedom* (2007), challenges existing notions of blackness driven exclusively by the somatic – color. Invoking the Canadian multiculturalism experiment, he argues for an ontological blackness that minimizes color. Foster's approach echoes Clarence Sholé Johnson's earlier study which proposes a "reconceptualization of blackness that is both counterhegemonic and color transcending" (174). Without attempting to do the impossible here – a comprehensive analysis of rethinking blackness – the most important point of the many reexaminations of blackness must be stated: as many questions as they attempt to answer, they reveal the multiplicity of blackness and its ever-shifting interpretations.

As the many debates on modernity versus modernities, and blackness and black modernities rage on, the scholarly works they produce will continue to explain the diverse and fascinating ramifications of blackness in modernities.

The Volume

At the height of the rethinking and reexaminations, the Collegium for African American Research (CAAR) held its Seventh International Conference in Madrid, Spain. The Call for Papers (CFP), issued in the summer of 2006, underscored the Collegium's attention to the unfolding intellectual and scholarly developments: the 2007 conference was planned to address Blackness and Modernities. The essays in this book began as plenary and panel presentations at this conference. While the conference was itself a reflection of the growing discourses on modernity and modernities, blackness and black modernities, it did not set out to rigidly address prescribed alternative modernities or suggest definitive paradigms of blackness. Rather, it appealed to flexibility, broad interpretations, and diverse narratives. As the CFP put it:

> The African American Experience of the modern world can be dated to 1500, to 1776, to 1865, to 1920, to 1965, to 2000? The experience is multiple, the people many, and the modern manifold. [...] We want to consider ways in which peoples originated in Africa and living in the Americas have created as well as come to terms with modernism.

Although the following essays have developed further since the conference, they still reflect the essence of the call of 2006.

The volume is divided into four thematic sections, representing a broad chronology, from the era of the Atlantic Slave Trade to the last quarter of the twentieth century: "Literary and Cultural Perspectives," "Race, Diasporas and Modern Encounters," "Harlem Renaissance: Legacies of an African American Epoch," and "Racialized Bodies, Activist Minds." Multiplicity in being black, in being "modern," is a significant element of commonality among the essays gathered here. So, too, is the influence, whether overt or implied, acknowledged or mediated, of W. E. B. Du Bois. It would seem that in discussions of African American expressive output in the twentieth century and beyond, engagement with Du Bois in one form or another is practically required – if only to refute or question his work. Clarence Sholé Johnson's opening essay not only engages with the vastly influential theory of double consciousness, it does so in order to challenge a reading of Du Bois by one of the most arresting scholars in present-day African American studies, Molefi K. Asante, who provocatively asserts: "there is no double consciousness. I announce an end to Du Bois's errant conclusion."

Focusing on the rhetorical device of narrative viewpoint – who tells the story – Johnson argues that the double point of view inherent to Du Boisian theory, whether it is white racism that is 'telling the story' of black inferiority, or black voices who are contesting that story, the two narratives of a single reality necessarily confirm double consciousness. Moreover, they are mutually reinforcing or 'inclusive.' Thus, insofar as Asante's 'contestational' vantage point is in response to the 'denigrating' vantage point, he is inevitably partaking of double consciousness. Citing the work of Jane Anna Gordon, Johnson also and crucially frames the insight afforded by double consciousness as "a *theoretical gift/contribution* from the colonized to the Western canon" (emphasis in original). The enlisting of African American epistemology as a means to engage with texts and lived subjectivities not obviously (or not only) representative of an African American tradition, reminds us that Du Bois articulated a mode of being-in-the-world that has become – consciously or not – central to much intellectual practice today. Double consciousness has not only been adopted as a critical and analytical tool for twentieth- and twenty-first-century texts, it is also central to innumerable studies focused on historical periods prior to Du Bois' formulation; that Johnson extensively references Paul Gilroy's seminal work *The Black Atlantic,* whose sweep encompasses Enlightenment philosophy to Toni Morrison and twentieth-century "diaspora musics," is no accident.

Whether explicitly referenced or not, Gilroy's strategy of "unwhitening" Western modernity by adducing the presence and active participation of (forcibly displaced) Africans and peoples of color, also underpins many of the essays in this volume. María García Lorenzo's contribution is a case in point. She notes that the gothic genre emerges with the Enlightenment, the rise of scientific racism and the phenotypical taxonomy of human groups, and the consolidation of racial slavery in the Americas. The mastery of letters, additionally, became a crucial index of a person's human status. García Lorenzo advances the argument that while American gothic appropriates black history, present-day African American subversion of gothic codes serves to re-narrativize that appropriated history.

Insofar as gothic is concerned with transgression, that is, the observance or not of boundaries, the genre naturally accommodates coeval fears of racial admixture and supposed degeneration. García Lorenzo notes that gothic literature "involves both assertion and subversion of established patterns of authority," allowing for those anxieties to be mediated. Notions of and anxieties about authority framed, for example, questions of authorship related to slave narrative. The "authorial passing" associated with the genre, argues García Lorenzo, entails what might be termed "cultural ventriloquism" in turn implying the seizure and mobilization of a white discursive space. This act of repossession by the "culturally dead" (echoes of Orlando Patterson, here) overturns the genre, so that we find slave narrative foregrounding certain motifs – enclosed spaces, violent family dispersals, sexual transgression – associated with gothic.

Discourse is of course a two-way street, so that to the extent that American gothic has undergone a process of "unwhitening" enacted by African American cultural expressiveness, so too has the reader: "The gothic as genre [...] (re)emerges as a racialized discourse [...]. The point is that the reader can be unwhitened, too," declares García Lorenzo. This last may be the most transgressive act of all, recalling Du Bois' invitation to the white reader to "step within the veil" and participate in a racialized reality – an invitation, in short, to embrace (a discursive) miscegenation.

If critical readings of gothic must accommodate its racially hybrid formulation then, equally, "Modernity, the Modern, and Modernism" cannot be constructed exclusively as white, Anglo-American practices. Christopher Mulvey's essay explores the work of James Weldon Johnson in order to arrive at "a special understanding of Modernity." Mulvey drives his point home by, among other things, comparing Johnson with America's proto-citizen, Benjamin Franklin. A comparativist approach tends to reveal even as it contrasts two components and, in this case, Franklin emerges as being "distinguished by his lack of talent" precisely in those areas where Johnson excelled: poetry, music, and writing novels. Mulvey inscribes Johnson's life and works within an African American tradition of modernity, inevitably framed by (a belated) race consciousness and strategies of resistance to discrimination. Collective as these experiences may be, Mulvey stresses Johnson's specificity – he was not "'any kind of Negro'" but of "a special kind." For one thing, he "strenuously resist[ed]" self-portrayal as victim in his 'real' autobiography, *Along This Way: The Autobiography of James Weldon Johnson* (1933). For another, he was multi-talented – massively so. His gifts manifested themselves not just in his mastery of several artistic forms, but also in an ability to adapt to and take control of any situation, from speaking Spanish to averting his own lynching, to wearing a Panama hat. This protean gift reminds us that modernity and blackness are not undifferentiated, homogeneous, and immutable categories; there are many modernities, many forms of being black.

If Johnson's *Autobiography of an Ex-Colored Man* takes the reader into the terrain of fiction, then that fiction is not "any kind" of fiction but of a "special kind." Its embracing of the passing genre places it within the Harlem Renaissance tradition even if its re-gendering of the tragic mulatto theme acts to complicate passing narrative conventions. Further, the filtering of reality through an *individual* consciousness reaches out to modernism as much as its *race* consciousness places *The Autobiography* within the discursive tradition of William Wells Brown and Charles Chesnutt. What Mulvey designates as the "relocation of the genealogy of the Ex-Colored Man" seems to echo the protean skills of its author; in addition to the multiple discursive allegiances just noted, Mulvey reminds us that the work was also published twice: once anonymously in 1912, once with full acknowledgement of authorship in 1927, this second publication "relaunch[ing] the novel as a special contribution to the Harlem Renaissance."

Mulvey places Johnson within Anglophone modernity itself, a "direct descendant" not just of "the ships that very shortly after 1492 [...] began to take Africans across the Atlantic," but also of such intellectual and race leaders as Douglass, Wells Brown, Crummell, and Delaney. Drawing on Gilroy, Mulvey cogently argues that, ultimately, the African in the Americas is at the heart of modernity and deserves consideration as the "prototypical modern being," not least as a result of the experience of deracination, alienation and existential loss: "The Americas were the Waste Land."

Claude Julien's essay reminds us that the discourse of race is not circumscribed to representations of blackness, nor indeed that race consciousness is closed off to white authors. Taking two contemporary novels, *Killing in This Town* (2006) by African American author Olympia Vernon, and *Wolf Whistle* (1993) by white male author, Lewis Nordan, Julien explores the novelistic appropriation of two racially motivated murders, Emmett Till's and James Byrd's. The narration of these gruesome events reminds us that the racial terror associated with the Black Atlantic and also an intrinsic element in the forging of Western modernity, is part of our living memory as well as the present. Once more, African American epistemology – a racialized body of knowledge – reveals itself to be critical to the ways in which we reconstruct and mediate ("exorcise") our collective past: black and white, Western and non-Western, Anglophone and not Anglophone.

Paul Gilroy's phrase "the volatile core event of Afro-Atlantic cultural creation" (73) even if not written with jazz expressly in mind, orients us toward what he also terms "the phatic and the ineffable" (ibid.), that is, black musics. That black cultural forms, including music, are modern as well as modernist, Gilroy has no doubt, characterized as they are by "their hybrid, creole origins in the West" (ibid.). Alexander Beissenhirtz builds on that constituent legacy to explore multiple and evolving ways of critiquing jazz and arrive at a "politicized counter-discourse to traditionalist 'master narratives'" on jazz. Framing his arguments in light of Bernd Ostendorf's formulation of jazz as a "*vernacular modernist* idiom" (emphasis in original), Beissenhirtz, stresses also jazz's multiple sources: "jazz is not exclusively Western. [...] it is deeply rooted in the black folk and its music." Perhaps its most remarkable attribute is its conjoining of a "[vernacular] subculture" with "an aesthetic avant-garde," or what Beissenhirtz identifies as jazz's ability to "mediat[e] a cultural contradiction."

This cultural contradiction is reflected in the various debates on its formal qualities and in which seemingly irreconcilable positions are staked out. Amiri Baraka links jazz to bebop and the drive to exceptionalize it ("to restore jazz [...] to its original separateness"), while traditionalists such as Wynston Marsalis, Stanley Crouch, and Albert Murray strive to situate jazz at the heart of American cultural expressiveness. This latter view is perhaps most closely associated with Ken Burns' "controversial" documentary television series, *Jazz* (2001), which posits a teleological, uninterrupted, and "coherent" jazz trajectory from folk to middle class idiom. The traditionalist narrative thrust of Burns' documentary excises non-traditionalist elements such as "jazz avant-garde, jazz-derived experimental music and fusion" as well as performers from Europe and other parts of the world.

Beissenhirtz identifies thus the battle lines around which discussions and interpretations of jazz are drawn: on the one hand, "official history," "built-in limitations," "an exclusionary version"; on the other, "complicated and variegated cultural phenomena," "revisionist history." It is the latter stance with which the New Jazz Studies concerns itself, promoting an "inclusive narrative" that identifies jazz as a "discourse of alterity" and "hybridization." Ultimately, Beissenhirtz's arguments reveal how the inclusive project of the New Jazz Studies in fact honors the "volatile core event" that led to black musics, brought to the West literally on the backs of Afro-Atlantic peoples.

In the second section in this volume, "Race, Diasporas and Modern Encounters," David Abulafia actually focuses on that inaugural moment in modernity, the "foundations for the intensive trans-Atlantic slave trade of the sixteenth to the early nineteenth centuries." Abulafia adds to the growing body of scholarship (including his own) on the role of the Iberian powers in the Atlantic and trans-Atlantic slave trade during the early modern period. In so doing, he also complicates Gilroy's narrative which, however persuasive, is emphatically Anglophone and centered on the Enlightenment and post-Enlightenment. What Abulafia's shift in emphasis demonstrates is that early modern and Renaissance Portugal and Spain both "laid the foundations" for the Atlantic slave trade even as they, especially the Spanish, grappled with the semantic field of slavery and racial othering, in particular as it related to the matter of who could and could not rightfully be considered a slave.

Abulafia notes that Atlantic slavery actually preceded that of the New World, commencing with the invasion of the Canary Islands in the late pre-modern era. Slave raids led to a dramatic depopulation of the Eastern Canary islands and the importing of Berber slaves from the facing West African coast. To these African slaves were later added slaves from further South, creating thus the precedent for the later trans-Oceanic event, "when African slaves were carried to the Caribbean to replace the rapidly declining Taíno Indian population." By the mid-fifteenth century Portugal was "acting as a middleman" for European, especially Spanish, slave markets, such as the "great slave emporia of Seville and Valencia." While notions of race or *raza* at this point, in Spain at least, were linked to non-Christian lineage, Abulafia strongly suggests that this was the scenario from which emerged later practices of differentiation and discrimination as a result of skin colour:

> Although some of the Africans seen in Iberia were free, most of those at liberty were freedmen or freedwomen who had first arrived as slaves; unfreedom seemed to characterise dark-skinned people, in the eyes of those Europeans who encountered them, whether as slave traders, slave owners or passers-by. From this developed the notion that their inferiority was something inherent, conferred by their racial distinctiveness.

If, in the ensuing millennium the Iberian inductive role in the Black Atlantic has been occluded by, among other things, a dominant Anglo-American scholarship, Paul Delaney reminds us that present-day Spain cannot be disengaged from the migratory routes of the black diaspora. Delaney begins by invoking twentieth-century African American connections with Spain: Langston Hughes, the black Abraham Lincoln Brigaders, Richard Wright, Chester Himes... As an African American himself, he can add his own experiences commencing with his first visit when, as a G.I. stationed in Bordeaux in the

1950s, he caught the train across the Franco-Spanish border to Barcelona. Race inevitably rears its problematic head in an unfortunate episode involving white Americans who barred Delaney's entrance to a July 4th party at a Zaragoza hotel to which he had been invited by the manager.

Much like Langston Hughes' brief to cover the involvement of peoples of color in the Spanish Civil War, Delaney takes "special note of color in Spain on the occasion of my every visit." His response to a society still recovering from a devastating civil conflict is not as scathing – or idiosyncratic – as Richard Wright's in *Pagan Spain* (1957) based on his visit during the same period. For Delaney, Spaniards "were not sensitive to nor knowledgeable about other races, especially mine." They had "a kind of simple, if not simplistic, notion of black people" which was, nevertheless, distinct from the hatred-infused "low regard American whites held of blacks." Delaney shrewdly notes, "Spaniards had *seen* black people throughout [Spain's] history, but they had not really *experienced* us" (emphasis in original).

In 1987 and as *New York Times* Bureau Chief stationed in Madrid, Delaney is struck by huge changes in Spanish society, including a growing racial diversity driven by decolonization of North African territories and the lure of Spain's new-found wealth. The North African and sub-Saharan immigrants that were making their way to Spain were at that time mostly moving on to France and other Northern European countries. Small pockets remained in Spain, however, providing the vanguard of what has become an influx that has grown exponentially in the ensuing decades.

Even during slavery African Americans were traveling back and forth across the Atlantic and establishing "the importance of mobility" in accessing "a better life in freedom," according to Mar Gallego. Gallego's gendered reading of voluntary displacement or travel also draws on slave narrative as a precursor genre in relation to later travel narratives. Thus Mary Prince's 1831 slave narrative *The History of Mary Prince* creates the parameters for travel narratives by freedwomen such as *A Narrative of the Life and Travels of Mrs. Nancy Prince* (1850), Mary Seacole's *The Wonderful Adventures of Mrs. Seacole in Many Lands* (1857), and Julia Cooper's *A Voice from the South* (1892).

Travel narratives are a form of life writing that, when produced by women of color, engage tropes of mobility in very gender- and race-specific ways. European sojourns by African American women in the early twentieth century extend the empowerment project linked to travel that was articulated by nineteenth-century slave foremothers. The narratives of Addie Hunton, Gwendolyn Bennett, and Jessie Fauset not only nod in the direction of these past accounts, but also undertake to "dispel [...] racist and sexist stereotypical images of black women." Personal enrichment and the ability to switch cultural and linguistic codes are yoked in these narratives to the metaphor of travel – a sort of reverse middle-passage, if you will – in order to deconstruct prevailing racist and patriarchal ideologies surrounding women of color.

Gender conjoins with mobility once more in Ime Kerlee's comprehensive portrait of racial, cultural, and linguistic *mestizaje* among "transmigrant" Dominicans in Santo Domingo and New York. Central to this narrative is the construction and re-construction of racial identity which, in Kerlee's analysis, emerges as plural and fluid, challenging historical attempts to fix Dominicans in terms of racial categories. She notes the U.S. preference for racial binaries in contrast to Dominicans' embracing of fluidity.

Not the least interesting aspect of Kerlee's essay is its deconstruction of whiteness, mediated through strategic attempts by Dominicans to claim it in order to survive in a local and global context. Blackness and African lineage were suppressed while whiteness was "redefined in order to include those who were not visibly white." Kerlee also links these strategies to other forms of ontological and political constructedness: those of nation, sexuality, and reproduction. Whiteness thus became framed by "an ideological struggle for power," that could and did, where expedient, ignore actual skin color. Kerlee identifies two key textual instances in this process: *Enriquillo* (1882) by Manuel de Jesús Galván, and the creation of the *campesino Cibeaño*. Both centered on figures who represented a fusion of Taíno (indigenous) and Spanish (colonizing) cultures, the ensuing hybridity of which served to suppress further Dominican links to African influence even as it reinforced the cultural fantasy of whiteness.

It goes almost without saying that the *Enriquillo* and *campesino Cibeaño* constructs enlisted masculinity in their parable of white nation-building. The Trujillo regime extended the discourse of whiteness to Dominican women, placing light skinned and/or white women at the center of national representation – and Trujillo's own sexual preferences, revealing once more ways in which the politics of race intersect with the politics of gender.

Comparing racial politics of the Dominican Republic ("[a] contradictory fluidity and fixity") with those of the U.S. ("a binary system of white and black"), Kerlee observes that upon arriving in the U.S., Dominican migrants were forced to "beg[in] the process of racialization anew." It is this process of re-racialization that makes migrants (as opposed to non-migrants) more alert to the constructedness of race, even if the Dominican Republic already accommodates a questioning of racial discourses.

In the first essay in the section "Harlem Renaissance: Legacies of an African American Epoch," Simon Dickel places two Harlem Renaissance texts at the heart of modernism, thus adding to the body of critical work that complicates the view of Western literary modernism as prevailingly white and Euro-American. Dickel implicitly endorses claims such as Toni Morrison's that "there is no escape from racially inflected language" (13) as well as Gilroy's proposition of a creolized Western modernity, and forges connections between Harlem Renaissance writers Richard Bruce Nugent and Wallace Thurman, and contemporary artists Steven Corbin and Isaac Julien. He further prizes open the time frame of the Harlem Renaissance even as he vexes that period's "disregard" for the "bisexual, interracial and polyamorous aspects" of Nugent's text, noting also that our ability to reference these elements at all reflects the critical shift in the late 1980s prompted by the HIV/Aids crisis.

Nugent's text, then, is both transgressive in its portrayal of the intersections of race, sexuality, and gender and groundbreaking in its anticipation of present-day queer aesthetics. Thurman's *Infants of the Spring* subtly evokes Nugent's "Smoke, Lilies and Jade" and takes up the central concern of that text with transgressive sexual and racial allegiances. Over half a century later, Corbin's 1989 novel, *No Easy Place to Be*, returns the reader to the Harlem Renaissance and Nugent's foundational queer text. Racial politics (including passing) once more intersect with sexuality and gender choices. However, Corbin rewrites the sexual ambiguities and ambivalences of "Smoke, ..." by fixing his characters' sexuality and positing unambiguous homosexual and heterosexual identities. Dickel argues that Corbin thus "strengthens black gay identity and supports an afrocentric black gay agenda."

The self-consciously avant-garde aesthetics of Isaac Julien's film *Looking for Langston* (1989) situates this work within a context of modernity; the engagement with black modernism through voice-over readings from Nugent and Langston Hughes establish its transgressive sexual pedigree. If Julien's narrative looks to Nugent and Hughes as early exponents of queer poetics, he crafts a narrative of queer allegiances over time through allusions to white gay artists such as Carl Van Vechten and photographers George Platt Lynes and Robert

Mapplethorpe. Yet Julien's film, according to Dickel, is more in tune with the agenda of disambiguation of Corbin's novel. *Looking for Langston* suppresses references to whiteness throughout, thus "unequivocally support[ing] the project of constructing a black gay literary heritage." Ultimately, while Julien subtly rewrites the transgressive poetics of Nugent's text, *Looking for Langston* nevertheless honors the "modernist experiments of the Harlem Renaissance."

The remaining three essays in this section likewise identify the Harlem Renaissance as a locus of creativity and modernist aesthetics. Alison Goeller's essay on Zora Neale Hurston returns us to the role of African American vernacular, this time in language, as a constituent element of the expressive output of that period. The vernacular not only challenges *normative* discourse, it also and strategically complicates *white* normativity. Adding gender to this cumulative challenge, Hurston articulates her resistance to racial and gender paradigms principally through the "power of language" and, specifically, voice. According to Goeller, Hurston's novel *Moses, Man of the Mountain* (1939) can be read against the author's struggle to assert her artistic identity, in which the function of voice and the work it does, are central.

Goeller suggests that Moses be read as a sort of alter ego for Hurston, to the extent that his uncertainties about who he is are reflective not only of Hurston's own "struggle with her identity as an artist," but also her straddling of multiple expressive forms: "writer, anthropologist, folklorist, playwright, performer, teacher." This vocational ("schizoid" according to her biographer, Robert Hemenway) multiplicity, makes her richly representative of modernism and the Harlem Renaissance, as well as a precursor of "the post-Modernist penchant for collapsing generic boundaries." *Moses* is a remarkable text, notes Goeller, not only because of its efforts to fuse "black creative style, biblical tone, ethnic humor, and legendary reference," but also because of its quest for "an authentic [black] vernacular voice."

If Zora Neale Hurston is a major proponent of the expressive brilliance of African American vernacular (and one of its major *ex*ponents), then a similar claim can legitimately be made for Duke Ellington and jazz. Małgorzata Ziółek-Sowińska advances that the African American specificity of Ellington's music as a promoter of "a new sense of black pride" is consistent with an aesthetic centered on "'racial feeling'" which took its inspiration from vernacular musical idioms such as "ragtime, blues, work songs, and the Negro spirituals." Ziółek-Sowińska declares that Ellington combined innovation with more canonical forms, sophistication with tradition, and "contributed towards modernism in African American aesthetic expression" in the early twentieth century."

Analyzing *Black Symphony* and the suite *Black, Brown and Beige*, she argues that Ellington harnessed his musical talents and agenda of racial pride and uplift to Harlem Renaissance modernist aesthetics. Throughout, he put in conversation the vernacular and rhythmical idioms of black music with highly elaborate musical compositions. Ellington's music, then, straddles the broad span of African American music, referencing the earliest forms introduced into the Americas by African slaves and the innovative brilliance and complexity of the twentieth century which he himself helped to establish. He combined the orthodox with the unorthodox and the modern, acknowledging the investment of modernity ("tomorrow") in the vernacular ("popular music"): "blues is the rage in popular music. And popular music is the good music of tomorrow." Ziółek-Sowińska concludes by stressing Ellington's intense relevance to later jazz icons – Miles Davis, for example – and the key position he occupies in American music as a whole.

Staying in the world of black music, Emil Sîrbulescu's essay in fact approaches the trumpeter through his literary, and not musical, craft. Armstrong produced two autobiographies – *Swing that Music* (1936) and *Satchmo: My Life in New Orleans* (1954) – as well as a not inconsiderable amount of "life" writing in the form of letters and transcribed interviews, the last providing the content for two biographical works – Robert Goffin's *Horn of Plenty: The Story of Louis Armstrong* (1947) and *Louis Armstrong, In His Own Words* (1999), attributed to Thomas Brothers and Armstrong himself. Sîrbulescu notes the formal affinity between Armstong's music and his writing, both combining "disciplined craftsmanship with inspired, exuberant improvisation." Indeed, Sîrbulescu describes Armstrong's written style as "word-jazz: a spicy gumbo of standard English, Black English, street slant, Bronzeville and Harlem jive, down-home colloquialisms, Southern regionalisms, Louisiana pidgin, Creole patois." It hardly needs to be stressed that Armstrong's collapsing of formal boundaries as well as his use of source materials in themselves mixed and fluid (vernacular idioms, blues, jazz), are strategies that are congruent with modernist aesthetics.

The fourth and final section of this volume, "Racialized Bodies, Activist Minds," presents essays in which the black body is the focus of attention, whether analytically, performatively, or as a racialized object. All three essays remind us once again that there is no single, undifferentiated black subject, but multiple and complex ways of being-black-in-the-world. The first and last focus on the black female body as a site of "securitization of regimental policing," as Simone A. James Alexander puts it. Taking Audre Lorde's well-known struggle with breast cancer, Alexander notes that perhaps the single most effective way of countering the aggressive policing of the black female body is to fight fire with fire, that is, with a "corresponding militancy." The case of Audre Lorde adds further layers of specificity – her lesbian orientation and committed feminism. Normative enforcement in the case of Lorde thus takes on an extra edge. The embodied subjectivity that conforms to the triad of white, healthy (i.e., two-breasted), and straight, materializes chillingly at Lorde's beside. Lorde records the dissonance between her own subjectivity and that of the female representative of the American Cancer Society's Reach for Recovery Program: "'As a forty-four year old Black Lesbian Feminist [...] my primary concerns two days after mastectomy were hardly about what man I could capture in the future.'" Alexander notes that in light of history and the commodification of African women's bodies, especially healthy women's bodies (she provides an extensive analysis of the case of Saartjie Baartman, the Hottentot Venus, for example), Lorde forces us to consider the very nature of women's health. Alexander links the struggles of black women today with those of their foremothers, militantly seizing a metaphorical auction block in order "to be seen and heard as subjects and producers of knowledge."

Inherent to André Lorde's account of her struggle to define health in her own terms is the interrogation of (white) compulsory heterosexuality and patriarchal norms. Models of white and black masculinity and related codes likewise come under scrutiny in Georg Bauer's essay. The history of black American boxing of course cannot be disengaged from the battles royal in which black, frequently slave, boxers fought each other bare-fisted, blindfold, and in a group. The winner was the last fighter left standing. That a historically demeaning and exploitative ritual is today associated with individuals such as Joe Louis and Muhammed Ali, among others, bears witness to an extraordinary self-(re-)appropriation of the black body and attendant cultural codes.

Bauer heightens the performative aspect of boxing by examining its representation in modern film, without minimizing the historically specific racial codes: just as battles royal were a way of controlling *black* masculinity by whites, so Hollywood films about boxing tend to assume a default, i.e., white audience, and re-present historical anxieties about *white* masculinity, exacerbated by the success of Ali and co. Bauer quotes Spike Lee approvingly: "He was handsome, he was articulate; he was funny, charismatic. He was whuppin' ass too!" White boxers on film both feed (white) American audiences' chronic need for a champion, according to Bauer, and "tap into the American self-made-man myth." Black boxing success complicates "'American' [...] ideas of being any other colour than white" and intensifies the need "to re-establish the white boxer as an icon." For now, notes Bauer, white boxing iconography has the upper hand in the film industry ("New trends in boxing films paint a grim picture for African American pugilists"). Yet the last word must go to the likes of Ali, Louis, and Archie Moore who, off-celluloid, put their boxing skills to great ends: "Transcending color lines and highlighting them at the same time."

If black boxing refers us to modern ways of being black and male, then Angela Davis performs a similar service with regard to being black and female. Icons such as Ali and Davis further recall the weight of history and collective trauma constitutive of the black diaspora. Both figures tap into the experience of Africans in America, that is, slavery: Ali through boxing, Davis through her engagement of the rhetorical tradition of slave narratives in her political autobiography (*An Autobiography* [1974]). Indeed, both black boxing icons and Davis re-engage with the self-defining strategy of the slave narrative genre, a strategy prompted by a coercive white environment which oppresses even as it seeks reductively to define the black object/subject. One might be forgiven here noting how the ensuing (self-) perceptual breach once more echoes Du Bois. To paraphrase Gilroy, "Striving to be both American (or Western) and black requires some specific forms of double consciousness" (1).

In this volume's closing essay, Yvonne Gutenberger stresses Davis' co-ancestry with the slave narrators through the attempt "to correct public misconceptions both of herself and of the Black Power movement." Gutenberg argues that Davis' (and the slave narrators') purpose is ontological and political: the end-game is to take (back) control over who she is and to win hearts and minds to a political cause. Participation in the self-defining rhetoric of slave narrative also seals Davis' kinship with modern or *neo*-practitioners of the genre, such as Toni Morrison, David Anthony Durham, Margaret Walker, Charles Johnson, Sherley Anne Williams, to name but a handful. These latter-day writers of course have produced imaginative approximations to the horrors of slavery, while Davis' blood ties with slave narrative also extend to autobiography, which Gutenberger notes is "a typical African-American literary genre." The life-narratives of slaves were "sites of historiography, autobiography, and literature." African American life writing, in short, taps into collective experience even if mediated through a single voice ("me-ism" and "we-ism," according to Selwyn Cudjoe and quoted by Gutenberger). The collective ethos of African American life writing is at odds, however, with the greater self-referentiality at the heart of Western autobiography. Gutenberg argues that Davis cannot escape the latter's "tendency toward individuation" however much she tries to draw attention away from herself by locating her personal struggle in a context of the "fight against discrimination." In the last analysis, insofar as Davis has survived in the public imaginary as 'a hairdo,' Gutenberg questions the success of her "political self-construction" and collective political message.

The essays in this volume tackle an array of topics which shed light on the complex place of blacks and blackness in the equally complex space(s) of ever-shifting modernities. They demonstrate, among other things, that the Afro-Atlantic is not exclusively invested in the trauma of diasporic displacement, and that it does not end with the abolition of the slave trade or the emancipation of slaves in the Americas. By the same token, the history of race and race making is revealed to transcend a Northern, English-speaking hemisphere, just as the most nuanced race consciousness is frequently located in the racialized subject. Ultimately, these essays remind us that modernity, like the Black Atlantic, is an open-ended project, "always unfinished, always being remade" (Gilroy xi).

Works Cited

Caplan, Pat, and Farouk Topan, eds. *Swahili Modernities, Culture, Politics, and Identity on the East Coast of Africa*. Trenton: Africa World P, 2004.

Eisenstadt, Shmuel Noah. *Comparative Civilizations and Multiple Modernities*. New York: Koninklijke Brill, 2003.

---. "Multiple Modernities." *Daedalus* 129.1 (2000): 1-29.

---, ed. *Multiple Modernities*. New York: Transaction Publishers, 2002.

Foster, Cecil. *Blackness and Modernity: The Colour of Humanity and the Quest for Freedom*. Montreal: McGill-Queen's UP, 2007.

Gates, Henry Louis, Jr. "Authority, (White) Power and the (Black) Critic; It's All Greek To Me." *Cultural Critique* 7 (Autumn 1987): 19-46.

Gilroy, Paul. *The Black Atlantic: Modernity and Double Consciousness*. London: Verso, 1993.

Hlongwane, Gugu. "What Has Modernity To Do With It?: Camouflaging Race in the 'New' South Africa." *Journal of Literary Studies* 18.1 & 2 (2002): 111-31.

Ikonné, Chidi. *From Du Bois to Van Vechten: The Early New Negro Literature, 1903-1926*. Westport: Greenwood P, 1981.

Johnson, Clarence Sholé. "Reconceptualizing Blackness and Making Race Obsolescent." *White on White/Black on Black*. Ed. George Yancy. Lanham: Rowman and Littlefield, 2005. 173-202.

Kaiwar, Vasant, and Sucheta Mazumdar, eds. *Anatomies of Modernity: Essays on Race, Orient, Nation*. Durham: Duke UP, 2003.

Kamali, Masoud. *Multiple Modernities, Civil Society, and Islam: The Case of Iran and Turkey*. Liverpool: Liverpool UP, 2006.

Kolakowski, Leszek. *Modernity on Endless Trial*. Chicago: U of Chicago P, 1997.

Locke, Alain. "The Negro's Contribution to American Art and Literature." *The Annals of the American Academy of Political Science and Social Science* 140 (November 1928): 234-47.

Martin, Fran, and Larissa Heinrich, eds. *Embodied Modernities: Corporeality, Representation, and Chinese Cultures*. Honolulu: U of Hawaii P, 2006.

Perkinson, James W. *White Theology: Outing Supremacy in Modernity*. New York: Palgrave Macmillan, 2004.

Roniger, Luis, and Carlos H. Waisman, eds. *Globality and Multiple Modernities: Comparative North American and Latin American Perspectives*. Sussex: Academic P, 2002.

Rostow, Walt Whitman. *The Stages of Economic Growth: A Non-Communist Manifesto*. Cambridge: Cambridge UP, 1960.

Schmidt, Volker H. "Multiple Modernities or Varieties of Modernity?" *Current Sociology* 54.1 (2006): 77-97.

Sivaramakrishnan, K., and Arun Agrawal, eds. *Regional Modernities: The Cultural Politics of Development in India*. Stanford: Stanford UP, 2003.

Taylor, Charles, and Benjamin Lee. "Multiple Modernities Project: Modernity and Difference." *The Center for Transcultural Studies*. 7 Sept. 2010 <http://www.sas.upenn.edu/transcult/promad.html>.

Wagner, Peter. "Modernity – One or Many?" *The Blackwell Companion to Sociology*. Ed. Judith Blau. Oxford: Blackwell, 2000. 30-42.

Zeleza, Paul Tiyambe. "Rewriting the African Diaspora: Beyond the Black Atlantic." *African Affairs* 104.414 (2005): 35-68.

Clarence Sholé Johnson

Resistance to Modernity: Two Contesting Viewpoints*

Introduction

> The literary people among us have been trumpeting Du Bois's statement about double consciousness for the past twenty or so years to explain identity chaos or a sort of identity complication due to a racist society that privileges whiteness. [...]
> However, there is no double consciousness. I announce an end to Du Bois's errant conclusion and I question the strength by which it is promoted by academic literary scholars who are often not in contact with the ordinary African person in America. (Asante, "Blackness" 207)

These are the magisterial pronouncements of Molefi Asante in his essay "Blackness as an Ethical Trope." Asante's contention is that Du Bois's claim about double consciousness as a psychological fissure of the black person in America (and generally of people of color in a white supremacist world as a result of white supremacist practices), a fissure that sometimes occasions self-doubt, even self-devaluation, never existed for the ordinary black person in America. According to Asante, the phenomenon of double consciousness exists only on an individual (or personal) level for Du Bois and possibly some others of his ilk. But is Asante right?

It is this question that I propose to address in this paper. And I shall do so by examining the purported veracity of Asante's claim that the situation of those afflicted by Du Boisean double consciousness, including Du Bois, differs from that of ordinary African Americans, including Asante himself. Indeed, if Asante's assertion is correct, then one needs to look closely at the peculiarity of the situation of those for whom the phenomenon of double consciousness obtains. By so doing, one would come to appreciate Asante's declamation against Du Bois, and hence his own announcement of the end of double consciousness. But I hope to show that, despite Asante's protestations to the contrary, he is paradoxically trapped in the psychological cloud of the very phenomenon of double consciousness that he so vehemently repudiates. The reason is that, if we read Du Bois's concept of double consciousness as a cardinal feature of *resistance to oppression*, in that it illuminates the devaluation and dehumanization of oppression to which the oppressed respond by demanding recognition and respect, then, as I will show, Asante's own lifework in Afrocentricity logically entails a form of double consciousness notwithstanding his pronouncements to the contrary. In other words, Asante's existential undertaking is motivated by the very idea that drives Du Bois's existential quest although Asante might think otherwise. As such, Asante's announcement of the end of double consciousness is not just false; it even traps Asante into a logically incoherent position of which he seems completely unaware.

Toward Double Consciousness

I begin with a very thin sketch of the familiar story of how Du Bois discovered himself as raced. The main outlines of the story are worth recalling, even at the cost of tedium, both to provide a background for understanding Du Bois's claim about the phenomenon of double consciousness and for understanding Asante's problem with that claim.

As Du Bois tells it, his discovery of himself as raced was "in the early days of rollicking boyhood," at his New England school in Great Barrington, Massachusetts, following an idea that had come to the boys and girls that they buy and exchange visiting cards with each other. The exchange was merry, says Du Bois, until one of the girls, a tall newcomer, peremptorily rejected his card "with a glance" (2). It was there and then that Du Bois realized that he was *fundamentally* different from his schoolmates. I say "fundamentally" because Du Bois points to possible similarities he may have with his schoolmates: similarities "in heart and life and longing" (ibid.). But even so, he realized that the difference, one that he later will represent symbolically using the concept of a vast veil and sometimes an unscalable wall, ran very deep. This principle of difference, namely race, separates his schoolmates from him into two distinct and different worlds.

What Du Bois notices and represents through the metaphors of the veil and the wall is the social hierachization of American society along racial lines, with whites occupying the higher stratum of the social ladder because of whiteness and blacks occupying the lower stratum because of blackness. In other words, Du Bois notices a necessary relation between race and social location in the sense that the society is stratified between those who are socially advantaged because of whiteness and those disadvantaged because of blackness.

Obviously, Du Bois's realization of race-based social inequity followed his *personal* realization of being raced. This point is significant for two reasons: First, Du Bois seemed, at least conceptually, to separate these two realizations. Thus he responded to the realization that he was racially different from his schoolmates by treating the latter with benign contempt. And so, while treating his schoolmates with benign contempt, he triumphed whenever he defeated them at any competitive endeavor, intellectual or physical (ibid.). Second, as he tells us, with time his contempt began to wane when he realized that the very things he longed for in life had been appropriated by whites *by virtue of their race*. As he says, "the words I longed for, and all their dazzling opportunities, were theirs, not mine" (ibid.). This second realization, namely, that no matter how he triumphed in any competitive endeavor his accomplishments would not translate into correlative social benefits, made Du Bois resolve to wrest these appropriated social goods, these undeserved benefits or "prizes," as he calls them, from his white counterparts (ibid.). After all, these social goods had not been obtained on an equitable basis. Indeed, it would seem that for Du Bois they were ill-gotten gains.

One should not be particularly surprised, though, by Du Bois's conceptual separation of his self-discovery of being raced, on the one hand, and his awareness of the inequities in the society along racial lines, on the other. After all, it was in youthful innocence that he discovered himself to be raced. (The rejection by the tall newcomer lifted the veil, as it were, from his eyes.) Moreover, Du Bois was not from the South where such inequities were stark realities and a fact of life. So it is understandable that he would not have noticed social inequities along racial lines. However, the fact is that he eventually came to notice race-based social inequities and what he considered the debilitating effect of racism on the psyche of African Americans. It is this effect that he frames using the concept of double consciousness. His point is that the society in which the African American exists, in terms of its racial/social configuration, is one that precludes the possibility of the African American having a singular and cohesive self-identity. This is so because the society is shaped by the modalities of whiteness, and as such it only lets the African American "see himself [herself] through the revelation [or lenses] of the other [read white] world" (Du Bois 3). The phenomenon of double consciousness, as Du Bois puts it, is a way of "always looking at one's self through the eyes of others, of measuring one's soul by the tape of a world that looks on in amused contempt and pity" (ibid.).

The full consequence of this self-perception and evaluation through the prism of a white supremacist world is the psychological bifurcation that it occasions in the African American; the individual realizes that her/his humanity is being called into question by being required to see and judge her/himself, both ontologically and axiologically, from the perspective that the dominant society has imposed on her/him. In other words, the individual's worthiness as a *functional* human being is determined by white normative and aesthetic values. And this state of affairs creates tremendous psychological problems for the individual in the sense that s/he cannot see her/himself as she really is or cannot function as s/he would otherwise desire – i.e., free from anxiety and trepidation. Quite the contrary, s/he is subject to perpetual anxiety. It is in this context that we should appreciate Du Bois's examples of the effect of double consciousness on the black craftsman, the black professional, be he preacher or doctor, and the black savant or intellectual (Du Bois 3-4). There, Du Bois speaks of "the double aimed struggle of the black artisan" to maximize his potential only to be met with white contempt for black intellectual and productive capacity, while at the same time recognizing the urgency of meeting the basic needs of "a poverty-stricken horde" (4); of the conflicting tendencies of the black professional, on the one hand toward quackery and demagogy when among his folks, and, on the other hand, toward excruciatingly painstaking perfection over the most lowly and unchallenging of assignments when among whites (ibid.).

In each of these examples the individual does not have a single or unitary (read coherent, non-conflicted) consciousness. Instead, s/he has a fractured or bifurcated consciousness. But no human being can live in a wholesome manner with a bifurcated or conflicted consciousness. As humans, we seek to live as unitary (read coherent, non-conflicted and wholesome) selves and having a unitary consciousness. Du Bois takes this proposition to be axiomatic, and rightly so. Hence he suggests that the existential quest of the African American is to overcome double consciousness. Alternatively put, the existential quest of the African American is to construct a single unitary consciousness (or self-identity) from two distinct and antithetical identities and their attendant perspectives, or, as Du Bois metaphorically puts it, to construct a single unitary consciousness from "two souls, two thoughts […] two warring ideals [that exist] in one dark body" (3). To repeat, Du Bois takes the constant endeavor to overcome these conflicting perspectival and identity issues on a daily basis as constitutive of the existential struggle, the strife, for African Americans.

As is well known, Du Bois's suggested method of overcoming the problem of double consciousness is to reconcile both the two antithetical perspectives of the self and the two distinct identities, one African and the other American, to which the perspectives are pegged. Only then, he tells us, can the African American become "a co-worker in the kingdom of culture"; or "escape both [psychic] death and isolation"; or "husband and use his [her] best powers and latent [read innate] genius" (ibid.). I take this to be Du Bois's meaning in the assertion that the history of the African American is "the history of [...] this longing [...] to merge his double self into a better and truer self" (ibid.).

It is arguable whether or not Du Bois's suggested solution to the problem is feasible. Consider, for example, Black Nationalist alternatives to the United States' endemic racism and *a fortiori* to Du Bois's proposed solution. I have in mind here the views of Black Nationalists such as Martin Delaney and Marcus Garvey whose advocacy was for African Americans to be repatriated to Africa in order to be free of white racism thereby ensuring group survival.[1] But that is not what I wish to examine in this paper. My proposed aim is to examine Asante's challenge of Du Bois on the issue of double consciousness. In particular, Asante rejects the purported psychological state to which Du Bois applies the concept of double consciousness in respect of the lived reality of African Americans, and hence rejects the very meaningfulness of the concept itself (see also Asante, "Racism"). In so doing he claims that he announces an end to double consciousness. (See the passage quoted at the beginning of this paper.) But is he right in his repudiation of the concept of double consciousness? As I will show later, Asante is manifestly wrong in his view precisely because his Afrocentric undertaking necessarily entails a form of double consciousness. But first, what is the basis for Asante's rejection of Du Boisean double consciousness?

Asante's Issues

Like Du Bois, Asante draws upon his own experience of growing up in the United States to advance his thesis. He tells us that he was born in the strictly segregated town of Valdosta, Georgia, and that he grew up with the self-consciousness of a racialized Other. In Valdosta, blacks lived on the economically depressed and deprived side and whites on the economically affluent side.

Moreover, black and white children did not interact with each other as was Du Bois's experience growing up in Great Barrington. In the segregated world of Valdosta, which Asante takes to be a microcosm of Southern United States, there was no delusion or mistake about the relation between a person's material condition and her/his race. Nor were there any delusions or mistakes about the operating conditions that governed race relations. While he and other black boys anywhere between the ages of 6 and 12 would assemble at dawn to be carted off in a pick-up truck to labor all day in tobacco and cotton fields, young white boys of similar ages would be going fishing or camping. What we have here is a contrast between a life of labor experienced by black boys and a life of leisure enjoyed by white boys. This state of affairs was a fact of life. Asante registered this contrast as two distinct and different modes of being, two worlds inhabited by two distinct and different types of souls: one completely and thoroughly white and the other completely and thoroughly black. It is in this connection that Asante goes on to tell us that he was not only "[s]haped in the mold of segregation," but also that he "knew at a very early age that the world of America was black and white." Hence, he concludes, he is "for all practical purposes a made-in-America person" ("Racism" 14). The import of Asante's remarks is that he, unlike Du Bois, grew up with an awareness of the necessary connection between race and social (dis)advantage in American society as symbolized by Valdosta, Georgia. Du Bois, on the other hand, had to *discover* this connection between race and social inequities about the society somewhat later albeit in his youth.

For Asante, while economic deprivation and hardship constituted the material reality of black life in the South, it was a permanent state of angst that constituted its existential/spiritual reality. Blacks lived under perpetual fear and terror of white violence, contempt, cruelty, brutalization, and lynching. Along these lines, Asante relates a story about a black man who was lynched in a part of Valdosta that came to be known by the local blacks in the community as "Kill-Me-Quick."

> To remind us of just how cruel the whites could be in the South an African man was killed and his body dragged through the dirt roads of the two black sections of town, Southside and Westside. I was barely six when this happened, but the fumes rising from the anger in the black community colored the mental skies of a thousand children for several years. [...]
>
> So lynching registered early and substantially on my mind; the effect of the monstrous crimes against innocent and often defenseless African Americans was permanent. (Ibid.)

Asante also informs us of a downright cruel and humiliating treatment he received from a white man when he was only twelve years old. At the time, he wanted desperately to contribute to his family's income. So he set himself up as a shoeshine boy and "found a white barber shop" in close proximity to his neighborhood whose owner was willing to give him a chance to shine the shoes of the white customers. The narrative continues as follows:

> My very first customer, demonstrating for others in the shop his contempt for Africans, even a child, spat on my head as I leaned over his shoes. I knew what had happened. I did not say a word as I gathered up my shoeshine box, forgot about my payment, and walked out of the barbershop to the laughter of the man and a few other customers. ("Racism" 16)

Let me pause for a moment to observe that the foregoing narrated experiences significantly helped to shape Asante's reaction to white supremacy – a point to which I return later. Meanwhile, as Asante goes on to tell us, the terror of racism, the economic hardships visited upon blacks because of racist practices and racial segregation, and the overall powerlessness of blacks to challenge and overturn these practices, far from occasioning in blacks a desire to seek to belong to the dominant society, had the unintended consequence of occasioning cohesiveness in them and instilling in them a sense of self-confidence. As Asante says, the blacks of Valdosta did not have a double consciousness, for they did not wish or long to be a part of the larger society, and so did not plead for social acceptance. Nor did they try to fashion an identity that would be acceptable to the larger society – precisely what constitutes double consciousness. Instead, they cultivated an insular consciousness, a unitary consciousness of self-confident selves inhabiting their black bodies as a bulwark against white racism. There was no confusion about their black identity or the social reality of their existence. Asante sums up this point by saying, "There existed no reference point outside ourselves despite the economic and psychological poverty of our situation" (ibid.). A final point Asante makes on this score is that white violence against blacks, and white cruelty and general antipathy towards blacks, as manifestations of antiblack racism, led blacks to have no positive expectations from whites. It is against this background, then, that we are to understand Asante's repudiation of Du Bois's concept of double consciousness as "madness" ("Blackness" 208).

Three points are implicit in Asante's critique of Du Bois. First, Du Bois had positive expectations from whites and American society at large, expectations which were thwarted symbolically in the peremptory rejection of his visiting card by the tall girl, the newcomer to his school, during the visiting card exchange mentioned earlier. And so he was disappointed. Second, Du Bois must have mistakenly thought that he shared a similar heritage, and hence a common identity, with whites; so it came as a rude shock when he realized otherwise. This was another disappointment. By contrast, Asante says of himself that

> Since I was a child I have always known that my heritage was not the same as that of whites. I never thought we came over here on the *Mayflower*. When I got up in the mornings to go to the fields, little white children got up to go fishing in the lakes or to camp. ("Racism" 18)

And third, Du Bois thought that he had a place in an American society that had not only fashioned its identity in terms of whiteness, but that also, through its institutional mechanisms, deliberately chose to reject anything black. Recognizing, however, that his identity as black makes him an outsider (or Other), Du Bois nevertheless desired or longed to belong to America. Yet this desire was challenged by the stark realities of racial dynamics in the society. Hence he found himself in internal conflict with a tortured soul, trying to reconcile the conflicting psychic pulls of (i) recognizing the fact of his blackness and (ii) desiring acceptance in a white society that repudiates blackness. Contrasting his own perspective with that of Du Bois and like-minded blacks, Asante asks rhetorically:

> Did I think that I shared something with these whites? Was I that crazy? Did I believe that I was an American in the same way whites were? Did I want to be like whites? [...] It might have been another matter if I had gone to school and to church with whites when I was younger. I might have suffered confusion, double-consciousness, but I did not. (Ibid.)

Asante attributes his supposed lack of double consciousness to his insular upbringing, saying that the segregated schools, among other things, kept him "away from the longing to be white or to be accepted by whites that Du Bois must have felt in Great Barrington, Massachusetts" (ibid.).

Afrocentricity and the Ghost of Double Consciousness

Let us suppose for the sake of argument that Asante is right in his criticisms of Du Bois's concept of double consciousness. And let us also accept his claims about his insular upbringing in racially segregated Valdosta, Georgia. Still, does it follow that he is free of the very double consciousness that he disparages? I answer "No." By way of demonstration, let me direct attention to Asante's Afrocentric preoccupation. Afrocentricity is meant to be a counterweight to Eurocentricity and white supremacy. Eurocentricity itself, traceable to European expansionism in The Age of Conquest since Columbus, affirms whiteness as normative for humanity. Blackness, the antithesis of whiteness, was deemed a deviation from the norm of humanity; hence we have a denigration of blackness in its manifold forms and an ascription of ontological inferiority to blackness. It is these twin features of white supremacy, namely, its normativity of whiteness and devaluation of blackness, that Asante is contesting in his affirmation of Afrocentricity. More precisely, Afrocentricity is both a repudiation of the normativity of whiteness and an affirmation of blackness as an authentic form of human identity.

Seen this way, there is absolutely nothing wrong with Afrocentricity. It is a form of resistance to whiteness and a form of self-definition of a historically despised people; it is positive valuation of black identity. So I applaud it. But, then, such an enterprise, as is clear, is intelligible only against the backdrop of the specter of whiteness that has haunted Asante since childhood and throughout his formative years of living in the United States. Recall Asante's boyhood experience as a farm worker in sharp contrast to the experience of many (if not most) white boys of a similar age. Recall also the cruel and humiliating treatment Asante received from the white patron at the barbershop. These experiences crystallize Asante's response to white supremacy. Because Asante finds white supremacy repugnant, he therefore sets out to wage an all out assault on it via Afrocentricity. True, he is certainly not measuring his soul, in the sense of assessing his humanity, through the lenses of whiteness, and so is not susceptible to *one* sense of double consciousness that Du Bois, in my view, considers negative and disparaging[2]. This is the sense in which African Americans are compelled by white racism to determine their worthiness as humans by seeing themselves through the lenses of whites. This sense of double consciousness is negative and disparaging because it denies the humanity of African Americans by devaluing the authentic self that is only perceived intimately and subjectively *from a first-person point of view.*³ This negative and disparaging sense of double consciousness precludes the individual having any authentic view of herself/himself. Be it noted that Du Bois bemoans the kind of society that occasions in some of its citizens such a mode of existence, and so he repudiates, at least in my view, the state of affairs evoked by this sense of double consciousness.⁴ So, like Du Bois, Asante repudiates this sense of double consciousness, for he is contesting the very lenses through which white supremacy measures and values individuals.

However, by virtue of the fact that Asante has to affirm the authenticity of blackness, both ontologically and axiologically, and has to doggedly affirm his black identity, he cannot but be subject to double consciousness in *another* sense. This is a sense in which double consciousness is a psychological predisposition, a mental propensity, to demand recognition and respect from forces that are presumed white supremacist in nature, and that are wont to deny him his humanity. It is in responding to these forces that he devotes every fiber of his being. I shall refer to this as the contestational sense of double consciousness. The point to note here is that both this psychological predisposition and Asante's affirmation of his authentic African identity exist only because and against the backdrop of such hostile forces mentioned, namely white supremacy. It is precisely in this way that double consciousness as contestation manifests itself. In this regard, therefore, Asante's Afrocentric quest is as much existential as was Du Bois's undertaking in *Souls*, articulated as the end of the spiritual strivings of African Americans. Put another way, for both Asante and Du Bois, we have an existential quest for recognition and respect from a society that has a history and strong propensity to do otherwise. This quest is articulated in slightly different ways; but it is one and the same in nature.

Additional support for this reading of Asante's position can be seen by considering that, even as a teenager, long before he became the recognized Afrocentricist that he is now, Asante was always in a *mental state of readiness* to contend with white supremacy wherever he encountered it. He tells us as much in saying that, among the vows he made to his great-great-grandmother, Frances Chapman who lived and died in Dooly County, Georgia, was "never to allow white racial supremacy to go unchallenged" ("Racism" 16-17). To that end he informs us that, while attending elementary school in Tennessee, where he had moved from Georgia, "my friends looked to me in any confrontation with whites because I maintained an understanding in my relationships with whites that demanded mutual respect" ("Racism" 17).

This statement suggests that Asante was consistently conscious of the *possibility* of being denigrated at any moment because he is black, and so was always mentally prepared to counter such sources of denigration. One can assume that there were times when such a possibility was actualized, and that there were other times when it was not. The fact, however, is that Asante was always ready for it whenever it occurred. If so, then surely, he cannot be a "unitary and holistic" consciousness ("Racism" 18), as he says, thereby implying that he was in a state of tranquility about his identity. He may be certain about his blackness (or black/African identity) but he was certainly haunted by the specter of white supremacy then as now. The reason is that, while being conscious of his authentic blackness, Asante was also conscious of white society's view of him as black. And there can be no doubt that he was not calmly accepting of white America's response to his blackness. In sum, Asante was in a perpetual state of angst created and imposed on him by external (read white supremacist) forces over which he had no control and which were indirectly influencing his very mode of being on a daily basis. It is in this way, I submit, that Asante manifested then, as he does now, double consciousness in the contestational sense specified.

But are the two senses of double consciousness, the disparaging/denigrating and the contestational, mutually exclusive as might appear? I think not. On the contrary, to the extent that the contestational is resistance to white supremacy *as mediated by the denigrating and disparaging sense of double consciousness*, the two senses are thus mutually inclusive. If this is the case, then Asante may not have been subject to the denigrating and disparaging sense of double consciousness that he reviles and that Du Bois bemoans, but he is certainly subject to it in another way through the contestational sense. Either way, he, like others who live under the social atmosphere of racial (or even other forms of) oppression, is not free from the psychological state that Du Bois so very aptly describes as double consciousness.

Further Considerations against Asante
The phenomenon of double consciousness, its meaning and scope, as well as attempts to overcome it, unquestionably have generated lively and sometimes vigorous debates among scholars.[5] Even so, notwithstanding the diversity of viewpoints on the subject, the verdict in the previous section is upheld almost

universally by contemporary scholars who have examined the issue of double consciousness. For example, Cornel West extols the virtue of double consciousness even as he brings out what he considers Du Bois's failure to see its wider implication for the Euro-American struggle for self-identity (*Prophecy* 30-31; *Reader* 58). This wider implication, for West, is that African Americans' struggle for self-identity, foisted upon them by white racism in America, is part and parcel of a larger struggle for self-identity with which white America itself was grappling. The identity crisis for white America consisted in "being provincial but [yet] yearning for British cosmopolitanism, of being at once incompletely civilized and materially prosperous, a genteel Brahmin amid uncouth conditions" (*Prophecy* 31). Given this larger context, West construes the concept of double consciousness as being aimed principally at capturing the psychic turmoil of African Americans within the dynamics of a hostile, racially circumscribed existence, yet also giving expression to a similar psychic turmoil of white America that was (and still is) suffering from a debilitating European inferiority complex while trying to forge an identity somewhat distinct from Europe.

Evidently for West there is no problem about the adequacy of Du Bois's use of the concept of double consciousness to capture the existential lived reality of blacks in the United States and of the psychological effect of the phenomenon of double consciousness on blacks. West speaks of the temptations that the phenomenon of double consciousness often induces in black subjects: doubt, despair, self-hatred and hate. (*Reader* 108-15) In fact, West reduces black double consciousness to black namelessness and invisibility that derive from white supremacist architectonic. Accordingly, he sees black strivings (to address the issue of double consciousness) as consisting in various attempts to forge an identity that will enable blacks to overcome namelessness and invisibility. And he tells us that the mechanism through which such attempts are realized is "those forms of individual and collective resistance predicated on a deep and abiding black *love*" (*Reader* 106; emphasis in the original).

One criticism that West brings against Du Bois, though, is that despite Du Bois's powerful conceptualization of the existential predicament of African Americans as one of double consciousness and also despite Du Bois's lifelong struggle against white supremacy, Du Bois offered what West calls an "inadequate interpretation of the human condition." This is so, says West, because Du Bois manifested an "inability to immerse himself fully in the rich cultural currents of black everyday life" (*Reader* 89). The thrust of West's criticism is that

Du Bois was an elitist whose theoretical insights did not have the kind of weighty significance they otherwise might have had they been sufficiently grounded in the concrete life of everyday black people. Indeed, West puts the point very bluntly: Du Bois "adopted a mild elitism that underestimated the capacity of everyday people to 'know' about life" (*Reader* 90). The evidence that West adduces in support of Du Bois's alleged elitism is Du Bois's notion of the Talented Tenth, the ten per cent that comprised the educated black elite in post-Emancipation United States, whose supposed role and duty was to pull up and transform the ordinary illiterate mass from a condition of uncouthness (or near primitiveness) to one of refinement that would make black people acceptable to white America.[6] West contends that Du Bois did not believe that he, and by extension the educated class, could learn anything from the ordinary uneducated folk. The consequence of this alleged elitism is that Du Bois, despite his genius, could only offer a very narrow or limited characterization of the condition of the ordinary folk for whom he attempted to speak. But Du Bois's elitism should come as no surprise because, says West,

> Du Bois was a child of his age. He was shaped by the prevailing presuppositions and prejudices of modern Euro-American civilization. [...] [He] was, in style and substance, a proud black man of letters primarily influenced by nineteenth-century Euro-American tradition. (*Reader* 88)

I shall not pause to examine whether or not this criticism of West is fair. I can only say in passing, and in agreement with Lucius Outlaw, that West's claim that Du Bois failed to immerse himself in the life of the ordinary folk is grossly mistaken.[7] Chapter Four of *Souls,* entitled "Of the Meaning of Progress," demonstrates otherwise. There, Du Bois catalogues his journey as a young teacher to rural Tennessee, living among the ordinary illiterate and poor folk, trying to educate them, and in the process sometimes breaking bread with them and even attending church with them. That said, what matters for me in the present discussion is that, even despite West's criticism of Du Bois, and even despite what West might refer to as Du Bois's anxiety-ridden concern about white perception of blacks, West upholds the value of the concept of double consciousness as a powerful intellectual and analytical device to characterize the phenomenon that has shaped black strivings since modernity. And on this score, Asante would again seem to be on the losing side.

Jane Anna Gordon sees the concept of double consciousness not only as an epistemic device that Du Bois uses to characterize an existential phenomenon, but also, and more importantly, as a *theoretical gift/contribution* from the colonized to the Western canon. It is an epistemic device because Gordon takes the concept as describing a viewpoint that is peculiar to the racially/colonized oppressed and that equips the colonized/oppressed with a peculiar vantage point from which s/he perceives and evaluates both her/his oppressor and the distinctive features of the oppression. This vantage point, being peculiar to the oppressed, is epistemically closed off to the oppressor, and necessarily so. (Recall Du Bois's view of the African American being gifted with a second sight!) It is in light of this peculiarity of the state of double consciousness, or, better still, the epistemic vantage point that it offers the colonized/oppressed, that the colonized/oppressed can affirm her/his agency and subjectivity in dealing with her/his oppression.[8] On this showing, double consciousness, for Gordon, is an attribute that the oppressed/colonized should embrace rather than shy away from or deny as does Asante. It is a testament to Du Bois that, positing the concept of double consciousness, he theorized the peculiar perspectival access the oppressed has to her/his oppressor and the condition of her/his oppression.

And it is precisely because Du Bois uses the concept of double consciousness to provide a theory that gives expression to the peculiar epistemic access the oppressed/colonized has to her/his condition and, indeed, the phenomenon of racism (and oppression as a whole) that Gordon refers to the concept as a theoretical gift of the colonized to the colonizer. The background context for Gordon's reading of double consciousness in this way is Western colonialism itself as founded upon white supremacy and antiblack racism. This is a context in modernity within which the (colonized) black is ontologized in the white mind as an object, an entity devoid of reason and rationality. Thus ontologized, the black is deemed incapable of any form of cognitive activity. Indeed, how can there be cognitive activity where there is no cognition? It follows from such a conceptualization that the black is a fit candidate for slavery and colonization.

Hegel draws precisely such a conclusion, as Gordon observes, grounding it on the premise that Africa is not a part of world history and that Africans lack self-consciousness, the defining characteristic of rational agency (Jane Anna Gordon 146).[9] Similarly, other key modern philosophers such as Hume, Kant, and Locke, short of drawing the conclusion Hegel draws, advance views about the supposed cognitive deprivation of blacks. Indeed, we are all too familiar with the Hume-Kant characterization of Africans as ontologically incapable of producing any arts or engaging in any industry or intellectual endeavors.[10] I speak of the Hume-Kant characterization because both philosophers are in complete agreement about black (or Negro) supposed cognitive deprivation.[11] Here is Hume's view to which Kant gives his unqualified intellectual blessing:

> I am apt to suspect the negroes and in general all other species of men (for there are four or five different kinds) to be naturally inferior to the whites. There never was a civilized nation of any other complexion than white, nor even any individual eminent either in action or speculation. No ingenious manufactures amongst them, no arts, no sciences. On the other hand, the most rude and barbarous of the whites, such as the ancient Germans, the present Tartars, have still something eminent about them, in their valour, form of government, or some other particular. Such a uniform and constant difference could not happen, in so many countries and ages if nature had not made an original distinction between these breeds of men. Not to mention our colonies, there are negroe slaves dispersed all over Europe, of whom none ever discovered any symptoms of ingenuity; though low people without education will start up amongst us and distinguish themselves in every profession. In Jamaica, indeed, they talk of one negroe as a man of parts and learning; but it is likely he is admired for slender accomplishments, like a parrot who speaks a few words plainly. (33)[12]

Although Gordon does not explicitly furnish this larger background context in modernity for her discussion, save for her specific observation about Hegel, there is no doubt that this is the historical context that frames her interpretation of the concept of double consciousness.[13] The significant point that Gordon makes in advancing the aforementioned interpretation of the Du Boisean concept of double consciousness in question is that she sees a deliberate reluctance or refusal by the dominant group, the historical colonizer, to incorporate this theoretical concept into the western canon. And Gordon considers this reluctance a deliberate attempt to further deny black agency and subjectivity. Gordon draws a parallel here between this deliberate endeavor to deny black agency and subjectivity in the realm of black intellectual production with a similar historical denial of black agency and subjectivity in the context of black labor that was appropriated and exploited under slavery and colonialism.

Gordon's point, in essence, is that whether one examines the issue of black agency and subjectivity from the point of view of the physical (labor) or the cognitive (theory/ideas), the notion of blacks as rational agents capable of engaging in *the volitional act of giving or contributing* is what modernity categorically denied. And it is in response to this deliberate denial, particularly in the realm of the intellectual, that Gordon takes double consciousness as a *theoretical* contribution of the colonized to the Western canon, an epistemological tool to characterize an existential situation. Saying that the concept is theoretical entails that it has universal validity and general applicability *qua* theory. What this means is that the concept, like any theoretical device, transcends the very particularity and concrete situatedness of the experiences that immediately occasioned it and to which it gave initial expression. It is instructive in this regard that subaltern groups such as feminists, gays and lesbians, the disabled, the aged, and, yes, postcolonial subjects, are invoking this concept to give expression to their various forms of oppression and to affirm their humanity (Jane Anna Gordon 153-54; Young ch. 2).

How does all this relate to Asante's repudiation of the concept of double consciousness? Given Gordon's reading, Asante's disavowal of the concept of double consciousness and his attempt to dismantle it, as he says, would have the paradoxical consequence of constituting a rejection of the very black agency and humanity that Asante himself is very anxious to affirm via his Afrocentricity. In other words, granting Gordon's analysis, Asante would again be on the losing side.

Finally, Paul Gilroy considers the concept of double consciousness principally as giving expression to the existential predicament of African Americans in the twilight of modernity and, by extension, as expressing what Du Bois takes to be the nature of the experiences of formerly colonized peoples the world over. As Gilroy puts it,

> Double consciousness was initially used to convey the special difficulties arising from black internalisation of an American identity [...]. However, I want to suggest that Du Bois produced this concept at the junction point of his philosophical and psychological interests not just to express the distinctive standpoint of black Americans but also to illuminate the experience of post-slave populations in general. Beyond this, he uses it as a means to animate a dream of global co-operation among peoples of colour which came to full fruition only in his later work. (126)[14]

This observation by Gilroy, like Gordon's, is significant because it points to the universality of the concept of double consciousness in giving expression to the experiences of those diverse peoples whose existence has been shaped by Euro-American hegemony under slavery and colonialism. But above all, for my purpose, Gilroy's view is in line with the views of both Gordon and West especially in seeing the concept of double consciousness in contexts that go beyond the particularity of the African American situation.

Of course, it does not follow from the fact that there is a chorus of views extolling the virtue of double consciousness that the concept is legitimate, and that, it might be said, is exactly Asante's point in challenging and repudiating the concept. My response to this objection, however, is as follows: if the concept is illegitimate, as Asante claims, then the burden of proof is on him to demonstrate its illegitimacy. But I do not believe that he has met that burden. Merely proclaiming that a concept is illegitimate does not make it so. I understand and sympathize with Asante's motivation for rejecting the concept. Asante believes that the mental fortitude to overcome racism comes from an environment other than that which causes the racism itself. And he believes that he has acquired such mental fortitude to deal with racism on his own terms from Valdosta. But one can agree with him on this last point about the preparation he received from Valdosta to contend with racism without necessarily denying as he does that racism and white supremacy, as a conjunctive form of oppression, produce the psychic condition that Du Bois describes. What I have tried to show is that Asante's denial cannot be sustained even by his own testimony that purports to show otherwise.

Conclusion

I have examined two alternative responses to modernity's imposition of racial inferiority on people of color, and central to my discussion is Du Bois's concept of double consciousness to characterize the psychological effect of this act of dehumanization. As I have shown, Asante rejects this consequence of modernity even as he disparages modernity. But I have argued that Asante is wrong in denying this consequence. And to support my view, I have called attention to certain autobiographical facts about Asante himself which show that white supremacy is an albatross strapped to his neck as much as it haunts all of us living in the twilight of modernity. Metaphorically, an albatross is (i) something that causes deep concern or anxiety; and (ii) something that greatly hinders accomplishment: that is, an encumbrance. My position is that, unquestionably, this is what white supremacy is to all of us who live under hegemonic structures of race(ism). In various ways we are contesting it. And so, like Du Bois, Asante and all people of color refuse to be measured by lenses that deny us our identities. But in doing so we must admit, notwithstanding Asante's denial, that we are living in a state of double consciousness, in the sense of a state of racial anxiety and desire for respect and recognition.

But the usefulness of the concept goes beyond race and color, for it is a similar refusal to be measured by male supremacist lenses in patriarchal societies that animates feminist quest for recognition and respect. And a similar resistance to (be measured by) the gaze of the colonialists is what animates much of postcolonial critical discourse. What this shows is that there are hegemonic structures other than race to which the concept of double consciousness applies – patriarchy and colonialism being two such structures. This being the case, Du Bois' concept of double consciousness very aptly characterizes the phenomenon of the presuppositions of resistance in any social setting. In this regard, the concept gives expression to a cardinal feature of oppression to which victims of oppression are responding, namely, the denigration of oppression and the demand for recognition and respect by victims of oppression.

It follows from the foregoing considerations that Asante's demand for recognition and respect unquestionably leads him to tacitly use the very concept he so vehemently repudiates. Has he then really brought an end to double consciousness as he set out to do? The answer is certainly "No." He may *think* that he has brought an end to it, but his pronouncement is belied by the specter of white supremacy that motivates his very Afrocentric undertaking. I conclude therefore that while Asante is explicitly disavowing the phenomenon of double consciousness, he is implicitly acknowledging it in some form through his Afrocentric challenges to white supremacy. As such, his overall position generates a logical incoherence of which he seems completely unaware.[15]

* I wish to thank Middle Tennessee State University for the award of an FRCAC Summer Research Grant that enabled me to revise this paper for publication in this volume.

[1] See Martin R. Delaney "The Condition, Elevation, Emigration, and Destiny of the Colored People of the United States" and "Philosophy and Opinions of Marcus Garvey." Both selections are reprinted in James A. Montmarquet and William H Hardy, eds., *Reflections: An Anthology of African American Philosophy* (Belmont: Wadsworth, 2000).

[2] I argue below that Asante is indirectly subject to this denigrating and disparaging sense of double consciousness. If I am right, then clearly Du Bois's concept of double consciousness admits of more than one reading.

[3] For an exemplary discussion of the subjectivity of conscious experience see Thomas Nagel, "What Is It Like to be a Bat?" *Philosophy: The Quest for Truth*, ed. Louis P. Pojman (New York: Oxford UP, 2006), ch. 32.

[4] Asante claims that the state of affairs does not exist, at least for most ordinary African Americans, and I consider that assertion to be simply false.

[5] The following is just a sample of scholarly examinations of the subject: Paul Gilroy, *The Black Atlantic: Modernity and Double Consciousness* (Cambridge: Harvard UP, 1993); Cornel West, *Prophecy Deliverance! An Afro-American Revolutionary Christianity* (Philadelphia: The Westminster P, 1982), ch.1; West, *The Cornel West Reader* (New York: Basic Civitas Books, 1999), 58-59; Ernest Allen Jr., "Du Boisean Double Consciousness: The Unsustainable Argument," *The Black Scholar* 33.2 (2003): 25-43; T. Owens Moore, "A Fanonian Perspective on Double Consciousness," *Journal of Black Studies* 35.6 (2005): 751-62; Jane Anna Gordon, "The Gift of Double Consciousness: Some Obstacles to Grasping the Contributions of the Colonized," *Postcolonialism and Political Theory*, ed. Nalini Persram (Lanham: Lexington Books, 2007), ch. 7.

[6] If West is correct, then Du Bois would seem to be suffering from an inferiority complex comparable to that from which white America suffered in relation to Europe. And this would be rather ironic. But is West right?

[7] See Lucius T. Outlaw, "On Cornel West on W. E. B. Du Bois," *Cornel West: A Critical Reader*, ed. George Yancy (Malden: Blackwell, 2001), ch. 14.

[8] Gordon proceeds to characterize double consciousness as "potentiated second sight," a characterization she borrows from Paget Henry. By this characterization she means that double consciousness, though initially deemed a liability, turns out also to be an asset to its possessors because of the special insight it offers them (147-49).

[9] See G. F. W. Hegel, "Geographical Basis of World History" / "Colonialism in the Internal Logic of Capitalist Modernity," *Race and the Enlightenment*, ed. Emmanuel Eze (1857; Cambridge: Blackwell, 1997), ch. 10.

[10] Hume's view is expressed in his essay "Of National Characters," and Kant's approval is given in his "On National Characteristics." Both essays are reprinted in the 1997 reader, *Race and the Enlightenment*, ed. Emmanuel Eze, chs. 3 and 4, respectively. What I take to be Locke's view can be reconstructed from his investigation of the concept of a person and his attendant discussion of the problem of personal identity in Book Two, ch. 27, of his *Essay*

Concerning Human Understanding, ed. Alexander Campbell Fraser (1690; New York: Dover, 1959). I take Locke's discussions therein to have implications for his political views, especially about the issue of slavery, in both the *Two Treatises of Government*, ed. Peter Laslett (1689; Cambridge: Cambridge UP, 1960), and "The Fundamental Constitutions of Carolina: March 1, 1669," *The Avalon Project at Yale Law School*, 26 Feb. 2008 <http://avalon.law.yale.edu/17th_century/nc05.asp>, item no. 107. For a discussion of this aspect of Locke's thought see my *Cornel West & Philosophy*, ch. 6, entitled "Modernity, Philosophy, and Race(ism)."

[11] See my *Cornel West & Philosophy*. Others who have similarly provided in-depth analyses of some, if not all, of these philosophers' views of blacks in the Western canon include David Theo Goldberg, *Racist Culture: Philosophy and the Politics of Meaning* (Oxford: Blackwell, 1993), ch. 2, esp. pp. 21-40; Eze, "The Color of Reason: The Idea of 'Race' in Kant's Anthropology," *Postcolonial African Philosophy: A Critical Reader*, ed. Eze (Cambridge: Blackwell, 1997), ch. 4; West, *Reader* ch. 5, and *Prophecy* ch. 2; Lewis Gordon, *Her Majesty's Other Children* (Lanham: Rowman and Littlefield, 1997), ch. 2, esp. pp. 25-28; Tsenay Serequeberhan, "Eurocentricism in Europe: The Case of Immanuel Kant," *The Philosophical Forum* 27.4 (1996): 333-56; Serequeberhan, "The Critique of Eurocentricism and the Practice of African Philosophy," *Postcolonial African Philosophy*, ed. Eze, ch. 5; Richard H. Popkin, "The Philosophical Basis of Eighteenth-Century Racism," *Studies in Eighteenth-Century Culture*, ed. Harold E. Pagliaro (Cleveland: Case Western Reserve U, 1973), 245-62; Harry M. Bracken, "Essence, Accident and Race," *Hermathena* 116 (Winter 1973): 81-96.

[12] For Kant's endorsement of Hume's overall view see the following remarks in his essay "On National Characteristics": "The Negroes of Africa have by nature no feeling that rises above the trifling. Mr. Hume challenges anyone to cite a single example in which a Negro has shown talents, and asserts that among the hundreds of thousands of blacks who are transported elsewhere from their countries, although many of them have been set free, still not a single one was ever found who presented anything great in art or science or any other praiseworthy quality, even though among the whites some continually rise aloft from the lowest rabble, and through superior gifts earn respect in the world" (55).

[13] Admittedly, there is a lot more to Gordon's discussion than I have outlined here. But the brief exposition I have offered will suffice for my purpose.

[14] In the succeeding page, Gilroy elaborates this point by giving the origination of the concept of double consciousness in Du Bois's thought saying, "Double consciousness emerges from the unhappy symbiosis between three modes of thinking, being and seeing. The first is racially particularistic, the second nationalistic in that it derives from the nation state in which the ex-slaves but not-yet-citizens find themselves, rather than from their aspiration towards a nation state of their own. The third is diasporic or hemispheric, sometimes global and occasionally universalist. The trio was woven into some unlikely but exquisite pattern in Du Bois's thinking" (127).

[15] I thank Lewis and Jane Gordon for inviting me to present an earlier version of this paper in a session with Asante as part of the Conversations Series of the Institute of Race and Social

Thought of Temple University, March 23, 2007. I should note in this respect that although Asante disagreed with me on some of the issues I have raised here, nevertheless he was very gracious in his response and the ensuing discussion, for which reason I most sincerely applaud him. Also, I presented a version of this paper at the Third Annual Caribbean Philosophical Association conference in Montreal, August 1-3, 2006, and wish to thank the discussants at my session whose responses inspired me to pursue the subject further. I wish also to thank the anonymous reviewers of FORECAAST whose comments enabled me to expand and sharpen my analysis in parts of my discussion. Finally, I thank Tina Johnson, Jane Gordon, and George Yancy for their invaluable comments on earlier drafts of this paper.

Works Cited

Allen, Ernest, Jr. "Du Boisean Double Consciousness: The Unsustainable Argument." *The Black Scholar.* 33.2 (2003): 25-43.

Asante, Molefi. "Blackness as an Ethical Trope: Toward A Post-Western Assertion." *White on White/Black on Black.* Ed. George Yancy. Lanham: Rowman and Littlefield, 2005. 203-16.

---. "Racism, Consciousness, and Afrocentricity." *Reflections: An Anthology of African American Philosophy.* Ed. James A. Montmarquet and William Hardy. Belmont: Wadsworth, 2000. 13-22.

---. *The Afrocentric Idea.* Rev. ed. Philadelphia: Temple UP, 1998.

Bracken, Harry M. "Essence, Accident and Race." *Hermathena* 116 (Winter 1973): 81-96.

Delaney, Martin R. "The Condition, Elevation, Emigration, and Destiny of the Colored People of the United States." *Reflections: An Anthology of African American Philosophy.* Ed. James A. Montmarquet and William Hardy. Belmont: Wadsworth, 2000. 73-81.

Du Bois, W. E. B. *The Souls of Black Folk.* 1903. New York: Bantam Books, 1989.

Eze, Emmanuel, ed. *Postcolonial African Philosophy: A Critical Reader.* Cambridge: Blackwell, 1997.

---, ed. *Race and the Enlightenment.* Cambridge: Blackwell Publishers, 1997.

Garvey, Marcus. Excerpt from *Philosophy and Opinions of Marcus Garvey*. *Reflections: An Anthology of African American Philosophy*. Ed. James A. Montmarquet and William Hardy. Belmont: Wadsworth, 2000. 92-97.

Gilroy, Paul. *The Black Atlantic: Modernity and Double Consciousness*. Cambridge: Harvard UP, 1993.

Goldberg, David Theo. *Racist Culture: Philosophy and the Politics of Meaning*. Oxford: Blackwell, 1993.

Gordon, Jane Anna. "The Gift of Double Consciousness: Some Obstacles to Grasping the Contributions of the Colonized." *Postcolonialism and Political Theory*. Ed. Nalini Persram. Lanham: Lexington Books, 2007. 143-62.

Gordon, Lewis R. *Her Majesty's Other Children*. Lanham: Rowman and Littlefield, 1997.

Hegel, Georg Wilhelm Friedrich. "Geographical Basis of World History." 1857. *Race and the Enlightenment*. Ed. Emmanuel Eze. Cambridge: Blackwell, 1997. 110-49.

Hume, David. "Of National Characters." 1748. *Race and the Enlightenment*. Ed. Emmanuel Eze. Cambridge: Blackwell, 1997. 30-33.

Johnson, Clarence Sholé. *Cornel West & Philosophy*. New York: Routledge, 2003.

Kant, Immanuel. "On National Characteristics." 1764. *Race and the Enlightenment*. Ed. Emmanuel Eze. Cambridge: Blackwell, 1997. 49-57.

Locke, John. *An Essay Concerning Human Understanding*. 1690. New York: Dover Publications, 1959.

---. "The Fundamental Constitutions of Carolina: March 1, 1669." *The Avalon Project at Yale Law School*. Item no. 107. 26 Feb. 2008 <http://avalon.law.yale.edu/17th_century/nc05.asp>.

---. *Two Treatises of Government*. 1689. Ed. Peter Laslett. Cambridge: Cambridge UP, 1960.

Moore, T. Owens. "A Fanonian Perspective on Double Consciousness." *Journal of Black Studies* 35.6 (2005): 751-762.

Nagel, Thomas. "What Is It Like to be a Bat?" *Philosophy: The Quest for Truth*. Ed. Louis P. Pojman. New York: Oxford UP, 2006. 285-93.

Outlaw, Lucius T. "On Cornel West on W. E. B. Du Bois." *Cornel West: A Critical Reader*. Ed. George Yancy. Malden: Blackwell, 2001. 261-79.

Popkin, Richard H. "The Philosophical Basis of Eighteenth-Century Racism." *Studies in Eighteenth-Century Culture*. Ed. Harold E. Pagliaro. Cleveland: Case Western Reserve U, 1973. 245-62.

Serequeberhan, Tsenay. "The Critique of Eurocentricism and the Practice of African Philosophy." Ed. Emmanuel Eze. *Postcolonial African Philosophy: A Critical Reader*. Cambridge: Blackwell, 1997. 141-61.

---. "Eurocentricism in Europe: The Case of Immanuel Kant." *The Philosophical Forum* 27.4 (1996): 333-56.

West, Cornel. *Prophecy Deliverance! An Afro-American Revolutionary Christianity*. Philadelphia: The Westminster P, 1982.

---. *The Cornel West Reader*. New York: Basic Civitas Books, 1999.

Young, Iris M. *Justice and the Politics of Difference*. Princeton: Princeton UP, 1990.

María M. García Lorenzo

The Unwhitening of Discourse: The Gothic in African-American Literature

> The terrain, slavery, was formidable and pathless. To invite readers (and myself) into the repellant landscape (hidden, but not completely; deliberately buried, but not forgotten) was to pitch a tent in a cemetery inhabited by highly vocal ghosts.
>
> (Toni Morrison, foreword to *Beloved*)

Jerrold E. Hogle opens his introduction to *The Cambridge Companion to the Gothic* by asserting that gothic fiction "is hardly 'Gothic' at all" (i). Indeed, histories of gothic literature locate the beginning of the formula at the end of the eighteenth century, that is, during the Enlightenment. The Age of Reason defined or redefined the social markers (for instance, literacy) that set classes and species apart, drawing a division line between me and not-me, human and non-human, citizen and slave (see Gates 24-25). Therefore, modern ideals were born side by side with their terrors, celebrating freedom while finding room for slavery. In this context, black mastery of arts and letters questioned the assumptions that constructed modernity and the Enlightenment – the age of "light" that tried to leave all "darkness" behind – and that relegated non-whites to the status of non-citizens and virtual non-humans. The discussion that follows addresses two nuclear ideas. First, that American gothic texts have always engaged in a cross-fertilization between black history and white imagination where history has remained mostly silenced by the dominant discourse. Second, that recent African-American texts relive and rewrite that history by deconstructing the conventions of the gothic formula.

Gothic literature articulates abjection and cultural contradictions. Its basic rhetoric is that of terror, violence, destruction and the grotesque. At the center of the formula, the "fascination with transgression and the anxiety over cultural limits and boundaries" (Botting 2) found, in its American version, a suitable breeding ground in the cultural anxieties of racial hybridism and degeneration.

The symbolic shadows, the mythical obscurity, the legendary fear of darkness that vertebrated the genre had an actual counterpart in the non-white races that populated the American territories. However, gothic literature – as a paradoxical form that involves both assertion and subversion of established patterns of authority – provides a space for the re-enactment of power positions and cultural resistance. George Piggford rightly asserts that Fiedler's influential study on the bond between the American gothic tradition and slavery focused mainly on the use of the trope of blackness by *white* authors (143). *Love and Death in the American Novel* (1960) did not debate blackness as a gothic ingredient in African-American texts, Piggford argues. Taking the issue further, the use of *whiteness* as a gothic component was equally ignored. Teresa Goddu, in *Gothic America: Narrative, History, and Nation*, calls for a re-evaluation of the gothic, frequently buried in debates over psychological/theological notions of the dark, in order to focus on history and slavery as the true origin of such blackness (10). She thus subscribes to the "ghost in the machine" metaphor, Morrison's trope for the absent presence of race in American Literature ("Unspeakable" 11).

"American gothic" is a very elastic term, inclusive enough to cross the boundaries of literary genre and to express more an attitude or an impression than a set of rigid conventions. In this comprehensive sense, American history and American culture are themselves gothic, both encouraging and welcoming the literary formula. Goddu, for instance, points to the country's corruption under a veil of innocence and purity, like a solid and apparently respectable building that shelters decay and eventually collapses (10). Ignorance of its own moral decadence regarding racial matters was not the only gothic feature of the country's past, since it was joined by the threatening reality of biological and cultural hybridism. Additionally, slave riots were an impending menace on the American economic system for decades.

At this point, literacy enters the discussion once more. As mentioned before, in the Age of Reason literacy set apart the citizens and those that did not deserve citizenship, the rightful and the right-less. But American culture became Gothicized – and, therefore, subject to notions of transgression – with, for instance, the ambiguity of authority. On occasion, doubt was cast on African-American assertions of having actually written the texts they claimed as their own, which is a truly gothic instance in its imprecise contours and ominous possibility: someone looks like the author of a book, but maybe isn't.[1] (Obviously enough, disbelief emerges when something does not comply with the constructed categories that systematize our existence.) Black voices are heard that should remain silent, an actual restoration of Poe's black cat (which threatened to haunt whiteness and return to claim revenge). This distrust of authorial passing can be seen as a sort of appropriation of voice, a cultural ventriloquism emulating Francis Carwin's in C. Brockden Brown's novel *Wieland* (1798). African-American history, so to speak, was gothic because it implied the return of the culturally dead.

Those "voices" and "mobility" where there was no whiteness and where a void should be – a negation on the part of the community in tune with Oscar Patterson's social death – found a proper set of metaphors in the literary gothic. The imaginative rendering of the fears of miscegenation in white texts, nevertheless, walked side by side with the abominable facts of black history, so the literal horrors of bondage merge with the essential features of the American gothic narrative, among which the torment of innocent victims stands out. Since slavery embodies a heritage bleak enough in itself to be perceived as a gothic theme, slave narratives of the eighteenth century can be read as gothic accounts of enslaved Africans or African-Americans, well before the publication of the so-considered founder of American gothic texts, Brown's *Wieland*. Also, well-known phrases such as "being possessed" or "invasion of the body snatchers" have participated in the white gothic imagination for centuries, but were actualities in the lives of enslaved men and women. Thus the uncanny, the familiar but disturbing, has been used by African-Americans since before the American Civil War either to represent the horror of their reality or to reverse the formula in order to subvert the binary opposition that bonds blackness to evil or threat. Traditional gothic devices (immeasurable and disproportionate misery, the claustrophobic environment of slave ships, familial disruptions, the cruelty of the plantation system, and abusive body politics) appeared in their texts to express cultural resistance through the reversion of the formula. In other words, by encoding their own history in gothic narratives they challenged the white conception of modernity.

Throughout the nineteenth century we seem to have two parallel lines of texts conforming to or adapting the gothic code: fantasies that demonize racial otherness (Edgar A. Poe or Nathaniel Hawthorne, to name only two), and historical accounts that presumably appropriate gothic imagery or settings in order to portray the cruelty and violence of enslavement (Hanna Crafts, Harriet Jacobs, or Frederick Douglass). In other words, "white gothic" and "black gothic." However, I would point to the constant cross-fertilization of both throughout the nineteenth century. Crime or rebellion stories concerning blacks, or the confessions pronounced by convicted slaves fuelled the blossoming of a specifically American gothic imagination, haunting the minds of a national consciousness that silenced crucial political and social issues. Meanwhile, the reports of such confessions in newspapers and chronicles adapted the discourse of gothic narratives. Such cross-fertilization consolidated the genre – as a white form, that is, conforming to the dominant discourse – and for centuries now it has been approached as an Anglo-American tradition. As a result, we usually speak in terms of the black race's "appropriation" of the gothic convention, when maybe we should question whose appropriation of what occurred first.

The most famous and critically appraised kind – "white gothic" – reinforced the very binary oppositions, so specific to the formula, that the second kind was trying to subvert. In particular, we are dealing here with color imagery:[2] white versus black, light versus darkness. As we all know, the Judeo-Christian discourse has crystallized horror and evil in linguistic units referring to blackness and absence of light: the Prince of Darkness, the black mark of Cain, the "dark side of the force" my generation grew up with. On the contrary, God is white-skinned and dressed in white. In the States, racial difference and, therefore, white supremacy was highlighted by means of the monstrosity ascribed to the black race. The fear of racial boundary transgression was mythologized in the horrors of *any* boundary transgression (sexual, intellectual, biological, etc.), for which reason "blackness" could also be ascribed to some white characters. By this "othering" device, characters such as Hawthorne's Dimmesdale in *The Scarlet Letter* (1850) or Faulkner's Popeye in *Sanctuary* (1931) are read as black. Blackness as agent or setting of horror, then, populates the formula that encodes racial anxiety; blackness as victim of horror, however, requires further consideration and will be paid proper attention below. The gothic genre, if understood as a monolithic white discourse, conceptualizes the Self and the Other in terms that some African-American texts deconstruct and defy. They decentralize whiteness, deprive it of its authoritative position, by exposing whiteness as an alien other that generates horror, violence and destruction.

Hence, gothic discourse has been both white and black from its very beginning. What whitened the discourse, in truth, was the overpowering presence of social constructions regarding color and fear, decades of literary criticism that popularized the genre and therefore downplayed its subversive power, and the assumption of a white audience, as Toni Morrison accurately claims in *Playing in the Dark*. Consistent with this line of thought is Teresa Goddu's argument that the recurrent associations of the gothic with the sensational and its "apparent lack of connection to reality and intellectual purpose" have generated

> a resistance to examining African-American narratives in relation to the gothic. [...] However, instead of accepting traditional readings of the gothic as unrealistic and frivolous, thereby excluding African-American narratives from this genre, we should use the African-American gothic to revise our understanding of the gothic as an historical mode. (139-40)

In recovering African-American gothic's relationship to history, we should bear in mind that white and black are non-colors, devoid of chromatic significance. White and black, then, are reversible and therefore exchangeable. I have already alluded to the othering device of ascribing blackness to white characters or settings to attach an evil quality to them – in other words, with a view to making us read them as black. Blurry outlines is one of the defining features of the gothic, one that exposes the anxiety of transgressing cultural positions: half here *and* half there; alive *and* dead; organic *and* artificial; human *and* animal; black *and* white;[3] ours *and* other's (or even multiplicity, like Doctor Frankenstein's monster, who belonged to several classes at the same time). The white middle-class faces the uncertainty of these cultural positions, which becomes terrifying because its very definition depends on these categories: in between, ambiguous, composite, as Kristeva puts it (4). National consciousness abjects ambiguous identity territories, as Goddu argues, to avoid the abyss of non-identity.

Some African-American writers employ the same devices of non-identity, and subsequently unwrite history and national narratives. Hanna Crafts' protagonist of *The Bondwoman's Narrative* passes for white, for instance. In *The Narrative of the Life of Henry Box Brown* the protagonist escapes slavery confined in a box that hides his color. This image powerfully resembles the fears of buried-while-alive that haunted Edgar A. Poe, serves as a metaphor for slavery, and also is a reversion of the racial implications of the gothic. The central character in Ralph Ellison's *Invisible Man* is equally unreadable through the usual color code because he cannot be seen, and this imprecision of color category is precisely what makes a "spook" of him, a social specter. These authors, then, make a point of the ambiguity that created so much anxiety in American culture.

Instead of constructing Otherness, they are deconstructing the gothic means through which Otherness is constructed.

This racial variation on the formula is very much alive in the twentieth century. In fact, it has never ceased to impregnate African-American literature. Zora Neale Hurston's *Their Eyes Were Watching God* (1937), Richard Wright's *Native Son* (1940), Ralph Ellison's *Invisible Man* (1952), Amiri Baraka's *Dutchman* (1964), Toni Morrison's *Song of Solomon* (1977) and *Beloved* (1987), or Gloria Naylor's *Linden Hills* (1985) are revealing examples of the unwhitening of the white discourse in gothic literature. A form of resistance has been thus exerted by African-Americans through the gothic tradition, but this whitened tradition has been subverted by white authors too. Melville's white whale already subverted the ideological opposition based on color. Joseph Conrad's *Heart of Darkness* (1899) reversed the color dichotomy to serve a deep suspicion of the deadly whiteness of European culture. William Faulkner's "A Rose for Emily" (1931) shows that black and white are reversible.

Racial reversion of gothic devices can be observed and has been duly analyzed in Wright's *Native Son* (for instance in Sisney; George; Butler; or Smethurst), not a gothic novel in the usual sense but definitely one that incorporates gothic tropes and structures:

> Bigger turned and a hysterical terror seized him, as though he were falling from a great height in a dream. A white blur was standing by the door, silent, ghost-like. It filled his eyes and gripped his body. It was Mrs. Dalton. He wanted to knock her out of his way and bolt from the room. (Wright 85)

Race and gender are gothicized at this key moment of the novel. The scene presents a triangle of passive and active poles, each trespassing their constructed ontological categories: frightened blackness (Bigger), threatening whiteness (Mrs. Dalton), white blindness and silence, black power exerted on whiteness through fear and violence. Bearing such reversions in mind, James Smethurst defines the novel as an "anti-gothic" text (29) in his review of gothic elements in *Native Son*. His analysis does not neglect Bigger's constant reference to the whiteness of the things he sees: walls, smoke, clouds, hair, etc, including a white cat that functions as a reversal of Poe's black, watching cat (34). Bigger's menacing environment, then, is shrouded in a confusing whiteness out of which he makes very little, thus contesting the characteristic, and menacing, gothic darkness.

Their Eyes Were Watching God also falls into this group of texts that unwhiten the gothic symbolic system. Hurston employs gothic elements – such as brutal nature or unexpected radical changes in a character's attitude – to unveil the whitening of the black folk community and its catastrophic consequences. In other words, as Erik D. Curren argues,

> As soon as the folk community is threatened by an outside force – in this case, the power of nature – it begins to display white attitudes. The first of these is a modern dismissal of tribal lore, a short-sighted and close-minded empiricism that discounts other ways of knowing nature [...]. Related to this are bigotry and materialism more typical of white America than of black folk culture. (20)

At the same time, an ideological reversion has taken place: Hurston deprives Christianity, one of the sources of the white/black opposition, of its redeeming values and darkens it, while she deprives voodoo of its presumed diabolic implications and brings it to the center of the novel's discourse. This gothicization of the Christian dogma, together with her treatment of the black vernacular, contributes to the whole architecture of black empowerment that Hurston erects.

Similarly, Amiri Baraka's *Dutchman* problematizes class, sex, and race oppression by deconstructing gothic conventions. The play's setting – a claustrophobic subway train that imprisons characters – echoes other gothic environments too intensely to be overlooked. Therefore, readers are readily prepared to approach the text with a set of conventions to make meaning of it. But we soon find that the binary oppositions (black/white, male/female) on which the play is based do not work in the traditional way. Indeed, Baraka disempowers the black male character, Clay, and casts the threatening factor on Lula, the female white character. Clay, as the assimilated (white and black at once) and oppressed black youth, is powerless in the face of Lula's sexual advances and awakening words. Entrapped by American history as he is in the subway train, Clay's reaction, in Piggford's words, is "a gothic vision of race revolution and murder, an inversion of the dominant structures of power" (155). Clay's vocalization of murder and devastation in the following passage evidences Baraka's use of the contesting strength of the gothic in order to unveil white dominance (political and discursive) and suggests its end:

CLAY: Tell [your father] not to preach so much rationalism and cold logic to these niggers. Let them alone. Don't make the mistake, through some irresponsible urge of Christian charity, of talking too much about the advantages of Western rationalism, or the great intellectual legacy of the white man, or maybe they'll begin to listen. And then, maybe one day, you'll find they actually do understand exactly what you're talking about, all these fantasy people. And on that day [...] they'll murder you, and have very rational explanations. Very much like your own. They'll cut your throats, and drag you to the edge of your cities so the flesh can fall away from your bones, in sanitary isolation. (2313)

Toni Morrison's novels, too, can be approached as texts that resist the white construction of race through the deconstruction of the white gothic. Although Morrison has manifested her dislike of the term "gothic" in relation to her texts, she has repeatedly gothicized them. *Beloved* is likely to stand out as the most remarkable of her novels in terms of gothic resources (among others the classic haunting past, ghosts, bodily possession and infanticide). But I'd like to highlight some other elements at play, specifically those that contribute to the unwhitening of the gothic formula. In *Beloved*, we find a description of the Ku-Klux-Klan (the "talking sheets" that resemble specters and materialize haunting presences) inspired by vampiric imagery: "Desperately thirsty for black blood, without which it could not live, the dragon swam the Ohio at will" (79). Halberstam defends that the vampiric allusion mirrors in the capitalist nature of slavery, where the body is appropriated for consumption (12), and where Sethe tries to consume her own children who, by law, are not her property.

Gothic literature, it should be remembered at this point in my discussion, unveils and debates various forms of oppression, among which economic and social oppression is fairly common. *The Castle of Otranto* (1764), for instance, develops a well-known gothic convention: that of the lawful/unlawful inheritance of property, usurpation and restoration. Ruth Bienstock Anolik examines the bond between gothicism and property in the masterplots of several traditional gothic texts, and concludes: "We may say, then, of the gothic that it posits a ludic, supernatural world in which the principles of legal ownership grounded in rationality and an existing social order, must give way to the irrational, to ghostly possession" (668). Anolik's study engages in the invisibility or even civil death of disempowered citizens, such as women (and slaves, I should add), whose rights to property are neutralized by the dominant system. Gothic fantasies would then allow for an alternative version of ownership. In the United

States, African-Americans *became* properties, in other words objects – not subjects – in the processes of ownership and transmission. Bodily possession like the one we read about in *Beloved* is, we should remember, a typical gothic trope that in this case invites reflection, bearing in mind that the actual possession of people – i.e., slavery – originated Beloved's story.[4]

Song of Solomon is another novel providing examples of reversion of gothic conventions in order to contest the white discourse associated with them. If *Beloved* draws on possession and haunted houses, Milkman Dead's story reverses the gothic code as related to violence, environment, and color imagery. In the novel, black activist groups reenact on white people the violence and horror once inflicted on blacks. But in a ceremonial scene, following a hunt, Milkman Dead understands black history as he participates in the evisceration of a bobcat. However lyrical the fragment may sound, its diction powerfully reminds us of hardcore gothicism:

> "Everybody wants a black man's life [...]. It's the condition our condition is in."
> Omar cut around the legs and the neck. Then he pulled the hide off.
> "What good is a man's life if he can't even choose what to die for?"
> The transparent underskin tore like gossamer under his fingers.
> "Everybody wants a black man's life."
> Now Small Boy knelt down and split the flesh from the scrotum to the jaw [...]. He dug under the ribcage to the diaphragm and carefully cut around it until it was free. (281-82)

Morrison, however, subverts the gothic code by transforming the scene into a ritual of love and respect, not of destruction, that contributes to Milkman Dead's racial resurrection. As with the scene from *Native Son* mentioned above, black characters become empowered through the same imaginative devices traditionally used to disempower African-Americans. In other words, the classic gothic tradition ascribed violence and destruction to blackness, thus cultivating the discourse that marginalized the black Other.

The following passage presents us with another instance of generic reversion and subversion in *Song of Solomon*:

> Milkman ducked under the boughs of black walnut trees and walked straight towards the big crumbling house. He knew that an old woman had lived in it once, but he saw no signs of life there now. [...] From where he

> stood, the house looked as if it had been eaten by a galloping disease, the stores of which were dark and fluid. (219-20)

The scene rescues gothic settings of thick, gloomy vegetation and decayed architecture, so it seems to encourage the usual reading of such settings. Our reading of the passage – and, accordingly, of the complete text – is conditioned by Morrison's reversing practices, by which the "old woman" (Circe) bears a witch's name but lacks her devious manners, and the derelict house stands on as a symbol of resistance against white mischief. Similarly, the white bull in the novel, which precipitates Freddie's mother's labor and subsequent death, cannot be read as a symbol of racist oppression exclusively. It invokes terror, as well as the pain involved in labor and the distress caused by the disruption of Freddie's family. It is a gothic device that falls out of "normalized" horror imagery, but whose disturbing potential is as effective as the usual ghostly presence.

Gloria Naylor's *Linden Hills* deserves a reference in my deliberation of representative texts that challenge ideological assumptions through gothic devices. Charles Wilson states that "In *Linden Hills*, almost any physical or philosophical concept is reversed" (80), including generic conventions. To name two examples, five generations of Nedeeds have erected the black community of Linden Hills, an attractive space even for whites, where moving down – not up – the hill is a sign of social improvement. Regarding gothic tropes, Willa Nedeed is locked by her husband in the basement, not in the attic, for bearing a light-skinned child whose "ghostly presence […] mocked everything his father had built" (18). Whiteness, then, is once more seen as the origin of abuse and destruction. But Willa's confinement and torture ultimately empower her through the memories and writings of past Nedeed women who, like her, suffered oppression:

> She wasn't like these other women; she had coped and they were crazy. They never changed […]. Anger began to scratch at the scars in her mind and she trembled as fresh blood seeped through the opening wounds. That's why Luther never talked about them: there wasn't a normal one in the bunch. But there was nothing wrong with her. She remembered loving the seasons, loving life. And there just couldn't have been anything wrong with what she had wanted. A home. A husband. Children. That was all, and that was so little. To ask for so little and to have it taken away. No, it wasn't wrong. It wasn't sick. If there was any sickness, it was in this house, in the air. It was left over from the breaths of those women who

had come before her. [...] Blood from the open scars dripped down behind her eyes as she looked around the basement, futile and bewildered. (204)

In the above extract, the typical use of female captivity and pain (her emotional and physical scars are mentioned) has been altered to celebrate life and domesticity. Willa emerges from her captivity – that is, from the socially dead – a determined woman, not the consumed and demented victim we might expect from classic gothic literature. By drawing on recognizable gothic conventions, Naylor invites us to read this as a symptom that the house has been exorcised out of a history of patriarchal abuse, and a woman is now bound to dislocate domestic power positions. The Nedeed's homeplace, consequently, burns to ashes so as to annihilate the "unnatural" – i.e., resistant – creature that can't be controlled.

Toni Morrison's words aptly restate the central arguments of this paper:

> Black slavery enriched the country's creative possibilities. For in that construction of blackness *and* enslavement could be found not only the non-free but also, with the dramatic polarity created by skin color, the projection of the not-me. The result was a playground for the imagination. What rose up out of collective needs to allay internal fears and to rationalize external extrapolation was an American Africanism –a fabricated brew of darkness, otherness, alarm, and desire that is uniquely American. (*Playing* 38)

Morrison's thesis in *Playing in the Dark* asserts that the implicit or explicit Africanist presence is ubiquitous in American literature, serving to define Americanness – i.e., whiteness – through its other. Such a presence transformed African-Americans into objects, not subjects, unable to write their histories and define their selves. Therefore a gothic ingredient such as darkness, omnipresent in American texts, is an othering device, a metaphor that maps out an ideological territory. But American gothic was not the prerogative of white authors, for American history and culture was gothic enough to favor gothic literature – regardless of race. But it has been revered as a white invention, hence the frequency with which the terms "appropriation" and "subversion" appear when we deal with African-American gothic.

The gothic as genre or effect, as a set of conventions or as the impression of unbearable, disproportionate and unprecedented suffering, can be read as a racialized discourse that becomes unwhitened, and its readers repositioned, in the works of some African-American writers. Fiedler has already argued that "horror is essential to our literature" (26). The point to discuss is not how frequently horror is present in American literature, nor how frequently it is imagized through blackness. The point is that the reader's position can be unwhitened, too. Deconstruction of gothic conventions like the white/black distinction by black and also white authors were well under way before critics began to unwhiten the genre themselves. Gothic literature can be approached as the underside of the American ideal, as an expression of the racialized other, or even as the oldest postcolonial literature on the American continent. By negotiating literary conventions, such as gothic codifications of race, African-American history is rewritten, and the black gothic exerts the subversive power that popular genres possess.

---

[1] In this line of thought, frontispiece portraits were used as authenticating devices by slave narrative authors who wished to prove their authorship, thus eliminating a discontinuity with their own texts that could erase their social and artistic identity.

[2] In *Playing in the Dark* (35) Toni Morrison claims the term "gothic" instead of the racially-emptied "black" or "dark," which seem to have replaced the former when referring to the genre under study here (for instance, in Harry Levin's *The Power of Blackness*).

[3] Needless to say, passing novels participate in this ambivalence of being and evidence another gothic element in American fiction.

[4] Equally related to a system that "cannibalizes" part of its members to feed other is Sethe's feeling that, outside her house, the world will "swallow her up."

Works Cited

Anolik, Ruth Bienstock. "Horrors of Possession: The Gothic Struggles with the Law." *Legal Studies Forum* 24 (2000): 667-86.

Baraka, Amiri. *Dutchman*. 1964. *Norton Anthology of American Literature*. Ed. Nina Baym. 6th ed. Vol. E. New York: Norton, 2003. 2301-14.

Botting, Fred. *Gothic*. London: Routledge, 1996.

Brown, Charles Brockden. *Wieland; or The Transformation* and *Memoirs of Carwin the Biloquist*. 1798. Ed. Emory Elliott. Oxford: Oxford UP, 1994.

Butler, Robert. "*Native Son* Is Set in a Gothic Ghetto." *Readings on Richard Wright*. Ed. Hayley R. Mitchell. San Diego: Greenhaven, 2000. 120-24.

Curren, Erik D. "Should Their Eyes Have Been Watching God? Hurston's Use of Religious Experience and Gothic Horror." *African American Review* 29.1 (1995): 17-25.

Fiedler, Leslie. *Love and Death in the American Novel*. 1960. Illinois: Dalkey Archive P, 1997.

Gates, Henry Louis, Jr. *Figures in Black: Words, Signs, and the "Racial" Self*. Oxford: Oxford UP, 1987.

George, Stephen K. "The Horror of Bigger Thomas: The Perception of Form Without Face in Richard Wright's *Native Son*." *African American Review* 31.3 (1997): 497-504.

Goddu, Teresa A. *Gothic America: Narrative, History, and Nation*. New York: Columbia UP, 1997.

Halberstam, Judith. *Skin Shows: Gothic Horror and the Technology of Monsters*. Durham: Duke UP, 1995.

Hogle, Jerrold E., ed. *The Cambridge Companion to the Gothic*. Cambridge: Cambridge UP, 2002.

Kristeva, Julia. *Powers of Horror: An Essay on Abjection*. 1980. Trans. Leon S. Roudiez. New York: Columbia UP, 1982.

Levin, Harry. *The Power of Darkness: Hawthorne, Poe, Melville*. New York: Alfred Knopf, 1970.

Morrison, Toni. *Beloved*. 1987. London: Vintage, 2005.

---. *Playing in the Dark: Whiteness and the Literary Imagination*. New York: Vintage Books, 1993.

---. *Song of Solomon*. 1977. London: Picador, 1989.

---. "Unspeakable Things Unspoken: The Afro-American Presence in American Literature." *Michigan Quarterly Review* 28.1 (1989): 1-34.

Naylor, Gloria. *Linden Hills*. 1985. Harmondsworth: Penguin, 1986.

Patterson, Orlando. *Slavery and Social Death: A Comparative Study*. Cambridge: Harvard UP, 1982.

Piggford, George. "Looking into Black Skulls: American Gothic, the Revolutionary Theatre, and Amiri Baraka's *Dutchman*." *American Gothic: New Interventions in a National Narrative*. Ed. R. Martin and E. Savoy. Iowa City: U of Iowa P, 1998. 143-60.

Sisney, Mary F. "The Power and Horror of Whiteness: Wright and Ellison Respond to Poe." *College Language Association Journal* 29.1 (1985): 82-90.

Smethurst, James. "Invented by Horror: The Gothic and African American Literary Ideology in *Native Son*." *African American Review* 35.1 (2001): 29-40.

Wilson, Charles E., Jr. *Gloria Naylor: A Critical Companion*. Westport: Greenwood P, 2001.

Wright, Richard. *Native Son*. 1940. New York: Perennial Classics, 1998.

Christopher Mulvey

The Modernity of James Weldon Johnson and the African American Twentieth Century

Notions of Modernity, the Modern and Modernism were crucial to the thinking of early twentieth-century cultural criticism when an anxiety to be Modern, to become Modern, to be seen to be Modern possessed artists, futurists, activists alike. The conflicts and the claims can be used to situate the African American in the twentieth century, and one African American in particular can lead to a special understanding of Modernity. That African American is James Weldon Johnson.

Before an address is made to the Modernity of this man, it would be well to wonder at certain considerations in his life story. Sondra Kathryn Wilson identifies the remarkable nature of the remarkable work of a remarkable man when she points out that:

> Some historians have written that Johnson's contribution to his race was most effectively expressed through his literary works. Conversely, some assert that his greatest contribution was made in the arena of civil rights. (ix).

If we were to compare him with another American, it might be that we should compare him with Benjamin Franklin, another political activist, journalist, linguist, diplomat and writer, except that Johnson was also a poet, musician and novelist, working in areas in which Franklin was distinguished by his lack of talent. Franklin was D. H. Lawrence's little man in a snuff-colored suit, despised because he had no soul (Lawrence 24). Johnson by contrast dressed very well and had plenty of soul. In James Weldon Johnson, we have then a paradoxical man, a trained lawyer who could sound God's trombones.

Both Benjamin Franklin and James Weldon Johnson lived successful and, as far as we can say it of another person, happy lives. Franklin, it is true, died in his bed at the age of eighty-four while Johnson died in an automobile accident at the age of sixty-seven, but automobiles were not a liability in Franklin's day. "Johnson's later years were filled with honors," Ladell Payne tells us,

> He was awarded the Spingarn Medal by the NAACP for his achievements as "author, diplomat, and public servant." He received the Harmon Award for *God's Trombones* and was elected a trustee of Atlanta University. [...] In 1930 he became the Adam K. Spence Professor of Creative Literature at Fisk University, a position he held until his death in 1938. (44)

Johnson's successful, prosperous and honored life emphasizes the fact that in him we have one of those people so talented that they have enough reserve ability and stored energy to succeed in many ways in a long life and at all points; they make the living of life seem easy. Robert Fleming's description expresses the point precisely: "James Weldon Johnson [was] 'truly the "Renaissance man" of the Harlem Renaissance'" (qtd. in Tuttle, "Johnson" 1053).

Everyone knows that Franklin had a hard start. His story of success following his arrival in Philadelphia in 1723 with no more than two bread rolls in his pocket is the stuff of American legend. Only in the last half century have parents and teachers stopped using Benjamin Franklin as a model for aspirant youth. Perhaps not everyone knows that James Weldon Johnson had a considerably easier childhood than Franklin. The first son of James and Helen Louise Johnson was born as he says, "June 17, 1871, in the old house on the corner" of a block in Jacksonville, Florida. There Mr. Johnson was soon to build a new house, a "mansion," in which the boy grew up in an atmosphere of art, culture and decorum (*Along This Way* 8).

However, the date of Johnson's birth, 1871, and its place, Florida, tell us that no matter how pleasant home was for that black child, he had been born into a world infinitely more dangerous than the Massachusetts of 1706 into which the white child Benjamin Franklin had been born. In 1871, the Civil War was over but six years, and, if slavery had not been ended, it is almost certain that Johnson's parents would not have emigrated from the Caribbean island of Nassau to live in the American South. This was the period that Charles Chesnutt would call "Post-Bellum-Pre-Harlem," and it is plain from the way Johnson tells his story in *Along This Way* that a New South was emerging at about the same rate that he was growing up. That New South was a world in which the practice of lynching, relatively rare in the Old South where black people were considered property, became increasingly virulent and increasingly directed at African

Americans in the years from 1870 onward. It reached a peak in 1892 when there were 230 victims, 161 of whom were African American (Tuttle, "Lynching" 1211).

It is surprising to learn, therefore, that, in 1871, the baby Johnson was nursed by a white woman: "When I was born," Johnson writes,

> my mother was very ill, too ill to nurse me. Then she found a friend and neighbor in an unexpected quarter. Mrs. Cleary, her white neighbor who lived a block away, had a short while before given birth to a baby girl. When this baby was christened she was named Angel. The mother of Angel, hearing of my mother's plight, took me and nursed me at her breast until my mother had recovered sufficiently to give me her own milk. So it appears that in the land of black mammies I had a white one. (*Along This Way* 9)

Nothing should surprise us in the variations of human behavior, but Johnson's own comment suggests that a white woman's nursing a black baby was an unusual act. Because of the bad taste of white Southerners who boast about "their black mammies," Johnson says that he will not boast about his "white mammy"; nonetheless, it is clear that he was proud of his distinction. That it was a rare one is demonstrated to some extent by a poem that Langston Hughes wrote toward the end of his life:

> Comes the COLORED HOUR:
> Martin Luther King is Governor of Georgia,
> Dr. Rufus Clement his Chief Adviser,
> A. Philip Randolph the High Grand Worthy.
> In white pillared mansions
> Sitting on their wide verandas,
> Wealthy Negroes have white servants,
> White sharecroppers work the black plantations,
> And colored children have white mammies:
> Mammy Faubus
> Mammy Eastland
> Mammy Wallace
> Dear, dear darling old white mammies –
> Sometimes even buried with our family.
> *Dear* old
> Mammy Faubus! (92-93)

What had been a fact in 1871 had become a fantasy by 1967, and a white mammy as unreal as a black plantation.

Along This Way provides another contrary Southern snapshot in the generosity shown to Jimmie Johnson, the college student, by a white physician called Dr. Summers. The dates are vague, but it must have been about the year 1888. Student and physician developed a relationship "on a high level," says Johnson. "It was not that of employer to employee. Less still was it that of a white employer to a Negro employee. Between the two us, as individuals 'race' never showed its head" (*Along This Way* 95). Dr. Summers's behavior was by no means as remarkable as that of Mrs. Cleary, but that it was unusual is demonstrated by that fact that when Dr. Summers took Jimmie traveling, they ate together: "I am sure that it was at Dr. Summers's suggestion, perhaps on his insistence, that I ate at the captain's table. He followed the same course at the hotels in New York and Washington" (*Along This Way* 99).

Through these years, Johnson gives the impression that he lived a charmed life, one unscarred by the brutal segregation that was growing increasingly more effective and restrictive in his world. It was as if he preserved some talismanic shielding from bad treatment. On the first occasion of his going to university, he traveled with his wealthy Cuban friend Ricardo Rodríguez from Jacksonville to Atlanta. A conductor asked them to move from the first-class car to the Jim-Crow car. The two discussed the situation in Spanish: "As soon as the conductor heard us speaking a foreign language, his attitude changed; he punched our tickets and gave them back, and treated us just as he did the other passengers." This, says Johnson, was his first experience of "race prejudice as a concrete fact" (*Along This Way* 65).

It is remarkable that the revelation of race came so late in the life of James Weldon Johnson living in Florida when the revelation came so early in the life of a contemporary living in Massachusetts. Of the chilling moment, W. E. B. Du Bois says:

> It is in the early days of rollicking boyhood that the revelation first bursts upon one, all in a day, as it were. I remember well when the shadow swept across me. I was a little thing, away up in the hills of New England, where the dark Housatonic winds between Hoosac and Taghkanic to the sea. In a wee wooden schoolhouse, something put it into the boys' and girls' heads to buy gorgeous visiting-cards – ten cents a package – and exchange. The exchange was merry, till one girl, a tall newcomer, refused my card, – refused it peremptorily, with a glance. Then it dawned upon

me with a certain suddenness that I was different from the others; or like, mayhap, in heart and life and longing, but shut out from their world by a vast veil. (2)

However, despite Johnson's being seventeen years old when he saw the vast veil, it should not be inferred that Florida was free of racial prejudice. More importantly, it might be inferred that James Weldon Johnson was loathe to see himself as a victim.

The lesson learnt from that incident – "that in such situations," as Johnson says, "any kind of Negro will do; provided he is not one who is an American citizen" – is one that he draws again at the end of chapter 8 (*Along This Way* 65, 89). In that chapter, he talks about the dangers of the railroad car, and he gives details of three experiences. He does not emphasize the fact, but they all took place in the state of Georgia. On one occasion, the conductor was "rather apologetic" as he explained "that we had just crossed the Georgia line, and it was against the law in Georgia for white and colored people to ride in the same railroad car" (*Along This Way* 86). Johnson does not usually give a precise date for these incidents, but this he says took place in 1896, and the reference to the infamous Supreme Court judgment on segregation in *Homer A. Plessy v. John H. Ferguson* of April 1896 would have escaped no reader in 1933.

Episodes in which the ingenuity and courage of the black passenger overcome the prejudice and stupidity of the white conductor are very like episodes that appear in Josephine Brown's telling of her father's life, *The Biography of an American Bondman* (56-60), episodes which her father, William Wells Brown, tells in fictional form in *Clotel; or The President's Daughter* (172-74). But there is a difference. There is a deadly earnestness about William Wells Brown that is missing in James Weldon Johnson. Brown, a fugitive slave who had had to teach himself to read once he had escaped from a man who then forced him to live in exile in Great Britain until his price was paid, shows himself as having nothing to fall back on but his wit and wits. Johnson, by contrast, shows that "in such situations any kind of Negro will do; provided he is not one who is an American citizen." One way of not being an American Negro was to speak Spanish and another was to wear "a genuine Panama hat" (*Along This Way* 88). Class underlay these stratagems. Johnson traveled in first-class and Pullman cars, and his bearing, clothes and speech marked him as a gentleman. Though his story mimes to some extent that of a fugitive slave, Johnson was not "any kind of Negro'; rather, he was showing himself to be a special kind.

In 1933, Johnson strenuously resists presenting himself to the reader as any kind of victim, and his story reads as a story of American success. There is, however, a story within that story that arguably came close to bringing the success story to an abrupt end. It is an episode that can be described as a near lynching, and it took place in his home town of Jacksonville in 1900. There he was confronted in the city's Riverside Park by a squad of white soldiers who believed that he had been molesting a white woman; the military sent out "a detachment of troops with guns and dogs" to get him. The full danger of the South confronted him, and James Weldon Johnson was as close to being a victim as at any point in his charmed life as the soldiers began to shout: "'Kill the damned nigger! Kill the black son of a bitch'" (*Along This Way* 167).

Speaking Spanish or brandishing a Panama hat would not put things right, and Johnson initially panicked, but realizing that was the way to get himself murdered, he took command of first himself and then of the situation.

> As the rushing crowd comes, yelling and cursing, I feel that death is bearing in upon me. Not death of the empty sockets, but death with the blazing eyes of a frenzied brute. And still, I am not terror-stricken, I am carrying out the chief command that has been given me, "Show no sign of fear; if you do you are lost." (*Along This Way* 167)

A lieutenant breaks through the mob of soldiers: "We look at each other; and I feel that a quivering message from intelligence to intelligence has been interchanged." Johnson demanded the name of the officer's officer and called himself the man's prisoner. The near lynching was averted. Taken before the senior officer, a man whom Johnson knew, Johnson ended the incident by explaining: "'The lady with me is white, but not legally so'" (*Along This Way* 169). Johnson's self-possession meant that he not only escaped death; he also escaped public humiliation. He makes it clear that what saved him was his matching the bearing of the officer, and he was accorded the treatment of a gentleman in return. To that extent, his bearing was the equivalent of the Spanish language or a Panama hat. Once again, he had not behaved like "any kind of Negro," to repeat his repeated phrase. As with the railroad car incidents, Johnson wants to make light of the situation: "The quick turn taken by fate had buoyed me up. [...] my sense of relief had mounted almost to gayety" (ibid.), but gayety did not last. Instead, the incident preyed on his mind and disturbed his sleep for months (*Along This Way* 170). He had learned that he was, indeed, some kind of Negro. There is something quintessentially Modern in Johnson's role playing of selves, in his capacity to be simultaneously "any kind of Negro" and in the detached attachment to life that that enabled.

In 1912, Johnson published a novel that he called *The Autobiography of an Ex-Colored Man*, and in it the hero stands close to a lynching in which a man is burnt alive:

> He squirmed, he writhed, strained at his chains, then gave out cries and groans that I shall always hear. The cries and groans were choked off by the fire and smoke; but his eyes, bulging from their sockets, rolled from side to side, appealing in vain for help. Some of the crowd yelled and cheered, others seemed appalled at what they had done, and there were those who turned away sickened at the sight. (*Ex-Colored Man* [1927] 90-91)

As Eric Sundquist says: "The lynching scene is all the more provocative for having been inspired by an incident in Johnson's own life" (42). The hero decides then and there to become an Ex-Colored man; that is, to allow himself to be taken for a white man, and, instead of pursuing the improvement of his race, to pursue business success. The near lynching presents the Negro as quintessentially a victim, the role that *Along This Way* rejects, denies and underplays. The near lynching in the novel resonates with the near lynching of the author when he heard the words unspoken in the novel: "'Kill the damned nigger! Kill the black son of a bitch'" (*Along This Way* 167). Unlike Johnson, the Ex-Colored Man cannot take command of the situation, and, shaken to his soul, in his terror, anger and shame, he reaches for a new identity: "I had made up my mind that […] I was not going to be a Negro" (*Ex-Colored Man* [1927] 95). *Along This Way*'s "any kind of Negro" would echo *The Autobiography*'s no kind of Negro.

The Autobiography is commonly classed as a novel of passing, but there is considerable dispute about the kind of passing. Herman Beavers says that the Ex-Colored Man is a "'tragic mulattto' who passes for white" (39). Michael Hardin says the Ex-Colored Man is "passing as heterosexual" (103). Martin Japtok says the Ex-Colored Man "is passing for black more than he is passing for white" (37). Moreover, Japtok raises the issue of the narrator's class, and that might suggest the question, Is the Ex-Colored Man passing as a gentleman? In *Passing and the Rise of the African American Novel*, Giulia Fabi provides a route out of these dilemmas: "Johnson's pioneer fictional play with both the autobiographical mode and an unreliable first-person narrator is indicative of a new interest in portraying how reality is filtered, recreated, and mystified by individual consciousness" (92). Here, we have a classic concern of Modernity – the ambiguity of the human condition reflected in a Modernist pre-occupation with formal questions of narrator perspective. That places *The Autobiography of an Ex-Colored Man* in a tradition that began in the nineteenth century with *Notes from the Underground* and passed by way of *The Waste Land* and "The Metamorphosis" to *The Stranger*. In the genealogy of Modernism, James Weldon Johnson's Ex-Colored Man is kin to Fyodor Dostoyevsky's Underground Man, T. S. Eliot's Son of Man, Franz Kafka's Gregor Samsa and Albert Camus's Meursault as much as he is, in the genealogy of the African American novel kin to William Wells Brown's Clotel, Frank Webb's Clarence Gary, Frances Harper's Iola Leroy and Charles Chesnutt's John Walden.

Relocation of the genealogy of the Ex-Colored Man allows a confrontation with the most anguished reading of the novel – Robert B. Stepto's in the study of African American narrative that he called *From Behind the Veil*. "*The Autobiography*," he says,

> is conventionally and routinely delivered unto us as a "modern novel," or, more boldly, as a "modern Afro-American novel." In retrospect, the only thing more extraordinary than this conception and delivery is the deliberate nurturing that has been bestowed upon this illusionary child. (95-96)

Stepto's emotion suppressed is anger that a classic African American text fails the racial test. Stepto is too good a reader not to be aware of how good Johnson is a writer, and he knows that something is up: "Johnson is up to something different from what Douglass, Washington, and even Du Bois pursue in their autobiographical narratives. For this reason it may be said that *The Autobiography* is on the verge of achieving generic stature." But what that something is, says Stepto, makes *The Autobiography* "something less than a novel" (127). Stepto thinks that Johnson is sacrificing fiction to the demands of fact when the problem is Stepto's demand for the novel to be more true to race than to art.

Emory University's Woodruff Library possesses James Weldon Johnson's own copy of the 1912 *Autobiography of an Ex-Colored Man*, and the Emory catalog lists *The Autobiography* under the two headings: "African American men – Fiction" and "Mulattoes." The Boston Public Library has similar headings: "African American men – Fiction" and "Racially mixed people – Fiction." The New York Public Library has a much longer list of headings, but they are of a kind with the Boston Public. To say that *The Autobiography of an Ex-Colored Man* is about African American men is incomplete and not because the book is also about African American women. The Emory catalog might better have said that the subject of *The Autobiography of an Ex-Colored Man* is the "Son of Man" because the Ex-Colored Man lives:

> where the sun beats,
> And the dead tree gives no shelter, the cricket no relief,
> And the dry stone no sound of water. (Eliot 61)

He lives, that is, in Eliot's Waste Land. The truth is that *The Autobiography of an Ex-Colored Man* is a great Modernist text, and this very difficulty in categorizing *Ex-Colored Man* is itself a mark of its Modernity, its representative status of early literary Modernism. Its border crossing strategies supports this, and it also supports, in turn, the growing consensus that Modernism was by no means an exclusively white, Anglo practice.

The bad faith of his existential tragedy makes the Ex-Colored Man an unhappy man, but the tragedy of a rich white man with a sad black secret is not what *The Autobiography of an Ex-Colored Man* is about. It is about a tragedy of a larger kind. He lives in a twilight zone, one that he stumbled into when, told as a child, not to stand with the whites (*Ex-Colored Man* [1927] 7). After the lynching, he decides to stand with the whites anyway. But with whom, does he truly stand? In his own life, James Weldon Johnson allowed no such ambiguity. He firmly stood with the blacks, but James Weldon Johnson the novelist created a hero who declines entirely "work so glorious" (*Ex-Colored Man* [1927] 103). Partly this is the artist exploring the road not taken, writing an anti-autobiography as a form of spiritual exercise. Herman Beavers says that "Johnson's novel is the first to give voice in fictional form to 'the Veil'" (39), but, as Mar Gallego argues in *Passing Novels in the Harlem Renaissance*, there is a conflict between Johnson's text and Du Bois's *Souls of Black Folk* because "Johnson's novel negates both the positive image of the 'Talented Tenth' and the idealistic possibility of a 'third self'" (qtd. in Yupei 721).

The 1912 Publisher's Preface goes so far as to say, "In these pages it is as though a veil had been drawn aside: the reader is given a view of the inner life of the Negro in America, is initiated into the 'freemasonry,' as it were, of the race" (*Ex-Colored Man* [1912] v). That infamous preface – said to be by "The Publishers" but in fact written for them by Johnson (Goellnicht 19) – is the first-page move of a hero who labels himself a coward and a deserter on his last page. It is part of the duplicity of the Modernist novel that it involves its readers in ambiguities, half-truths, evasions and self-reflections, reflections, that is, on the readers who cannot agree that the hero is a coward and a deserter without implicating themselves in the same judgment. There is another dimension to the duplicity of *The Autobiography of an Ex-Colored Man* – the two ways in which Johnson published it. In 1912, Johnson published the book anonymously with its cryptic preface. In 1927, Johnson republished the book with his name on the title page and an Introduction by Carl Van Vechten. There are small and interesting changes in the text of the two versions, but the real difference is that, by the act of republishing, Johnson gave the world two completely separate novels. The republication relaunched the novel as a spectacular contribution to the Harlem Renaissance. It was now taken to be the work of the New Negro celebrated by Alain Locke, and he along with Van Vechten made *The Autobiography of an Ex-Colored Man* into a novel of the 1920s. The Moebius-like half-twist of Johnson's elusive text, now a novel, now an autobiography, moves in Modernist manner to disconcert the reader and, in so disconcerting, challenges traditional certainties.

A link between the condition of the Irish and the condition of African Americans was one that underpinned the thesis of Alain Locke's *The New Negro*, published in 1925, and it is fully worked through in Tracy Mishkin's *The Harlem and Irish Renaissances*. The argument is that the contributors to *The New Negro* were engaged in creating a Renaissance exactly as the Irish writers were doing. It is worth noting that Locke did not use the term "Harlem Renaissance"; he used the term "The Negro Renaissance" (1), and the Negro Renaissance was explicitly matched to the literary and political struggles not only of the Irish but of the world's liberation movements. "As in India, in China, in Egypt, Ireland, Russia, Bohemia, Palestine and Mexico, we are witnessing the resurgence of a people" says Locke (xvii). The terrible processes, delays and outcomes of those many liberations, interrupted as they were by World Depression and World War, could not be known in 1925.

In his own critical writings, James Weldon Johnson more than once made a connection between African America and Ireland, especially in the areas of poetry and folk song. However, it is an Irish novelist with whom Johnson has the strongest Modernist link. A novel that began to appear in serial publication just two years after James Weldon Johnson published *The Autobiography of an*

Ex-Colored Man was James Joyce's *A Portrait of the Artist as a Young Man*. Stephen Daedalus, the artist hero, achieves a joyous optimism that might indeed have been a statement of an African American artist of the 1920s: "I go to encounter for the millionth time the reality of experience and to forge in the smithy of my soul the uncreated conscience of my race" (Joyce 253). That is very much the impulse to which James Weldon Johnson gave expression in 1922 in his Preface to *The Book of American Negro Poetry*: "The final measure of the greatness of all peoples is the amount and standard of the literature and art they have produced." This voicing of late-Victorian, Pateresque aesthetics shows Johnson to be educated in the same school as Eliot, Joyce and Pound and learning, like them, the first lesson of political Modernism – that its art and its artists are the test of a people: "No people that has produced great literature and art has ever been looked upon by the world as distinctly inferior" (Johnson, Preface v). Nonetheless, there is another dimension to the Joycean creed. It is summed up in a passage fundamental to the self-identity of the Modernist artist:

> I will not serve that in which I no longer believe whether it call itself my home, my fatherland or my church: and I will try to express myself in some mode of life or art as freely as I can and as wholly as I can, using for my defence the only arms I allow myself to use, silence, exile, and cunning. (Joyce 247)

Stephen Daedalus is kin to the Underground Man, the inhabitant of the Waste Land, the Ex-Colored Man.

That returns us to what is remarkable about Johnson: he is not only a representative of Modernism. He is also a representative of the Modern, and the Modern is a term that historians use to identify the point at which the culture of the Modern World might be said to have begun. A popular date for that start is 1492. However, in *The Black Atlantic*, Paul Gilroy asks us to look away from the ships that took Columbus across the Atlantic and to look towards the ships that very shortly after 1492, perhaps as early as 1500, began to take Africans to the Americas. Gilroy's world does not become the Modern World until Africans had learned enough of the languages and cultures of their European enslavers to engage in the Western discourse and challenge the presumptions of the Enlightenment. In the Anglophone world, that might have been as early as the eighteenth century, but for Gilroy, the incontestable African challenge to the Western agenda comes in the nineteenth century when he asks us to consider

> Frederick Douglass's relationship to English and Scottish radicalisms and to meditate on the significance of William Wells Brown's five years in Europe as a fugitive slave, on Alexander Crummell's living and studying in Cambridge, and upon Martin Delany's experiences at the London [...] International Statistical Congress in 1860. (17)

James Weldon Johnson was a direct descendant of that first group of Black Intellectuals, and in *The Autobiography of an Ex-Colored Man*, his hero expresses admiration for the greatest of them:

> As I grew older, my love for reading grew stronger. I read with studious interest everything I could find relating to colored men who had gained prominence. My heroes had been King David, then Robert the Bruce; now Frederick Douglass was enshrined in the place of honor. (*Ex-Colored Man* [2004] 21)

Douglass, Wells Brown, Crummell and Delaney had either been slaves themselves or were children of slaves; they grew to be intellectual giants and race leaders; they were self made. And in making themselves, they were making the Modern World. *The Black Atlantic* gives us a genealogy that is anticipated in a comment Harold Cruse made in 1967 in *The Crisis of the Negro Intellectual*. "There is an almost direct line of development," he wrote, "from [Frederick Douglass] to the NAACP and the modern civil rights movement" (5).

In *The Black Atlantic*, that deliberately difficult book, Gilroy shapes six chapters around six themes: the Ship, the Slave, Music, Consciousness, Violence and Tradition. These, he argues, have created Black Atlantic culture. The four abstract notions need less immediate explication than the two concrete ones: the Ship and the Slave. The image of the Ship informs the first chapter, and Gilroy asks us to think of ships as "the living means by which the points within that Atlantic world were joined. [...] getting on board promises a means to reconceptualize the orthodox relationship between modernity and what passes for its prehistory" (16-17). That link between the Modern World and the slave ship is fully developed in *The Black Atlantic*'s next chapter, that focuses on the Slave: "I propose," says Gilroy,

> that the history of the African diaspora and a reassessment of the relationship between modernity and slavery may require a more complete revision of the terms in which the modernity debates have been constructed than any of its academic participants may be willing to concede. (46)

The African in the Americas is premised as the prototypical Modern being. The African in the Americas experienced the deracination, alienation and existential loss that are the characteristics of Modernism. The Americas were the Waste Land.

That is why the Emory Library Catalog is missing the point when it says that *The Autobiography of an Ex-Colored Man* is about "African American men." When the same catalog says that the book is about "Mulattoes," it is again not inaccurate, but it is again misleading. It is misleading if it is using that dated term to suggest that Johnson was writing about a marginal group of interest only to themselves or to those with a specialist interest in American turn-of-the-century racial types. The "mulatto" nonetheless can lead to the universalizing core of *The Autobiography* if it is allowed to invoke what Paul Gilroy describes as "the theorization of creolisation, metissage, [...] and hybridity" – terms he uses as a way of rejecting "ethnic differences as an absolute break in the histories and experiences of 'black' and 'white' people" (2). Gilroy is teaching us that the English word "mulatto" might be retrieved for decent use if we recognize that all men and women, T. S. Eliot as much as James Weldon Johnson, are mulatto, and that it is the Modernist fate, and privilege, to be mulatto. James Weldon Johnson the Modernist author of *The Autobiography of an Ex-Colored Man* is in remarkable complement to Johnson the Modern secretary of the NAACP. The protean, Franklin-like multiplicity of Johnson brings together the strands that are contained in the twentieth century's fascination with the word "Modern."

Works Cited

Beavers, Herman. "*Autobiography of an Ex-Colored Man.*" *The Oxford Companion to African American Literature*. Ed. William L. Andrews, Frances Smith Foster, and Trudier Harris. New York: Oxford UP, 1997. 39-40.

Brown, Josephine. *Biography of an American Bondman. By His Daughter*. Boston: R. F. Wallcut, 1856.

Brown, William Wells. *Clotel; or the President's Daughter: A Narrative of Slave Life in the United States*. London: Partridge & Oakey, 1853.

Camus. Albert. *The Stranger*. 1942. Trans. Matthew Ward. New York: Vintage, 1989.

Chesnutt, Charles W. *The House Behind the Cedars*. Boston: Houghton Mifflin, 1900.

---. "Post-Bellum-Pre-Harlem." *The Colophon: A Book Collectors' Quarterly* 2.5 (1931): n. pag.

Cruse, Harold. *The Crisis of the Negro Intellectual*. 1967. New York: Quill, 1984.

Dostoyevsky, Fyodor. *Notes from the Underground*. 1864. Trans. Andrew R. MacAndrew. New York: Signet, 1961.

Du Bois, W. E. B. *The Souls of Black Folk; Essays and Sketches*. Chicago: A. C. McClurg & Co., 1903.

Eliot, T. S. *Collected Poems 1909-1933*. London: Faber, 1958.

Fabi, M. Giulia. *Passing and the Rise of the African American Novel*. Urbana: Illinois UP, 2001.

Franklin, Benjamin. *The Autobiography of Benjamin Franklin and Selections from his Other Writings*. Ed. Nathan G. Goodman. New York: Modern Library, 1932.

Gallego, Mar. *Passing Novels in the Harlem Renaissance: Identity, Politics and Textual Strategies*. Hamburg: LIT, 2003.

Gilroy, Paul. *The Black Atlantic: Modernity and Double Consciousness*. 1993. London: Verso, 1996.

Goellnicht, Donald C. "Passing as Autobiography: James Weldon Johnson's *The Autobiography of an Ex-Coloured Man*." *African American Review* 30.1 (1996): 17-33.

Hardin, Michael. "Ralph Ellison's *Invisible Man*: Invisibility, Race, and Homoeroticism from Frederick Douglass to E. Lynn Harris." *The Southern Literary Journal* 37.1 (2004): 96-120.

Harper, Frances E. W. *Iola Leroy, or, Shadows Uplifted.* Philadelphia: Garrigues, 1892.

Hughes, Langston. *The Collected Works of Langston Hughes: The Poems, 1951-1967.* Ed. Arnold Rampersad. Columbia: Missouri UP, 2001.

Japtok, Martin. "Between 'Race' as Construct and 'Race' as Essence: *The Autobiography of an Ex-Coloured Man*." *The Southern Literary Journal* 28.2 (1996): 32-47.

Johnson, James Weldon. *Along This Way: The Autobiography of James Weldon Johnson.* New York: Viking P, 1933.

---. *God's Trombones: Seven Negro Sermons in Verse.* New York: Viking P, 1927.

---. Preface. *The Book of American Negro Poetry: Chosen and Edited with an Essay on the Negro's Creative Genius by James Weldon Johnson.* New York: Harcourt Brace, 1922. vii-xlviii.

---. *The Autobiography of an Ex-Colored Man.* Boston: Sherman, French & Company, 1912. [James Weldon Johnson's own copy, originally published anonymously, held at Emory University's Manuscript, Archives, and Rare Book Library]

---. *The Autobiography of an Ex-Colored Man.* New York: Harcourt, Brace, 1927.

---. *The Autobiography of an Ex-Colored Man.* 1927. Boston: IndyPublish.com, 2004.

Joyce, James. *A Portrait of the Artist as Young Man.* 1916. London: Penguin, 1974.

Kafka, Franz. *The Metamorphosis and Other Stories.* Trans. Willa and Edwin Muir. London: Penguin, 1961.

Lawrence, D. H. *Studies in Classic American Literature.* 1923. Ed. Ezra Greenspan, Lindeth Vasey, and John Worthen. Cambridge: Cambridge UP, 2003.

Leavis, F. R. *New Bearings in English Poetry: A Study of the Contemporary Situation.* London: Chatto and Windus, 1932.

Locke, Alain, ed. *The New Negro.* 1925. New York: Atheneum 1975.

Mishkin, Tracy. *The Harlem and Irish Renaissances*: *Language, Identity, and Representation*. Gainesville: Florida UP, 1997.

Payne, Ladell. "Themes and Cadences: James Weldon Johnson's Novel." *The Southern Literary Journal* 11.2 (1979): 43-45.

Stepto, Robert B. *From Behind the Veil: A Study of Afro-American Narrative*. Urbana: Illinois UP, 1979.

Sundquist, Eric J. *The Hammers of Creation: Folk Culture in Modern African-American Fiction*. Athens: Georgia UP, 1992.

Tuttle, Kate. "Johnson, James Weldon." *Africana: The Encyclopedia of the African and African American Experience*. Ed. Kwame Anthony Appia and Henry Louis Gates Jr. New York: Basic Books, 1999. 1053-54.

Tuttle, Kate. "Lynching." *Africana: The Encyclopedia of the African and African American Experience*. Ed. Kwame Anthony Appia and Henry Louis Gates. New York: Basic Books, 1999. 1210-12.

Webb, Frank J. *The Garies and Their Friends*. London: Routledge, 1857.

Wilson, Sondra Kathryn. Introduction. *Along This Way: The Autobiography of James Weldon Johnson*. By James Weldon Johnson. N.p.: Da Capo, 2000. ix-xviii.

Yupei, Zhou. "Rev. of *Passing Novels in the Harlem Renaissance: Identity, Politics and Textual Strategies* by Mar Gallego." *African American Review* 38.4 (2004): 720-23.

Claude Julien

Wolf Whistle and *A Killing in This Town*: Two Ways to Exorcise Racial Hatred

> Horror is tied to events never to be forgotten. In this respect, it constitutes the ultimate ethical motive in telling the histories of victims.
> (Paul Ricoeur, *Time and Narrative*)[1]

If modernism in fiction consists in breaking codes, Lewis Nordan's *Wolf Whistle* (1993) and Olympia Vernon's *A Killing in This Town* (2006) pertain to modernist stories. Indeed, both novels have arisen from two particularly gruesome racist murders that resurface in stories that are far removed from this world. In one of them, a character sees in a raindrop a proleptic film of events to come, and a parrot directly designates a murderer in a courtroom. In the other, too, animals become actors or sensitive witnesses, sometimes both.

Both fictions have been produced by authors born and raised in the rural Deep South. Vernon, a black lady, was in her early thirties when *A Killing in This Town* was published; Nordan, a white man, was in his early fifties. Other differences must be pointed out at the outset. In an essay that appeared in *The Oxford American* two years after the book's publication, Nordan declared Emmett Till's[2] lynching in 1955 was at the heart of the story and told of his reactions at the time as a youthful resident of the very county where the murder took place, a small town where everyone knew almost everyone else. On the contrary, Vernon denied in an unpublished personal interview (04-15-2009) that my intuition that the equally horrid murder of James Byrd, a crippled war veteran beaten, then dragged to death in Texas behind a pickup truck, in 1998 inspired her writing at all. She holds she sees "images," visions whose amanuensis she becomes.[3] Other deep differences call attention. Temporality is one of them: Nordan's *Wolf Whistle* was published thirty-eight years after the death of Emmett Till while Vernon's *A Killing in This Town* appeared barely eight years after the lynching of James Byrd. A creation closer to the racial anger the murder may have provoked, *A Killing in This Town* is physical, macabre. *Wolf Whistle* is no less intense, but its descriptions of bodily violence are not so graphic.

My thesis here is that in both novels, odd companions as they are in the same essay, younger white Southerners are the ones that seek a way out of ghoulish racial hatred, fascism at its rawest. Horror is partly resolved through distinct channels. Repentance is essential in *Wolf Whistle* that moves from the bleak Southern past to an elusive better future when two socially far apart white women find a crystal ball in a junk store. The ball tells them nothing but they discover they both hold similar hopes. Much deeper than this quaint resolution is the novelist's sense of personal guilt embodied in two characters. That questioning of self provides a strong moral center that Vernon's book lacks. *A Killing in This Town* also ends on a faint gleam of a new life beyond a faraway railroad terminal. That hopeful escape of the Klan's projected black victim and his wife has been engineered by two young white men who are ready to go to any length, including murder of the Klan leader, to put an end to racial violence in their town. But the characters lack substance. Their minds are not probed as they prepare and carry out their revolt against racist practices.

Focusing on discourse as I intend to do here is always a moot exercise. How do magic elements address racial hatred and violence? Assuming my intuition about *A Killing in This Town* is right, we have two fictions that have not "emplotted" history, as Paul Ricoeur would say, but appropriated horrendous events to weave them into stories that are factually implausible and invite the reader to take a leap from history to characters haunted by an evil that must be eradicated. There is no atonement other than positive feelings in *Wolf Whistle*. On the contrary, *A Killing in This Town* seems to be inspired by a visceral urge to retaliate. This essay will start with *Wolf Whistle*, perhaps easier to approach due to Nordan's comments, a post word in the 1995 edition and the essay published in *The Oxford American* that same year.

Wolf Whistle: Racist Memory and the Absurd

Nordan's first point in these crucial commentaries is that, slow writer as he usually is, *Wolf Whistle* sprang into existence in just one year after a TV interview in which a thoroughly unprepared answer had him declare that his next book would be about the Emmett Till tragedy. According to him, the novel was "a complete surprise", a "phantasmogoria based upon history's broadest outlines. It was a fairy tale" ("Making" 76). *Wolf Whistle* is set in Arrow Catcher,

Nordan's pre-existing fictional Mississippi backwater, a world at once funny and terrifying, coherent and discontinuous, tender and brutal. In the setting we are steeped in this time, a bird speaks a truth the judge and jury will not hear, a dead eye sees. In Nordan's own words, it is as if "monsters and angels roamed the Delta flatscape on some other planet" (ibid.) – the here transplanted elsewhere. The gist of these essays is that Nordan feels he was not in command as an author, that his story grew upon him and imposed a plot line involving fantastic elements.

Beyond literary aspects, and perhaps more relevant for our purpose here, Nordan's essays also discuss his long-lasting obsession with the Emmett Till tragedy: that he was about the same age as the victim. That he lived in the very county where the murder was perpetrated. That, although his parents knew relatives of the Bryant and Milam families, neither the murder nor the trial were ever discussed at home; and that he himself failed to raise the issues with his parents or friends in town. In short, Nordan felt implicated by race and geography – all the more so as, at a deeper personal level, he had perhaps[4] smiled at the joke then circulated about a black youth "who stole a gin fan and tried to swim across the lake with it" (*Wolf Whistle* 204). Regretting his passive acceptance of dominant attitudes, he envied the one class mate whom everyone detested and who, in the gymnasium locker room, spoke up against the murderers and the prevailing racism. To what extent the novel's Roy Dale stands for the young Nordan of 1955 is impossible to say; but his regrets suggest he certainly owes a lot to the author of 1993 who sardonically describes a Delta society mired in hierarchy, a world where no one is allowed to stray beyond prescribed roles, be they a modern higher class lady or a school master principal. As Lord Poindexter Montberclair reminds Solon, the white "trash" he will recruit for a henchman, that the world places decent white people on top:

> Poindexter said, "Decent whitefolks have always needed the likes of you."
> Solon said, "They have?"
> Poindexter said, "We need people like you to help keep our niggers in line."
> Solon said, "Well –"
> Poindexter said, "That how I see it, Solon, don't you agree? Isn't that how you see it?"
> Solon said, "Well –"

Poindexter said, "It gives you lower classes, you white-trash boys, some *raison d'être*, wouldn't you say so?" (118)

Nordan kept the hulk of history intact. Such is the case for the trial that exculpated the murderers, and especially the courage of Emmett's uncle as a witness in a hostile courtroom. But, otherwise, *Wolf Whistle* turns history on its head, even the circumstances of that denial of justice, as we shall see later. The real life murder involved lower middle class whites only (at least officially, according to court records). The crust of white society, Lord Poindexter Montberclair, is also a party to the case in the novel. The murder of the real Emmett Till resulted from pure and simple racist hate. Bobo's death verges on the absurd as Solon feels for the lad and is ready to renege on his contract ("Got to be uncomfortable, sho does, even for a nigger" [169]), but finally kills him in self-defense after being wounded when Bobo takes hold of his discarded hand gun, a mere .25 caliber.

One needs to summarize *Wolf Whistle* to point out its departure from fact. Solon Gregg, a petty thief and a brutal husband who wants to impress the local citizenry with his importance, is miffed when liberal Lady Montberclair offers Bobo a ride home in her Cadillac rather than acknowledge him, a white man, in the store. So, he goes to the Montberclair mansion to hint at the lady's supposed affair with a black youth who carries her photo in his wallet.[5] The great man first turns Solon's tale down. Only when he hears of his wife's romance with a known homosexual who plays the organ at church does he seek Solon out to negotiate a contract on Bobo's life. He finds him in the run down local hotel on the verge of committing suicide – again a measure of Arrow Catcher's absurdist streak. With Solon bragging that they are out after Bobo, the pair leave in the great man's El Camino red pickup which Solon has haggled out as a getaway car, together with Montberclair's German Luger and one thousand dollars in cash. However, their association turns short when Montberclair discovers the white lady in Bobo's wallet is not his wife, but an actress. Solon who is now in possession of the Luger orders Montberclair out of the car at gun point and leaves him stranded in a downpour. Solon's mood turns friendly to the abducted youth. He throws his own gun and his wad of banknotes out the window, and offers to take him fishing. His captive jumps out instead, recovers Solon's discarded weapon and shoots at him from the ditch. Solon is wounded in his face and fires back with the Luger, shooting one of Bobo's eyes out. He next drives to a deserted mill where he steals a gin fan to sink the body in a flooded spillway – not a river as in real life.

Phantasmagoric elements surface in moments of extreme tension or of outright horror. In the courtroom, for instance, when a parrot that cannot speak passes judgment by dropping a huge bird-do on Solon's shoulder as Bobo's uncle points at the murderer. The situation is farcical in so far as the parrot has been introduced into the courtroom by Alice's uncle (the town gravedigger) to please his estranged wife who is allergic to feathers on her returning home. But farce also makes sense. The accusing parrot has a significant function. It is not from just any country. It is from Africa, and a more recent arrival than Uncle, "generations closer to their shared homeland" (250), the text adds ironically. The novel's otherworldliness is multi-faceted and speaks the unspeakable by reaching out into fantasies that suggest beyond conventional expression. Another key example occurs when the students practice "arrow catching," a weird sport played in teams of two, an "archer" and a "catcher" who must clutch the arrow while it is still in flight. Roy Dale misses his usual partners (they have discovered Bobo's body as they were fishing) and is made to pair up with Smoky Viner, the not-so-smart boy with a forehead like a ram.[6] Roy hates Smoky, all the more so now he envies him for having had the courage to speak up against racism. Roy Dale's arrow is aimed deliberately at Smoky Viner and flies with "all his rage, his emptiness and loss, outward, outward forever away from his heart" (208). To Smoky Viner who is hit in his forehead and knocked unconscious, the arrow means a strange, foreign oppression, seems "to emerge from another world into his own [...]. Sucking up [...] all the available oxygen from the atmosphere and into its hungry, insatiable self," and provoking unrelated miraculous events:

The atmosphere rarefied.
Birds fell from the air.
Cattle toppled over in a field.
Car motors stalled on the highway. (208)

Roy Dale's spiteful arrow also has the effect to confirm Smoky in his opinion that racism must be abolished: indeed, Bobo's martyred body wearing aquatic creatures and the stigma of its own death returns to life and his fateful whistling becomes a mere adolescent prank:

> The body of the Bobo child, dressed in heavy garment of fish and turtles and violent death, reversed all its decay, and flesh became firm once more, eyes snapped back into sockets and became bright, bones unbroke themselves, feet became swift, laughter erupted like music, and bad manners and disrespect and a possessive disdain for a woman became mere child's play, a normal and decent testing of adolescent limits in a hopeful world. (208-09)[7]

The (blunt) arrow shot with a vengeance reaches into the complexities of life. It reads as a way for Roy Dale to conform to the dominant opinion – detestation of Smoky – but also as a way to vent his rage against the life his parents and grandparents have handed down to him, and also against himself for having lacked Smoky's forthrightness. Indeed, the whole class sees hope in the unlikely disintegration of the arrow into "chards of wood and a spray of sawdust" (209). Hope "For themselves, for the Delta, for Mississippi, maybe for the world" (210). Roy Dale empties his quiver onto the field. He seizes the one arrow he likes to play with, shooting it for practice into his bedroom wall. That arrow is not blunt, but has a steel point. Its warped shaft makes it date from long gone pre-Civil War days, but it still flies well. Roy breaks it across his knee, saying "I'm sorry, I'm sorry, I'm sorry" (ibid.), a symbolical renunciation of the violence inherited from the past.

The reader's imagination is called upon to link Roy Dale's violent instincts with Mississippi's past embodied earlier by the red-headed buzzards which learned ornithologists have named for local politicians (James Vardaman, Theodore Bilbo, Hugh White, J. P. Coleman, Ross Barnett, etc.), who, perched on telephone poles, watch over Balance Due (the poor white part of the town rife with crime and misery, also known as Scumtown), like "a glorious Festival of Dead Rebels [...] content for now with road kill" (70). *Wolf Whistle* is a highly political novel charging that Old South politicians and ideologies still reign. No longer as grand Civil War combatants soaring toward the sun, but as scavengers feeding on carrion and watching over "Balance Due" – a sore of the nation's unkept promise – to keep poor whites in line. It does not take much imagination to leap from Roy's blunt arrow to Solon's bullet knocking Bobo's eye from its socket, dead but lucidly seeing the world through his racially-conditioned eyes: how Solon should have waited for him, "a strapping young man" (172), to help him carry the gin fan before killing him:

he waited for Solon, could see all this through the demon eye upon his cheek, without fear or anger, or even a sense of injustice, but only with an appreciation of the dark and magical and evil world in which he had been killed. (177-78)

This memory of the gin fan haunts the novel. With devastating irony, Nordan changes history by having dead Bobo's hand brush Solon's to help him load the gin fan into the truck.[8] Liberation to come is also written, a dim hope, in the crystal ball Alice (the humble school mistress devoted to her poor-white students) and Lady Montberclair stumble upon in the magic corner of the junk store. Alice is the reader's guide through the looking glass from the outset. Not only does she see Bobo's death refracted through a drop of rain – desperate as she is at her inability to deflect death. She also visits the Gregg home in the first chapter, and realizes a mere ditty like "Here Comes Santa Claus" helps Ms. Gregg overcome her pathetic stammering: "Santa Claus had broken her chains and set her free" (17). The whole world is waiting to be set free, she thinks. This passage includes a proleptic vision in which Alice is "born again," not religiously but freed from the racial oppression she detests, and sees the rewards and the many hurdles and hardships of the coming struggle:

> She saw the ancient star rising over Bethlehem. [...] She saw what was unimaginable, classrooms in the swamp with black faces and white faces together. [...] She saw children holding hands with grown-ups, black and white, signing "We Shall Overcome" in long lines and in churches. She saw a church bombed in Montgomery, dead children, marchers in Selma, freedom riders in Selma. She saw bombs flying over the miraculous desert, Baghdad burning, Emmett Till dead, Medgar Evers dead, Martin King, the little blue figure of her still-born child, years hence, herself an abandoned child as well, names, faces, geographies not yet known to her, for in the extremity of her pain and need, linear tile disappeared and became meaningless. (17-18)

Wolf Whistle is full of humor and satire, but also compassion. It is one of a kind that manipulates the chronology of events, leaps forward and backward, makes Bobo's martyred eye see in death and ends when civil rights campaigner to come, Alice, and liberal Sally Anne Montberclair, the murderer's wife, browse among a junk shop's cluttered scraps – a Civil War sword, cooking utensils, farm implements, leg irons, etc. The crystal ball in the shop's magic aisle is translucent, the size of a cantaloupe. Nothing is to be seen through it, nothing at all. But emotion overcomes them. Perhaps they do weep in each other's arms. Perhaps they do not. Perhaps, they do hold each other tight. Perhaps they do not. "Nobody but Bobo knows for sure what happened" (290).

A Killing in This Town: Racial Memory and Revenge

In *Wolf Whistle*'s rewriting of history, Solon Gregg whom Poindexter Montberclair has called "trash" (53) has no personal motive to carry out his contract on Bobo. On the contrary, he detests Montberclair who has insulted him and, forgetting racial etiquette, even tries to befriend his captive. Does this forgetting himself suggest or deny the existence of any real bond between rich and poor whites short of greed and the lust for power? *A Killing in This Town*'s rewriting of history also seems to refute a supposed alliance between rich and poor whites when Gill Mercer and Adam Pickens revolt against the local time-honored Klan ritual maintained by the descendants of the founders who gave their name to the town they owned.

A Killing in This Town's locale is Bullock,[9] an isolated rural Mississippi town crossed by a railroad line to Memphis. The events take place under the reign of Jim Crow possibly in the 1920s or 1930s. Three men, Salem and Hurry Bullock, assisted by Hoover Pickens, keep alive a Klan coming-of-age ceremony in which young members first don a robe on turning thirteen when they recite the Klan commandment,

> We are white men, born unto the earth
> And land, which is ours and belongs to us, as
> Free and automatic white men.
> All niggers must be obedient.
> They are not part of the human thread,
> But are animals and must be dragged from
> Their properties and stricken from the
> Blood of the nation.
> The same thing goes for hypocrites. (114)

This commitment to white superiority leads them to proving their manhood by calling out a designated black man to be horse-dragged to death tied to a pulley. Young Adam Pickens has reached this stage in life and hates to think of dragging a man to death, then taking the body home in a wheelbarrow.

The novel's current events are haunted by the earlier dragging of Curtis Willow whose only crime consisted in coming out naked from swimming in the river, crossing the path of Lenora Bullock (Hurry's wife) who charged him with whistling, offended as she was after he ignored her advances. This time, the designated victim is preacher Earl Thomas who offended the Bullock clan for daring to bring into the open a health department official letter warning the community against the noxious fumes from the plant. The town reeks of evil, not just the people.[10] Insistent, recurrent metaphors bring up the lack of air, the dust, the oppressive heat, the rot that is eating the table on the Pickens's breakfast porch. Mostly, there is the factory-related lung disease the men had rather ignore, a canker that gnaws at them from within. Lives revolve round this Pauer plant, a name which (perhaps too obviously) conjures up the specter of *power* that affects everyday relationships. Frustrated and ugly wives (orphans picked up in the railroad station waiting room) are unloved, despised, even raped in D. D. Pickens's case.[11] These characters are mere profiles inhabiting a dichotomous world, for, contrary to white characters, harmony and mutual love reign among black couples.[12] The all-evil white world suffers only three exceptions: the nameless salesclerk at the fabric store, Adam Pickens and Gill Mercer. Gill resents being made to drag Curtis Willow to mark his passage to Klan adulthood when he was thirteen, and especially Hurry Bullock's making him pop the eye of the dead man with a shovel blade. He now nurtures the wish to punish the Klansmen. He knocks Hurry Bullock unconscious as the latter is crying over his wife's dead body and carries him to Earl Thomas's home where Emma New swathes[13] the still unconscious man in white gauze and brings him out on the porch, as if he were her husband for Adam to drag to death through the woods that separate the white and black districts. Once this murder has been carried out, the novel ends with Gill and Adam seeing Curtis's widow and the Thomas couple away toward another future at the end of the Memphis line. A speechless (presumably white) accordion player who has ruined his instrument and at last benefits from the *mercy* (120, 239) of the accordion seller is also, symbolically, on the trip. So is a woman with a naked baby.

A Killing in This Town is a difficult book to read. Not because of its leaping backward or forward (for instance, the fatal encounter between Curtis Willow and Lenora Bullock is split between pages 61 and 166-67); but mostly because it is marred by an affected "poetic" style that can make meaning evanescent. Images can be useful to create or bolster an atmosphere, as in "the sun's dictatorship" (17) or "the door that caged the tools" (51), but one runs across numerous cases of gratuitous verbosity like "the paralysis of her gown" (97), or "the sperm of floating molecules" (134) to refer to dust, or again "the sentiments of the dust" (179) to refer to footprints.

Physical violence abounds in Vernon's story. Kicks breaking ribs loose, skin and flesh scraped through to the bone, Curtis's eye forced from its socket, or Hurry Bullock's eye, lost after the dragging while he still has his shoes on, as Hoover Pickens notes. These elements, the rib and the eye, conjure up memories from the Bible, but photos of Emmett Till's murdered body may also interfere here. And, like Bobo's, Curtis's eye can still see though it is dead.

Discussion: Magic, Revolt and Creation
The time has come after these synoptic presentations to bring these two novels by black and white authors together to assess the functions of magic elements and to discuss their discourses against racial violence.

Magic plays a more important role on the events in *Wolf Whistle* than it does in *A Killing in This Town*. Two magic elements figure prominently in Nordan's work. They do not change history, but they provide keys to the characters' psyches. Firstly, there is Runt's green African parrot that takes to its wings from Runt's lap, circles around the courtroom, lands on Solon's head and graces his shoulder with "great farting blobs of liquid white bird dooky" (255) which introduces an insistent hammering of the epithet *white*. Secondly, there is the arrow hitting Smoky Viner, not so bright a lad and the butt of many jokes at school, whose denunciation of racism induces Roy Dale's change of heart illustrated by his decision to take a shower "most every day from now on, feet smelling bad as they do" (205). That apparently trivial and discordant detail about personal hygiene has two sides, of which comedy is perhaps the least notable. The other more symbolically significant side is the intention to extirpate oneself from one's own (or society's?) all-pervasive dirt. Nordan's book consistently offers dual, or more, readings. So does magic which serves to represent the horror of violence and, mostly, link it with the region's history and current oppressive racist policies. Also, by way of contradiction, magic brings release, visions of hope, blue, unclear – as the Santa Claus song does to relieve Solon's wife of her stutter due to marital maltreatment. Magic knows limits: the crystal ball in the junk store teaches Alice and Sally Anne Montberclair nothing. There is absolutely no magic there. The murder and the trial have made them see a light already present in their hearts.

The function of magic is more restrained in Vernon's *A Killing in This Town*. There is the watchful hummingbird, a symbol of elegance, lightness and grace that flits in and out or perches on the maple tree under which the Klansmen pronounced Curtis dead and loaded him onto their squeaky wheelbarrow. There is Midnight, the healer dog that helped ailing baby Adam find his breath by lying next to him. Midnight that howls its disapproval on seeing Adam try his Klansman's robe on. Midnight that finds Earl Thomas in the woods, wounded for falling from the same maple tree (his rib "glowing" [71]), and goes to warn Emma New of her husband's predicament – not with words, but enticing her to follow him the way dogs will do. But no magical intervention allows the characters of *A Killing in This Town*, whether white or black, to glimpse a vision of a better future, or even of a hard liberation struggle. Evil is entrenched in that society, nothing will shake its hellish grip off. Adam (the first man?) is alone as the book ends ambiguously. Alone in his past – when he learned the news Hurry Bullock had shot Midnight in the leg for fleeing rather that lie down by his dying brother.[14] Alone in his future, now that he has come into the world by freeing himself of the right the Klan's constitution gave him to be "the naked proprietor of a killing in this town" (246). Free… as the willing perpetrator of an execution. Not of an evil idea, but of a man. Free… or deprived of consciousness.

A Killing in This Town's discursive program hinges on the punishment of the Klan as suggested by the heading from Matthew XXI-44, "And whosoever shall fall on this stone shall be broken: but on whomsoever it shall fall, it will grind him to powder." An eye for an eye… says the *Book of Matthew* 5-38 – Hurry's eye for Curtis's eye. Memory of days of oppression, the "symptoms of suffocating history in their bones" (19) fuels the story line; but neither does the shadow of the James Byrd lynching nor retaliation lead to any questioning. Three whites are involved in Klan violence, just as there were three murderers that 1998 night in Texas, and murder is perpetrated in the same way – dragging with the added gratification of sadistic kicks in the rib cage.[15] Vernon who was born in Louisiana transposed her story to the heart of the Jim Crow era, the Mississippi where she spent part of her young life for a mental geography of racism.

The agents of punishment (can we say *revenge*?) are white. Gill and Adam represent youth and team together for the ultimate slaying of the Jim Crow past. Lenora Bullock, the Klan's seamstress, shoots herself in her head through her birthmark under the posted Klan mantra in the barn. Salem Bullock dies from suffocation by the local disease he would not acknowledge when Earl Thomas, thirteen years earlier, brought a letter from the health department warning the men that the Pauer plant was injurious to health. His brother Hurry is dragged to death as Adam acts under Hoover Pickens's, his own father's, guidance. Later, as he comes with the wheelbarrow to carry the body to the morgue, Hoover finds the health department letter dangling from a pocket and realizes that "Earl Thomas had simply come to save them" (232). The realization makes him turn from the corpse and vomit, and only then does he see, "beneath the eye of the wheelbarrow" (ibid.), that the dead man is in fact his Klan officer, Hurry Bullock. Black characters are not actively vengeful, merely complacent in Gill's scheme. Sonny, Curtis's widow, builds a cross written with Hurry's name on it and places it in the wheelbarrow to mark his grave, an action the text leaves unaccounted for. Similarly, Earl Thomas's thoughts remain a sealed book. He was ready to submit to death, to sacrifice himself out of his sense of duty toward his flock as a preacher, but becomes complicit in Hurry's death that begins from his home when Emma New brings the white man's swathed body out. He is no direct executioner and is absent from the text during the deed. He is just present on the page in the train station. The text proposes no inside view of his feelings. We read nothing about pangs of conscience. Has a pastor forgotten the sixth Commandment, "Thou shalt not kill"?

The murderers in *Wolf Whistle* incur no punishment. Nordan's story follows history in this respect. Solon and Lord Montberclair are acquitted, but the novel focuses on characters who vent their detestation of their action, or of their own passive neighbors and friends. Alice somehow feels responsible for not trying some kind of a charm, such as a mojo, when she saw Bobo's death refracted through a rain drop. She speaks her outrage and when she makes her students draw their memories of the trial, all assignments turn out to be pictures of the parrot who made her exclaim *"Thar she blows"* (256) in the courtroom – a strange unexpected allusion to Captain Ahab's obsession with the elimination of evil which he never sees is within himself in Melville's *Moby Dick*. Like his niece, Runt also feels responsible because he might have saved Bobo by giving word of the threat on him to his uncle: the lad could have been put on the train back to Chicago. Runt becomes Nordan's mouthpiece when expressing with Coach Heard (who has had one drink too many) a sense of hurt and dismay that town folks could carry on with their lives as if nothing had happened, murder or trial. Bizarre satire of a masochistic South steps into the story when, to Runt's astonishment, some people line up in repentance to be hit on their heads with an ax handle – and one of them goes back in line for more. It's the crippled high school Coach, a veteran of the second world war,[16] who expresses with very homely and moving words what no one seemed to care to say or think: "I never knowed about this emptiness inside me, until that little colored boy got killed and Solon and Dexter got let loose" (273). Coach Heard's words are spoken to Runt whose parrot he offers to adopt. They do not register at once and the men's dialogue ends as a childish fantastic world evaporates into adult resignation and Coach Heard finally calls Runt by his real name, Cyrus:

> Runt said, "What do you want with a parrot?"
> Coach said, "I don't know. I already got me a peg leg. Seem like all I need now is a parrot."
> Runt said, "You gone sail the high seas, ain't you, Coach?"
> Coach said, "I'm gonna get me a Jolly Roger."
> Runt said, "It's a bad world, Coach. It's an evil world we live in."
> Coach said, "I know, Cyrus, I know. We'll just have to make do." (276)

This is not the way the book ends, however. The dream of a world that may, or may not, come into being lingers in the hopes entertained by poor-white Alice and rich Sally Anne in the junk store. Will magic hold its own and change the world? Only Bobo knows whether Alice and Sally Anne wept together, in each other's arms, finding like-minded thoughts in their hearts.

Rounding Up the Discussion

The power of magic in *A Killing in This Town* mostly pertains to Midnight's compassion toward good people in pain. Midnight is an unusual name for a dog. Can it signal the beginning of a new day while still in the dark hours? We remember Midnight brings baby Adam back to life, brings Emma New the news of her husband's fall in the woods, howls when Adam wears his Klan robe and later refuses to relieve Klansman Salem Bullock of his lung affliction. Nordan's story takes a different route where magic rests in the accusing parrot and in dead Bobo's remaining eye that is able to reveal what it sees. *Wolf Whistle* is the more realistic fiction because, for all its supernatural elements and satiric bent, it keeps focused on the mindset of the mid-1950s rural South. Bobo's shooting at his (former) abductor after finding his "pea-shooter" (59) by the roadside in the dark is improbable but steeped in America's future because, on an interpretive level, it embodies the spirit of resistance that was to take wings in Montgomery and elsewhere.

We have seen that the most manifest distinction between our two books has little to do with magic. It resides in the characters' minds, probed in one novel and neglected in the other. *A Killing in This Town*, streamlined, dichotomous, fantastic and humorless as it is, seems to be more superficial because it lacks human depth and historical perspective. Emmett Till's tragedy is not the only *terra firma* that gives *Wolf Whistle* its backbone or, again in Nordan's words in his "Growing Up White in the South" essay, its "moral center." Pairing supernatural elements with an accurate representation of the region's mores, the real and the unreal is Nordan's way to express the unbelievable yet true situation of this Delta backwater, as well as a gleam of hope. *Wolf Whistle* also achieves that, incidentally, by blaming American society at large through the name of the poor-white district, *Balance Due*, possibly an oblique comment upon the ravages of social inequality suggesting the root of racism may be that too many white people have been left by the side of the road to prosperity and taught to hate difference.

A Killing in This Town reads like a revenge on that past madness that still perverts many white minds today, a fictional explosion against racist iniquity. Rather than just a brutal revenge against Jim Crow insanity, *Wolf Whistle* is also self-rebuke, or, more exactly, a denunciation of the teenager Nordan then was, molded by the milieu he was growing up in. Smoky's rise to dignity is not due to his just speaking up against injustice: most importantly, he also admits to his first conforming, reflex-like, to local behavior:

> Smoky Viner said, "It ain't right."
> Somebody said, "We ain't said it was right, Smoky. We just kidding around."
> Smoky Viner said, "I laughed too, I couldn't help it."
> Well.
> Smoky Viner said, "I hope I live long enough to forgive myself for that laugh." (206)

If we pair up Smoky's declaration with Nordan's 1995 confession in "The Making of a Book" – "perhaps I laughed" –, Smoky impersonates a better young man than the author admits he then was. That the older Nordan is directly present behind Smoky Viner's words is obvious and extremely moving. Nordan's essay gives deep creative insight in two other instances. Firstly when he mentions the letter he wrote to Emmett's mother, after enlisting his wife's help, to tell her that her "son's life and death changed [his] own life" (78). In the second passage, he tells of his phoning "the boy in the locker room" (80), the original Smoky Viner in real life. Their conversation ends the essay and must be quoted at length because it helps understand how sensitivity can trigger an author's creation over thirty years later: the novel's source from which Nordan's sense of guilt arose never happened in the original Smoky's memory:

> "Do you remember when you first heard of the murder?" He said, "No, Buddy, I'm sorry I don't." I said, "There were some terrible jokes being made, do you remember that?" He said yes, he did remember, and then he recalled the same awful joke about the gin fan. I said, "I'm thinking of the day in the football locker room. I was the team manager, and the team was dressing out, and everybody was talking about the murder. Do you remember that? He thought for a few seconds. He said, "No I don't think I do. I remember people talking about it." I said, "The day I'm thinking of, we were all talking about the murder, and making jokes, and then you stood up for the dead boy. You said, 'I'm for the colored boy,' or something like that. Do you remember that?" He thought again. He said, "No Buddy, I'm sorry. I really don't." I said, "The way I remember it, you said this and the rest of us stopped talking. I thought you were so courageous. I wished I had said it. I think about that moment all the time. I've thought of you for all these years. You don't remember?" He said, "No, I'm sorry. I don't." I said, "It took so much courage. I admire you for it." He said, "Well, thank you. Thank you, Buddy. He said, "I'm real glad you called. This has been nice." (81)

There is no comparable personal emotion at work in the creation of *A Killing in This Town* that just describes Adam's and Gill's physical reactions in front of horror – vomiting – but skips their thoughts.

However different the impulses to create may be, I will conclude this essay with another line of investigation that has been barely broached here. Both novels address C. Vann Woodward's thesis in *The Strange Career of Jim Crow*, as well as the "white problem" Lerone Bennett Jr., described in his famous *Ebony* article. In so doing, they reconfigure the events in such a way as to represent the young and the white lower classes as the main agents seeking liberation from the past.

[1] "L'horreur s'attache à des événements qu'il est nécessaire de ne jamais oublier. Elle constitue en cela la motivation éthique ultime de l'histoire des victimes." My translation from Ricoeur's *Temps et récit* (Paris: Seuil, 1985) 1.

[2] Only in the galley version was Emmett's first name turned to the youth's nickname, "Bobo." Nordan adds he liked the nickname better for its allowing him more leeway in the creation of a character he could feel closer to.

[3] Vernon makes the same point in an interview with Dee Stewart, then speaks of purpose: "It is not my job to worry about what the world is doing, only to write the story of injustice of the world through the characters. [...] Let the characters create the purpose" (Stewart 5). I still stand by my intuition for two very factual reasons. Firstly, that James Byrd's death is the only instance of lynching by dragging I have ever heard of or read about in any book or media. Secondly, that Vernon studied criminal law before turning to a writing career. She was about twenty when this lynching occurred, and James Byrd's fate must have been a case study in college. And so, thinking of the obsessive "eye" motif, must have been Emmett Till's because an action was still pendant against Carolyn Bryant. As I see it, the 1988 circumstances made a strong impression on Vernon's mind, returned to her as a novelist, however unconsciously, and organized themselves into a fiction. "What happens to a dream differed?" asks a Langston Hughes poem. Maybe Vernon's novel is a fictional explosion. Understandably. Creation is mysterious.

[4] He says he has no precise recollection: "Probably I smiled at the joke. I don't remember" ("Making" 76).

[5] Emmett's favourite brag to impress his rural friends was that he, a Chicago resident, had a white mistress whose photo he carried around.

[6] Smoky likes to boast about his main accomplishment: that he has butted a toilet door flat to the ground with his forehead.

[7] Emmett's mother testified in court that what was perceived as an insulting whistle may have been the sound her son used to control the stutter he was afflicted with in moments of excitement. He was showing off in a group of peers.

[8] In their confession that was published in *Look* after they were discharged, Bryant and Milam said they made Emmett carry the gin fan. Nordan's representation clearly blasts away at the murderers' racist mindset.

[9] One is tempted to read in that name the impetuosity and eventual brutality of a young bull, but "bullock" also means a castrated bull. Maybe the name cuts both ways, suggesting violence and/or frustrated manhood.

[10] Nordan's Arrow Catcher (as in the other works located there) is peopled with all kinds: some foolish, some lazy, drunkards, gossips, drudges, ordinary men and women struggling to get by in a backwater; but the people in Bullock are only imprisoned on either side of the color line.

[11] Adam was born from that rape. His mother once contemplated pushing her baby's fontanel in for this reason.

[12] A shining instance is Curtis Willow's morning greeting to his wife: "Now I know why the garden of Eden was so beautiful. There was a woman in the middle of it" (30).

[13] There is possible irony beside the factual need to hide the body's identity. James Byrd was stripped before he was dragged over three miles of country road, his body dismembered, one arm found there, his head elsewhere, his torso again in some other location.

[14] Emma New finds Midnight under the maple tree. She tends its wound and wraps its leg in gauze, the same material she uses to heal her husband's broken rib and to later enshroud Hurry Bullock.

[15] Brewer, one of the two defendants who were given a death sentence, only admitted to giving James Byrd a kick in the chest to break up the fight. Berry, the owner of the truck who received a life imprisonment sentence, asserted during his trial that Byrd was stabbed dead before the dragging began. Was that done out of mercy – a word that comes up twice in *A Killing in This Town* in connection with the accordion player? The truth of it will probably never be known. The three men, two of whom officially joined the Ku Kux Klan in jail, have appealed. In a letter sent to co-defendant Brewer from jail, King wrote: "reguardless [sic] of the outcome of this, we have made history and shall die proudly remembered if need be. [...] Gottago. Much Aryan love. Respect and honor my brother in arms." Qtd. in Paul Duggan, "Racist Convicted in Texas Murder," *The Washington Post* 24 Feb. 1999, 22 June 2004 <http://www.washingtonpost.com/wp-srv/national/longterm/jasper/guilty022499.htm>.

[16] A war against the horrors of racism.

Works Cited

Nordan, Lewis. "The Making of a Book." *The Oxford American* (Mar.-Apr. 1995): 75-81.

---. *Wolf Whistle*. 1993. Chapel Hill: Algonquin, 1995.

Stewart, Dee Y. "Finding Logic: An Interview with Olympia Vernon." *Suite 101.com: Insightful Writers, Informed Readers* 21 July 2004. 4 Mar. 2009 <http://www.suite101.com/article.cfm/african_american_women_writers/109979>.

Vernon, Olympia. *A Killing in This Town*. New York: Grove P, 2006.

Alexander Beissenhirtz

Theorizing the Vernacular Modernism of Jazz: The *New Jazz Studies*

Introduction
In recent years, a large number of scholars from diverse academic backgrounds has systematically assessed and theorized the discourses surrounding jazz music. Contemporary jazz studies conceptualize their object as a cultural formation with significant non-sonic implications and therefore approach it from a transdisciplinary, cultural studies perspective. Jazz scholarship thus accounts for developments that have shaped musicology in general: Traditional concepts of this academic discipline have yielded to a *New Musicology* from which notions of an emergent *New Jazz Studies* are partly derived. This tendency can be considered a consequence of Edward Said's assertion that "the study of music can be more, and not less, interesting if we situate the music [...] in a social and cultural setting" (xvi). Thus, the *New Jazz Studies* aim at shedding light on the figurations and functions of jazz within culture and society, thereby accounting for contemporary debates in critical theory. This new critical awareness involves a scepticism towards conventional constructions of a coherent jazz tradition and history. In order to contextualize this point, I will draw on the historical debate about the implications of the bebop revolution because, as Scott DeVeaux has argued, "in order to understand jazz, one has to understand bebop" (*Bebop* 3). Bebop represents a decisive juncture in jazz history not only because the musical vocabulary of jazz changed significantly, but also because it strongly foregrounded the subcultural aspects of jazz culture. As Eric Lott points out, the bebop movement "merit[s] the spin of subculture theory: zoot, lip, junk, and double-time became the stylistic answer to social contradictions [...] experienced by the makers and followers of bop" (459). Investigating the space between the music and the culture surrounding it as described by Lott and others,[1] I want to suggest in this essay that the new revisionist approach to jazz and its history can be considered a politicized counter discourse to traditionalist "master narratives" about the music, its history, and its practitioners.

Defining the Field

Ralph Ellison, who frequently commented on jazz and its socio-cultural, historical, and aesthetic implications in his writings, asked in his essay, "On Bird, Bird-Watching, and Jazz": "Who knows very much of what jazz is really about? Or how shall we ever know until we are willing to confront anything and everything which it sweeps across our path?" (224-25). Although critics, journalists, musicians, and fans have dealt extensively with the music and the lives of its practitioners since its beginnings, jazz studies as an academic discipline was a somewhat marginal phenomenon for a long time. As Krin Gabbard points out, jazz scholars and researchers more often than not have backgrounds in diverse academic fields, dealing with jazz "within, outside, or around their work in departments of English, philosophy, African American studies, history, music, American studies, comparative literature, and film studies" (*Representing* vii). Therefore, much recent jazz scholarship, such as Gabbard's research on jazz and film,[2] takes a transdisciplinary approach, moving away from strictly musicological and historical analysis in favor of questions concerning the functions of jazz within society and its figurations in culture. In that manner, jazz studies have begun to thoroughly confront "anything and everything that jazz sweeps across our path," to repeat Ellison's words. Numerous anthologies, monographs, and other publications of the last 20 years share the assumption that jazz, as Eric Porter puts it, is "a business enterprise and a set of institutional relationships, a focal point for political and social debate, a vehicle for individual and communal identity formulation, and, eventually, an idea" (6). Of course, the understanding of jazz as a multi-faceted cultural phenomenon with major extra-musical implications is not new: significantly, one of the pioneering works of the *New Jazz Studies*, Robert G. O'Meally's anthology *The Jazz Cadence of American Culture* (1998), contains various essays, articles, and interviews ranging from early writings on jazz by authors like Sterling Brown or Zora Neale Hurston to contemporary jazz scholarship. In this way, the scholarly and intellectual tradition on which the new approach to jazz studies builds is being acknowledged.

The emergence of the *New Jazz Studies* must be understood in the broader context of theoretical developments that had an impact across the humanities during the last decades, including "classical" musicology which, through a reversal of its traditional methods, has developed into a *New Musicology* – a term which implies a conceptual affinity to the *New Jazz Studies*.[3] As Stephen Paul Scher points out, in modernizing and revising the traditional musicological approaches and methods, the *New Musicology* has incorporated "certain terms that connote postmodernist awareness [...] like 'meaning, value, criticism, literary theory, deconstruction, narrative, canon, women, gender, sexuality, feminism, society, culture, politics, ideology'" (11-12). Thus, both the *New Musicology* and the *New Jazz Studies* account for contemporary critical theory by constructing the music as a complex, multi-faceted discursive field, thereby focusing especially on non-sonic aspects like race, class, and gender as inscribed in the apparatus of the music. In that manner, the study of jazz is no longer a largely apolitical analysis of aesthetics, but takes into perspective the political implications of the music. In the following, I want to contextualize this new, revisionist approach to jazz history and culture.

Approaching music, whether jazz or other genres, primarily through its apparatus (as opposed to a focus on the music as such, that is, its aesthetic features), naturally carries certain risks: in *The Jazz Cadence of American Culture*, for example, jazz aesthetics for O'Meally are related to seemingly far-fetched phenomena such as skyscrapers, Michael Jordan, or the American Constitution. But as awkward as some of those comparisons and analogies may seem, one should not downplay the impact of the "jazz factor" as it becomes visible and audible in American and global culture, because, as O'Meally writes,

> in spite of the curse of seeing jazz everywhere, we must not commit the matching crime of refusing to see it (to see jazz, meaning to *understand* it in profound ways as well as to visualize the music in its not strictly musical incarnations) anywhere. (ix)

The distinction between "understand[ing jazz] in a profound way" on the one hand and extra-musical visualizations on the other illustrates two major concerns of the *New Jazz Studies*: one is musico-historical and/or musicological in the broadest sense, including related questions of the modes of production of jazz music, its history, etc. The other deals with jazz from the perspective of other fields of inquiry, aiming at shedding light on literary works or periods, painting and sculpture, sociological and historical questions, etc. This is achieved by investigating how artifacts, society, or cultural constellations of any kind are informed by jazz or jazz aesthetics, and vice versa, how sociohistorical factors relate to jazz music and its practice.

Like any other musical idiom, jazz music is inseparable from the discourses surrounding it, because, as John Gennari suggests in his comprehensive study on jazz criticism, "the meanings we attach to the music and the musicians [...] are very deeply influenced by the filters that stand between us and the sound that comes out of the musicians' bodies and instruments" (4). The reception of the music is thus dependent on a textual level which precedes and frames the act of listening itself (ibid.). Thus, jazz writing, be it scholarly or else, needs to be understood as a discursive site in which extra-musical referentiality is constructed in the context of the non-referential sign-system of music. I want to extend Gennari's argument by suggesting that not only jazz criticism, but all kinds of jazz discourse – including jazz journalism and scholarship, song-titles, biographies and autobiographies, jazz-related fiction or poetry, jazz on TV and in the movies, even commercials using jazz as background music – provide a framework in which certain meanings are attributed to the music, thereby contributing to, commenting on, or challenging our understanding of what we consider jazz to be and to mean.

Political Blues

As Lewis Porter has observed, "when jazz began, and each time it changed, there was a controversy. And each time it changed, the debate revolved around the question, What is jazz?" (vii). This seemingly simple question, which has prompted countless heated debates during the first century of jazz, has significant ideological implications. Scott DeVeaux has touched on the essence of the problem by persuasively arguing that "the struggle is over possession of [jazz] history, and the legitimacy it confers" ("Constructing" 485). He suggests that jazz historians, commentators, scholars, and musicians – from Hugues Panassié's 1934 *Le jazz hot* to contemporary debates about neo-classicism in jazz – have repeatedly tried to "impose a kind of deadening uniformity of cultural meaning on the music" ("Constructing" 505).

Before discussing how the *New Jazz Studies* figure in the controversies about the "cultural meaning" of jazz that were and continue to be a constant backbeat of the music itself, its production and reception, I want briefly to recapitulate the problem in the light of Berndt Ostendorf's conceptualization of jazz as a "vernacular modernism":

> The drive for innovation which is so characteristic of jazz identifies it as a truly Western child of Modernism. There is that discipline of making it new. Yet, jazz is not exclusively Western. [...] it is deeply rooted in the black folk and its music [...] and it has repeatedly been revitalized by

black folk energy, such as blues and gospel. At the same time it is a global, Modernist idiom. [...] Jazz mediates a cultural contradiction: though socially a subculture, it has been an aesthetic avantgarde since Armstrong's Hot Five. (167, 171)

I suggest that the mediation of black vernacular culture and modernism in jazz as described by Ostendorf has significant political implications. In this context, the concept of the vernacular requires brief explanation: Sieglinde Lemke has defined vernacular art as being "produced by non-hegemonic artists [...], defined by a structural opposition, or *difference*, to a dominant standardized term" (155). Aiming at achieving recognition and canonization by highlighting difference, she characterizes the vernacular as "a style with politics in view" (168). In order to grasp the political dimension of the vernacular modernism of jazz, it is useful to turn to the controversies about the bebop movement as an example.

It is common knowledge that the innovations and abstractions of bebop – for better or worse – moved jazz away from dance halls and into bohemian nightclubs and concert halls, thus significantly changing the function of the music. Even if the vernacular elements of jazz were by no means abandoned altogether, bebop foregrounded the modernist aspects of jazz. This turn toward abstraction was interpreted by Amiri Baraka (then Leroi Jones) as the articulation of a "willfully harsh, *anti-assimilationist* sound" (181) that functioned as an intentional assault on middle-class values. From his perspective, these were represented by the predominantly white swing big bands, whose music he characterized as "a stylized reflection of a culturally feeble environment" (ibid.). By interpreting the intellectualisms of bebop as expressive of a genuine black folk or vernacular sensibility, that is, by constructing aesthetic difference as racial and social difference, he identified black vernacular culture as a countercultural force against white hegemony to which the swing bands, from his point of view, had assimilated. This radical view of the function of jazz was contradicted within the black intellectual community: Albert Murray, for example, did not consider bebop as a rupture within the jazz tradition, but rather viewed it as a continuation, as musicians like Charlie Parker and Dizzy Gillespie tried, in Murray's words, "to make the music swing harder" (166). Even though Murray and Baraka both acknowledge that bebop was built upon the vernacular roots of black music, their respective conclusions differ fundamentally from each other: For Murray, the vernacular functions as a continuum within African American musical expression as he regards both the swing big bands so harshly criticized by Baraka as well as the bebop movement as not only an integral part of black American culture, but a constitutive element of American national culture and society at large. The notion of jazz as "America's classical music" is also prevalent in Ralph Ellison's writings on jazz. Baraka's black nationalist, counter-hegemonic conceptualization of bebop prompted Ellison to comment polemically:

> The tremendous burden of sociology which Jones [Baraka] would place upon this body of music is enough to give even the blues the blues [...]. It is unfortunate that Jones thought it necessary to ignore the aesthetic nature of the blues in order to make his ideological point, for he might have come much closer had he considered the blues not as politics but as art. [...] For the blues are not primarily concerned with civil rights or obvious political protest; they are an art form and thus a transcendence of those conditions created within the Negro community by the denial of social justice. ("Blues People" 249, 257)[4]

Ellison's situating of jazz within, and not in opposition to American national culture, involves an emphasis on aesthetics, that is, on the status of jazz as an autonomous art form that requires no referentiality and meaning beyond its own formal features. By insisting on the status of jazz as a "fine art" that needs to be approached with what Pierre Bourdieu has called an aesthetic attitude, Murray and Ellison claim that the African American musical tradition of jazz can be considered "America's classical music." Yet while Bourdieu has argued that the aesthetic outlook can serve as a strategy to distinguish oneself socially from others, it would be highly misleading to interpret Ellison's and Murray's position as mere snobbery. As different as their conception might seem from Baraka's, I suggest that it can be conceived of as a different kind of effort to re-functionalize bebop, which, by moving jazz out of the dance hall, seemed to have lost its social relevance: whereas Baraka conceptualized bebop as a symbolic weapon to oppose the hegemonic power structure that forced jazz musicians into the role of entertainers playing for dances, Ellison's and Murray's argument also implicitly acknowledges the emancipatory force inherent not only in bebop or jazz but in all of black music, not by constructing it as protest music, but by elevating it to the status of an autonomous form of (American) art, thus also dismissing the racist, reductive view of the black jazz artist as entertainer. It is necessary to add that for neither Ellison nor Murray, did the notion of jazz as dance music diminish its status as art; quite to the contrary, both writers considered danceable rhythms to be a crucial element of jazz music.

Toward the Margins: The *New Jazz Studies* and Revisionism
Although jazz studies have come a long way since the controversies about bebop, the respective conceptualizations of jazz and the accompanying rhetoric resonate through contemporary debates about jazz and its function within culture and society. Baraka's claim that bebop musicians strived "to restore jazz, in some sense, to its original separateness" (181) ironically resembles efforts since the 1980s by traditionalists – usually associated with trumpeter Wynton Marsalis and writer Stanley Crouch (one might also add Albert Murray to the list) – to "restore jazz." However, the aim was not a realm of "original separateness" à la Baraka; rather, the traditionalist movement took up Ellison's ideas, though decades later, as it aimed at institutionalizing the music at the center of American national culture. Stanley Crouch, in somewhat bombastic rhetoric, linked this vision of jazz – as a music firmly rooted in African American vernacular culture yet representative of traditional values of the American middle-class – to a distinctly bourgeois lifestyle:

> There is a large dream in the world of jazz, and that dream is much richer than anything one will encounter in the ethnic sentimentality of Afrocentric propaganda. What those young jazz musicians symbolize is freedom from the tastemaking of mass media and an embracing of a vision that has much more to do with aesthetic satisfaction than the gold rush of popular entertainment […]. They have a healthy respect for the men and women who laid an astonishing tradition down. In their wit, their good grooming, their disdain for drugs, and their command of the down-home and the ambitious, they suggest that though America may presently be down on one knee, the champ is about to rise and begin taking names. (159)

A similar view as Crouch's dominates large parts of Ken Burns's impressive yet controversial TV-series *Jazz* (2001), an exhaustive documentary in which jazz history is shown as a coherent development from a folk idiom into a bourgeois art form in the United States. Louis Armstrong, Duke Ellington, and other jazz heroes are covered extensively, whereas musicians from Europe and other continents, as well as the jazz avantgarde, jazz-derived experimental music, and fusion are almost entirely omitted.

The *New Jazz Studies* challenge narratives such as Burns's by approaching jazz music and history from a revisionist perspective. Krin Gabbard has characterized this challenge as the expression of "a profound discomfort with the idea that an official jazz history *can* be written or that any representation of the music can transcend its own built-in limitations" (*Representing* 3). In a similar manner, Scott DeVeaux stresses the constructedness of the jazz tradition by describing it as "an overarching narrative that has crowded out other possible interpretations of the complicated and variegated cultural phenomena that we cluster under the umbrella *jazz*" ("Constructing" 488). The replacement of an exclusionary version of jazz history by a revisionist one that embraces popular music, fusion, and the jazz avantgarde, can be considered one major concern of the *New Jazz Studies*. This inclusive narrative is intertwined with another equally important aim, namely, to regain an awareness of the sociopolitical relevance of jazz. The work of scholars like DeVeaux, Brent Hayes Edwards, Daniel Fischlin, Krin Gabbard, Ajay Heble, George Lewis, George Lipsitz, Ingrid Monson, Eric Porter, Sherrie Tucker, and several others has brought forth a paradigm shift in jazz studies: the aesthetic imperative has increasingly become replaced by an approach focused on the social contexts of the music, thus echoing Baraka's conception of jazz as a site of resistance against hegemonic power. In jazz discourse today, race relations are one of several socially relevant issues. Thus, the *New Jazz Studies* not only conceptualize jazz as a discourse of alterity, but also critically investigate how alterity figures within jazz discourse itself, as a large number of recent publications on the role of women in jazz exemplify (e.g., see Tucker; Oliveros; Smith; Monson). Likewise, the *New Jazz Studies* have explored similarly marginalized musical tendencies in jazz by focusing on the hybridization of the music through contemporary popular music as well as experimental languages of jazz and improvised music as played and listened to all over the world.[5]

Conclusion
The revitalized interest in jazz academia in what Fischlin and Heble describe as "an identifiable and radical form of improvisational practices in which concepts of alternative community formation, social activism, rehistorization of minority cultures, and critical modes of resistance and dialogue" (2) can be considered a counter-discourse to the neo-classical tendencies that dominated large parts of public jazz discourse during the 1980s and '90s. The *New Jazz Studies* approach

seems to have developed into the leading paradigm in jazz academia as it has replaced traditional conceptions of jazz history as a "linear progression from genius to genius" (Lipsitz 22) by narratives that account for the aesthetic hybridity and socio-cultural complexities and conflicts that have characterized jazz music and jazz culture since its beginnings. At the same time, though, *Jazz at Lincoln Center* has emerged as a powerful organization that successfully put into institutional practice the Ellisonian vision of jazz as an autonomous, respectable, genuinely American fine art: By presenting jazz in a similar way as European classical music, including pre-concert lectures by noted experts, the notion of jazz as "America's classical music" is strongly asserted. In that manner, *Jazz at Lincoln Center*, despite a certain narrowness of artistic vision, has helped to foster recognition for and appreciation of a historically marginalized African American art form. As this process of canonization has arguably not yet been sufficiently theorized in jazz academia, it will be one of the future tasks in jazz studies to provide a scholarly framework that accommodates the canonized mainstream of American jazz (as represented, for example, by *Jazz at Lincoln Center*) with the multitude of other musical and cultural figurations of the vernacular modernism of jazz in its second century.

---

[1] On the socio-cultural contexts of jazz, see also, e.g., Jost. On the status of the music as a subculture, see, e.g., Sidran.

[2] See her *Jammin' at the Margins*.

[3] In their introduction to the anthology *Uptown Conversation: The New Jazz Studies*, O'Meally, Edwards, and Griffin name the *New Musicology* as one transdisciplinary influence on the *New Jazz Studies* (6).

[4] Baraka and Ellison use "the Blues" as an umbrella term under which the several forms of African American musical expression, including jazz, are grouped together. In the work of both Baraka and Ellison, jazz figures most prominently among the various idioms of black music.

[5] For jazz and contemporary popular music, see, e.g., Kelley; Neal. For the avantgarde, see, e.g., Lewis, "Experimental Music"; Lewis, "Improvised Music."

Works Cited

Baraka, Amiri. *Blues People: Negro Music in White America*. New York: Morrow Quill, 1963.

Crouch, Stanley. "Blues to Be Constitutional: A Long Look at the Wild Wherefores of Our Democratic Lives as Symbolized in the Making of Rhythm and Tune." *The Jazz Cadence of American Culture*. Ed. Robert G. O'Meally. New York: Columbia UP, 1998. 154-65.

Ellison, Ralph. "Blues People." *Shadow and Act*. 1964. New York: Random House, 1995. 247-58.

---. "On Bird, Bird-Watching, and Jazz." *Shadow and Act*. 1964. New York: Random House, 1995. 221-32.

DeVeaux, Scott. *The Birth of Bebop: A Social and Musical History*. Berkeley: U of California P, 1997.

---. "Constructing the Jazz Tradition." In: O'Meally 1998, 483-512.

Fischlin, Daniel, and Ajay Heble, eds. *The Other Side of Nowhere: Jazz, Improvisation, and Communities in Dialogue*. Middletown: Wesleyan UP, 2004.

Gabbard, Krin. *Jammin' at the Margins: Jazz and the American Cinema*. U of Chicago P, 1996.

---. *Representing Jazz*. Durham: Duke UP, 1995.

Gennari, John. *Blowin' Hot and Cool: Jazz and its Critics*. Chicago: The U of Chicago P, 2006.

Jost, Ekkehard. *Die Sozialgeschichte des Jazz*. Frankfurt am Main: Zweitausendeins, 2003.

Kelley, Robin D. G. "Beneath the Underground: Exploring New Currents in 'Jazz.'" *Uptown Conversation: The New Jazz Studies*. Ed. Robert G. O'Meally, Brent Hayes Edwards, and Farah Jasmin Griffin. New York: Columbia UP, 2004. 404-16.

Lemke, Sieglinde. "Theories of American Culture in the Name of the Vernacular." *Theories of American Culture: Theories of American Studies*. Ed. Winfried Fluck and Thomas Claviez. Tübingen: Narr, 2003. 155-74.

Lewis, George E. "Experimental Music in Black and White: The AACM in New York, 1970-1985." *Uptown Conversation: The New Jazz Studies*. Ed. Robert G. O'Meally, Brent Hayes Edwards, and Farah Jasmin Griffin. New York: Columbia UP, 2004. 50-101.

---. "Improvised Music After 1950: Afrological and Eurological Perspectives." *The Other Side of Nowhere: Jazz, Improvisation, and Communities in Dialogue*. Ed. Daniel Fishlin and Ajay Heble. Middletown: Wesleyan UP, 2004. 131-62.

Lipsitz, George. "Songs of the Unsung: The Darby Hicks History of Jazz." *Uptown Conversation: The New Jazz Studies*. Ed. Robert G. O'Meally, Brent Hayes Edwards, and Farah Jasmin Griffin. New York: Columbia UP, 2004. 9-26.

Lott, Eric. "Double V, Double Time: Bebop's Politics of Style." *The Jazz Cadence of American Culture*. Ed. Robert G. O'Meally. New York: Columbia UP, 1998. 457-68.

Murray, Albert. S*tomping the Blues*. New York: Da Capo, 1976.

Monson, Ingrid. "The Problem with White Hipness: Race, Gender, and Cultural Conceptions in Jazz Historical Discourse." *Journal of the American Musicological Society* 48 (Fall 1995): 397-422.

Neal, Mark Anthony. "'... A Way Out of No Way': Jazz, Hip-Hop, and Black Social Improvisation." *The Other Side of Nowhere: Jazz, Improvisation, and Communities in Dialogue*. Ed. Daniel Fishlin and Ajay Heble. Middletown: Wesleyan UP, 2004. 195-223.

Oliveros, Pauline. "Harmonic Anatomy: Women in Improvisation." *The Other Side of Nowhere: Jazz, Improvisation, and Communities in Dialogue*. Ed. Daniel Fishlin and Ajay Heble. Middletown: Wesleyan UP, 2004. 50-70.

O'Meally, Robert G., ed. *The Jazz Cadence of American Culture*. New York: Columbia UP, 1998.

O'Meally, Robert G., Brent Hayes Edwards, and Farah Jasmin Griffin, eds. *Uptown Conversation: The New Jazz Studies*. New York: Columbia UP, 2004.

Ostendorf, Berndt. "Anthropology, Modernism, and Jazz." *Ralph Ellison*. Ed. Harold Bloom. New York: Chelsea House Publishers, 1986. 145-72.

Porter, Eric. *What is This Thing Called Jazz? African American Musicians as Artists, Critics, Activists*. New York: Columbia UP, 2002.

Porter, Lewis. *Jazz: A Century of Change: Readings and New Essays*. New York: Schirmer, 1997.

Said, Edward. *Musical Elaborations*. New York: Columbia UP, 1991.

Scher, Stephen Paul. "Melopoetics Revisited." *Word and Music Studies: Defining the Field*. Ed. Walter Bernhart, Steven Paul Scher, and Werner Wolf. Amsterdam: Rodopi, 1991. 9-24.

Sidran, Ben. *Black Talk*. New York: Da Capo, 1981.

Smith, Julie Dawn. "Playing Like a Girl: The Queer Laughter of the Feminist Improvising Group." *The Other Side of Nowhere: Jazz, Improvisation, and Communities in Dialogue*. Ed. Daniel Fishlin and Ajay Heble. Middletown: Wesleyan UP, 2004. 224-67.

Tucker, Sherrie. *Swing Shift: "All-Girl" Bands of the 1940s*. Durham: Duke UP, 2000.

David Abulafia

The First Atlantic Slaves, 1350-1520: Conquest, Slavery and the Opening of the Atlantic[1]

I

What I want to show in this essay is how the slave trade underwent a number of crucial transformations over five hundred years ago, which laid the foundations for the intensive trans-Atlantic slave trade of the sixteenth to the early nineteenth centuries. We shall see how, at the end of the Middle Ages, an Atlantic slave trade developed out of the much older Mediterranean slave trade; how it came to encompass first the Canary Islands and then West Africa; how it then became extended to the first areas of the New World to be visited by Europeans; and finally how a slave trade came to link Africa to the New World, as labour shortages in the first Spanish colonies created demand for the slaves sold by the Portuguese, to replace the notionally free subjects of the Crown who were worked to death in the *encomienda* system. Some parts of this history will be more familiar than others; but it seems to me to be important to stress the interconnections between what may at first seem rather disconnected histories.

This takes us at once to problems of definition which are central to what I have to say here. The Spanish authorities differentiated between free subjects who had obligations in taxes and labour services, and slaves who were owned and could be traded. But at the same time the Spanish authorities in Hispaniola and elsewhere had no qualms about forcibly moving the indigenous population, about separating parents from children for long periods, about making stringent demands for tribute in gold. By the time of the Laws of Burgos, in 1512, the physical abuse of the natives was outlawed, but this legislation was generally honoured in the breach. *De jure*, the Taíno Indians were free; *de facto* they were placed in an abject, servile condition, so that their great defender, Bartolomé de las Casas, could say that they were treated like excrement in the road. Moreover, legal freedom could be compromised by what the philosophers called a condition of 'natural slavery.' Aristotle, several of whose major works became known in the thirteenth century, differentiated between those who could play a full role in society as citizens and the 'banausic' elements, humans who in his view were naturally suited to subordinate roles; he considered that as 'natural slaves' they lacked the mental capacity to govern themselves effectively. So we shall see that the history of Atlantic slavery spills over beyond the slave trade into problems of definition of which the opponents and the proponents of slavery were well aware even in the early sixteenth century. Thus, before her death in 1504, Queen Isabella of Castile repeatedly and emphatically demanded that Canary islanders and Taíno Indians (other than rebels) should not be enslaved, since they were her subjects, even if they were not Christian; they could be seen as weak humans, child-like (as las Casas himself observed), in need of protection and completion, that completion to be achieved by making them into Christian converts and, by extension, into fully-fledged human beings, able to take part in civilised life.

This raises the question of the status of non-Christians already living within late medieval western Europe. Jews, and by extension Muslims, were described in Sicily and Spain as the *servi* of the king. On the other hand, this servitude, which, in the case of the Jews, had roots in the theology of St Augustine, was not generally understood to be anything like slavery. I understand a slave to be someone who is bought and sold, who has little or no property (at least according to the law), and who may be subject to the corrective authority of a master or mistress, even, in Roman law codes, to the point where the slave-owner has power of life and death over slaves. As the English historian Maitland observed, the Jews were free in respect of all people except the king; they could not be bought and sold as slaves. But Iberian kings could interpret the subjection of Jews to their authority in both positive and negative ways, treating their Jewish advisers as their honourable ministers, as an extension of their own voice, or, at the other extreme, insisting that 'the Jews and all they have are ours,' words employed by Ferdinand the Catholic at the time of the expulsion of the Spanish Jews in 1492. The Muslims under Christian rule were regarded in a very real sense as part of the 'Royal Treasure.' The term *servi* was capable of very many interpretations; after all, the pope himself was 'the servant of the servants of God.' Although the term *servi* was not ascribed to the American Indians (indeed, one important writer insisted that they were free – *liberi et ingenui*), there are certainly some analogies between their status and that of subject Jews or Muslims in Spain, and I intend to return to this point later.

II

Slavery was a well-established feature of Mediterranean life in the late Middle Ages; slavery persisted, particularly in the Mediterranean lands and on the eastern frontiers of Europe, regions where war captives were easy to obtain. On the other hand, slaves ceased to be a significant source of agricultural labour. The origins of slaves varied from decade to decade; the northern coasts of the Black Sea, for instance, provided late medieval Genoa with thousands of Circassians whom they sold in Egypt (where some became members of the elite Mamluk guard, and even became sultan); the highlands of Libya were an important source in the fourteenth century; more dramatically, the entire population of Muslim Minorca was sold into slavery by the island's Christian conquerors in 1287, and the Saracens of Lucera in southern Italy, descendants of the free Muslim population of Sicily, were sold *en masse* as slaves in 1300. For centuries, Muslim raiders from North Africa had been carrying off the inhabitants of Mediterranean Europe, and the mariners of Spain, France and Italy had responded in kind. Enslavement was in fact often used as a means of demanding ransoms, so that captives of high rank or wealth had some hope of redemption; and Jews, Christians and Muslims all had institutions of their own which worked for the ransoming of slaves, notably the Trinitarian and Mercedarian brothers in Mediterranean Spain and southern France. Palermo, Majorca, Barcelona, Valencia were among the places to which those looking for a household slave would gravitate; Lisbon was soon to be added to the list.

Slaves were acquired to clean and cook and serve in the home, in the main, or to perform menial tasks in artisan workshops. Female slaves were certainly abused by their masters, whether they were bought solely for sexual gratification or sexually exploited while working as domestics. There were precocious developments in the Iberian sphere, with some slaves working on sugar plantations in Valencia (Saunders 62-112; Blumenthal).[2] These were still small-scale enterprises, however. The most recent research indicates that the sugar industry in the Mediterranean, even though it was very labour-intensive, did not depend heavily on slave labour; this was a link that would develop gradually, and later, in the Atlantic world.

Slave raiding in the eastern Atlantic is first of all associated with the discovery of the Canary Islands. In 1341 a Portuguese expedition arrived in the Canary Islands, where the crew encountered people of Berber descent who had lived in isolation from the African mainland for many centuries. To European

Christians, the islanders were deeply puzzling. They were neither Christian nor Muslim; they lived in conditions of great simplicity, lacking metals, often dwelling in caves, rearing their goats, sheep and crops in what were to all intents Neolithic societies. The great Italian writer Boccaccio heard of this encounter and wrote a short essay about it, emphasizing the innocent simplicity of the near-naked islanders, for they seemed to be living out a pastoral idyll from Ovid or Virgil; others, including his friend Petrarch, laid stress instead on what he regarded as the savagery and solitude of Canary island life, seeing the inhabitants more as animals in human shape. The contrast between these two views of 'primitive' peoples in the Atlantic was developed independently again and again as more peoples were discovered beyond the boundaries of Christendom, varying between the view that they lived in the prelapsarian Golden Age of the classical writers and the view that they were barbarous, bestial, ignorant and irrational. It was assumed that if the inhabitants of these new worlds were less than fully human, they could and should be placed under the authority of Christians and work for them.

The Portuguese expedition was only one, and not necessarily the first, of a sequence of expeditions down the coast of Africa to the Canaries, in search of profit – ideally, gold, but if that could not be found, there were dyestuffs such as orchil and dragon's blood. And then, because all the indications are that these expeditions made less money than they had hoped from such products, there was the chance to fill the hold with human cargoes. Thus human beings became already a sort of ballast. For Canarians taken back on later expeditions were certainly enslaved. In 1342 the Catalan king of Majorca sent an expedition south to conquer the islands, which was beyond his abilities; but three years later a document from Majorca reports that 'a certain captive from Canaria' was working in a vineyard near the island capital, and the casual way he was described hints at the existence of plenty more Canarian slaves (Rumeu de Armas 40). The novelty of the Canary islanders consisted in the fact that they had been brought in from the Atlantic and from the fact that they were 'pagan,' unlike the Muslim slaves who were so well known in Majorca at the time.

Against this, the idea that the islanders would be better of as free Christians than as heathen slaves gained ground very rapidly. In 1351, the king of Aragon and the pope sent ships from Majorca to the Canaries, as part of an ambitious plan to bring the islanders into the Christian fold. They planned to carry along as well twelve Canary islanders who had been brought back to Europe by an earlier expedition and had been instructed in the Catalan language and in the Christian faith. These islanders were said to be full of zeal to work for the conversion of their fellow-islanders The king of Aragon wrote that the Canary islanders 'lived according to no law but acted in a bestial way in all things.' The idea of living without 'law' may simply mean that they had no recognised religion, for in Spain it was common to talk of the 'law' of the Jews and the Muslims, meaning not just the Torah and the Koran, but their religion. Still, that underlined the point: these newly-identified people had no identity, and did not fit within the established categories of Spanish religious experience. The islanders remained suspicious of the European visitors they encountered, and the reason seems to have been their well-justified suspicion that they usually came to seize islanders and carry them off into slavery.

The islanders responded in kind: sometimes European slave-raiders were themselves captured, enslaved and put to work in humble occupations such as slaughtering animals, a task reserved for the very lowest caste in island society. A fifteenth-century chronicle relates that the island of Lanzarote in the eastern Canaries had been largely depopulated by slave raiders by 1400, and the other islands were also treated as good hunting grounds. One result of the fall in the population of the eastern islands was that Berber slaves began to be imported from the facing coasts of Africa, supplemented later by other slaves from further south. The Canaries thus set a precedent for what would happen across the vaster distances of the open Ocean, when African slaves were carried to the Caribbean to replace the rapidly declining Taíno Indian population.

In the fifteenth century, the Canaries became a battleground between rival Iberian powers. Prince Henry the Navigator despatched repeated expeditions from Portugal to the islands from 1424 onwards; and it is hard to see where to draw the line between his grandiose dreams of conquest and his willingness to exploit the human resources of the islands by carrying off the inhabitants into slavery. The pope received complaints from the missionary bishop of Lanzarote; the bishop begged him to take action to defend the islanders, for some were already turning to Christianity, but they were being molested by Portuguese raiders – if they were not actually taken captive, their food and goods were stolen from under their eyes. Henry, for his part, was very proud of this outcome: he boasted that he had won 400 converts; for 'converts' read, it has been suggested, 'slaves,' Canary islanders transported back to a Christian life in Portugal, precursors therefore of the African slaves who, just over ten years later, would become staple element in Portuguese trade in the eastern Atlantic. The argument was that they would be better off as slaves in Portugal, with some hope of Christian salvation, than as pagans in their dusty islands.

Henry saw his activities in the islands as a chance to score points against his rivals the Castilians. It was not simply a political question; there was a moral issue that had remained unresolved: did pagans possess the right to govern themselves without interference? Against the view that stretched back to Pope Innocent IV and Thomas Aquinas stood a solid phalanx of arguments that the Christian Church must give its warm approval to what were to be wars of conquest for the purpose of conversion.

III

It would be easy to jump to the conclusion that Henry had a particular use in mind for these slaves. From the 1420's he had established himself as master of the previously uninhabited island of Madeira, and by the 1440's it had begun to emerge as a significant centre of sugar production. By 1500, some 2,000 out of a total population of about 15,000 were slaves; however, the main labour force on Madeira consisted of free Portuguese and Italians (Russell 97-98). By 1500, slaves from West Africa were an all-too common article of Portuguese trade, and many passed through Madeira on their way to Portugal, simply because the standard sailing routes went that way. However, the original slave population of Madeira seems to have consisted of Canary islanders, for example Guanches seized on the coast of Tenerife by raiding parties. They were considered troublesome; they were said to lack docility. This apparently meant that in the longer term there was a preference for slaves from the shores of Africa. The other uninhabited islands of the eastern Atlantic also played a significant role in the history of Atlantic slavery, though each in a slightly different way. Thus, once they had been claimed for Portugal, the Cape Verde Islands, discovered around 1460, eventually became a vital way-station for slaves exported from Africa to the Americas, as well as a supply station for ships heading from Europe to the west.[3] The royal privilege establishing Portuguese settlement in the Cape Verde Islands, dated 12 June 1466, grandly talked of the rivers, woods, fisheries, coral, dyes and mines on islands that could offer very few of these resources; more importantly, the islanders could trade freely on the Guinea coast, and slave trading and raiding was to become their real speciality (Blake vol. i, doc. 1, 64-67).

Still further east, right on the Equator, the Portuguese colony on the island of São Tomé, explored in 1472, was a collection point for slaves from the bend of Africa, linked after 1482 to the important Portuguese trading station at Elmina on the African coast (Vogt 19-92; Hair; DeCorse; Ryder 42-45). São Tomé is now known for its fine chocolate, a product unknown in Africa and Europe before the discovery of Mexico; but at the end of the fifteenth century, the Portuguese tried to make São Tomé into a centre of sugar production (Blake vol. i, doc. 13, 89-92; Saunders 177). In 1493, King João II conceived a brutal plan to settle the island with enslaved Jewish children, forcibly taken from their parents in Portugal in order to ensure that they were baptised and brought up as Catholics. A Christian writer asserted that 2,000 were despatched, but only 600 were still alive in 1510 (Garfield 74). The harsh conditions – the searing heat, the insect-borne diseases, the uncleared jungle, the heavy manual work involved in sugar production – killed many of the Jewish child slaves, and it was for that reason that African slaves began to be imported from the mainland to work the sugar estates. Along with the Cape Verde Islands, São Tomé also functioned as the collection point for slaves bound for the Caribbean at the start of the sixteenth century. By 1517 slave-traders were by-passing Portugal and sending black slaves directly to Hispaniola, where their labour compensated for the loss of that of the native Indian population, whose numbers had fallen precipitously in the years after the Spanish conquest.

The history of Canarian slaves, Jewish slaves and later of Caribbean slaves was, as will already be obvious, intimately bound up with that of African slaves. Raiding rather than trading laid the foundation of the Atlantic slave trade; the trade began piratically with raids into both the Canaries and Berber territory on the oceanic edge of Africa; in 1444 240 Sanhaja Berbers were captured and sent back to Portugal on six caravels. They arrived in Lagos, the major town of the western Algarve, and Prince Henry himself was awaiting them. The Berber slaves were mixed together with a number of darker slaves from further south. Although he cruelly mocked the facial features of these slaves, Henry's biographer Zurara expressed his horror at their misery, at the sight of families being split apart and the great distress this caused (Zurara vol. i, 83; Saunders 35). For Thomas Aquinas had insisted that, while slavery was permissible, the separate sale of parents and children, husbands and wives, was not. Still, Zurara piously thought that there was 'some consolation amid their current distress' in the opportunity to be saved as Christians, for 'many died in this faith,' 'remembering that they too are of the generation of Adam' (Zurara vol. i, 81, 84; Wolf). Such comments conveyed a mixed message about the human status of these people. Henry the Navigator seems to have viewed this breach of Aquinas' principles (if he was even aware of them) with equanimity, and this serves as a reminder that theory and practice stood a long way apart as far as the treatment of indigenous peoples was concerned.

The opportunity now seemed to exist for a Portuguese slave trade, with Portugal acting as middleman for Europe. This was made real the next year, when much larger numbers of Africans were taken directly to Lisbon, exciting great wonder among the citizens, who came aboard the caravels to see these people; so many flooded aboard that there was a worry the ships would capsize. The slaves were then marched to Henry's palace in Lisbon, thereby displaying to any sceptics what profits Henry's slow-maturing schemes could produce. Before long the great slave emporia of Seville and Valencia were turning to Portuguese suppliers in order to keep their slave markets stocked (Blumenthal). It is thought that Henry and his agents were responsible for the import of up to 20,000 slaves from Africa south of the Sahara, from the Berber lands facing the Canaries and from the Canaries themselves.

In 1482 the trading station of Elmina (Sao Jorge da Mina, in modern Ghana) was established as a base for the trade in gold and slaves (De la Fosse 26-33). And, as the slave trade developed, Africans became a familiar sight on the streets of Lisbon and other European cities, as never before. There were certainly ambiguities in the way white Europeans reacted to different skin colour; on the one hand, black was seen as a negative colour, but on the other Caspar, one of the three Magi, was portrayed as an African king in Flemish, Spanish and Italian paintings of the Adoration produced at this time. Although some of the Africans seen in Iberia were free, most of those at liberty were freedmen or freedwomen who had first arrived as slaves; unfreedom seemed to characterise dark-skinned people, in the eyes of those Europeans who encountered them, whether as slave traders, slave owners or passers-by (Lowe and Earle 1-47; Blumenthal). From this developed the notion that their inferiority was something inherent, conferred by their racial distinctiveness.

IV

It was Castilian conquistadores who finally completed the subjugation of the Canary Islands between 1483, when Pedro de Vera pacified Grand Canary and

1496, when Alonso de Lugo overwhelmed the last resistance among the Guanches of Tenerife. Pedro de Vera urged 600 Canarians to join him on a raid to Tenerife, supposedly to replenish depleted supplies on Grand Canary; instead he locked them in the holds of his ships and carried them all to southern Spain. Equally, on Tenerife, the unsentimental de Lugo had no qualms about enslaving three hundred islanders who had arrived to fight on his side; once in Spain, they appealed to Ferdinand and Isabella, who ordered that 'they should be set free, and remain free' (Espinosa, iii. c. 6). This was an act Isabella would repeat several times when she learned of the arrival shiploads of enslaved Taíno Indians from the Caribbean. But it would be a mistake to exaggerate the degree of control the queen could exercise, for Genoese merchants based in the islands continued to export enslaved Canary islanders to Seville (Otte).

Meanwhile, Iberian slave traders acquired captives from the western edges of the Sahara, especially the coasts facing the Canaries; these slaves were put to work in the Canary islands themselves (Fernández-Armesto 36-38; Blumenthal). To some degree, particularly in the eastern islands, this was in order to replenish the population, which had fallen calamitously as a result of disease and enslavement. Many of these arrivals were Muslims (though some became Christian); and Ferdinand and Isabella were worried that the Muslim population would grow dangerously large, so they discouraged the arrival of free Muslims, and encouraged the importation of African slaves who were increasingly put to work in the sugar factories (Fernández-Armesto 213-14).

V

When Columbus arrived in the New World he was immediately struck by the similarity between the Taíno Indians he encountered in the Bahamas and the Canary islanders (indeed, the term 'New Canaries' was sometimes used to describe the islands he had found). As he said in his logbook, 'none of them are dark, but rather the colour of Canary islanders, nor should one expect anything else, since this island is in the same latitude as the island of El Hierro in the Canary Islands' (RC vi, DB c. 29) – a clear expression of the common belief that skin colour was simply determined by latitude, and that the closer one came to the Equator and to the Sun, the more one would be burned brown and then black. But he also rapidly took the view that 'they ought to make good and clever servants' (RC vi, DB c. 28). During his first voyage he mulled over the commercial possibilities of the lands he had found: he saw some gold, much cotton, a few spices, but also human cargoes of slaves, which, he was well aware, could be used to make up for a shortfall in gold. Still, it was not until January 1493, when he entered lands which were apparently inhabited by the people he called the Caribs, that his thoughts turned fully to the question of enslavement. Against the image of the peaceful, innocent, weak Taíno Indians he set another image, that of violent, ugly, cannibalistic Caribs who were said to prey on the Taínos, and from whom the Spaniards needed to protect the Taínos. When he met some threatening Indians painted in black 'he believed they were the ones from Carib and that they ate people' (RC vi, DB c. 107). If the king and queen decided they wanted him to bring slaves from the lands he had discovered, it was these people, who in his view needed to be tamed, whom he would try to bring back to Spain (Ife 40-41).

As Columbus' disappointment at not finding vast piles of gold mounted, the idea of supplying Europe with slaves became ever more attractive. During his troubled second voyage Columbus wrote to Ferdinand and Isabella, asking for supplies of cattle and other necessities to be sent to Hispaniola; in return he would send payment in the form of slaves

> from among these cannibals, a people very fierce and suitable for the purpose, and well-proportioned, and of very good understanding, who, having abandoned their inhumanity, will be better than any other slaves, which inhumanity they will lose when they are outside their land. (Jane, i. 91-93)

In fact, the Spaniards rapidly began to enslave Taíno Indians as well. The chieftain Guatiguaná had ordered the killing of twelve Christians; five hundred of his people were enslaved and packed off to Spain in a fleet that set sail from Hispaniola on 24 February 1495. The queen would prove to be very unhappy at the enslavement of Taíno Indians, even of Indians accused of rebellion, 'a move undertaken without doubt without the consent of the king and queen' (RC vii, 5.4.51). As reports filtered through to the royal court, arriving on the same ships as the slaves, perplexity grew. And among the conditions imposed by the king and queen before Columbus' disastrous fourth voyage in 1502-04 was one to the effect that he must not bring back any slaves.

Still, theory – in Spain – and practice – in the Indies – could be far removed from one another. And, even if the great debates involving las Casas took place so many decades after Columbus' voyages, there were already doubts and uncertainties in the years around 1500. The question was posed to lawyers and theologians whether it was permissible to sell into slavery Indians sent to Spain by Columbus. From 1501, the royal court ordered its agent Ovando not to enslave the Taínos of Hispaniola, and tried to ensure that slave-raiding was confined to enemy territory – in other words, the Caribs were ideal slave material, but the Taínos were not. But life as a domestic slave in Spain or Portugal had its advantages over life as a notionally free Taíno: the evolving tribute system, the *encomienda*, formally guaranteed the legal freedom of the Taínos while at the same time placing on their shoulders heavy burdens in tribute, and leaving them at the mercy of callous and greedy settlers. This *encomienda* system was derived from medieval Castilian practice, where the king would draw up a division (*repartimiento*) of conquered lands, and assign them to his vassals (*encomenderos*); in the New World it underwent swift and significant adaptation, so that these were rights not over land but over a work force whose task was to produce tribute in gold or possibly cotton (Chamberlain). As for that workforce, it was not legally owned by the *encomendero*. The Taínos were free in the sense that they had their own leaders; while working in the goldfields they lived in their own reserved areas, though the mere fact of requiring men to work in the mines for months away from home destroyed family life and led to a dramatic decline in the birth rate among the Taíno population. Only in 1512, with the Laws of Burgos, was an attempt made, many thousands of miles away, to guarantee the position of the Indian workers. But few settlers cared whether these people were legally free, 'natural slaves' or indeed unfree. These lawyers' distinctions meant nothing to the greedy, ambitious men who sought their gold.

VI

A clearer idea of the scale and ruthlessness of slaving expeditions in the western Atlantic can be obtained by looking at the sequence of voyages that broke Columbus' monopoly on exploration in the New World from 1497 onwards. There were two arguments which were thought to justify slave raids. One was that some of the lands the slavers visited lay beyond the areas where Columbus had planted the flag of Castile; some, indeed, lay in the lands assigned to Portugal by the pope's division of the world between the two Iberian powers in 1494. The second issue was the conduct of the indigenous peoples. Those who were said to consume human flesh, or those who reputedly had no regard for the laws of incest, behaved in what was understood to be an inhuman, bestial way, and had to be tamed; equally those who conducted themselves very aggressively could be classified as enemies. Later, as we shall see, this doctrine was enshrined in the curious document called The Requirement, which did license the enslavement of those who opposed the Crown of Castile on the lands it claimed as of right.

In what purports to be an eye-witness account of the capture of hundreds of slaves in 1497, Amerigo Vespucci described the arrival of the Spanish ships at a place called 'Iti'; naked, painted and plumed warriors shot their arrows at the ships to prevent the sailors from landing (Vespucci ep. VI, 75; lettera, f. 8r; Notes 191). But they were easily enough beaten off by the far superior weapons on board the ships; 222 were captured, and the sailors, after more than a year at sea, were anxious in any case to turn homewards, potentially enriched by their cargo of slaves (Vespucci ep. VI, 76; lettera, f. 8v). But others argued that attacks of this sort were completely unjustified. Bartolomé de las Casas later fulminated against Vespucci:

> although these natives are without faith, yet those with whom Amerigo went had neither just cause nor right to make war on the natives of those islands and to carry them off as slaves, without having received any injury from them, or the slightest offence. (Vespucci, app. E, 151)

The impression is that there were some basic rules of engagement: slaves were taken in great numbers when the inhabitants turned hostile; equally the Europeans were only too glad to find an excuse to seize them. If gold was not to be had, slaves were a good substitute.

Many details of the slave raids were included in depositions made by opposing parties in the long-running legal dispute between the Crown and the Columbus family about the rights of the Columbuses in the New World (RC viii, TCL). Vicente Yáñez Pinzón had captained the *Niña* on Columbus' first voyage; now he set out under royal licence for the New World in 1499. He was ordered not to bring back Caribbean islanders as slaves, though Africans were acceptable if he entered eastern Atlantic waters. In fact he took thirty-six slaves from the New World, and then toured the smaller islands of the Caribbean, finding them deserted as a result of Carib or European predations (RC v, PM 1.9.8). Luis Guerra and a colleague went to Brazil in 1500 to 1501, taking slaves from 'Topia,' that is, the lands of the Tupí Indians, and selling one girl named Sunbay in Spain for six thousand *maravedís*, though this was an exceptionally high price, and it was not a good deal – Sunbay then fell ill. These captives were called *in-*

dios bozales – the term *bozales* indicated that they were regarded as primitive, even savage, and was also used of untrained slaves from West Africa (Blumenthal):

> in the case of *indios bozales* who come from a distant land, they undergo so much change and such trials, that the vendor is not obligated and cannot be held responsible for anything that may affect the health and frame of mind of the slave. (Vigneras 92)

This is a revealing recognition that the journey and life in Iberia entailed both physical and psychological damage (see RC viii, TCL, 13.4; Verlinden 399-400). Guerra was back again soon after, with his brother, once again looking for slaves, but he was reprimanded on his return for taking slaves from Bonaire Island, 'the said Indians being our subjects,' and therefore immune from enslavement. The Spanish historian Oviedo wondered about these actions:

> I do not know if these merchants were authorised to enslave the people of that land because they are idolaters, savages, sodomites, or because they eat human flesh. (Vigneras 124)

In other words, a sad routine of slave-raiding developed, to the horror of las Casas. Still, the emphasis, while Isabella was alive, was on the free status of the Indians, which, even in the *encomienda* system, was formally recognised: the gold the Indians had to provide was a tax or tribute, and indeed precisely because it was a tribute it confirmed that they were not slaves but subjects with obligations. The Crown therefore benefited from the fact that they were legally free and had financial as well as ethical reasons for not wishing them to be enslaved.

Still, as has been seen, a lucrative slave trade continued. An explanation for the neglect of these high-sounding principles can be found in the aggressive policies King Ferdinand was pursuing back home. He sought to establish bases in North Africa – at Oran in Algeria in 1509, at Tripoli in Libya in 1511 (Doussinague). All this was formidably expensive, and had tragic consequences for the Indians (Ladero Quesada). What mattered most to Ferdinand was not their welfare; it was their usefulness in meeting his financial needs. The Bahamas were cleared of inhabitants. Further south, two hundred slaves were taken in Curaçao in 1514, but a massive twelve hundred the next year, a scale of action justified by the proclamation of a holy war against the cannibalistic Caribs.

VII

There was a further problem: there was not a single answer to the question about the status of unconverted indigenous peoples. Not everyone agreed with Thomas Aquinas' argument that they had the right to govern themselves if they observed the basic principles of natural law. Nature could be seen as brutal; or it could be seen as ennobling. Taínos could be painted in glowing colours as men and women who lived a simple existence, in harmony with one another and with the natural world, as in the writings of Columbus and Peter Martyr; Caribs could be painted in dark colours as brutal and bestial warriors whose taste for human flesh was clear proof that they were savages from the forest. In addition, South American Indians could be portrayed as people who had no instinctive understanding of the rules of incest, no modesty – or the effective opposite, a pure innocence that would lead them instinctively to Christ once they had set eyes on the cross. Similar distinctions can be seen in the way the Canary islanders were observed, discussed and treated. The variety of views became a clash of views when las Casas and Sepúlveda passionately argued their cases in Valladolid in 1550-51 in the presence of Charles V and his morose son Philip II of Spain. These issues were also argued passionately in the works of the early sixteenth-century historians. Gonzalo Fernández de Oviedo (1478-1557) saw the Indians as to all intents lapsed Christians, whose ancestors had been blessed like all peoples at the ends of the earth with a visit from St Thomas the Apostle, but then, out of their fundamental stupidity and ignorance, they had lost their knowledge of Christian truth:

> Because these people of the Indies, although they are rational and descended from the family of Noah, had become irrational and bestial with their idolatries an infernal ceremonies and sacrifices, so the Devil had control of their soul for centuries. (RC ix, RC ix, Oviedo, 3.30.1, 3.3.1, 3.8.5)

They were therefore in a sense rebels against the Christian Church, but in any case their limited capacity for understanding meant that they always had to serve. They were also in a sense rebels against Spain, for Fernández de Oviedo he related an absurd tale of the conquest of the Americas by a prehistoric and pre-Christian king of Spain named Hesperus 3193 years earlier, meaning that Spain was only reviving its standing claim to rule the peoples and lands of the New World: 'God returned the sovereignty of the Indies after so many centuries,' decreeing that they should join Granada and Naples as the perpetual possessions of Spain (RC ix, RC ix, Oviedo, 3.4.2). In sum, they were *indios bestiales*, 'bestial Indians,' consumed by their vices and immersed in incest (RC ix, RC ix, Oviedo, 3.25, 3.25.1).

These ideas could also be linked to key texts from the ancient past, notably Aristotle's *Politics* and *Nicomachean Ethics*, which became known to readers in the Catholic world in the thirteenth century and had an enormous influence on Aquinas and on the teaching of philosophy, law and theology in the universities. What Aristotle conveyed was the idea of degrees of humanity (Pagden 17; Aristotle, *Politics* 1252a1, 1253a5-10). He presented a powerful image of the 'barbarian' as someone who possesses a natural cruelty; but cruelty is characteristic of beasts, not humans, therefore a barbarian who acted cruelly could be said to have lost the right to be called human (Aristotle, *Nicomachean Ethics* 1145a31). Eating human flesh was one sign of animal-like barbarity (Pagden 18; Aristotle, *Nicomachean Ethics* 1148b17-19; Aristotle, *Politics* 1338b19). Or, put differently, men (this is not the place to consider Aristotle's view of women [Aristotle, *Politics* 1260a7-14; Garnsey 114-15]) must learn to control their animal nature, using 'reason'; this will enable them to realise their potential. Building on ideas derived from Cicero, Thomas Aquinas expounded the idea of a society based on 'natural law,' in which certain fundamental practices and ideas could be found, such as knowledge of one Creator God, a horror of incest, and a system of justice; while missions should be sent to such a society, there was no automatic right of conquest if it caused no offence to Christians (McGrade 751-53; Luscombe 760-61). On the other hand, humans who did not associate with one another, but lived asocial lives, rather like Petrarch's Canarians, or the 'wild men of the woods,' failed to create a society based on justice. Their behaviour could descend to that of animals, living off raw meat, drinking out of skulls, refreshing themselves with draughts of blood (Aristotle, *Politics* 1280a31-35).

If there were barbarian people whose humanity was not fully developed, then it followed that they should not exercise dominion over Aristotle's Greeks, for their natural condition was to serve those who were fully human. Only by being mastered would barbarians like the American Indians, 'who, it is said, are like talking animals' reach a full state of existence, according to the Spanish legal scholar Gil Gregorio (qtd. in Pagden 48). The concept here is that of the 'natural slave' (Garnsey 107-27; Aristotle, *Politics* 1254a20-24). Someone who is a natural slave may or may not be a legal slave, for the natural slave may not yet have come into the power of his master. And the legal slave may simply be a captive of war, a Greek who has suffered misfortune, and is fully rational (Aristotle, *Politics* 1255a5). Natural slavery, as Anthony Pagden has stressed, is a psychological condition (42, 45, 47; see also Garnsey): the natural slave benefits from being under the control of his master, performing mechanical or 'banausic' tasks such as, in the years around 1500, the heavy labour required in a Canary sugar mill or the tiresome task of panning for gold in the riverbeds of Hispaniola (slaves were 'living tools,' Aristotle said, 'just as a tool is an inanimate slave' [*Nicomachean Ethics* 1161a30-b6; see Garnsey 119). Thus the Taínos might be seen as slaves by disposition, though legally, of course, they were the free subjects of Queen Isabella. One writer, Mesa, insisted that they were natural slaves, lacking full mental capacity, and in the same breath insisted that they were the subjects of the Crown and that therefore they could not just be traded on the slave market like merchandise (Pagden 49); so they were natural slaves but not legal slaves; where this left the *mestizos*, those of mixed parentage, who were increasingly common by now, is a moot point. Debates about these problems gathered pace at the beginning of the sixteenth century: King Ferdinand called together a meeting of theologians and lawyers, a *junta de letrados*, in 1504 (Pagden 28-31). While the very fact of debate indicates that the Indians had their stalwart defenders, there was an increasing emphasis on the idea that the American Indians were 'talking animals': barbarians, natural slaves, legitimately subject to the exercise of harsh corrective authority. For the main issue for many of those involved in the debates was not so much the rights of the Indians as the rights of the Castilian Crown in the New World.

Still, by accepting the sovereignty of Castile, conquered peoples could in theory protect themselves against enslavement. In particular, they must accept the right of Christian preachers to spread the Faith among them. There was a valuable reward, expressed in the curious document of 1511 known as The Requirement, which was to be read to uncomprehending inhabitants of the lands the Spaniards proposed to take under their authority:

> If you do so [i.e. submit], you will do well, and that which you are obliged to do to their Highnesses, and we in their name shall receive you in all love and charity, and shall leave you, your wives, and your children, and your lands, free without servitude, that you may do with them and with yourselves freely that which you like and think best. (*Requerimiento*)

This, then, was the way in which the Indians and other conquered peoples could guarantee their status as free subjects rather than as slaves of the Crown. (Of course, the phrase 'without servitude' did not mean exemption from the harsh requirements of the *encomienda* system and of tribute payment). But The Requirement ruthlessly set out the alternatives for those who did not comply, expressing with startling clarity the two extremes of the Spanish reaction to indigenous peoples:

> But, if you do not do this, and maliciously make delay in it, I certify to you that, with the help of God, we shall powerfully enter into your country, and shall make war against you in all ways and manners that we can, and shall subject you to the yoke and obedience of the Church and of their Highnesses; we shall take you and your wives and your children, and shall make slaves of them, and as such shall sell and dispose of them as their Highnesses may command; and we shall take away your goods, and shall do you all the mischief and damage that we can, as to vassals who do not obey, and refuse to receive their lord, and resist and contradict him; and we protest that the deaths and losses which shall accrue from this are your fault, and not that of their Highnesses, or ours, nor of these cavaliers who come with us. (Ibid.)

The lawyer who drafted The Requirement, Juan López de Palacios Rubios, also composed a tract in which he insisted that the American Indians were *liberi et ingenui*, 'free.' His arguments were profoundly rooted in the scholastic tradition of late medieval scholarship – in points of canon and civil law and theology, in the close reading of the authorities of past time.

VIII

It can be seen, then, that the problem of enslavement was not simply an economic issue, concerned with the substitution of slaves for the gold which seemed so far unobtainable, nor with the need to find additional labour for the mines, fields and plantations in both the New World and the Old. The question whether the newly discovered peoples of the Spanish lands in the Canaries and the Caribbean were subjects of the Crown of Castile was of critical importance in judging whether they could be enslaved – more important, in fact, than their status as pagans or heathens. This was no help to those who had been bought as slaves from Portuguese traders; these people elicited little pity. Even the great defender of the American Indians, Bartolomé de las Casas, for much of his career was not moved by the plight of the African slaves whom he saw as useful substitutes for the overworked peoples of the New World. Nor were these distinctions sufficient to limit the enormous human damage that was effected by a greedy and uncompromising tribute system, constructed on the backs of the Taíno Indians. Indeed, the argument went that precisely because they were subjects, they were liable to tax and tribute, just as all the subjects of the Emperor Augustus had been obliged to pay taxes in precious metals and salt a millennium and a half earlier. St Paul in his letter to the Galatians had tried to ignore the distinction in God's presence of slave and free: 'there is neither Jew nor Greek, neither slave nor free' (Gal. 3.28). We may conclude that the Spanish conquerors also ignored that distinction between slave and free, but not in the way St Paul intended.

Abbreviations

RC = *Repertorium Columbianum*

[1] This essay is an adapted version of the Millennium Lecture delivered by the author at the University of North Carolina in 2008.

[2] On the sugar industry, see Abulafia.

[3] See the documents and letters by Diogo Gomes, da Mosto, and da Noli in Crone 101, 63, and 106.

Works Cited

Abulafia, David. "Sugar in Spain." *European Review* 16.2 (2008): 191-210.
Aristotle. *Nicomachean Ethics*. Ed. and trans. H. Rackham. 2nd ed. Cambridge: Harvard UP, 1934.
---. *Politics*. Ed. and trans. H. Rackham. Cambridge: Harvard UP, 1932.
Blake, John William, ed. *Europeans in West Africa, 1450-1560: Documents to Illustrate the Nature and Scope of Portuguese Enterprise in West Africa*. 2 vols. London: Hakluyt Society, 1942.
Blumenthal, Debra. *Enemies and Familiars: Muslim, Eastern and Black African Slaves in Late Medieval Valencia*. Ithaca: Cornell UP, 2009.
Crone, Gerald Roe, ed. *The Voyages of Cadamosto and Other Documents on Western Africa in the Second Half of the Fifteenth Century*. London: Hakluyt Society, 1937.
Carrillo, J., ed. *Oviedo on Columbus*. Volume IX of the *Repertorium Columbianum*. Turnhout: Brepols, 2000.
Chamberlain, Robert S. "Castilian Backgrounds of the *Repartimiento-Encomienda*." *Contributions to American Anthropology and History* 5.25 (1939): 33-52.
DeCorse, Christopher R. *An Archeology of Elmina: Africans and Europeans on the Gold Coast, 1400-1900*. Washington, D.C.: Smithsonian Institution P, 2001.
Doussinague, José M. *La política internacional de Fernando el Católico*. Madrid: Espasa-Calpe, 1944.
De la Fosse, Eustache. *Voyage d'Eustache Delafosse*. Ed. and trans. Denis Escudier. Paris: Editions Chandeigne, 1992.
Fernández-Armesto, Felipe. *The Canary Islands after the Conquest*. Oxford: Oxford UP, 1982.
Garfield, Robert. "A Forgotten Fragment of the Diaspora: The Jews of São Tomé Island, 1492-1654." *The Expulsion of the Jews: 1492 and After*. Ed. Raymond B. Waddington and Arthur H. Williamson. New York: Garland, 1994. 73-87.
Garnsey, Peter. *Ideas of Slavery from Aristotle to Augustine*. Cambridge: Cambridge UP, 1996.

Griffin, Nigel, ed. *Las Casas on Columbus: Background and the Second and Fourth Voyages*. Volume VII of the *Repertorium Columbianum*. Turnhout: Brepols, 1999.

Hair, Paul Edward Hedley. *The Founding of the Castelo De Sao Jorge Da Mina: An Analysis of Sources*. Madison: U of Wisconsin African Studies Program, 1994.

Ife, B. W. *Letters from America: Columbus' First Accounts of the 1492 Voyages*. London: King's College London School of Humanities, 1992.

Jane, Cecil, ed. *The Four Voyages of Columbus*. 2 vols. London: Hakluyt Society, 1929-32.

Ladero Quesada, Miguel Angel. *El primer oro de América: los comienzos de la Casa de la Contratación de las Yndias (1503-1511)*. Madrid: Real Academia de la Historia, 2002.

Lardicci, Francesca, et al., ed. *A Synoptic Edition of the Log of Columbus's First Voyage*. Volume VI of the *Repertorium Columbianum*. Turnhout: Brepols, 1999.

Lowe, Kate, and Thomas Foster Earle, eds. *Black Africans in Renaissance Europe*. Cambridge: Cambridge UP, 2005.

Luscombe, D. E. "The State of Nature and Origins of the State." *The Cambridge History of Later Medieval Philosophy*. Ed. Norman Kretzmann, Anthony Kenny, and Jan Pinborg. Cambridge: Cambridge UP, 1982. 757-70.

McGrade, A. S. "Rights, Natural Rights, and the Philosophy of Law." *The Cambridge History of Later Medieval Philosophy*. Ed. Norman Kretzmann, Anthony Kenny, and Jan Pinborg. Cambridge: Cambridge UP, 1982. 738-56.

Otte, Enrique. *Sevilla y sus mercaderes a fines de la Edad Media*. Sevilla: Universidad de Sevilla, 1996.

Pagden, Anthony. *The Fall of Natural Man: The American Indian and the Origins of Comparative Ethnography*. 2nd ed. Cambridge: Cambridge UP, 1986.

Phillips, William D., Jr., ed. *Testimonies from the Columbian Lawsuits*. Volume VIII of the *Repertorium Columbianum*. Turnhout: Brepols, 2000.

Requerimiento. Archivo General de Indias, Audiencia de Panamá. Leg. 233, lib. 1, ff. 49-50v. N. d. <www.dickinson.edu/~borges/Resources-Requerimiento.htm>.

Rumeu de Armas, Antonio. *El Obispado de Telde: misioneros mallorquines y catalanes en el Atlántico*. Telde: Ayuntamiento de Telde, 1986.

Russell, Peter Edward. *Prince Henry "The Navigator": A Life*. New Haven: Yale UP, 2000.

Ryder, Alan Frederick Charles. *Benin and the Europeans, 1485-1897*. London: Longmans, Green and Co. Ltd., 1969.

Saunders, A. C. de C. M. *A Social History of Black Slaves and Freedmen in Portugal, 1441-1555*. Cambridge: Cambridge UP, 1982.

Verlinden, Charles. "Le 'Requerimiento' et la 'Paix coloniale' dans l'Empire espagnol d'Amérique." *Recueil de la Société Jean Bodin* 15 (1961): 397-414.

Vespucci, Amerigo. *Letters from a New World: Amerigo Vespucci's Discovery of America*. Ed. Luciano Formisano. Trans. David Jacobson. New York: Marsilio Publishers, 1992.

Vigneras, Louis-André. *The Discovery of South America and the Andalusian Voyages*. Chicago: U of Chicago P, 1976.

Vogt. John. *Portuguese Rule on the Gold Coast, 1469-1692*. Athens: U of Georgia P, 1979.

Wolf, Kenneth Baxter. "The 'Moors' of West Africa and the Beginnings of the Portuguese Slave Trade." *Journal of Medieval and Renaissance Studies* 24.3 (1994): 449-69.

Zurara, Gomes Eanes de. *The Chronicle of the Discovery and Conquest of Guinea written by Gomes Eanes de Azurara*. Ed. Charles Raymond Beazley and Edgar Prestage. 2 vols. London: Hakluyt Society, 1896-99.

Paul Delaney

From Tourist to Bureau Chief: Witnessing Spain's Racial Emergence

I never knew what the lure was, what force pulled me towards Spain. But it was there, as natural as gravity. The influence could have been the language of Langston Hughes and Hemingway, or the bravery of the Lincoln Brigade, or splashy pictures and posters of bullfights and the passion of flamenco. Or zesty paella.

And, of course, it could have been all of that.

Or, it could have been the brown skins of most depictions of Spaniards I had seen when in my youth, of people who were near my color – and skin color was a fanatical obsession in the place of my birth, Montgomery, Ala. Tour books I read touted Spain's Moorish connections and history books romanticized those links.

But, one year after President Eisenhower signed America's first treaty with Generalissimo Francisco Franco, as Richard Wright traversed Iberia and as Chester Himes began his love affair with Spain, I was an American soldier stationed in Bordeaux. There, I met some French Basques who turned me on to their cousins across the border. Young, foolish, naive, immature, inexperienced, but curious. In fact, I'd never heard of Chester Himes and I did not agree at all with Eisenhower's pact with the dictator.

Under those circumstances and backdrop, I began my own affair with Spain and paid my first visit to Iberia. I endured a slow, bumpy train ride out of Bordeaux, traveled east, through Toulouse, Perpignan, then, south across the Pyrenees to Barcelona.

I stepped off the train and into a world I never expected and never got over. However, I was startled by the military presence, the guns and soldiers and military vehicles at every intersection, sights and scenes I'd never before known first-hand, not even in ultra-racist, police-state Alabama, although the sight and presence of vicious white cops struck fear in most black men.

I found Spain to be a very poor country, surprisingly, as poor as Alabama.

On the other hand, I was immediately smitten by the overwhelming and magnificent beauty of the city. I stayed in a pension off the Ramblas, hopefully, near the one Langston Hughes chose when he showed up to cover the civil war in 1937.

I wandered up and down, back and forth, day and night. Soaking in the sounds and smells; enjoying side streets, Barrio Chino, Barrio Gótico, the waterfront. Restaurants, tapas bars, sidewalk cafes. Birds. Flowers. Life on the Ramblas. I was fascinated by the Mercado de la Boquería, Teatro del Liceo. I also saw for the first time Spaniards who looked more European than I'd come to expect – blond hair, blue eyes. Like white Americans. Or French. Barcelona did remind me of Paris.

Stationed so close in southern France, I returned several times to feed and nurture my passion and what was to become my lifelong affair with Iberia and its people.

My first trip to Madrid was also by train, a terrible overnight ride from Bordeaux, more uncomfortable than the trips to Barcelona, to my utter disbelief. My Spanish was much worse than it is now – if that were possible. Upon midnight arrival at Atocha Station, I jumped into a cab and told the driver, Hotel Sur. He apparently did not understand my elemental Spanish. Or, pretended not to, but he started driving anyway. After about 10 minutes, it came to him. "Ahhh," he declared, and dropped me at the hotel.

I slept all morning, bushed from the train ride. When I awoke near noon, I opened the shutters and, voila: Atocha was directly across the street. In fact, Hotel Sur is still there, more modern, I found on a recent trip.

I later visited Zaragoza on a Fourth of July. This is my white American holiday story. At the Gran Hotel, a manager invited me to a commemoration of our independence, sponsored by the hotel for American guests. I dropped by the party room, only to be turned away by several white American men. They insisted it was a private event and physically barred my entrance.

Well… even sober I was no match to fight those guys. So, believing a good run is always better than a bad stand, I managed something like, "happy Fourth fellows" and bade them adiós to celebrate their red, white and blue freedom in lily-white comfort. Guess you can see that the incident left an impression that I never let leave my mind.

Being black and sensitive, I took special note of color in Spain on the occasion of my every visit.

What I found back then was a nation that seemed shaky about its sovereignty, a kind of civic naïveté that I attributed to the multi-scars of civil war, the dictatorship, World War Two alliance with the Axis and, perhaps, the natural isolation of the Iberian Peninsula – along with Spain's wracked and sometimes wretched colonial history. On later visits to Mexico, I was to hear bitter comments about the country that I equated to the ubiquitous post-World War Two "Yankee go home" signs and sentiment all over France. And, I was not as harsh in my judgment as Richard Wright was in his "Pagan Spain."

I found a lovely, sweet, fun-loving people who simply were not sensitive to nor knowledgeable about other races, especially mine. A kind of simple, if not simplistic, notion of black people. Yet, those views were different, and my reactions to them were different from what I felt on that hot Fourth of July day in Zaragoza, different from the low regard American whites held of blacks, which was pure hostility and hatred... remember, this was the 1950s.

In contrast, my French experience was the exact opposite – they were a bit more sophisticated in dealing with non-whites, having deeper and more emotional and complicated relations with American blacks and certainly African blacks. France was a haven for black artists, musicians and ex-GI's who chose it over home after the war.

But, I must add, the U.S. military, the American government enforced a racist policy in France that prevented GI's from associating with Arabs in France. We were barred from visiting Arab neighborhoods, under threat of arrest and court martial.

On our base in Bordeaux, and at all American military installations, there were maps that outlined Arab areas where we were not to wander. We were barred from the homes and restaurants in those sections. The restricted neighborhoods were outlined in red ink. It was my first encounter with redlining. Of course, we GI's took our chances and gambled we would not be caught breaking American laws in Europe that were reminiscent of jim crow in the American South.

In Spain, I was somewhat surprised by the lack of real and substantive contact and historic knowledge about non-whites, even though Africa is about a canoe ride away. Spaniards had *seen* black people throughout its history, but they had not really *experienced* us.

Even in the big cities – Madrid and Barcelona – I had to endure unending stares from people obviously not used to being around a black man casually walking the streets or eating in restaurants.

But, most annoying, eventually, were people feeling and rubbing my skin and sometimes my head and hair. I took those actions as signs of admiration, not condescension, more fascination, curiosity. But, it did become irritating. The stares I accepted as more natural than the touching. I got used to the gawking and learned to ignore most of it. Between you and me, I did enjoy the attention some of the time, especially telling them about the U.S. On one visit, my wrist was in a cast from a basketball accident; some Spaniards misunderstood (due probably to my poor Spanish, plus, basketball was still strictly American) and thought I was a prize fighter. They started called me "Sugar Ray" (for Robinson) and buying me drinks in bars.

That was my introduction to Spain.

There was a 30-year interim before I found my way back, in 1987. And what a difference three decades made. I had graduated from college, had become a journalist, made my way to the *New York Times* and eventually to Madrid as the paper's bureau chief.

Spain had been tossed into the modern world, but not in moderation. Franco had been dead for over a decade, yet the people were still in a celebratory mood; the country was adjusting and adapting fast. The shy, bashful nation I lapped up previously was rapidly disappearing, almost gone. Taboos from the dictatorship were fading fast, replaced by a flaunting of freedom that I interpreted as a nation gone wild, awash in freedom and liberty, unabashed.

The prolonged celebrating was to the consternation of quite a few conservatives I met who longed for the good old days, or, the old traditions. It seemed modern Spain had adopted our New York, Studio 54 motto: party till you drop.

Fortunately, no more rubbing my skin or feeling my hair. Spain, indeed, was growing up. Spaniards were opening up their minds, their heads, their hearts, propped up by an expanding, explosive economy, propelled by La Movida, the arts; abetted by the brilliant movie director, Pedro Almodóvar, and a host of others. Not only did I write about that rapid change, I indulged in it and enjoyed it.

I wrote about what seemed to be a fledgling feminist movement, and a fledgling anti-bullfight movement. I missed the fledgling anti-smoking movement that surfaced after I departed. The dizzying pace of change was almost beyond belief. I thought the pace was much too out of control, building condos, malls, mansions and developments with wild abandon, reminding me of suburban expansion in America. My hope was that Spaniards would wise up and avoid catastrophe before it was too late.

But, guess what else I found 30 years later: black people, and it seemed that Spaniards were getting used to us. Somewhat. The change had occurred as more and more sub-Saharan Africans, escaping poverty, war and politics at home, made their way north across the Strait of Gibraltar.

But, Spain was not their real destination. The country was enjoying an economic boom, even as it continued struggling to shake off poverty and its status as Europe's economic and social doormat. Iberia, along with Ireland and Greece, was the poorest of Western Europe. So black Africans, along with North Africans, were trying to find their way farther north and most did, using Spain as a stepping-off point, a way-station.

However, a few remained in Spain. I saw a sprinkling of them in Madrid. But the majority were in Catalonia, picking fruit and vegetables. I wrote a story on their plight and complaints.

They had formed a fledgling civil rights organization to carry their arguments for decent salaries and more money, humane working conditions, adequate housing and better personal treatment by local citizens. Racism was the accusation.

A small cadre of Spaniards agreed with the Africans and they worked together pressing local officials to address the complaints. The coalition put on a play in Mataro, north of Barcelona, hoping to sensitize the locals about their new African neighbors. The effort to use drama was a total flop, perhaps, because of the choice of Gide's "The Blacks," which left the Spaniards scratching their heads.

In Madrid, there were small pockets of black residents, again, primarily African immigrants, who authorities said were in the country illegally.

They worked at menial jobs, lived quietly in small pockets on side streets, mainly keeping to themselves, probably for protection, to avoid unnecessary contact, especially with police, and possible exposure and expulsion.

I had almost no contact with the African community – my wife's hairdresser was African. When we saw each other – passing on the street or while shopping – it was like ships passing in the night – they did not know who I was, I did not know who they were.

I had good intentions of eventually writing more about the community of

Africans, but my assignment ended before I got around to it.

During my reporting stay in Spain, I tried to give my American readers some idea of what the country was going through during that period of its rapidly changing status.

My article on women dealt with the first survey on sexual harassment of women. Coincidently, I wrote an article on the treatment of women in North Africa – a fledgling women's movement.

I wrote about the saga of Morocco's first magazine for women. The publication suffered several bouts of closure after printing articles the government did not like, such as male homosexuality in Morocco. Needless to say, the magazine eventually was shut down for good after a couple more pieces that displeased the government.

My biggest story on race was the article on migrant workers. I quoted Madrid writer and sociologist, Amando de Miguel, acknowledging, yes, there was racism in Spain, but the "Spanish temperament is to ignore problems."

Barcelona Mayor Pascual Maragall said: "Spain doesn't have the colonial past of England or France, or the racial history of the United States… it's more of a cultural than racial thing."

The mayor seemed to confirm Senor de Miguel's observation.

He obviously mis-spoke and ignored history. I disagreed strongly with the mayor's take on Spain's colonial past, but as a reporter, I did not argue with him or try to correct him.

In my story, I pointed out that there were 151,000 Africans in Spain out of a population of 40 million. The number of illegal immigrants was put at 400,000, most of them Arabs from North Africa.

Gypsies also complained about racism, and I heard a lot of racist comments against them. Spanish attitudes about Gypsies were no different from the kind of slander Gypsies suffer worldwide. I personally never heard similar remarks against blacks in Spain, but the attitude towards Gypsies reminded me of how white Americans, especially southerners, regarded blacks.

But, I talked to black American students studying in Spain. Nearly all said that they had experienced some racism, but, interestingly, they noted that it was not as vicious or as deeply embedded as the racism they knew in the U.S.

Señor de Miguel, the writer, pointed out that there were, "only 400,000" blacks in Spain, and wondered, "What's going to happen when there are a million." That day must surely be here by now, or close to it.

One glaring example I found was the use of racist stereotypes in the media, especially in advertising, on billboards and in television commercials. Several products featured bulging eyes, thick red lips and extremely dark color to depict blacks, reminding me of our American past, much of which was disappearing fast.

American advertisers of Uncle Ben's rice and Aunt Jemima pancakes long ago toned down not only those racist images, but also got rid of other stereotypes – gone are Frito Bandito, Gold Dust Twins and soft drinks such as Injun orange and Chinese cherry. But Spaniards seemingly still see nothing wrong with stereotypical depictions.

Parenthetically, I should note that Spanish cartoonists drew President Felipe Gonzalez with thick lips, I assumed because he was from Andalucia, presumably of Moorish heritage, therefore, deserving such depiction.

To sum up, during my reporting years, and subsequent visits, I found Spain's race relations mixed: like the American students, I saw nothing similar to the racism from my childhood in Alabama or from my experiences in the rest of our country, where I lived or visited.

Nevertheless, Spain and Europe have very serious race problems today, problems that seemingly will only worsen, and that they seem absolutely clueless about how to deal with them. European leaders scratch their heads over social, religious and racial crises as they occur in country after country.

I cringe when I see Europeans following in the footsteps of Americans, making the same mistakes on race that we did. Crackdowns on Muslims wearing burkas and head scarves are not solutions.

To a large extent, we in America and Canada have learned to celebrate our different heritages. Similar to our experiences, Europeans are now dealing with the racism of politicians, European versions of our own George Wallace.

Jean-Marie le Pen, the French politician, was quoted saying that, "You can't dispute the inequality of the races… blacks are much better than whites at running, but whites are better at swimming." Many American white racists made such comments long before he did, and some still do, but, for the most part, they are in a minority.

We in America, been there, done that – and I am saying that we have overcome, compared to our European friends.

Our – that is, America's – current obsession with terrorism and the focus on people of color – Arabs in particular – and religion – notably Islam – as the root causes of terrorism will not go away soon. Like Europeans and race, we'll be dealing with those issues for decades.

That fact helps to prevent Americans from contributing our expertise to assisting Europeans. I once thought that Europeans could learn lessons from our civil rights movement, as well as post-civil rights activity, that the NAACP and other American organizations and leaders could share their tactics and strategies, that we could go to Madrid, Paris, Berlin, Copenhagan, wherever, and help out.

It may still take a European NAACP, street protests, boycotts and other activities to force Europeans to face the changes that occurred in America.

It seems that Spain has been spared the worst of the vicious lashing out that has occurred in Britain, France, Germany and other northern nations. So far.

I am not overlooking the response to the Atocha station bombing and other incidents with racial overtones. But Spain has a long history of dealing with terrorism, something lost on most Americans.

That experience may put Spain in a better position to show the way in Europe, to be the European bridge to the non-white nations to the south, possibly averting a long racial quagmire. Or worse. Or not.

My reasoning: even though Spain does not have a stellar history of dealing with non-whites – Mayor Maragall was wrong, Spain has a colonial reputation that is very similar to that of Britain, Holland, Portugal, Belgium and France – and even though Spain has little experience in civil rights, it still may be able to offer genuine and substantive assistance to the rest of Europe.

One of the most amazing sights I saw in writing about Spain was the annual trek of millions of North Africans on their way back home on summer vacation in July and August.

From northern Europe, they wend their way through Spain in cars and vans and trucks, to Algeciras for the short ferry ride across the strait to Morocco. Spain becomes a funnel for massive waves of humanity heading home.

It was a sight to behold. I did a story on the newly-organized cooperation between the governments of Spain and Morocco to make such a journey safe and humane. I believe it will take that kind of cooperation of all European nations, along with those across the strait, to solve the growing racial crisis.

It's not too late, but, as I said, I'm not optimistic. If we don't get a handle on it now, we'll be reading and writing about that crisis for generations.

Mar Gallego-Durán

African American Women Travelers: Claiming Voice and Transgressing Boundaries[1]

Travel narratives have been traditionally identified with the prototypical Ulysses myth, and therefore codified as male and white. However, African American women travelers have significantly contributed to the debunking of this myth, while simultaneously creating their own tradition of travel writing. These women not only anticipated Victorian women's renowned travel narratives, but they also managed to overcome racist and sexist misconceptions by placing their black bodies and subjectivities in motion. It is particularly interesting to track these women's journeys throughout the nineteenth century up to the first decades of the twentieth century, when many African American women traveled to Europe, and specifically to France. Although their travel narratives share both their personal quest for wholeness and their unremitting social (and even political) critique, each of these works reflects in unique ways an understanding of their self-positioning in relation to diverse historical circumstances and cultural codes. Thus, these narratives reveal a (hidden?) social and political agenda that disallows any monolithic conception of what an American may be by laying bare the inner workings of sexist and racist prejudice in their home country.

The editors of *A Stranger in the Village,* Farah Griffin and Cheryl Fish, claim in their introduction that African American mobility swings between two poles: the forced migration of the international slave trade and "the impulse for increased opportunities and the desire to find a home or homeland as well as for the purpose of pilgrimage, exile and pleasure" (XIII).[2] While this may be applicable to African American travel in general, I would like to contend that the case of African American women travelers is a particular one. Through their personal search for self-definition and self-articulation in their dealings with racial and cultural difference, these narratives engage in a process of both claiming voice and transgressing socially imposed boundaries. This is especially true if we analyze the evolution of female travel narratives from the origins in the nineteenth century to the travel narratives published in the crucial decade of the twenties within the so-called Harlem Renaissance period.

Nineteenth-Century Precursors: Public Commitment and True Womanhood

In the nineteenth century the few African American women who could travel were quite aware that racist and gender discrimination meant that they were exceptions or anomalies and, consequently, their journeys were guided by a clear sense of public commitment to both their race and their gender. In her study of the radical and political tradition of African American women's early autobiographies Mary Mason states that "travel or journey became synonymous with action and commitment to social change" (339). Moreover, as I argued in "Escritoras afro-americanas y relatos de viajes: desde el otro lado del cristal,"[3] these early autobiographies and slave narratives anticipated Victorian ones in the use of the trip as a means of self-affirmation, something which involved risking their own integrity and freedom in an enslaving country like the United States. Mason also comments that the main difference between the first travel narratives written by women in Europe, which became the source for Victorian women's narratives, and those early ones authored by African American women was that the latter ones were based on an "account of actual travel" (339). The constant emphasis on mobility becomes thus a leitmotif in their writings, which reflects the claustrophobic experience of many African American women who felt trapped in a racist and sexist society. Indeed, they became the embodiment of what was considered taboo and needed to be repressed: racial confrontation and female sexuality. So they undertook a crucial twofold task: in the first place, to interrogate the nature of race/gender divides in an attempt to lay bare their deceitful foundations. And secondly, to represent themselves as "speaking subjects"[4] by writing themselves back into the national discourse and defying social conventions of what was considered proper of "true women."[5]

This code of appropriate womanhood was mainly a cult of domesticity that secluded women at home and dictated their behavior as "pure" women devoted to their roles of wives and mothers. In general, African American women did not qualify as "true" women because of their race and their sexuality. As Hazel Carby explains: "Black women were not represented as the same order of being as their mistresses; they lacked the physical, external evidence of the presence of a pure soul" (26). This was even more evident in the case of black women travelers, because they placed themselves outside the home sphere and were left completely unprotected. Both in racial and sexual terms, they did not conform to this socially sanctioned model, and therefore had to pay a very high price for their disobedience, which consisted of facing social ostracism and constant sexual aggression. These historical origins marked the tradition of African American women's travel narratives in that they tried to disprove the negative and demeaning stereotypes imposed on them and propose new ways to interpret black female bodies in space, which involved not only the access to public places but also the possibility to inhabit those places neither as servants nor public women. These writers thus claimed the right to a new identity that could be defined from their own point of view with their newly acquired voices.

So the female authors of autobiographies in the nineteenth century would tend towards the second pole identified by Griffin and Fish and pointed out above: they see in mobility a liberating potential that also guarantees increased opportunities, encoded as life in freedom in slave narratives. Moreover, in these autobiographical narratives mobility also leads to a redefinition of the concept of self that propounds humanity and truth for all slaves.[6] A compelling example can be found in *The History of Mary Prince* (1831). When she escapes slavery by fleeing to England, she writes: "I am very happy to be in England. [...] I am very glad to have come to England, to know who God is. I should like much to see my friends again, but I do not now wish to go back to them: for if I go back to my own country, I might be taken as a slave again" (242). In the opposition between her country of origin and England, Prince acknowledges the importance of mobility to secure increased opportunities and a better life in freedom. Therefore, mobility also becomes an act of resistance against the racist ideology of enslaving countries, as it disproves its false premises based on seclusion and negation of the self.

But I would also like to read Mary Prince's slave narrative as a direct precursor of later travel narratives. Especially in her illuminating strategies of presenting the "I" as writing/speaking subject, she dispels myths about slavery by seeking to restore the "other of the other's" perspective.[7] To do so, Prince breaks the imposed silence, her voice representing all slaves' voices, in an effort to produce a socially committed communal autobiography. She portrays a very thorough picture of slave life, constantly commenting on the differences between enslaving myths about slaves and their actual feelings, and becoming a "more reliable authority on slavery than any white man and fully capable of speaking for all her fellow slaves" (Andrews qtd. in Gates, *Classic Slave Narratives* XVI). It also embodies an interesting mode of female authorship, as Henry Louis Gates confirms: "hers is a tale that has not been told before, the very tale of the female slave who heretofore had been spoken for but who had not yet spoken *for herself*" (*Classic Slave Narratives* xv). Her tale recounts the terrible situation of slave women who were subjected to both sexual brutalization and heartbreaking denial of their maternal roles. Following the code of true womanhood, they could not qualify as actual mothers to their children because of their excessive sexuality and animality. Besides, what is also important in the case of Prince's narrative is that it can be defined as a "travel slave narrative" due to the scope of her work, since she decides to expand her picture of slavery to include Bermuda, Turkey and Antigua.[8] The fact that she evokes different scenarios whereby slavery is enacted has the effect of bringing home the denigrating and dehumanizing impact of all kinds of slavery. Her indictment of slavery is thus generalized as her trips serve to bring to light the same atrocities inflicted upon unprotected slaves everywhere, and especially the very difficult life of slave women.

The parameters of female slave narratives were established thanks to texts like Mary Prince's, and by mid-nineteenth-century actual travel narratives were being published by African American free women, texts that articulated the need to ensure their right to their own voice in order to continue to reveal the dark and hidden side of the national picture. A highly relevant example is *A Narrative of the Life and Travels of Mrs. Nancy Prince*, printed in Boston in 1850. Born to free black parents in Massachusetts, Prince was compelled to travel out of the need to take care of her brothers and sisters first to Boston and then to Russia, where she spent nine years, and finally to Jamaica for two years. Hers is an interesting narrative that celebrates her discovery of actual voice while simultaneously investing in mobility as "a form of resistance, struggle, and freedom" (Griffin and Fish 68). Like Mary Prince, she also highlights the aforementioned social commitment in a conversation with a reverend that takes place prior to her trip to Jamaica: "I told him it was my intention to go if I could make myself useful, but that I was sensible that I was very limited in education" (69). But she also endorses Mary Prince's objective in writing her narrative: the denunciation of racial prejudice and slavery. Thus, she explains the terrible conditions of Jamaican inhabitants and the cruel way in which they were mistreated as if they were still in bondage. However, she loses no opportunity to enhance their freedom –

"yet their present state is blissful, compared with slavery" (70) – with respect to the horrid fate of the slaves on the ship that takes her back to the States.

The same observations can be noticed when she travels to Russia with her husband, Nero Prince, an African American who served in the tsar's guard. She describes the poor situation of Russian peasants comparing them to slaves who are also abused by the nobility. In this sense, her depiction of the way in which a peasants' revolt against the new emperor is suppressed is remarkably vivid:

> The scene cannot be described; the bodies of the killed and mangled were cast into the river, and the snow and ice were stained with the blood of human victims; as they were obliged to drive the cannon to and fro in the midst of the crowd, the bones of those wounded, who might have been cured, were crushed. (202)

Yet once again, the lot of the Russian peasants is far better than that of black slaves in her own country. Prince even aligns herself with the emperor's cause justifying this harsh treatment in order to draw to a close the plot against imperial power. Besides, she shows admiration for the emperor and empress, especially for her: "she carries power and dignity in her countenance, and is well adapted to her station" (204). All in all, she seems to be satisfied in her nine-year stay in Russia and the linen business she sets up there. In her case, Prince is able to combine conventions of Western travel narratives in her detached depiction of Russian society with the tradition of social and political commitment to denounce slavery that we have seen in previous travel writing by African American women.

But especially interesting for the purposes of this chapter is the travel narrative entitled *The Wonderful Adventures of Mrs. Seacole in Many Lands*, published in 1857. The daughter of a Scottish father and a Jamaican mother, Mary Seacole writes about her experiences in Jamaica and Panama and her participation in significant events like the Crimean war (1854-56).[9] Her narrative was quite popular at the time, which actually led to unheard-of visibility for the author. This narrative foregrounds the articulation of an actual voice and the deconstruction of dominant race/gender discourse through the strategy of "usefulness." In her stay in Panama, she mainly highlights the fact that she was especially needed during a cholera epidemic inscribing her black female self in an empowered position. She narrates her difficulties to keep men and cheaters at bay:

> it was often more difficult for an unprotected female to manage them, although I always did my best to put them in good humour. […] It was no easy thing to avoid being robbed and cheated by the less scrupulous travellers; although I think it was only the "cutest Yankee" who stood any fair chance of outwitting me. (Seacole in Griffin and Fish 17-18)

Seacole adopts the convenient role of a vulnerable woman by resorting to an appropriation of the code of "true" womanhood, whereby women are presented as fragile and in need of male protection.

However, as the narrative unfolds, what the author desires to emphasize is her enduring commitment to the soldiers of the Crimean war and her direct help to the troops, a service that was publicly acknowledged by those soldiers who invited her to address their regiment and even celebrated her after the war. Precisely for that reason, the end of the conflict meant a terrible drawback for her:

> And yet all this going home seemed strange and somewhat sad […] clearly had no home to go to […] What better or happier lot could possibly befall me? And alas! How likely was it that my present occupation gone, I might long in vain for another so stirring and useful. (Seacole in Pettinger 247)

Complicating notions of home/homeland, Seacole points to the difficulty of considering the United States as her home, as it denies her basic rights to citizenship and identity. Again the access to the public sphere is at the center of the debate, together with a plea for her individual freedom and free expression, and by extension, for all black women. Seacole's narrative thus combines the need to fashion a self in tune with appropriate notions of femininity with the sense of usefulness or social involvement which presides over her narrative.

The last narrative I would like to mention in this section is Anna Julia Cooper's *A Voice from the South* (1892), another autobiography that is a travel narrative of sorts, and which also exposes a deep commitment to unraveling race and gender hierarchies. As she puts it, she travels through "a land over which floated the Union Jack […] there can be no true test of national courtesy without travel" (93). She is obviously quite critical of the ideological tenets of her nation underlining the moments in which she is forced to choose between her allegiance to her gender or to her race as in, for example, the episode of the bathrooms: one "for ladies" and another "for colored people" (96). Cooper's anxieties are well summarized by Elizabeth Alexander: "Where does Cooper's body, both a 'lady' (which encompasses gender and class) and 'colored' (which encompasses race and humanity) belong? She is resistant to the direct challenge here presented to her fully coherent self" (68), revealing the interstices of dominant ideology. Cooper's other objective in authoring the narrative is to subvert the derogatory image of black women, a purpose that was shared by many of these women travelers. As Mary Helen Washington writes:

> The literature of black women at the turn of the century is a literature frozen into self-consciousness by the need to defend black women [...] against the vicious and prevailing stereotypes that mark nineteenth-century American cultural thought [...] the most common attack on the image of black women was to portray them as immoral women, licentious and oversexed. (73)

Indeed, all these women were able to claim a voice at the time, and therefore to speak the unspoken, or in Toni Morrison's arresting words, unspeakable things unspoken. By resisting to conform to suffocating and derogatory definitions of black femininity, they would actively contribute to deny those prevailing images by offering nurturing alternative configurations.

"France on my Mind": Travel Narratives Heralding a New Century
Keeping these precursors in mind is important in order to decipher African American female narratives in the first decades of the twentieth century, especially during the decade of the twenties. By constantly transgressing racial and gender boundaries, the latter are worthy heirs to their social and political commitment. I would like to focus on the European sojourn of three quite divergent women: Addie Hunton, Gwendolyn Bennett and Jessie Fauset. I have selected these three writers because they illustrate the desire to escape the suffocating experience of living in a segregated country such as the United States by exploring the possibilities afforded by moving temporarily to France and encountering cultural difference. All three were well-educated African American women who enjoyed a privileged status compared to that of their predecessors, although they were acutely aware of their status of second-class citizens in their own country.[10]

As Mary Elkins points out, Europe has been the traditional haven for African American male artists. However, in her analysis of the novels by Nella Larsen, Toni Morrison and Andrea Lee, she affirms that the "European experience fails as affirmation of self" (271). I contend that, on the contrary, these women's travel narratives are instrumental in revealing a female self that continues to uphold social and personal commitment. Being able to switch between cultural and linguistic codes facilitated their appropriation of European public spaces, and the comparison with the difficult integration back in the States. Moreover, their reflection on the very conditions upon which modernity was predicated on both shores pointedly exposed once more racial and gender discriminatory practices at work "back home."[11] I would like to argue, therefore, that there is a generational continuity between their predecessors and these three women's accounts of affirmation of self as well as the dispelling of racist and sexist stereotypical images of black women.

Addie Hunton participated actively in the war in France and narrated her experiences with her colleague Kathryn Johnson in *Two Colored Women with the American Expeditionary Forces* (1920). They undertook educational and welfare work among black American soldiers in France during World War I under the auspices of the YMCA. The narrative bespeaks deep fascination with France, a fascination that was shared by many contemporary travelers of the time, together with a quasi-identification with the French population, noted in the observation that everyone that comes to France ends up becoming "in some small way a part of it" (161). As a trained observer, Hunton depicts the places she visits on her free days, what she calls "Stray Days," positioning herself not as a tourist, but a connoisseur: "away from the beaten paths of travelers" (164). In these highly detailed depictions her interest in the culture and history of the country is quite evident:

> Looking out upon the huge dark form of the Louvre or letting the eye wander past the remains of the palace to the Place de la Concorde, it would be most natural that the thoughts or conversation would turn to the long struggle of France for the attainment of an ideal democracy. (161)

Her allegiance to the French cause is unquestionable, as is her representation of France as an "ideal democracy" in opposition to her own country. Moreover, she tries to avoid any connection to the limited vision of a tourist in order to distinguish herself from the rest of sightseers, in a way anticipating the postmodern difference between tourists and travelers.[12] Hunton carefully weaves her narrative always seeking identification with "native" people. Even when she confesses to go sightseeing, her main objective is to disclaim it as a mere distraction: "to gather new strength, new vigor for the important task back in the Y hut" (166). Thus, the actual pleasure she experiences from sightseeing is mainly tied up with the important mission on which she was sent to France.

Despite such interest in French culture, her position is gradually destabilized as the text progresses, because of her constant insistence on her patriotism. She seems to be torn between two warring allegiances: her defense of Frenchness and the sense of freedom that stems from her sojourn versus the homage she feels she should pay to her country of origin despite it all. Even when she could have denounced American racism, she seems unable to raise to the occasion. A telling instance takes place when Johnson and herself encountered the secret service man who was posing as a Frenchman: "Our secret service man was well-pleased with our Americanism, but we felt rather chagrined that we had missed so splendid an opportunity to share with him certain truths about colored folk at home that he probably had not learned" (163). The fact that they did not mention the racist attitudes they were witness to within the army undermines Hunton's seemingly committed account. Above all, what she wants to underline is her dedication to her duties during World War I, in which we can detect the idea of social commitment which is so crucial for many of these women travelers.

From the formal point of view, there is a very interesting trait in her constant use of the pronoun "one" instead of the usual first or third persons in most travel narratives. If we take into account the identity question this use poses, it complicates the narrator's perspective since it denotes a distance from the narrated events which is not frequent in African American women's travel narratives. It can be also read as the adoption of a presumed objectivity in order to deal with the difficult events she chooses to focus on, thus deviating attention from the female self to amplify the magnitude of and confer significance on those events.

In contrast to Hunton's ambiguous stance, the other two women writing in the 1920s share similar attitudes regarding their social and ideological positioning. Both Gwendolyn Bennett and Jessie Fauset belong to the artistic and intellectual African American elite of the time. This elite was aware of the modernist avant-garde and represented what DuBois called "the Talented Tenth";[13] it was also an elite that traveled quite frequently to Europe and, especially, to the cultural capital, Paris. In both narratives the fascination with France and its culture is also noticeable, as it is in Hunton's. Bennet and Fauset also have in common with Hunton the fact that they went to Paris as students, so their position is again not that of a tourist, but that of persons deeply interested in knowing more about the place and the society they encountered. Both admitted that their French stay had left a definitive mark on them.

In the case of Gwendolyn Bennett, she obtained a fellowship to study art in Paris in 1925 financed by the black sorority "Delta Sigma Theta," and after the trip she became a well-known poet, journalist and critic. Her narration under the title of *The Diaries of Gwendolyn Bennett* (1925), evokes once again the same sense of patriotism and nostalgia for her country that we see in Hunton: "A homesickness more poignant and aching than anything I imagine held me in its grip" (177), but which does not interfere with her critique of racist attitudes on the part of white Americans she meets while in Paris:

> A strange new patriotism has sprung up in me since I've been here in France [...] here are times that I'd give half my remaining years to hear the "Star Spangled Banner" played. And yet even as I feel that way I know that it has nothing to do with the same "home" feeling I have when I see crowds of American white people jostling each other about the American Express. (177)

Even though the social commitment we have already noted is not as clear as in Hunton's narrative, the author manages to emphasize the striking contrast between the absence of racist prejudice she perceives in France and the terrible situation of segregation that the African American community is subjected to at home. To bring this idea to the forefront, Bennett pays homage to the African American community exiled in France, but very especially to its artists' impressive contribution: "It makes my heart swell with pride to know these musicians who are black and yet so wonderful" (178), precisely to denounce the unjust racial relations back at home in the United States.

Jessie Fauset is particularly crucial for this overview of travel narratives, not only for her role as midwife to the Harlem Renaissance,[14] but also as a writer of extraordinary novels and nonfiction writings, especially her accounts of her trips to different places in Europe and North Africa. Keenly aware of what modernity meant from an intellectual point of view, she also acknowledged the indelible imprint that her French sojourn left on her confirmed by the fact that she returned to Paris, a visit she recalled in "Yarrow Revisited," printed in 1925 in *The Crisis*. "Yarrow Revisited" portrays the Paris she encounters upon her return which is quite different from her student's memories of "an enchanted city of gay streets, blue skies, of romantically history monuments, a playground, a court of justice of the world" (181). Her earlier account foregrounds that idealistic image of Paris and France in Hunton, where Fauset recalls her marked sense of freedom and *laissez-aller*; in short, she was able to experience the kind of joy that many African American expatriates felt in Paris at that time, and the sense of freedom from racial prejudice. I would also add here the experience of sexual liberation, subtly evoked by many expatriate women's accounts of their French sojourns, and embodied by the iconic figure of Josephine Baker in Paris in the twenties.[15]

Fauset seems to awaken from this somewhat unreal vision, which she calls her "faulty impressions" as a student (181) upon her return to a new Paris "crowded, but with Frenchmen now, not tourists" (181). Once again Fauset feels the need to distance herself from mainstream tourists, even physically, by seeking accommodation in a quiet hotel located in a residential area of the city. From this privileged standpoint, Fauset decides to shatter any false myths that her contemporaries may still hold about Paris. She achieves this by introducing the detail of her discomfort in the hotel summarized in the line of a Presbyterian hymn she remembers: "Change and decay in all around I see" (183). Once again, she tries to show that life in a residential area in Paris can be compared to a similar type of life the world over. And she concentrates on everyday routines that corroborate this, especially what she terms as the "hard common sense of the French" (183). What really impresses her is the commonsensical and hard-working population she meets in that neighborhood deprived of any romantic delusions. Indeed, what she finds is that their blunt matter-of-factness is undoubtedly "the Frenchiest quality about the French" (185).

What probably surprises the reader is that Fauset uses these features that are usually associated by Europeans with the American way of life in order to mark the difference between herself and French people. And again, as Bennett did before, she proclaims her patriotism: "In Paris I find myself more American than I ever feel in America. I am more conscious of national characteristics than I have ever been in New York" (185). She even goes on to argue that when she talks about doing things differently in America, she means that "Americans white and black do not act that way" (186). So even clearer than in any of the other writers Fauset seems to celebrate the distinct national character as a common trait to both blacks and whites. In her case, the motif of social denunciation retreats to the background in these observations, although she also seems to play the role of social commentator we have seen in the previous writers.

All in all, these narratives focus on the journey as a clear metaphor for a personal and collective search for identity against the racist and sexist ideology that prevailed in the United States at that time. Moreover, the journey itself turns to be a very useful interrogation into the social and political roles these women played by challenging the basic tenets of mainstream race/gender ideology and exploring alternative ways to place black female bodies in new geographies and cultures. In so doing, African American women travelers were able to assert their right to mobility and, more importantly, to articulation and agency.

---

[1] The author wishes to acknowledge the funding provided by the Spanish Ministry of Science and Research for the writing of this essay (Research Project FEM2010-18142).

[2] This selection of travel narratives established the field of African American travel writing together with Alasdair Pettinger's *Always Elsewhere: Travels of the Black Atlantic*, both published in 1998. In 1995, *"Who Set You Flowin'?" The African American Migration Narrative* by Farah Griffin opened new ground by focusing on the Great Migration to Northern cities in the twentieth century.

[3] This contribution was my first approach to the subject of African American women's travel narratives, in which I tried to outline the historical significance of these narratives mainly in relation to issues of mobility and female authorship.

[4] Borrowing Henry Louis Gates' apt phrase (*Signifying Monkey* 129), it clearly resonates with gender specificity when applied to the writings by these pioneering women.

[5] The historian Barbara Welter delineated the main parameters of "true women" in her classic "The Cult of True Womanhood, 1820-1860" (1976), summarizing them in three main virtues: beauty, purity, and piety.

[6] In his classic study of African American autobiographies, William Andrews argues that these writers felt the need to assert themselves "in the name of truth to self" (2).

[7] Adapting the Lacanian sense of the term, Nicole-Claude Mathieu used it to tackle the apparent paradox of the exclusion of women in ethnological research in 1986. Michelle Wallace first applied it to black women opposing the dominant paradigm of white maleness (53).

[8] In this sense, I follow Judith Misrahi-Barak when she mentions that "a new generation of writers […] have been opening new vistas in slavery literature" (14), arguing that links between slave narratives and travel narratives have not been sufficiently explored.

[9] I have included this author because I subscribe to the critical opinion that advocates for the important role played by her travel narrative in the evolution of African American travel writing.

[10] Although slavery had been legally abolished by the fourteenth amendment after the Civil War, the situation of the Reconstruction era and the first decades of the twentieth century deteriorated rapidly and the African American population did not enjoy many of the rights that had been legally recognized, such as voting or education. Lynchings and racial conflicts proliferated, but the worst lot was reserved for African American women since gender discrimination was added to them.

[11] I am particularly thinking here about the discourses of modernity as shaped by the diverse modernisms both in Europe and the States, but also the great influence of primitivism on the fashioning of more positive, although problematic, conceptions of blackness. For a perceptive account of the effects of Negrotarian ideology in the States, see Rhodes.

[12] As Mary Mulligan explains, many postmodern women travelers can be defined as "antitourist," since they make real efforts to differentiate themselves from conventional tourists (102-03).

[13] According to W. E. B. DuBois in *The Souls of Black Folk*, this intellectual elite would guide the destiny of African American masses and eventually reach complete integration in American society (62-76).

[14] She was the editor of *The Crisis* and promoted many literary careers at that time in *The Crisis*, including those of Langston Hughes and Wallace Thurman. An interesting reassessment of this figure can be found in Tomlinson.

[15] See Phyllis Rose's study of the significance of Baker in *Jazz Cleopatra* (1989).

Works Cited

Alexander, Elizabeth. "'We Must Be about Our Father's Business': Anna Julia Cooper and the In-Corporation of the Nineteenth-Century African-American Woman Intellectual." *In Her Own Voice: Nineteenth-Century American Women Essayists*. Ed. Sherry Linkon. New York: Garland, 1997. 61-80.

Andrews, William. *To Tell a Free Story: The First Century of Afro-American Autobiography, 1760-1865*. Urbana: U of Illinois P, 1988.

Bennet, Gwendolyn. "From the Diaries of Gwendolyn Bennett." *A Stranger in the Village: Two Centuries of African-American Travel Writing*. Ed. Farah Griffin and Cheryl Fish. Boston: Beacon P, 1998. 175-79.

Carby, Hazel V. *Reconstructing Womanhood: The Emergence of the Afro-American Woman Novelist.* New York: Oxford UP, 1987.

Cooper, Anna Julia. *A Voice from the South.* 1892. New York: Oxford UP, 1988.

DuBois, W. E. B. *The Souls of Black Folk.* 1903. New York: Bantam, 1989.

Elkins, Mary. "Expatriate Afro-American Women as Exotics." *International Women's Writing: New Landscapes of Identity.* Ed. Anne Brown and Marjanne Goozé. Westport: Greenwood P, 1995. 264-73.

Fauset, Jessie. "Yarrow Revisited." *A Stranger in the Village: Two Centuries of African-American Travel Writing.* Ed. Farah Griffin and Cheryl Fish. Boston: Beacon P, 1998. 180-85.

Gallego, Mar. "Escritoras afro-americanas y relato de viajes: una mirada desde el otro lado del cristal." *Relatos de viajes, miradas de mujeres.* Ed. Mar Gallego and Eloy Navarro. Sevilla: Alfar, 2007. 51-70.

Gates, Henry Louis, Jr. Introduction. *The Classic Slave Narratives.* Ed. Henry Louis Gates Jr. New York: Mentor, 1987. ix-xviii.

---. *The Signifying Monkey.* New York: Oxford UP, 1988.

Griffin, Farah. *"Who Set You Flowin'?" The African-American Migration Narrative.* New York: Oxford UP, 1995.

Griffin, Farah, and Cheryl Fish, eds. *A Stranger in the Village: Two Centuries of African-American Travel Writing.* Boston: Beacon P, 1998.

Hunton, Addie. "Stray Days." *Always Elsewhere: Travels of the Black Atlantic.* Ed. Alasdair Pettinger. London: Cassell, 1998. 161-66.

Mason, Mary G. "Travel as Metaphor and Reality in Afro-American Women's Autobiography, 1850-1972." *Black American Literature Forum* 24.2 (1990): 337-56.

Misrahi-Barak, Judith, ed. *Revisiting Slave Narratives: Les avatars contemporains des récits d'eslaves.* Montpellier: Presses universitaires de la Mediterranee, 2005.

Mulligan, Maureen. "La mujer viajera en plena crisis poscolonial: el ejemplo de Sara Wheeler." *Relatos de viajes, miradas de mujeres.* Ed. Mar Gallego and Eloy Navarro. Sevilla: Alfar, 2007. 95-118.

Pettinger. Alasdair, ed. *Always Elsewhere: Travels of the Black Atlantic.* London: Cassell, 1998.

Prince, Mary. *The History of Mary Prince, a West Indian Slave.* 1831. *The Classic Slave Narratives.* Ed. Henry Louis Gates Jr. New York: Mentor, 1987. 183-242.

Prince, Nancy. *A Narrative of the Life and Travels of Mrs. Nancy Prince.* 1850. *A Stranger in the Village: Two Centuries of African-American Travel Writing.* Ed. Farah Griffin and Cheryl Fish. Boston: Beacon P, 1998. 68-76, 201-05.

Rhodes, Chip. "*Writing Up the New Negro*: The Construction of Consumer Desire in the Twenties." *Journal of American Studies* 28.2 (1994): 191-207.

Rose, Phyllis. *Jazz Cleopatra: Josephine Baker in Her Time.* New York: Doubleday, 1989.

Seacole, Mary. *Wonderful Adventures of Mrs. Seacole in Many Lands.* 1857. *A Stranger in the Village: Two Centuries of African-American Travel Writing.* Ed. Farah Griffin and Cheryl Fish. Boston: Beacon P, 1998. 16-22.

Seacole, Mary. *Wonderful Adventures of Mrs. Seacole in Many Lands.* 1857. *Always Elsewhere: Travels of the Black Atlantic.* Ed. Alasdair Pettinger. London: Cassell, 1998. 245-49.

Tomlinson, Susan. "Vision to Visionary: The New Negro Woman as Cultural Worker in Jessie Redmon Fauset's *Plum Bun.*" *Legacy* 19.1 (2002): 90-97.

Wallace, Michelle. "Variations on Negation and the Heresy of Black Feminist Creativity." *Reading Black, Reading Feminist.* Ed. Henry Louis Gates Jr. Harmondsworth: Penguin, 1990. 52-67.

Washington, Mary Helen. *Invented Lives: Narratives of Black Women, 1860-1960.* New Cork: Anchor, 1987.

Welter, Barbara. "The Cult of True Womanhood, 1820-1860." *Dimity Convictions: The American Woman in the Nineteenth Century.* Columbus: U of Ohio P, 1976. 21-41.

Ime A. S. Kerlee

Somos una Mezcla?: Re-Constructing Race in *Dominicanidad*

Though it is generally agreed upon in the social sciences that race is a social construct, the lived experience of race remains salient. For migrants and their sending nations the experience of race privilege and racial discrimination can become a catalyst for the renegotiation and/or retrenchment of individual, national, and transnational definitions of race-based identities. Moreover, the language of so-called miscegenation and the privileges assigned to subsequent generations based on proximity to whiteness, makes racial negotiations a particularly gendered experience. For Dominican women migrants moving from a tripartite race-class system based on perceived phenotypic attributes and class-standing to a binary system based loosely on the one drop rule, racial negotiations become a key factor in the migration experience. By looking at the choices of Dominican women transmigrants we can see how individual experiences of identity expose the spatially bound social constructions of race. Their negotiations also show us the complex nature of racial privilege and how it impacts individuals' abilities to engage social, national, and transnational racial perceptions and definitions.

In this paper, I will discuss both the historical constructions of racial identity and my own research on current negotiations amongst Dominicans living in and outside of the Dominican Republic. The essay is split into two substantial sections: (1) the history of racial negotiations in the Dominican Republic and (2) participant data. Both historical and personal experiences are critical to the understanding of racial negotiation in the Dominican Republic. The history section discusses how whiteness became entrenched in the Dominican Republic and the subsequent moves by Dominicans to reinstate a sense of themselves as a mixture of Indigenous, African, and Spanish influences. My ethnographic research, on the other hand, points to contemporary understandings of the self as an unraced or racialized being.

My research found that Dominicans developed three key coping strategies that helped them deal with the shift between a somewhat fluid and multi-tiered race structure to the U.S. binary system: (1) rejection of blackness and the assertion of white privilege based on Dominican definitions of race, (2) recognition of racism based on U.S. definitions of blackness accompanied by a reification of the existing racial system in the Dominican Republic, or (3) a push toward a problematic multiculturalism and/or embrace of blackness. Though in many cases these strategies redefined racial definitions in the U.S., they often reinforced rather than dismantled ground level pigmentocracy in the Dominican Republic. Despite limited impact, race negotiations were multi-directional, originating within the Dominican Republic as well as the diaspora.

Methods

In order to determine how stories of race, gender, and migration are transmitted from abroad to households in the Dominican Republic, I conducted both historical research and semi-structured and unstructured interviews with Dominicans in both Santo Domingo and New York City. I also observed the impact of transmission of race and gender messages on self-identification over time. Everyone was asked to tell me stories about the following words: *indio*, black, feminism, racism, classism, migration, nation, and beauty. In order to further interrogate issues of race and gender, they were asked to (1) look at a series of pictures of women of different races and facial features and identify which ones they felt were the most attractive and explain why, and (2) watch documentaries on migration and on the *batey* and give their general responses to the accuracy of the material.

An initial opportunistic sample was carried out in several neighborhoods in Santo Domingo with a concentration on *Naco, los Prados* , the *Zona Colonial,* and to a lesser extent the neighborhoods in between these areas, supplemented by a judgmental sample in order to identify households and NGO members. Households were defined as any adult members of a family, or extended family, unit who have female friends or relatives living abroad in New York City or family, or extended family, with relatives and/or property remaining in the Dominican Republic. The study was stratified for race, class and gender to include *blancos, indios, negros*, and Dominicans of Haitian descent from the working, middle and upper middle class.

There were eight households and ten individuals in the study with a total number of thirty-five participants. Of these thirty-five, twenty-four were women, ten men, and one gender queer. Five middle class, twenty-five working class, and five subsistence level people participated. Nine participants were white or *indio/a claro/a,* twenty-one were brown or *indio* and *indio oscuro,* five identified as black (including two who also claimed *afro-dominicano* as their identity). There were three out queer participants, two gay males (one of whom is in the early stages of gender transition, noted above), and one lesbian. Of the participants who identified as heterosexual, twenty-three were currently in or had been in heterosexual relationships, two had been in heterosexual relationships but were questioning their sexuality, four participants who had occasional same sex encounters during the research process, and three participants who did not self-identify or provide information about their sexual orientation during the course of my research. Two NGOs and one organization[1] were also represented, Gay and Lesbian Alliance (GALA), Rural Women and Development (MRD), Dominican Haitian Women's Alliance (DHWA), either through interviews with their leadership or their members.

The Rhetoric of Whiteness
The desire for whiteness was historically located both inside and outside of the Dominican Republic. Outside of the Dominican Republic, colonial and neo-colonial powers fought to define Dominican racial identity for their own political and economic ends. Based on the assumptions of racial science, Spanish colonials created a pigmentocracy that named and illustrated racial difference based on parentage. These categories defined expected phenotypic traits and gradated status based on perceived proximity to whiteness.[2] The Spanish used this system to deny rights to Dominicans and dissuade other colonial and neo-colonial powers from doing the same. They justified control of the island by defining Dominicans as degenerate (Martínez-Fernandez 40). According to racial science, degeneracy was caused by either climate or interracial relationships. It implied a lack of whiteness for both those of bi- or multi-racial heritage and white Creoles who had been "tainted" by the environment and sexual relations with non-white people. By claiming Dominicans were degenerate, the Spanish de facto denied Dominicans' claims to whiteness.

Degeneration was also seen as indicative of laziness, licentiousness, inability to rule, ignorance, and violence (see Buckle; Gobineau; Ratzel). Spanish claims of Dominican degeneracy not only worked to disguise Spanish civil abuses in the 1860s but also helped support their refusal to grant Creoles positions in the government. Spanish officials and priests circulated derogatory racialized images of Dominicans in letters, open forums, and books, forcing the Dominican people to respond with assertions of their whiteness and the development of anti-black sentiment. The Spanish justified their behavior by referring to Dominicans as a "degraded race" and "colored population," and to the nation as a "black state" (Roorda 221). Spain used the language of racial science indiscriminately to describe the conditions on the island, reinforcing the idea of racialized backwardness that helped compromise Dominican sovereignty and discouraged white immigration.

When confronted with the possibility of U.S. expansion in the region in the 1840s, Spain openly called Dominicans black (Martínez-Fernández 40-41). This strategy played off of American racism in order to keep the U.S. government's growing interests in the region from challenging Spanish rule. Unlike Spain, whose policies remained fairly consistent throughout the period, the U.S. wavered regularly on the issue of Dominican identity.

> Virtually all agents dispatched there [to the Dominican Republic] were instructed to assess the proportion and the numbers of the different strengths of white element, the more ardently expansionist the reporter, the lighter the racial portrayal of the Dominican people. (41-42)

After the Haitian revolution and subsequent attempt to consolidate the entire island, Dominicans were unable to get support from the U.S. because of fears of "Africanization" (Atkins and Wilson 12-13). Without the support of the United States, Dominican people felt defenseless at a point in history that represented a watershed in racial identity for the nation.[3] Arguments also broke out in both Congress and U.S. papers about whether or not Dominicans were white. Southern fears of a "black nation" dominated the opposition and generally prevented the U.S. government from recognizing, overtly bargaining with, or otherwise working with the Dominican government until the 1900s (Martínez-Fernández 43-44, 166). Moreover, the U.S. government stated openly that they would side with white presidential candidates in the Dominican Republic (44), directly influencing Dominican governance at its highest levels.

U.S. involvement in the Dominican Republic in the 1900s further reinforced the idea that whiteness was quintessential to political power on the global stage. During the first occupation, 1916-1924, "The marines treated the Dominican people in a brutal, racist, and condescending manner" (Sagas and Inoa 135). Former President Monsignor Nouel was so disturbed by the racial overtones of the U.S. invasion and its subsequent violence that despite ailing health he returned from Rome to the Dominican Republic to protest. In a letter to the U.S. Minister, he described the Marines as engaged in the "hunting of men in the savannas as if they were savage animals" (Monsignor Nouel's letter to U.S. Minister Russell, qtd. in Sagas and Inoa 137). They also destroyed entire villages of *cimarrones* to eradicate free black communities living outside of state control (Martínez-Fernández 55). The destruction of free black communities represented a key reversal of the generalized acceptance of black alternative political power at the ground level, and ambivalence at the state level, that had existed since independence in 1844. State-sponsored racialized violence was repeated during the second U.S. invasion in 1961. Currently, pictures of white soldiers abusing brown and black Dominicans hang in the national museum and are reproduced in multiple Dominican history books. In each case the photographs were accompanied with a narrative on American racism, either in the form of the museum guide or the historians' text. The narratives also created the recognition that American racial binaries created fixity where Dominicans allowed fluidity. Finally, the narratives and images taken together with the historical memory they inculcated, reinforced the idea that access to white supremacy is the only route to Dominican sovereignty and respect on the international stage for multiple generations of Dominicans.

Dominicans were acutely aware of what racial classifications meant to their internal survival and global status. They used both language and immigration laws to claim whiteness for themselves. Dominicans used political, educational, and popular texts to erase blackness and redefine whiteness to include those who were not visibly white. Restrictions on and taxation associated with migration were used to increase the number of visibly white, European descended, peoples in the Dominican Republic while discouraging or expelling people of color. Embedded in these strategies was the engendering of the state, sexuality, and reproduction. The near absence of visible white people in the Dominican Republic and international discourses about their racial make up and competence transformed the use of the term "white" into an ideological struggle for power that superseded skin color.

As a counter to Spanish constructions of Dominicans as black people, Dominicans wrote countless letters and speeches asserting their Spanish origins and subsequent claims to whiteness (see Sagas and Inoa). In 1844 they sent an envoy to the U.S. Secretary of State who claimed that, "Dominican Republic whites largely held political power" and that "half [of the Dominicans] were white" (Atkins and Wilson 15). In the 1930s, Trujillo and Balaguer implemented the Dominicanization of the borderlands and the education system (Sagas 58). This policy involved the erasure of African influences and black Dominicans' contributions from the history books, public works and popular culture (Simmons, "Reconfiguring" 80, 85). Dominicans' references to themselves as white in both political and personal contexts, created an ideological link to whiteness for both Dominicans and people assessing their racial background abroad.

Two key figures emerged in the Dominican textual creation of whiteness: the *campesino Cibeaño* and Enriquillo. In 1882, Manuel de Jesús Galván wrote the so-called historical novel *Enriquillo* about a Taíno of the same name. The novel served two purposes in the racial narrative of the nation: (1) it created a popular fictional version of the actual rule of a Royal Governor who included indigenous people in whiteness and (2) it linked indigenous people and colonizers in the struggle against black people. The novel begins with the rule of the first Royal Governor of the Dominican Republic, de Ovando, and includes key historical figures and events. The inclusion of de Ovando is significant because he was the first governor to sanction interracial relations between white male colonists and Indian women. He also declared that any children from these unions would be considered white (Cassa). De Ovando's declaration relied on Columbus' observation that Taínos were white (Knight 12) on the one hand, and the assertion, by Rousseau and others, that indigenous people from the Americas were perfectible on the other.

Enriquillo embodies the perfectible noble savage/citizen whose story cemented hybridized national pride and whiteness beyond the skin. Though Enriquillo was painted as a nationalist hero, his education and religion were Spanish in origin. The narrative ensures Enriquillo's civility and loyalty to the Spanish while at the same time presenting Spanish abuses as anomalies. Although Enriquillo decides to rebel, his rebellion is based on European enlightenment principles that his fellow indigenous people lack; nor is his rebellion for freedom but rather to address abuses he sees as anomalous in an otherwise civilizing colonial regime. These distinctions are critical to the sense of white rule and indigenous potential for "whiteness under the skin" and are further cemented by Enriquillo's decision to stand with Spanish rule against African freedom efforts in the book. His actions not only erase real, historical, alliance between Taínos and Africans, but also the joint communities they created in the Dominican Republic.

In uniting Spanish and Taíno culture into one white culture, *Enriquillo* ushered in the nineteenth-century *indigenismo* movement. The movement became the primary literary and political tool for explaining Dominicans' visible brownness and supposed internal whiteness. It also displaced blackness in the Dominican Republic by allowing Dominicans to see themselves as white indigenous people and blackness as Other. "In order to varnish their common African past, the Dominican people essentially dropped the words black and mulatto from their vocabulary and replaced them with the less traumatic and more socially desirable Indio" (Simmons, "Reconfiguring" 35). The majority of Dominicans today identify as *Indio/a* despite widely held beliefs that Taínos were extinct by the mid-1500s and the attempts by President Fernández to include *mulatto/a* in the census and on state I.D. cards during his first term.

Like Enriquillo, the *campesino Cibeaño* relied on a masculine image of the nation. It both replaced and coexisted alongside the term *blanco de la tierra*; both refer to an imagined white man of the people. In the late 1500s *blanco de la tierra* was used by Dominicans to refer to hardworking agricultural workers who formed the basis of their society. Embedded in this phrase is the inscription of whiteness through the use of the term *blanco*. The concept erased people of color on two levels by: (1) labeling them white regardless of actual skin color or racial background, and (2) claiming that only white people contributed to the building of the nation. The latter negated the labor of Taínos and African-descended peoples in the mines and plantations upon which colonial fortunes and the Dominican economy were based. This erasure helped pave the way for the replacement of *blancos de la tierra* with the *campesino Cibeaño*. The Cibao valley has one of the longest standing agricultural communities in the Dominican Republic. It was built on the labor of single family farming supported by hunting that kept the country afloat during its multiple depressions. According to one participant from the region in my study, since Cibao's economy was based on the single family farming model, the region has some of the lightest people in the country living there. The term, then, relied on the entrenchment of the previous erasure of laborers of color and the open assertion of whiteness.

The shift to the term *campesino Cibeaño* also represented the government's attempt to locate visible whiteness in the nation for an international audience. This was done at a time, the 1930s, when the Dominican Republic was once again under scrutiny from the United States. Then president Trujillo courted the attention of the U.S. and tried to make political and economic ties with Europe through these discursive strategies. He also invited diplomats from the West to the Dominican Republic regularly. Thus locating the term in an actual region of the country – the Cibao valley – known for its visible whiteness served to reify the language of the term in ways that *blancos de la tierra* could not.

The 1930s further represented a critical shift in the racialization of the female body for national ends. Prior to this period, foreign observers circulated accounts of abundant sexually promiscuous Taíno women and women of African descent in the Dominican Republic (see Moya Pons). It was not until Trujillo entered office that the state began to seek out white or light-skinned Dominican women to represent the nation. White women were photographed with Trujillo regularly to circulate in both the national and international press (Simmons, "Reconfiguring" 85).[4] Trujillo's desire to whiten his own origins also made the position of white and light-skinned women in the Dominican particularly precarious. He chose women and young girls to represent the nation based on his own sexual preferences with no regard for consent. When he was bored with them Trujillo moved on to the next woman with little thought for their well-being. Since these women no longer fit the Catholic definitions of female purity it was unlikely that they were able to return to their homes and to relationships with men of their own choosing. The "eroticization of racial power" (Slocum 174) then, compromised any power white women gained by being written into the nation.

Migration

Dominicans also relied heavily on migration to increase the number of white European-descended people in the nation. As early as 1681, the Spanish government implemented an immigration program that moved *canarios*, white workers, to the Dominican Republic. They were seen as "a living frontier" to stop the French encroachment on Spanish soil (Moya Pons 65-66) as well as a way to increase white colonials on the island. Between 1681 and 1721, 706 families were relocated to the Dominican Republic (78). Despite the assumption that the *canarios* would integrate into the existing populace, these families created their own communities and ethnic enclaves, refusing to interact with Dominicans they saw as non-white. The inability to recruit people of European descent in the mid-1700s seemed to reflect the growing belief that the Dominican Republic was an unviable nation because of racialized degeneracy. Since *canarios* were visibly white, they most likely closed their communities to the Dominican people who were not.[5]

After independence, Dominicans tried a broader approach to increasing white immigration. The Immigration Act of 1847 encouraged migration from predominantly white settlements in the Americas and in Europe (Atkins and Wilson, 11-14). The Act was billed as the Dominicans' best hope of preventing Haitian attempts to reunite the island, writing the growing racial binary between black Haitians and white privileged Dominicans into the law. In 1932, tax laws were changed to further encourage white immigration. Law 279 taxed migrants based on their place of origin. People from Europe, Canada, and other predominantly white nations were charged $6 while Asians and Haitians paid $600. Asians and Haitians were also expected to pay the tax every 6 years of residence (Wucker 103). Two years later Trujillo echoed the *canarios* program by moving white settlers into the disputed border territories. Migrants and other chosen people were expected to live along the Haitian-Dominican border as part of the Dominicanization policy of the 1930s (105). Like the *canarios* before them, these migrants represented a visible boundary between supposed white Dominicans and black Haitians.

In 1938, in order to assuage the political backlash caused by the 1937 massacre of Haitians and black Dominicans, described in the next section, Trujillo offered to accept 100,000 Jewish refugees (see Levy). Jewish resettlement represented a major contradiction in Trujillo's policies as he had previously aligned himself with Nazi ideology. Nevertheless Jewish refugees were offered 80 acres of land, 10 cows, and a mule, and a horse in Sousúa. Of the 5,000 visas issued only 645 Jewish settlers actually arrived in the Dominican Republic. By the 1940s the vast majority of families had moved to the United States. Like the *canarios* before them, the Jewish settlers also remained a closed group. In fact Sousúa was an entirely Jewish town until the mid-1980s when tourism drew international visitors and Dominican workers to the region. Once again the attempt to create whiteness through immigration incentives failed.

Antihaitianismo

The narrative of the nation also depended on the Haitian Other and subsequent disassociation from blackness. Haitians are often depicted as people of African descent who were barbarians that threatened to overrun the country at any moment. This fear was so deeply embedded in the nation that the celebration of independence from Haiti continues to be the largest independence celebration in the Dominican Republic despite their not having gained full independence until 17 years later.

Embedded in the Haitian-Dominican binary was the location of blackness outside of *Dominicanidad*. This often resulted in the displacement of black Dominicans. In 1844 and 1861 it was feared that black Dominicans would side with Haitians against the nation if given the chance (Sagas 32). Although the fear of a universal black uprising resulted in the abolition of slavery for black Dominicans, it did not grant them equal rights.

Particularly in presidential elections, the specter of universal black allegiance over national pride remains a palpable tool in displacing black political power in the Dominican Republic. The presidential candidacy of Peña Gómez was compromised by accusations that he was in fact Haitian and would return the country to Haitian rule if elected. Potential candidates in the 2004 election were also discredited in this fashion. Images hinting toward the "Haitian origins" of black candidates, especially those who identify as black, circulate often during any election season.

In 1937, *antihaitianismo* and the rejection of African descent within the nation had lethal results for both Dominican and Haitian people living in the Dominican Republic. As part of the new migration laws designed to increase whiteness in the Dominican Republic Trujillo ordered that all foreigners on Dominican soil register with the government. Over 8,000 Haitians were expelled as a result of the registration effort (Wucker 47). Less than 3 months later, on October 3, 1937, Trujillo's army murdered between 12,168 and 25,000 Haitian and black Dominicans (Hicks 112). According to one comment maker in the documentary El Jefe, Trujillo intended to "remove the black taint from our [Dominican] blood." Visibly black Dominicans, particularly those closest to the border, were also killed as the national narrative of whiteness erased them from *Dominicanidad*.

Dominican women, regardless of skin color, who married Haitians, were targeted for the most extreme abuses because they were seen to have betrayed the nation. Priests along the border told stories of Dominican women hung outside their homes with their bellies split open and uteruses hacked out (participant data 2002). Though Trujillo himself was part Haitian, the national narrative he created denied *Dominicanidad* to Dominicans of Haitian descent. These women's children were also killed despite the fact that the Dominican constitution said they were Dominican from birth. The killing of women and children known to be Dominican represented a reversal of the longstanding whitening of the nation through intermarriage begun by de Ovando. Eugenicist racial science superseded historical realities and machetes proved more effective in enforcing whiteness than immigration laws or mythic texts.

Balaguer continued to deport Haitians well into the 1990s (Wilhelms 137). As in the case of the 1937 massacre, black Dominicans were not safe from forcible deportation. "Particularly during waves of repatriation, which are initiated by the government frequently after the end of the sugarcane season when little Haitian labor is needed for the following 6 months, the police stop every dark-skinned person in the streets" (68). Despite their own victimization at the hands *antihaitianismo* both Wilhelms and I found that many black Dominicans who have not traveled abroad believe that Haitians live better than Dominicans in the same socio-economic class. As one of my participants, Rosa, said, "It is not my fault they do not know their rights and so they let people take advantage of them. They have the same rights we [Dominicans] do! *And* they have international observers and American scholars looking out for them. What did I have? I mean, what do we have? Nothing!" Rosa's slip from the universal to the particular, and from the present to the past tense, in her statement spoke to abuses she endured for having features and jobs associated with blackness and/or Haitianness. Yet she was determined to write the abuses she endured as class conflict and state-level corruption rather than racism and *antihaitianismo*. To see incidents in which she was discriminated against as *antihaitianismo* would have required her to see herself as black rather than *india*. Like many other participants she would rather hold on to color privilege than risk losing it in an attempt to dismantle racism in the Dominican Republic.

The result of Dominican attempts to write/right a primarily brown and black nation in the face of global white privilege was general ambivalence toward racial categories based on skin tone alone. Dominicans moved from inherited Spanish racial categories (the casta system) that mapped bi- and multi-racial identities to ones based on an imagined past and redefined whiteness. In the 1970s, Guzmán identified nine hair colors, twelve skin colors, ten facial features, and six physical types (37-40). In 2000, both Rodríguez and Simmons found that whiteness was not only based on physical features but also other signs of status. "Hair texture, skin color, economics, education, and the like are indexes of how white one is" (Simmons, "Reconfiguring" 92). According to definitions and usages by participants, the complexities of these categories were often subsumed under the simple addition of *claro* or *oscuro* to any physical trait. Since most Dominicans had at least one *claro*, as well as one *oscuro*, attribute the result of this system was ambivalence toward visible skin color and blackness as an organizing principle. Moreover any one Dominican family contained black, brown and white members. As one female participant put it, "Our colors sit [with us] at the dinner table." Racial ambivalence was upheld by the ability of people of all colors to claim whiteness through not only features but associations, class, and education.

The contradictory fluidity and fixity of race in the Dominican Republic represented a radical difference in conceptualizing race when compared to the binary system in place in the United States. In the U.S., white supremacy was maintained by strictly dividing racial categories into a binary system of white and black. Although the constitution implemented the one drop rule and claimed black people represented three-fifths of a human being, these laws gave way to visible skin color. While in the Dominican Republic "to measure the living conditions of Dominican blacks and mulattos would mean no more than to assess the social status of the masses of the people, which would correspond more fittingly to an analysis of class inequalities and the social injustices bred by dependent capitalism than to a discussion of ethnic oppression" (Torres-Saillant 1089), class and social status often function as racial markers in the United States. Consequently, upon arrival, Dominicans migrants to the United States began the process of racialization anew.

Redefinition: Juana's and Manny's Stories
In my sample, white or light Dominicans living primarily in the U.S. were the most likely to embrace blackness as a part of *Dominicanidad*. Many of them found that racial binaries in the United States failed to allow them the kind of self-expression and freedom that they believed they had in the Dominican Republic. Identifying with blackness either linguistically or through association represented an opportunity to defy racial binaries by subverting the visual and/or become "cool" by embracing media stereotypes of black culture. These strategies were embraced primarily by Dominican migrants who were 35 and under and had spent more than 10 years living in the United States. Participants who were over 35 or newly arrived were more likely to remain firmly entrenched in the ethno-racial categories of the Dominican Republic and view American racial

categories through negative media stereotypes. While both men and women engaged in these strategies, men of all ages were more likely to choose race as coolness strategies while women, particularly 30 and over, were more likely to choose multicultural strategies.

When asked, Juana identified as either *blanca* or *india*. In her daily interactions and throughout the course of interviews and observations she did not self-identify without prompting and deftly avoided categories in conversations where they seemed to be natural parts of the discussion. Her avoidance was reflected in each story she told me and represented a strategy that argued for a universal humanism in social interaction to dismantle racism. Juana believed that by subverting the visual binaries through the racial composition of her own family, she would help force re-evaluation of racial categories in both countries. Given that Juana's family was part of the Dominican elite which has almost never engaged in interracial relationships, Juana's family's decision to weave visibly black people into their family tree represented a major challenge to the social mores of their social group.

Juana was a small woman with a thin frame, bony nose, thin lips, blue eyes, and straight brown hair. Her brothers, sisters, and mother had similar features to her own while her father is considered *indio claro*, with wavy black hair, and light tan skin. They were all college educated. Juana's father was a doctor and her mother was a retired professor. Her three brothers are all professors, while she and her sister were both married homemakers by choice. Her husband was a white American lawyer; her sister's husband, a white American neurosurgeon. Almost all members of the family owned property in both the Dominican Republic and the United States and traveled between both countries regularly. Their color, features, education, economic status, and transnational business ties marked them as members of the neo-elite white society in the Dominican diaspora.

She was generally labeled white in the U.S. until she spoke; she had a Spanish accent laced with the gruff tone of a long term smoking habit. The smokiness of her voice often eclipsed her accent. Her family's affluence had also prevented Juana from growing up in Dominican barrios that not only contained white, black, and brown Dominicans but also people of color from the English and Spanish speaking Caribbean, Asians and Asian-Americans, and African-Americans. Juana's neighborhood was predominantly white. Despite having access to whiteness in multiple ways, Juana's work and deep commitment to her community, led her and her sister to interact with Latinos of all colors. Juana believed the experience of hearing their economic and social struggles politicized her. Since these interactions would not have occurred in the Dominican Republic where Juana's family was among the secluded elite, the migrant experience was essential to her political and social awareness.

Juana's relationship to race contained both negative and positive definitions of blackness. She chose to participate in this project because she was "intrigued" by my research and felt "it is about time we [Dominicans] start talking openly about race." In our first unstructured interview she spoke at length about the preference for "white features" in the Dominican Republic and amongst older generations of Dominican migrants. When I asked about her own preferences, she said race was "irrelevant" to her, though she and her family did prefer the company of Latinos over other people.

After observing the family and their friends, I noted that their social group included only white Americans and white or light Latinos. Juana herself had recently moved to an area of town where there was less than 1% people of color, despite Latino enclaves and neighborhoods with racial and ethnic diversity of up to 65% in the area. Her sister lived in a similarly homogenous area. Juana explained her decision on the basis of class, "I have worked very hard in my life. My family and I came here with almost nothing because of the government corruption and we have managed to make something of ourselves. I think Dominicans all work very hard and who knows soon this neighborhood may be all Dominican. You never know." Her statement reflected comments made by most of my upper-class participants in that it implied that the American dream was still available to most migrants if they just worked hard while erasing the differences in economic status, race, and the American economy that post-1965 migrants face. Though Juana believed her family had come with nothing, a story they all repeated, her grandfather explained that they had in fact had substantially more money and connections than the average Dominican immigrant at the same period. They also had access to dual income households as the family had remained intact throughout the migration experience.

When I asked Juana why she and her sister had chosen to marry white Americans over Latinos of any color, while her brothers had chosen white or light Latina women, Juana located the decision in misogyny: "You know how they are; they picked women from the island so they could be the men, unquestioned. What they learned was, here or there, Dominican women are in charge."

The problem of Dominican men believing Dominican migrant women were "too independent" was highlighted in Dominican and American papers in 2001 when a Dominican baseball player lamented the lack of good nutrition and comfort in his home because he "could not find a good woman to take care of him." He stated that he intended to return to the Dominican Republic to find a wife because there were no "good women" in America (*Listen Diario* [New York] 10 October 2001). These comments sparked a debate in Dominican communities across the diaspora about relationships between Dominican men and women. Many of the women participating in these discussions agreed with Juana that it did not matter which side of the diaspora one lived on, women had far more power in their households than men believed. Though Juana was willing to discuss the gender dynamics between her brothers and their wives at length, she deftly changed the subject when the issue of their whiteness, or the whiteness of her own husband, was brought up.

Not everyone in Juana's immediate family was white or light, however, and the story she told about them illustrated the profound contradiction in her desire to dismantle racism in Dominican and American communities:

> My sister can't have children, so she adopted some. She wanted one boy and one girl. Even though she could have any child she wanted, she picked two black children from the Dominican Republic against my mother's protests. My mother is of that old generation that can't understand why you would choose children darker than you. But, my sister wanted to give these poor kids a better life.
>
> On their first day of school they were called names. I remember them coming home and asking why they were treated different than other kids at the school. We had to explain to them that people thought they were black. We told them to tell everyone that they were Dominican.
>
> A similar incident happened to my niece the first time she went with my sister back to the Dominican. One day she came in from playing and asked our Aunt why all the servants were the same color that she was but no one else was? None of us knew what to say, and now she does not like to go back for visits.

The decision to adopt black children represented a critical shift in the way Juana's family related to race. As white elites in the Dominican Republic they did not interact with people of color or engage in interracial relationships. Despite the existence of brown and black people at almost every level of the Dominican economy, for the most part they occupied the lowest levels of each class.

At the top of the class structure were people considered to be "pure whites." In a country where bi- and multi-racial identity was normative, and often necessary for survival of the nation, pure whites policed the racial boundaries of their society with unmatched vigor. The migration experience, and the subsequent exposure to people of color and working class people's issues, transformed Juana's and her sister's understanding of race to the point where they began to dismantle race at its most entrenched level.

Juana's story illustrated the ways in which many Dominicans check discussions of race with the assertion of ethnicity. When Juana's niece and nephew experienced racism at school, the family taught them to subvert the issue by claiming their Dominican ethnicity. On the one hand, the decision to assert Dominican identity in the face of American racism represented a desire to correct the erroneous assumptions about place of origin. By stating that they are Dominican, Dominicans hoped to remind Americans of all colors that identity goes beyond the visual. They also hoped to maintain their individuality and cultural integrity in the face of collapsing and totalizing terms like "black" or "Latino." Many of the Dominicans who also identified as Afro-Latino or black in my sample saw the issue of asserting Dominicanness as one of pride in one's heritage and community rather than a rejection of blackness.

On the other hand, the failure to think and speak critically about race and racism in the face of racial incidents also fostered ignorance and potential racism. It created a dichotomy between racial epithets for African-Americans and the supposed unraced body of the ethnic migrant. Worse still, it failed to equip visibly black children with critical tools for mediating, confronting, and potentially helping their communities move beyond racial inequality. Despite the comparative structure of Juana's story, her family's silence about the complexities of race also located racism in the U.S. while it exempted racial and color inequities in the Dominican Republic.

When Juana's niece returned to the Dominican Republic for her first visit she was unprepared for the racial disparity awaiting her. Having internalized the idea that racism consisted of offenses between European-Americans and African-Americans, Juana's niece could not help but be confused by the visible racial disparity in Dominican society. When she pointed it out to her family, they did not know "what to say, and now she does not like to go back for visits." It seemed the family's silences about race were not in fact about ethnicity but privilege. As white Dominicans at the top of the racial hierarchy in both countries they found themselves unprepared to discuss racial inequality. In the absence of critical discourse about race they had not seen their own recreation of racialized class structures until confronted. Rather than attempt to dismantle their own participation in the system of inequality they reverted to silence.

Unlike Juana's story, Manny's relationship to blackness was one of black as cool. Manny identified as *negro*, always said with a sly grin. Manny had dark black, straight hair, dark brown eyes, and light brown skin that was almost white. He had an M.A. from the most prestigious college in Santo Domingo and lived in an upper-middle-class home there with his family. Many of his siblings lived in New York and Manny went to New York regularly to visit them but always found a reason to return home. Manny's color, features, class, and education, marked him as *indio* with white privilege.

Of all of my participants, Manny was the most open about discussing race. In describing the racial situation of the Dominican Republic, Manny said "We are black. We are white. We are like you." The latter was a reference both to my skin color, brown, and my bi-racial identity. "We are mixed." As we saw in the beginning of this chapter, "we are mixed" was the national rhetoric of race in operation in the Dominican Republic at the time of my study. Manny used the phrase to call attention to the fact that both he and I were mixed despite the racial and ethnic categories of the U.S. that placed us in different categories. Although his statement exposed American inequities, it was also meant to highlight the spatial nature of race. While he and I stood in the Dominican Republic we were both "coffee colored children." If we were in the U.S. we would expected to compete for the limited resources allotted us as non-white people. He also used the phrase as an illustration of the fallacy of racial mixture as an indicator of equality in the Dominican Republic. He enforced the double meaning of the phrase by asking a woman with *oscura* features if I was *morena* (brown of African and white descent) or *india* (brown of Taíno and white descent). The woman identified me as *india* even though she knew that I was in actuality *morena*.

Despite the linguistic and performative games Manny engaged in to critically examine race in both countries, he was unwilling to tell me personal stories about experiences of racism. It was not until one of his friends sent a group mailing of Manny with a Hitler mustache and a swastika superimposed on his baby picture that Manny explained to me that "Racism is complex and situated. In the Dominican we make it a joke and anyone who doesn't laugh is..." His voice trailed off but then he continued, "I bet you did not know there were Nazis in the Dominican Republic. People think they came with Trujillo but they came with Columbus and they have not left. Everybody else leaves; [we are] a nation of migrants who can't ever get the right people to get out." Manny firmly believed that migration was a critical factor in shifting the way people talked and thought about race. He was uncertain if he thought migration could solve anything, however, because he felt the experience of being discriminated against in America created a new kind of silence about oppression that his linguistic games were meant to get around. He also admitted that the reason he had not wanted to talk about his own racial experiences with me was "because I am still angry. When I think about how we are treated in America, I don't ever want to go back. I want to stay here and be who I am, but I only get to be who I am if someone else gets to be who I am in America." Again his use of language played on duality; on the one hand, as we have seen, the Dominican economy was based on remittance income, without which Manny's family would not be middle class. On the other hand, Manny's statement called up the specter of both the poor and the Haitian migrants who occupy the same position in the Dominican Republic that Manny held in New York City.

Manny's "story" about blackness was particularly illustrative of the pitfalls of black-identified Dominican transnational migrants: "I am black. There is nothing cooler in NYC than a black man. And there is nothing cooler in Santo Domingo than me." Manny then stood up, spun around in a move from a Michael Jackson video, and began to sing the theme song to *The Fresh Prince of Bel-Air*.

Manny's performative "story" illustrated two key aspects of Dominican transnational migrants' relationships to American blackness: (1) the internalization of the myth of blackness as coolness and (2) the realization that race was constructed. Despite an increasing share of screen time for African-American and African Diasporic peoples in Hollywood, the criticism has remained that most of these roles are based in stereotypes, and are either about criminality, coolness, or a combination of the two (see Woll and Miller). Whether in blaxploitation films or mainstream films with only one or two black characters, there is an accepted inevitability that the black characters will be wise-cracking, stereotypical presences. In *The Fresh Prince of Bel-Air*, for instance, Will Smith's supposed intercity authenticity was juxtaposed with Carleton's bourgeois white-identified behavior in order to consistently criticize and deride upper class behavior perceived as white. Manny's adaptation of Will Smith capitalizes on the blurring of race and class and black stereotypes in order to refute binary racial constructions from which his own class and ethnicity should render him exempt. Unfortunately, the reliance on a stereotypical vision of blackness undermines the performative in this racial tale by reinscribing what Diawara called "transtextuality: an artifice which enables the performer to fill all the spaces that the old stereotype occupied and to be the star of the new show. If the old stereotype is the projection of white supremacist thinking onto black people, the new stereotype compounds matters by desiring that image, and deforming its content for a different appropriation."

Like Juana, Manny's attempts to subvert certain paradigms without critically examining others led to problematic resistance. Although Manny located his subversion in black performers that themselves critique rigid racial codes, the overall effect was to reify stereotypes of African-Americans. Moreover, since the myth of the black cool was also based on patriarchal masculinity that reinscribed female suppression while attempting to subvert racial oppression.

Finally, Manny's open embrace of blackness was met with amusement and derision from family and friends. When he spoke about race in a critical manner, his friends and family asked him to "sing that Fresh Prince song" or "do the subway guy."[6] For his Dominican peer group Manny's performative criticism was instead a kind of minstrelsy that reinforced their stereotypes about blackness rather than deconstructed them. As the Nazi photo incident illustrated, when Manny's discussions and/or actions became too transgressive, his friends and family reminded him of the racial boundaries that he was expected to uphold.

Reification: Adelina's Story
Critical to these failed attempts of subversion were an overarching discourse of social reification. Both Manny's and Juana's families reinforced whiteness even as they attempted to dismantle it. Other Dominicans in my sample openly embraced whiteness and *indio* as white privilege ideologies to maintain their own social status in the face of conflict and contradiction. Most of the Dominicans who identified as *indio/a* in my sample were visibly brown with a majority of *clara* features, middle class, and 25 or older. Their peer groups were made up of primarily white and light Latinos and white Americans. Although their families were more likely to have people with darker skin in their generation or the one

immediately preceding it, they referred to the racial incidents that these darker members endured as examples as to why American racial systems were too rigid and Dominicans were free of racism. When family members dared to tell stories of racial oppression based in blackness or to identify as black they were immediately silenced by an older member of the family or through name calling. Adelina's story represented the kind of parental policing and acquiescence typical of this group of participants.

Adelina identified as *india clara*. She had long, naturally brown hair, which lightened in summer months. Though it was not *pelo oscuro*, she still needed to blow dry her hair straight every morning or otherwise it was, in her own words, "too thick." She had a small nose, medium lips, and golden eyes and her skin was a soft honey brown. She and her siblings were all enrolled in small private colleges on the East Coast. Her grades were the best in the family. Her parents owned a small store. She had an aunt who owned a large beauty shop and an uncle who owned restaurants in both New York and the Dominican Republic. The remittance income from her family helped build the new community center in their sending community; one of the rooms in the center is named after them. Adelina's physical features, education, economic status, and transnational social capital mark her family as socially white by Dominican standards.

Adelina self-selected for my project after hearing a talk I gave about Dominican blackness. I was surprised when she chose to participate since she had bristled every single time I asserted that Dominicans were black during my talk. Despite the fact the panel was about blackness in Latin America and all of my quoted participants identified as black, Adelina took it upon herself to inform the audience "Dominicans are not black." This is the story she told the audience:

> I once came home and told my papi that several of my [Dominican] friends said we were black. Papi said "Adelina, you are the only one at the table who is black then." Everyone laughed.
> I am the darkest in my family and I am not dark. Everyone else is white. You know. We are not black.
> It is like... well... ok, I go to [a private liberal arts college in New England] and everybody there is white. There are so few Latinos it is amazing. So my [white] friend invited me to a party. They were Jewish. [long pause] So I went and they were all talking about how oppressed they were. I mean, they are rich [dramatic pause] and they are talking about how oppressed they are! People treat them badly. And there I was thinking how lucky I am. No one treats me like that.

The whole party they were talking about how people treat them, and how this party was to celebrate their survival. One of my friends offered me some food and I asked why everything had so much oil. They had to explain it to me: the oil represented their survival. I'm Catholic; I don't have to know about that. I felt so stupid.

I kept saying all of these stupid things. I mean, I'm Catholic and Spanish what do I know? I had the privilege. No one hunted us down. No one tried to kill us for being Dominicanos. I had the privilege to be ignorant about what their history is. Every time I opened my mouth, I had the privilege of offending them and having them apologize to me.

Someone who does not understand race [long pause] just sees color. That is what Americans do. But my friends were "white" [she made quotations in the air with her fingers] and I had more privilege than they did.

Adelina's story relied on several key elements in the construction of race in the Dominican Republic. It began by referring, verbally and non-verbally, to phenotypic traits that whitened Adelina. She reinforced these physical traits by referring to social class that also whitened her. Finally, Adelina used the language of whiteness established from Independence on in the Dominican Republic by referring to her Spanish heritage and Catholic faith. The reiteration of her Catholic beliefs was particularly significant since Adelina admitted later that she was not in fact Catholic. She was an atheist and her family was among the few Protestants in the Dominican Diaspora. Adelina's repetitive statement "I am Catholic" then works as code for "I am white."

Adelina also engaged in strategies of displacement in order to posit her definition of whiteness over the prevailing American one. First, she chose a group that is traditionally marginalized around the world: Jewish people. Then she relied on anti-Semitic rhetoric which posits Jewish people as wealthy and powerful, something she emphasized through strategically placed pauses, to set a stage in which she, as the supposed "oppressed Afra-Latina," should have been less powerful. Yet in her version of the story, she was not only more powerful than her hosts but also the unwitting oppressor. Lest we miss that she was equating power and race with privilege she used the word "privilege" several times in her story. Adelina's privilege negated an affiliation to blackness. Her power over visibly white people enforced her construction of herself as having access to white privilege.

The absence of a significant interrogation of either ethnicity or racism in Adelina's story served to reify Dominican narratives of whiteness. Had Adelina dealt with the ways in which Jewish people have been denied whiteness throughout history she would no longer have relied on the assertion of their whiteness to establish her own. Since privilege acted as the key element in establishing Adelina's whiteness, she also erased the oppressions Dominicans experience as Latinos and Afro-Latinos in the United States. In this way her narrative was typical of my survey sample in which the vast majority denied being discriminated against on the basis of their race while at the same time telling me stories of discrimination in open ended sessions that did not reference questions about race or racism.

In subsequent discussions, Adelina talked about the ways in which she was desired by young white and Dominican men. Again, the purpose of these stories was to reify her whiteness, since she felt that racial binaries in the U.S. precluded interracial desire. Although the exotic erotic was a typical trope in western narratives, these were often rewritten in the Dominican Republic where interracial marriages, if not color-variant marriages, were the norm. This did not mean that Adelina, or other Dominican women, were not aware of how the exotic erotic worked but rather that like other incidences of racism, Adelina willingly ignored racism in order to unrace herself. Her transnational travel reinforced this belief in her own whiteness by constantly labeling her as desirable in a language that links desire to whiteness.

Modified Reinvestment: Ramón's Story
The final group of participants whose experiences of race and racism in the United States led to new ways of thinking about race were Dominicans who identified as *indio/a, indio/a oscuro/a*, and those that most Americans would identify as dark black. Unlike white Dominicans whose experience of race allowed them to maintain their racial superiority or to modify it based on pre-existing images and metaphors, or *indios/as claros/as* whose lives in Dominican communities or constant transnational travel reinforced their proximity to whiteness and subsequent social standing, the participants in this category had experienced racism first hand. They were the most likely to be labeled black and experience racism in their daily lives in America. Their reaction to these experiences fell into two categories: a complete rejection of personal blackness or an embrace of blackness as a primary identity. The choice between the two was most often predicated by mobility. Dominicans who could return home or who believed that they would one day return home were the least likely to identify as black regardless of age or gender. Dominicans who could not return or who had

been born in the U.S. and saw it as their primary home were the most likely to identify as black. Ramón's story illustrated how those Dominicans who returned home took the stories of American racism with them but seldom used these as a launching point to discussing racism in the Dominican Republic in their daily lives.

Ramón identified as *indio*. His mother and father were Dominican; his grandparents on his father's side were Chinese. He, and most of the family, hid their Chinese heritage by dropping their last name on official documents. Like Adelina, Ramón was the darkest member of his family. He had dark brown skin, short black curly hair, a wide nose, and small, dark, eyes. His father served in the Dominican military and was a member of the Bosch cabinet. When Juan Bosch was ousted by Dominican elites and American forces, Ramon's family lost everything. Despite their economic decline, Ramon and his brothers were all college educated with at least one year spent abroad in the United States. One of his brothers owned his own business and Ramon worked for a joint Dominican and American intergovernmental agency. Though his physical features and name marked him as black, his economic, social, and educational capital granted him mediated whiteness.

Though Ramón told many stories about race in the Dominican Republic and in America, the story of his trip to a mall in Georgia was perhaps the most telling about his thoughts on race. He had gone to Georgia as part of his M.A. program and had been working with rural migrant workers to help them obtain their rights and a decent standard of living. As a result the relationship he had with them was one of privileged advocate. Yet the people he to whom he advocated treated him little better than their migrant workers and only because they knew he worked for a government agency. He had convinced himself that this dichotomy was based on rural backwardness and had gone with several white Georgians to the mall in Atlanta to unwind:

> Georgia is a racist hell hole. I don't know why anyone lives there or goes there. And the white people there are so stupid, they have absolutely no reason to think black people are less than they are. It is really amazing. [long pause] Although really it isn't any different than the way we [Dominicans] treat Haitians here [in the Dominican Republic]. In fact, the whole time I was advocating for [migrant] workers [in the U.S.] I was thinking about the Haitians [in the D.R.].
>
> One day, I went to the mall in Atlanta. I had been working really hard all week in Savannah and all I really wanted to do was get away

from rural life and be in a big city again. My friends and I drove for hours to come to the mall, and we spent almost our entire pay checks on stuff to take back [to the Dominican Republic]. I must have had like 6 or 7 bags.

On our way out of the mall, the police stopped me. I hadn't done anything! And they did not stop anyone else! They stopped me. He sighed deeply, and then continued. They made me empty out all of my bags and then show them the receipts. They actually stood there and checked every item!

When I asked them if someone had stolen something in the mall that day, they said "We don't know yet. Empty your pockets." I didn't want to because it was bad enough emptying my bags. So they started shoving me and one of them called me a "n--." He said, "You better empty your pockets boy before I do it for you." So I did.

They finally let me go, but not before they kicked all of my stuff all over the floor. I knew then that I was going home. I'm not a n--. I'm not black. He paused here to look at his skin and then looked at mine. Ramón was several shades darker than me and knew that I was proud of my blackness. Well, I am not black here [in the Dominican Republic] and I will never be black again.

Ramón's experience of working and shopping in Georgia gave him an insight into the constructed nature of race in both the Dominican Republic and the United States. His so-called "mall story" spoke to three key issues: (1) racism toward migrants in both countries, (2) disparities between definitions of blackness, and (3) the role of mobility in maintaining social status. Like Adelina's story, Ramón's story purposefully positions the speaker above and away from blackness. Unlike Adelina however, Ramón's experience of racism prevents him from erasing blackness even as he attempts to deny it power.

Although Ramón's narrative attempted to paint Georgia as unique, he ended up drawing a parallel between disparate treatment of migrants in the U.S. and the Dominican Republic. By framing his own experience of racism at the mall with the reference to disparate treatment toward migrants in both countries, his narrative also drew a parallel between racism and anti-migrant sentiment. Though these parallels are often drawn in the U.S., Dominicans traditionally eschew accusations of racism by recasting situations as national conflict between themselves and Haitians. Thus Ramón's narrative represented a critical shift in thinking about the treatment of Haitians as racism rather than nationalism.

Since he was considered black in rural Georgia he was treated as a second class citizen. His story of harassment in the mall not only contains emasculating and racist epithets but also the ready admission of state-sanctioned police that their only reason for suspecting him of shoplifting was the color of his skin. Blackness becomes synonymous with criminality in the same way that being Haitian is synonymous with criminality in the Dominican Republic. Though Ramón does not compare the incident in the mall to any such moment in the Dominican Republic, one could argue that his "mall story" begins with the parallel between the Dominican Republic and the U.S. precisely to point to this incident as another example of the racism embedded in *antihaitianismo*.

Interestingly, a similar incident did occur while Ramón and I were at a mall in Santo Domingo and my debit card was refused by a merchant. Although I was perfectly willing to go to an ATM around the corner to get money and make my purchase Ramón became openly agitated and argued with the merchant about my right to shop. He repeated several times that I was American to the shop owner to no avail. When we went around the corner to get the money he told me the shop owner did not take my card because I was black. He pointed to the racism behind constructions of Americaness in the Dominican Republic by adding, "If you were white like [my girlfriend] they would have let you use your card." The implication was that Dominican transnational dreaming crafted Americans as white; as a black woman in the Dominican Republic, it was still more likely that I was a thief than a legitimate American credit card owner.

Although Ramón's "mall story" compared the U.S. and the D.R. it also contrasted their definitions of blackness. His story ended with the statement "I knew then that I was going home. [long pause] I'm not black. Well, I am not black here [in the Dominican] and I will never be black again." This statement showed a keen understanding that race is spatially located. In the U.S. Ramón was seen as black and discriminated against in daily activities. In the D.R. Ramón was *indio* and his class, education, and ties to the government elite precluded most overt forms of disparate treatment. Prior to his incident in the U.S. he did not make connections between the treatment of Haitians and the treatment he experienced as a darker Dominican in certain situations as anti-black. Afterward, he became hyper-aware of race- and color-based oppression even as he maintained that blackness in the U.S. was more rigid and demeaning.

The conclusion of Ramón's story illustrated the desire to return to a place where he could regain his social standing. Though his skin color would not shift from place to place, the way it was interpreted would. His investment in regaining his privilege made him both aware of problems he had not seen before in his own country and less likely to challenge them when they affected his own standing. Having had the experience of blackness in an overtly anti-black situation made him invest in brownness and whiteness in a way that he had not prior to travel. His social capital remained tied up in proximity to whiteness as long as he remained in the Dominican Republic and he continued to pursue the markers needed to obtain that whiteness even as he criticized the ways blackness and Haitianness were crafted in the Dominican Republic.

Modern Interventions
Despite the preponderance of stories in which members of the Dominican diasporic community engaged in problematic re-constructions of race or in reifications of erasures of racial and color inequities, younger Dominicans in both countries were challenging racism in both cultures. In Adelina's story, for instance, it was her friends who called her black as part of their own insistence on a black consciousness in the Dominican community. They felt that Dominicans had rejected their African Diasporic roots in favor of whiteness and that particularly amongst the upper and middle classes, claims to whiteness prevented a true understanding of Dominican history.

The emphasis on Dominican racial history asserted by Dominicans like Adelina's friends represented a multidirectional discourse. In the 1960s, Dominicans themselves participated in literary movements and arts organizations that embraced co-equal racial identification through history and cultural such as *La Cultura Criolla*, *El Puño*, and *La Nueva Ola* (Atkins and Wilson 158-59). The latter was particularly important in combating the idea that racial awareness was a western construct; *La Nueva Ola* was anti-international, particularly anti-U.S., and looked specifically at Dominican racial history in order to define a new *Dominicanidad* in the post-Trujillo era. These groups were primarily urban and middle class and received state sanction from the Bosch administration (159).

The *indigenismo* movement also saw a resurgence in the 1960s that hoped to expand Dominican identity beyond the perfectibility conundrum to actual recognition of Taíno culture. Radical professional groups and university intellectuals began to write the history of Taíno cultural influences beyond rocks and drugs. They included the history of oppression endured under Spanish rule and the ties they between Taínos and African communities on the island (165).

These movements were a direct reaction to the eugenicist inspired racial narrative of the nation proposed by Trujillo. They came from an indigenous desire to revision the nation. Like most of the Caribbean, the Dominican Republic was influenced by pan-Africanism and civil rights (164-65). They were also influenced by socialist revolutions and revolutionary theories inciting indigenous cultural movements all over Latin America. It was these global and local histories that present-day movements turned to when building their own.

Despite the existence of the local and global connections to alternative racial narratives in the Dominican Republic, the racially repressive reign of Balaguer served to silence these movements. One of his first acts as President was to reverse Bosch's recognition of cultural groups as "anti-white" and to threaten those who might identify as Afro-Dominican (Atkins and Wilson 159). He also published several books on history and literature that once again erased the contributions of African and Taíno culture from *Dominicanidad*. His most famous work, *La isla al revés*, was in its eleventh edition in 2000 and is quoted widely in most cultural and history texts in the Dominican Republic. The reversal of racial discourse that Balaguer ushered into the Dominican Republic made the information from returnees and other migrants critical for the re-opening of racial discourse.

Both Ramón and Manny actively discussed race and racism in the Dominican Republic as returnees. Though their discussions lent themselves toward a reification of categories, they also opened space for racial discussions where previously there may not have been any. This kind of transformation of discursive space through border crossing was also quintessential in Juana's story where the border exists within her own family. By including black children in the make up of her rigidly policed upper-class white family, Juana reversed centuries of taboo.

Conclusion
However problematic and limited in scope trans/migrant strategies have been in challenging racial norms, they still impacted discourses in both the U.S. and the Dominican Republic. Migrants seem more aware of the constructed nature of race than non-migrants because, with the exception of the white elite, they now have the lived experience of being re-racialized. At the same time, challenges to racial discourse are also indigenous to the Dominican Republic itself. Although the experience of racism by migrants has often led to reification of racial categories in order to maintain status they have still encouraged discussion of racial paradigms. Unfortunately, as Manny's comments about racism implied, these stories were eclipsed by the promise of prosperity explored in previous chapters.

Women, like men, both challenged and internalized racism in their lived experience, organizing, and writing. In women's lived experience they were generally resistant to racial categories preferring to deal with ethnic conflict. Yet the preference for ethnic identification did not negatively impact the actions they took to confront constructions of race. Female-authored fiction, on the other hand, dealt explicitly with race and ethnicity from a gendered perspective. It provided the possibility for readers across the diaspora to discuss race and racism in both cultures.

---

[1] Note: names of organizations and participants have been changed for anonymity.

[2] The Spanish Crown commissioned paintings known as *castas* (castes) which illustrated each potential racial mixture in the colonies. Each potential racial mixture was given a name, mental and social characteristics, and status in colonial society. The paintings were meant to guide Spanish colonials in establishing order and maintaining racial supremacy. They were also painted by local artists to depict the lifestyles of various groups in the colonies and then sent back to Spain (for the most complete collection of essays on *castas*, see Katzew).

[3] Knight defined a watershed in racial identity as a moment in which the definition of a term of racial identity becomes solidified for the people who use it.

[4] Not surprisingly, when the state turned to tourism as a primary source of income, the image of promiscuous black and brown women once again circulated on the international stage. The use of images of women in traditional Haitian peasant clothes for a popular tourist newspaper to advertise nightly dance reviews, code for sex work in the Dominican Republic, had little impact on the incorporation into the national imaginary of blackness or people of Haitian descent.

[5] It is important to keep in mind here that although the Dominican Republic was still a colony in the 1600s and 1700s, slaves outnumbered white people by more than 4 to 1 (Moya Pons 40). In the sixteenth century the Spanish government also granted the bi-racial children of white and black parents the label of white to increase the overall 'non-black' population of the colony (Cassa). Thus, the number of visibly black people on the island was more accurately 5 or 6 to 1.

[6] "The subway guy" was Manny's impression of a homeless black man who asked people in the subway station closest to his sister's house for money. If they gave him money he sang blues songs for them; if they ignored him, he hurled white racial slurs at them regardless of their skin tone. Again, Manny's choice to emulate the homeless man spoke to the constructed nature of race by fixating on someone who located class oppression inside a certain racial

narrative of whiteness that superseded visible skin color. However, his performance reinforced the stereotype of the angry and shiftless black man and encouraged laughter at a black man rather than at a system that oppresses him and everyone else.

Works Cited

Atkins, G. Pope, and Larman Wilson. *The Dominican Republic and the United States: From Imperialism to Transnationalism*. Atlanta: U of Georgia P, 1998.

Buckle, Henry. *The History of the Civilization of England*. London: D. Appleton and Company, 1872.

Cassa, Roberto. "Movimientos sociales durante la intervacion military Norteamericana en la Republica Dominicana." *Ecos* 6.8 (1998): n.p.

Diawara, Manthia. "The Black Face Stereotype." *Black Cultural Studies*. N.d. <http://www.blackculturalstudies.org/m_diawara/blackface.html>.

Gobineau, Arthur. *The Inequality of the Races*. 1853. London: Howard Fertig, 1999.

Hicks, Albert. *Blood in the Streets: The Life and Rule of Trujillo*. New York: Creative Age P, 1946.

Katzew, Ilona. *Castas Paintings: Images of Race in Eighteenth-Century Mexico*. New Haven: Yale UP, 2004.

Knight, Franklin. *Race, Ehtnicity, and Class: Forging the Plural Society in Latin America and the Caribbean*. Waco: Baylor UP, 1995.

Levy, Lauren. "The Dominican Republic Haven for Jewish Refugees." *Jerusalem Post* 6 Jan. 1995. N.d. <http://www.jewishvirtuallibrary.org/jsource/Holocaust/sosua.html>.

Martinez-Fernandez, Luis. *Torn Between Empires: Economy, Society, and Patterns of Political Thought in the Hispanic Caribbean, 1840-1878*. Atlanta: U of Georgia P, 1994.

Moya Pons, Frank. *The Dominican Republic: A National History*. Princeton: Markus Wiener Publishing, 1995.

Ratzel, Friedrich. *Anthropogeographie*. N.p.: n.p., 1882.

Roorda, Eric. *The Dictator Next Door: The Good Neighbor Policy and the Trujillo Regime in the Dominican Republic*. Durham: Duke UP, 2003.

Sagas, Ernesto. *Race and Politics in the Dominican Republic*. Gainesville: U of Florida P, 2002.

Sagas, Ernesto, and Orlando Inoa. *The Dominican People: A Documentary History*. Princeton: Markus Wiener Publishers, 2003.

Simmons, Kimberly. "A Passion for Sameness: Encountering a Black Feminist Self in Fieldwork in the Dominican Republic." *Black Feminist Anthropology: Theory, Politics, Praxis, and Poetics*. Ed. Irma McClaurin. New Brunswick: Rutgers UP, 2001. 77-101.

---. "Reconfiguring Domincanness: Competing Discourses Surrounding Race, Nation, and Identity in the Dominican Republic." Diss. Michigan State U, 2002.

Slocum, Karla. (2002). "Negotiating Identity and Black Feminist Politics in Caribbean Research." *Black Feminist Anthropology: Theory, Politics, Praxis, and Poetics*. Ed. Irma McClaurin. New Brunswick: Rutgers UP, 2001. 126-49.

Torres-Saillant, Silvio. "The Tribulation of Blackness: Stages in Dominican Racial Identity." *Callaloo* 23.3 (2000): 1086-1111.

Wilhelms, Saskia. *Haitian and Dominican Sugar Cane Workers in Dominican Batayes: Patterns and Effects of Prejudice, Stereotypes, and Discrimination*. Hamburg: LIT, 1994.

Woll, Allen L., and Randall Miller. *Ethnic and Racial Images in American Film and Television*. New York: Garland, 1988.

Wucker, Michele. *Why the Cocks Fight: Dominicans, Haitians, and the Struggle for Hispaniola*. New York: Hill and Wang, 2000.

Simon Dickel

Modernism, the Harlem Renaissance, and Negotiations of Black Gay Identity in the 1980s

Ever since the publication of the first explicitly black and gay anthologies in the 1980s, such as Joseph Beam's *In the Life* (1986) and the Other Countries Collective's *Black Gay Voices* (1988), black gay writers have referred to two relevant periods within African American culture, the Harlem Renaissance of the 1920s and 30s and the Protest Era of the 1950s and 60s. What is more, they have established literary forefathers as role models, most notably Richard Bruce Nugent, Langston Hughes, and James Baldwin. The connection between 1980s black gayness, and the works and personas of Nugent, Hughes, and Baldwin serves a distinct function. The emphasis on black cultural traditions is a way to separate black gayness from the white dominated gay community. It is a means to gain self-empowerment as black gay men. But, more importantly, via the connection to periods and writers that are firmly rooted in and helped to establish the black literary tradition, black gay artists and activists aim to legitimize the existence of the black gay community in the eyes of the black community as a whole.

In the 1970s black (lesbian) feminist writers pursued a similar strategy with regard to their own heritage as black female and feminist writers. In 1975, Alice Walker published the essay "Looking for Zora," in which she describes her search for the grave of the Harlem Renaissance poet Zora Neale Hurston in Eatonville/Florida. As the exact place where Hurston is buried was in the midst of a neglected cemetery covered with weeds and was not visibly marked, Walker decided on the exact place herself and set up a gravestone with an engraving to remember Hurston. Walker's act of setting up a gravestone is a rather concrete act of constructing a black female literary heritage in order to empower herself and later generations of black female writers (107). Two years after "Looking for Zora," Barbara Smith published her landmark essay "Toward a Black Feminist Criticism," which was an important step for the emergence of a black feminist critique. In the 1980s, black gay writers used the same strategy.

Honoring Walker's essay on Hurston, Isaac Julien named his filmic meditation on Langston Hughes *Looking for Langston*. Similarly, the black gay literary critic Charles I. Nero pays tribute to Smith by naming his seminal essay on black gay writers "Toward a Black Gay Aesthetic: Signifying in Contemporary Black Gay Literature" (1991). In his essay, he draws on Henry Louis Gates's theory of Signifying. In *The Signifying Monkey*, Henry Louis Gates analyzes the ways Walker's *The Color Purple* relates to Hurston's *Their Eyes Were Watching God* as pastiche, "a joyous proclamation of antecedent and descendant texts" (xxvii).

Following Nero's approach of using Gates's theory of signifying for the analysis of black gay literature, I will discuss the relations between Richard Bruce Nugent's modernist short story "Smoke, Lilies and Jade" (1926) as antecedent text and Wallace Thurman's *Infants of the Spring* (1932), Steven Corbin's *No Easy Place to Be* (1989), and Isaac Julien's *Looking for Langston* (1989) as three descendant texts. "Smoke, Lilies and Jade" is widely regarded as the first text by an African American writer to present male homosexuality in unambiguous terms. Even if the depiction of male homosexuality is one of its transgressive dimensions and in deliberate contradiction of Alain Locke's ideal of black art formulated one year earlier in the introductory essay to his anthology *The New Negro* (1925), I will argue that the classification as a homosexual short story tends to disregard the text's bisexual, interracial and polyamorous aspects. On the basis of my reading of "Smoke, Lilies and Jade," I will then consider the ways in which the narrative was taken up in the three later texts. I will first consider Thurman's satirical Harlem Renaissance novel *Infants of the Spring* and early allusion to "Smoke, Lilies and Jade" and show how he, as Nugent's friend and contemporary, refers to all dimensions of the text's transgressive aesthetics. I will then focus on Corbin's and Julien's texts, *No Easy Place to Be* and *Looking for Langston*, both of which came out in 1989. Owing to several factors such as racism in the white dominated gay community, homophobia in the black community, and the threat of HIV/Aids, most black gay writers and filmmakers of the period proposed an explicitly black and gay aesthetics informed by discussions around identity politics. I will argue that the political context of the late 1980s is one reason for some crucial alterations in Corbin's and Julien's references to "Smoke, Lilies and Jade" that affect the story's interracial, bisexual and polyamorous dimensions.[1]

"Smoke, Lilies and Jade" (1926)

In the foreword of the anthology *The New Negro*, Alain Locke expresses his belief in the power of black art and literature for racial uplift. According to Locke, black artists should depict themselves positively in order to raise the public reputation of black people as a whole (3-16). In comparison, the younger generation of black artists and writers, among them Bruce Nugent, Langston Hughes, Zora Neale Hurston and Wallace Thurman, took a more radical approach towards art. They wrote about homosexuality and prostitution, were critical of an elitist concept of art and literature, and rejected the burden of representation, the notion that they should be representatives of and speak for the entire African American community. Often using a modernist aesthetics, they combined formal experiments with political concerns. For a long time, the modernist aesthetics of many Harlem Renaissance writers was not fully recognized. In his essay "Modernism and the Black Diaspora: Langston Hughes and the Broken Cubes of Picasso," Seth Moglen illustrates how critics have largely attributed the innovative formal experiments to white writers, whereas black writers of the period have been narrowly regarded as Harlem Renaissance writers, and he argues that, between the 1940s and the 1960s, modernism has been canonized in a "politically narrow and racially exclusionary" way, as a white aesthetic paradigm (1189). After surveying studies on modernism and the Harlem Renaissance, Moglen observes that the binarity between white modernism and the black Harlem Renaissance is deeply rooted. Black writers are excluded in important anthologies of modernist writers. According to Moglen, this canonization of modernism as a white phenomenon influenced studies of black Harlem Renaissance scholars, too (1189).[2]

Moglen's criticism does not apply to Joseph Allen Boone's study *Libidinal Currents: Sexuality and the Shaping of Modernism*. In his study, Boone has included a chapter on the "Queer Sites of Modernism," which explicitly refers to gay urban spaces of the 1920s and 30s, the Left Bank in Paris and Greenwich Village and Harlem in New York City. These gay urban spaces are the places of origin of what he calls "a neglected alternative modernism" (205) – as opposed to high modernism. The texts Boone considers as constituting this neglected alternative modernism are characterized by experimental styles of writing and by transgressive representations of gender, sexuality, and desire. Boone's argument corresponds with Moglen's emphasis on the political significance of the formal experiments of female, black, and working-class writers in the 1920s (1191).

Boone states that some of these texts "foreshadow the rise of what is now being called 'queer' in current gay studies, arts, and politics" (205). The literary anthology *Fire!!* (1926) is a prominent example of the combination of a modernist aesthetic with assumedly disrespectable topics like homosexuality and prostitution that contradicted Locke's ideals of black literature.

With the contribution of the story "Smoke, Lilies and Jade" to the first and only issue of *Fire!!*, Nugent published one of the first fictional accounts of homosexual desire in the United States. What is more, it is the first known text on that topic by an African American writer. However, this characterization runs the danger of producing an interpretation that focuses on homosexuality alone. In addition to the black protagonist's homosexual desires for a white man, the text presents various differences and their intersections, among them race, sexuality, and gender and can legitimately be categorized as a text about a black protagonist with interracial, bisexual, and polyamorous (sexual) desires.

Before reading the first sentence of "Smoke, Lilies, and Jade," the reader encounters it as a text whose experimental form is directly visible on the page. In large part, it consists of sentence fragments and ellipses. The story is written in a stream of consciousness style and is framed by the description of its protagonist, Alex, who is alone in his room lying on his bed and smoking a cigarette.

A sexual encounter between Alex and a man called Beauty whom he meets one night on the street is one of the narrative's transgressive elements. As Beauty's body is described as white several times, e.g. "two strong white legs [...] firm white thighs" (Nugent 37), the interracial nature of the encounter adds a second element of transgression. However, neither homosexuality nor interracial love is represented as an area of conflict in the text. Something else is troubling Alex's mind, namely his love for two persons. In addition to Beauty, he is in love with a black woman named Melva, and it is his affection for two persons that is the reason for his inner conflicts:

> he would like Beauty to know Melva... they were both so perfect... such compliments... yes he would like Beauty to know Melva because he loved them both... there... he had thought it... actually dared to think it... but Beauty must never know... Beauty couldn't understand... indeed Alex couldn't understand... and it pained him... almost physically... and tired his mind... Beauty... Beauty was in the air... the smoke... Beauty... Melva... Beauty... Melva... Alex slept... and dreamed. (36-37)

Alex's subsequent dream is the result of his initial belief that he has to decide between Beauty and Melva. He dreams that he is in "a field of blue smoke and black poppes [sic] and red calla lilies" (37). Searching on his hand and knees he first meets Beauty and later Melva. Beauty's and Melva's physical appearances are vividly described starting with their feet and legs and ending with their eyes. In the descriptions of their naked bodies, the differences in gender and race are clearly marked. Both of them utter a single identical sentence: "I'll wait Alex" (37). In his dream, Alex reacts in confusion each time he hears this sentence, he kisses Melva and continues his search. He cannot decide between the two.

After awaking from the dream in which he dreamed of kissing Melva only, Alex thinks "he would like to kiss Beauty's lips" (37), but he smokes a cigarette instead. In the narrative, a kiss on the lips between two men is represented as being more taboo and shameful than the sexual act. A little later Beauty kisses Alex's lips while Alex pretends to be asleep, and still later, Beauty and Alex kiss each other with their eyes open:

> Beauty's lips touched his... pressed hard... cool... opened slightly... Alex opened his eyes... into Beauty's... parted his lips... Dulce... Beauty's breath was hot and short... Alex ran his hand through Beauty's hair... Beauty's lips pressed hard against his teeth... Alex trembled... could feel Beauty's body... close against his... hot... tense... white... and soft... soft... soft.........(38)

Boone persuasively argues that this kiss signifies that "an ultimate barrier of self-actualization has been crossed" (231). After this kiss, Alex is no longer reluctant to introduce his lovers to each other (Nugent 38). In the text's last passage that is set at Coney Island, Alex's inner conflict is once again made manifest by the naming of opposites that stand for Alex's conflicted feelings for Melva and Beauty: the up- and downward movement of the rollercoaster and the ferris wheel, the change from day to dawn symbolized by sunset and subsequent moonrise, the contrast of the sound of the sea and the sound of the train, and finally Alex's memories of Melva's and Beauty's kisses. After the sensual experience of these opposites, Alex no longer feels the need to decide between his two lovers, and the conflict is resolved by Alex's thought: "one can love two at the same time" (39).

Infants of the Spring (1932)

In 1932, Wallace Thurman published *Infants of the Spring*, a satirical novel of the Harlem Renaissance, whose character Paul Arbian is based on Richard Bruce Nugent. The allusion to Nugent is indicated by Arbian's last name which evokes Nugent's initials RBN.[3] Arbian is depicted as a dandy and an artist who is very open about his sexuality (Glick 414-42). Being asked whether he prefers homosexuality or heterosexuality, Arbian answers: "'I really don't know. After all there are no sexes, only sex majorities, and the primary function of the sex act is enjoyment. Therefore I enjoyed one experience as much as the other'" (Thurman 47).

Thurman and Nugent were friends and belonged to the group of younger black artists who opposed the demand for positive representations of blackness. Next to "Smoke, Lilies and Jade," it was Thurman's contribution of his short story "Cordelia the Crude," which deals with prostitution, that made the magazine *Fire!!* scandalous. J. Martin Favor argues that *Infants of the Spring* is "both parody and documentary. Indeed that is what makes it effective satire" (203). In *Infants of the Spring*, the Harlem Renaissance is far from being idealized. Favor observes that

> the character Paul Arbian worships great artists, but remains stuck within the walls of "Niggerati Manor" when it comes to his own works. This house where the central characters live and work is far from a productive salon, generating ground-breaking works of art, music and literature. Rather, it is a kind of intellectual ghetto occasionally patronized by elites who have little genuine interest in advancing the careers of African American artists, except as they might be able to produce hackneyed "racial" art. (202-03)

In *Infants of the Spring*, Arbian tells his friends about a (homo-) erotic dream he had which clearly alludes to "Smoke, Lilies and Jade." He dreamed that he was in a field of beautiful flowers, among them "white lilies, red lilies, pale narcissi, slender orchids, polychromatic pansies, jaundiced daffodils, soporific lotus blossoms" (Thurman 45). This list of flowers signifies homosexuality. In his study *Gay New York*, George Chauncey states that the use of names of flowers for homosexual men, such as pansy, was so common in the 1920s and 30s that "they were sometimes simply called 'horticultural lads'" (15). The lilies directly refer to the lilies in the title of Nugent's story. And as Charles C. Eldredge has shown, for modernists, calla lilies were easily identifiable as a symbol of homo- and bisexuality. Arbian's narration of the dream continues and becomes more explicit:

> I lay down. Then I became aware of a presence. An ivory body exuding some exotic perfume. Beauty dimmed my eyes. The physical nearness of that invisible presence called to me, lured me closer. And as I crept nearer, the perfume pervaded my nostrils, inflamed my senses, anesthetized my brain. My hand reached out and touched a silken forelock. Involuntarily, my eyes closed and I was conscious of being sucked into it until there was a complete merging. For one brief moment I experienced complete ecstasy. (45)

By the use of the term "ivory," the body is marked as white whereas the gender is not specified. Like the male character in Nugent's "Smoke, Lilies and Jade," the presence is called Beauty. At the end of the quotation, Arbian makes the sexual nature of the encounter in the dream between himself and Beauty explicit, a reference to the sexually explicit narrative of "Smoke, Lilies and Jade." In the short account of Arbian's dream, Thurman has captured some of the key elements that made "Smoke, Lilies and Jade" scandalous, the homoeroticism indicated by the setting in a field of flowers, the interracial sexual encounter between the black Arbian and the white person, the indeterminacy of the body's gender, and the sexual overtones in Arbian's account of his dream. In the novel, Thurman gives a satirical account of the Niggerati, the group of younger Harlem Renaissance artists he belonged to himself. By depicting Arbian as a bohemian artist who does not care about sexual conventions Thurman once again questions Locke's ideal of the New Negro and the need for positive representations of blackness. As *Infants of the Spring* was written during the time of the Harlem Renaissance, the text's references to "Smoke, Lilies and Jade" have to be seen in a different political context than those in Corbin's and Julien's texts from 1989.

No Easy Place to Be (1989)

Steven Corbin's 1989 novel *No Easy Place to Be* is set during the time of the Harlem Renaissance and depicts the social and political life in 1920s Harlem. The Harlem Renaissance is represented as a microcosm, and the novel's characters are represented as types. For example, each of the three sisters, who are at the center of the novel, embodies a different facet of social and political life in Harlem. Miriam is a political activist and follower of Marcus Garvey and works as a nurse; Velma is a black writer associated with the writers and artists of the period and the very light-skinned Louise works as a showgirl at the Cotton Club and decides to pass as white.

In my analysis, I will limit my focus on how the characters Rudy, Melva, and Scott allude to the fictional characters of Nugent's story "Smoke, Lilies and Jade." The most direct reference to "Smoke, Lilies and Jade" can be deduced from the name "Velma," where Velma is an anagram of the name "Melva," the female lover in Nugent's story. I suggest that the constellation of Melva, Alex and Beauty in "Smoke, Lilies and Jade" serves as a basis for the relationship of the three friends Velma, Rudy and Scott. Rudy's character is loosely based on Alex, the protagonist of "Smoke, Lilies and Jade," and there are references to its author Nugent, as well, while Scott is broadly reminiscent of Beauty. The relationship between Velma, Rudy and Scott develops just after Rudy and Velma meet Scott for the first time. Scott invites them for a midnight picnic on Brooklyn Bridge. The time and place of their meeting is instructive. As "the nighttime walkways of the city's downtown bridges have traditionally been heavy homosexual cruising areas, practically since their opening" (Delany 213), a context open to sexual possibilities is directly evoked in this scene.

After drinking wine and smoking marijuana, Rudy, Scott and Velma emphasize their mutual friendship with an embrace. At first, Velma feels excluded from Rudy's and Scott's hug:

> She [Velma] walked toward [Scott], her arms outstretched for an embrace. Scott walked toward her, passing her, and threw his arms around Rudy, who half-heartedly returned the hug. Velma stood motionless, not knowing what to do. (100)

But when she joins the two men in their embrace a few moments later, the three of them become a "triangle of inebriated passion" (ibid.). The passage on the bridge is a foreshadowing of their relationship. During the course of the novel, each of them will have sex with the other two friends respectively. However, the constellation in *No Easy Place to Be* is more complicated than that in "Smoke, Lilies and Jade." The relationship of Velma, Rudy, and Scott is determined by jealousy as well as by their sexual identities. Whereas Velma loves both men and enjoys having sex with them, Rudy, after their first sexual encounter, does not want to pursue a sexual relationship with Velma. He is sexually attracted to Scott who in turn wants a monogamous relationship with Velma. Nevertheless, he once had an enjoyable homosexual experience when he lived in Paris, and on one occasion he tries to make Velma jealous by having sex with Rudy.

Velma points out to Rudy the complications arising from her being in love with two men. At the same time, her statement illustrates that being in love with two men – "one can love two at the same time" (Nugent 39) – is an excellent theme for literature, a twofold reference to Nugent's short story as well as Corbin's novel itself:

> "Everything's so damn crazy. I'm in love with Scott. You're in love with Scott; Scott loves me; I'm in love with you. Gosh! There must be a novel in there or something, wouldn't you say? At least." (309)

In highlighting the complications connected with Velma's being in love with two men and with Rudy's homosexuality, *No Easy Place to Be* points to the transgressive elements that Nugent presents in "Smoke, Lilies and Jade." Altering the bisexual and interracial dimensions of the short story to a narrative that presents only black characters who arrive at static, unambiguously homosexual and heterosexual identities, Corbin strengthens black gay identity.

On one occasion, *No Easy Place to Be* indirectly refers to "Smoke, Lilies and Jade." Rudy is awakened by Velma because of a quarrel that ends in a physical fight between the two friends. Like Alex in "Smoke, Lilies and Jade" Rudy had been lying in his bed dreaming, and he thinks afterwards, "had he known, or barely sniffed the nature of her 'emergency,' he wouldn't have budged from his Murphy bed. As it was, she'd awakened him from a wet dream he was having about Scott" (362). Because of the parallels between Melva and Alex and Velma and Rudy, the wet dream Rudy refers to is arguably an allusion to the dream described in "Smoke, Lilies and Jade."

Rather than homosexuality or bisexuality, it is the fact of Alex's being in love with two persons that Nugent presents as an area of conflict (Schwarz 135), and this is precisely the focus *No Easy Place to Be* takes in referring to "Smoke, Lilies and Jade." In contrast to Nugent who represents the perspective of Alex, Corbin puts the female protagonist Velma at the center of the narrative. Whereas "Smoke, Lilies and Jade" concentrates on Alex's adoration for Beauty rather than for Melva, she – as Velma – rather than Rudy is the one who has to come to terms with her love for two persons.

In "Smoke, Lilies and Jade," Beauty is represented as a white man, adding the transgressive element of interracial love to the topics of homosexuality and polyamory. This dimension is omitted in the relationship of Rudy, Velma and

Scott, all of whom are black. Nevertheless, the emphasis on Scott's physical beauty alludes to the character Beauty in Nugent's story. When Velma meets Scott for the first time, she thinks: "If Adonis was Negro [...] he would look like this" (Corbin 90). In his study *When Harlem Was In Vogue*, David Levering Lewis characterizes Beauty as a "Hispanic Adonis" (197). As it is not unlikely that Corbin knew Lewis's 1981 study at the time he wrote his novel, one could cautiously argue that he uses the name "Adonis" to refer to Beauty. Adonis, the symbol of male beauty stemming from Greek mythology, is frequently referred to in gay sub-culture and has thus become a gay icon. By comparing Scott, a black man, to the white Adonis, Corbin directs the reader's attention to the beauty of black men, making this strategy of empowerment of black men comparable to the 1960s slogan "black is beautiful." In the context of this black gay narrative, it is also an encouragement for black gay readers to recognize the beauty of other black men as well as their own.

Looking for Langston (1989)

Employing an avant-garde aesthetic, Isaac Julien's 1989 film *Looking for Langston* is constructed as a collage without a linear storyline. The black and white film consists of newly directed scenes and archival footage evoking a combination of three historical periods, the Harlem Renaissance, the 1950s and 60s, and the late 1980s. Two of the film's protagonists are called Alex and Beauty, and one scene is a direct adaptation of "Smoke, Lilies and Jade."

The scene is a dream sequence framed by cigarette smoke alluding to the title and main motif of Nugent's story. Throughout the scene, the soundtrack consists of the voice-over narration of a part of "Smoke, Lilies and Jade" illustrated by the images projected on screen. Alex imagines himself walking in a field of grass. He meets Beauty who is standing naked in a field of lilies. Alex touches his body. Beauty speaks one sentence "I'll wait." The second half of the scene takes place in a bedroom. Beauty and Alex are lying on the bed with Beauty resting his head in Alex's lap. The image is modeled after a photograph by the white homosexual photographer George Platt Lynes. Platt Lynes's 1952 photograph is entitled "John Leaphart and Robert 'Buddy' McCarthy" and it depicts two naked men, one black and one white (Leddick 152). The black man rests his head in the lap of the white man with his eyes closed. This reproduction of the Lynes image invites us to interpret it against the background of the film's critique of the practices of white male homosexual artists, particularly Carl Van Vechten and Robert Mapplethorpe.[4]

With regard to the scene outlined above, Henry Louis Gates states in his essay "The Black Man's Burden" that Nugent's story "receives perhaps the most elaborate and effecting tableau vivant in Julien's film" (232). Later in his essay Gates argues that "the importance of open-textured films such as *Looking for Langston* is in presenting an aesthetics that can embrace ambiguity" (238). If one looks at Julien's adaptation of Nugent's story, however, the sexual and racial ambiguity of "Smoke, Lilies and Jade" is recast as a rather unambiguous narrative. Instead of representing Alex's interracial and bisexual relationship to Beauty, a white man, and Melva, a black woman, the film depicts Beauty as a black man and leaves Melva out altogether. What is more, the excerpts from "Smoke, Lilies and Jade" that are read in the voice-over narration are deliberately altered. In addition to some minor omissions to make the passage more comprehensible for the viewer and the fact that wherever the name Alex is used in Nugent's text, the voice-over narrator uses the personal pronoun 'he,' there are two crucial alterations that change the sense of Nugent's text as a whole.

The first major alteration concerns Alex's inner conflict because of his love for two persons. The part of Alex's dream in which he encounters the naked Melva whom he kisses on the lips is left out altogether. His resulting confusion and inner conflict because of his love for two persons is altered to a conflict in which he has to come to terms with his homosexuality. The second alteration concerns the omission of the racial markers that can be found in Nugent's story. Whereas in "Smoke, Lilies and Jade" Beauty's naked body is repeatedly described with the adjective "white," the Julien scene shows a black man standing in the field of white Lilies. In "Smoke, Lilies and Jade," Beauty's whiteness is once again emphasized in the passage: "Alex trembled... could feel Beauty's body... close against his... hot... tense... white... and soft... soft... soft" (38). The voice-over narrator in the scene simply omits the word "white" in this very sentence and thus adjusts the narrative to the image of the two black men on the screen.

Whereas Julien's avant-gardist film language corresponds to the experimental style of "Smoke, Lilies and Jade," the adaptation of the story's contents unequivocally supports the project of constructing a black gay literary heritage. In the case of Corbin's and Julien's texts, black gay identity is strengthened through narrowing down of the sexual possibilities in Nugent's story. In their adaptations of "Smoke, Lilies and Jade," Corbin and Julien neglect the story's queer and polyamorous elements. Rather than deconstructing stable notions of hetero- and homosexuality and questioning monogamy in favor of polyamorous models of relationships, they affirm black gay identity and leave out the aspect of polyamory.

With their alterations of Nugent's short story, Corbin and Julien implicitly take sides in a political debate that started in the second half of the 1980s. At the time, black gay cultural activists debated the implications of gay interracial love and sexuality. Much of this debate was fueled by the slogan "black men loving black men is the revolutionary act of the eighties" which goes back to an influential article by the late black gay activist Joseph Beam written for the *Gay Community News* in 1985. The article was later re-printed in the anthology *Brother to Brother* as "Brother to Brother: Words from the Heart."[5] The slogan was taken up again in Marlon Riggs's 1989 film *Tongues Untied*. At the end of the film, the slogan appears on the screen and the reference to the 1980s is omitted. In his poem "Tongues Untied" which he performs in the film, Riggs vividly depicts his experiences of racism within the white gay community. He criticizes his own invisibility and the omnipresence of stereotypical images of black men as hypersexual within white gay contexts. He finally leaves the white gay community "in search of something better" (202), the promise of an autonomous black gay community. This autonomous organization can be seen in the publication of numerous black gay periodicals, the founding of black gay writers' workshops, such as the Other Countries Collective, and the publication of black gay anthologies, among them *In the Life* (1986), *Black Gay Voices* (1988), *The Road Before Us: 100 Black Gay Poets* (1991), and *Brother to Brother: New Writings by Black Gay Men* (1991). In his essay "Jungle Fever? Black Gay Identity Politics, White Dick, and the Utopian Bedroom," the literary critic and writer Darieck Scott reconsiders the emergence of black gay identity in the 1980s and explains the two sides of Beam's slogan "black men loving black men." He argues that on the one hand it can be understood as it was originally intended in Beam's essay as a demand for "mutual nurturing" but Scott also shows that at the same time it has become a "directive against interracial dating" (304). Scott warns against the implications of rigid constructions of black gay identity. He states that "the creators of black gay identity, while explicitly criticizing the hierarchy of desirability constructed in white gay social and political life, implicitly reinscribe that hierarchy's static concept of desire" (303). With his multi-layered depictions of interracial gay sexuality in his next films *Young Soul Rebels* (1991) and *The Attendant* (1992), Julien changed his approach and added new facets to discussions about black gay identity.

Conclusion

Owing to its modernist form and transgressive contents, "Smoke, Lilies and Jade" can be regarded as a text belonging to what Boone has termed a "neglected alternative modernism." Six years after the publication of "Smoke, Lilies and Jade," Thurman alludes to the text's transgressive elements in his satirical novel *Infants of the Spring*. As Thurman belongs to the younger generation of Harlem Renaissance artists who questioned the need to produce positive representations of blackness, his references to "Smoke, Lilies and Jade" fulfill a different function than those by Corbin and Julien. Whereas Thurman satirizes the artistic movement he belongs to himself and once again emphasized the transgressive elements of Nugent's short story, Corbin and Julien produce their texts in retrospect. In their 1980s references to "Smoke, Lilies and Jade" the story's bisexuality, polyamory, and interracial sexuality are altered in favor of coherent black gay narratives. On a formal level, Corbin and Julien choose different approaches. Because of its didactic aims, *No Easy Place to Be* is not laid out as experimental fiction, and it does not allude to the formal experiments of modernist texts. *Looking for Langston*, however, follows avant-gardist cinematographic traditions in order to pay tribute to the modernist experiments of the Harlem Renaissance writers and artists. Corbin's and Julien's alterations of Nugent's account of bisexual, polyamorous, and interracial love to confirmations of black gay identity have to be seen in the context of the newly emerging black gay culture of the 1980s. During this decade, strategies of confirming a black gay heritage and identity were an important step in the emancipation of black gay men who had to become visible in order to fight against the threats of white gay racism, homophobia, and Aids.

[1] In chapter four of my forthcoming book *Black/Gay: The Harlem Renaissance, the Protest Era, and Constructions of Black Gay Identity in the 1980s and 90s*, I have used and elaborated on the argument put forward in this essay.

[2] For a critical re-evaluation of the scholarship on the Harlem Renaissance, see Hutchinson.

[3] In his study on the Harlem Renaissance, Steven Watson even quotes a passage from *Infants of the Spring* that refers to Arbian in order to illustrate his biographical chapter on Nugent (90).

[4] For a discussion on the intersections of race and sexuality in the photographs of Mapplethorpe, see the essays by Mercer and Muñoz.

[5] In the article, while including all black men, Beam explicitly addresses black gay men. He wants his political demands to be understood as a strategy for all black men to survive in a racist society, an agenda "which is not rooted in any particular sexual, political, or class affiliation, but in our mutual survival" (242).

Works Cited

Beam, Joseph. "Brother to Brother: Words From the Heart." *Brother to Brother: New Writings by Black Gay Men*. Ed. Essex Hemphill. Boston: Alyson, 1991. 230-42.

---. *In the Life: A Black Gay Anthology*. Boston: Alyson, 1986.

Boone, Joseph Allen. *Libidinal Currents: Sexuality and the Shaping of Modernism*. Chicago: U of Chicago P, 1998.

Chauncey, George. *Gay New York: Gender, Urban Culture, and the Making of the Gay World, 1890-1940*. New York: Basic Books, 1994.

Corbin, Steven. *No Easy Place to Be*. New York: Simon and Schuster, 1989.

Delany, Samuel R. "Atlantis Rose: Some Notes on Hart Crane." *Longer Views: Extended Essays*. Ed. Samuel R. Delany. Hanover: UP of New England, 1996. 174-250.

Dickel, Simon. *Black/Gay: The Harlem Renaissance, the Protest Era, and Constructions of Black Gay Identity in the 1980s and 90s*. Berlin: LIT, 2011.

Eldrege, Charles C. "Calla Moderna: 'Such a Strange Flower.'" *Georgia O'Keeffe and the Calla Lily in American Art, 1860-1940*. Ed. Barbara Buhler Lynes, and Georgia O'Keeffe. New Haven: Yale UP, 2002. 4-37.

Favor, J. Martin. "George Schuyler and Wallace Thurman: Satirists." *The Cambridge Companion to the Harlem Renaissance*. Ed. George Hutchinson. Cambridge: Cambridge UP, 2007. 198-212.

Gates, Henry Louis, Jr. "The Black Man's Burden." *Fear of a Queer Planet: Queer Politics and Social Theory*. Ed. Michael Warner. Minneapolis: U of Minnesota P, 1993. 230-38.

---. *The Signifying Monkey: A Theory of Afro-American Literary Criticism*. New York: Oxford UP, 1988.

Glick, Elisa F. "Harlem's Queer Dandy: African-American Modernism and the Artifice of Blackness." *MFS Modern Fiction Studies* 49.3 (2003): 414-42.

Hutchinson, George. *The Harlem Renaissance in Black and White*. Cambridge: Belknap-Harvard UP, 1995.

Julien, Isaac. Dir. *Looking for Langston*. London: BFI, 2005. DVD.

Leddick, David. *George Platt Lynes 1907-1955*. Köln: Taschen, 2000.

Lewis, David L. *When Harlem Was In Vogue*. New York: Knopf, 1981.

Locke, Alain, ed. *The New Negro*. New York: Touchstone, 1997.

Mercer, Kobena. "Reading Racial Fetishism: The Photographs of Robert Mapplethorpe." *Welcome to the Jungle: New Positions in Black Cultural Studies*. New York: Routledge, 1994. 171-220.

Moglen, Seth. "Modernism in the Black Diaspora: Langston Hughes and the Broken Cubes of Picasso." *Callaloo* 25.4 (2002): 1189-1205.

Muñoz, José Esteban. "Photographs of Mourning: Melancholia and Ambivalence in Van der Zee, Mapplethorpe, and Looking for Langston." *Disidentifications: Queers of Color and the Performance of Politics*. Minneapolis: U of Minnesota P, 1999. 57-74.

Nugent, Richard Bruce. "Smoke, Lilies and Jade." *Fire!!* Ed. Wallace Thurman. Metuchen: Fire!! P, 1982. 33-39.

Other Countries. *Other Countries: Black Gay Voices*. New York City: Other Countries, 1988.

Riggs, Marlon. "Tongues Untied." *Brother to Brother: New Writings by Black Gay Men*. Ed. Essex Hemphill. Boston: Alyson, 1991. 200-05.

Schwarz, A. B. Christa. *Gay Voices of the Harlem Renaissance*. Bloomington: Indiana UP, 2003.

Scott, Darieck. "Jungle Fever? Black Gay Identity Politics, White Dick, and the Utopian Bedroom." *GLQ* 1.3 (1994): 299-321.

Thurman, Wallace. *Infants of the Spring*. 1932. Boston: Northeastern UP, 1992.

Walker, Alice. "Looking for Zora." *In Search of Our Mothers' Gardens: Womanist Prose*. Ed. Alice Walker. San Diego: Harcourt Brace Jovanovich, 1983. 93-116.

Watson, Steven. *The Harlem Renaissance: Hub of African-American Culture, 1920-1930*. New York: Pantheon, 1995.

Alison D. Goeller

Zora on the Mountain: Zora Neale Hurston's Artistic Exodus in *Moses, Man of the Mountain*

In 1939, a year after she published *Their Eyes Were Watching God*, the book that eventually secured her place in the American literary canon, Zora Neale Hurston published her third novel, *Moses, Man of the Mountain*, a text she had been working on since 1934 and had finished while she was employed by the WPA in her hometown of Eatonville, Florida. Like *Their Eyes* it received mixed reviews, the most disappointing coming from colleagues. Alain Locke, for example, labeled it a "caricature instead of a portrait," and Ralph Ellison noted that "for fiction it did nothing for the Negro" (qtd. in Hemenway 273). Hurston herself was not entirely happy with the book. "I have the feeling of disappointment about it. I don't think that I achieved all that I set out to do" (Kaplan 422), she wrote to Edwin Osgood Grover, a professor at Rollins College, an all-white coed institution in Winter Park, Florida. Grover had supported Hurston in her 1932 production of her play *The Great Day*, and she dedicated the book to him.

Exactly what Hurston had set out to do in this Modernist/African Americanist re-telling of the story of Moses leading his people to freedom has been the subject of critical debate ever since, though, living in the shadow of *Their Eyes*, *Moses* has not received the critical attention it deserves. Of course, it is perhaps understandable that readers of Hurston's beloved story about Janie Crawford Killicks Starks Woods' journey to self-fulfillment would be disappointed in a book about Moses, an Old Testament patriarch. Indeed, though one of its major themes is the liberation of African Americans thinly disguised as Old Testament Hebrews, one wonders why Hurston seems to have abandoned her theme of female liberation. After all, as Mary Helen Washington points out, Janie was one of the few – and certainly the earliest – heroic black women in the Afro-American literary tradition ("Zora Neale Hurston"16), and *Their Eyes*, with its strong female presence, was "inherently a critique of the male-dominated folk culture" (Foreword xiii), representing "a woman redefining and revising a male-dominated canon" (Foreword xiv). Indeed, Alice Walker's by now legendary defense of Hurston's text at the 1979 MLA Conference in San Francisco was based on the notion that Hurston's novel represented a critique of that canon and that "women did not have to speak when men thought they should" (Foreword xii). Perhaps even more importantly, as Washington points out, *Their Eyes* "shows us a woman writer struggling with the problem of the questing heroine as woman and the difficulties in 1937 of giving a woman character such power and such daring" (Foreword xiv). Had Hurston, then, given up on her "project" by turning to the story of Moses?

I would like to suggest that *Moses, Man of the Mountain* is, in fact, about a woman's journey towards freedom, a woman even more fascinating and enigmatic than Janie. That woman is Hurston herself. My premise is this: if *Their Eyes* is Hurston's interrogation of issues of gender and female freedom via the trope of finding one's voice, *Moses*, I contend, can be read as a narrative of what it meant for Hurston to be a writer in the first half of the twentieth century. Her story of Moses' uneasy leadership among the Hebrews, his efforts to liberate them from Egyptian bondage and to deliver the voice of a new God to his people, serve as a kind of palimpsest of Hurston's own uneasy "project" as a major literary figure of the Harlem Renaissance, a serious student of anthropology, and a gifted writer dedicated to securing her place, not just among African American writers, but among writers of the Modernist canon. In her special retelling of the Moses story, Hurston investigates what she felt to be her artistic responsibility, her mission to "translate" and represent her community's authentic linguistic identity, thus contributing to their cultural liberation and integrity. At the same time Hurston recognizes, in Moses' struggle, the challenges and obstacles she herself constantly faced in her own exodus to forge her unique path as a writer and a scholar.

It has become almost a cliché that Hurston was the undisputed champion of African American vernacular speech and that, in the words of Henry Louis Gates Jr. in his afterword to *Their Eyes*, it "became the fundamental framework for all but one of her novels" (197). From childhood she had been exposed to the porch talk in her hometown of Eatonville, Florida, the first all-black incorporated town in America, and was deeply affected by the vitality of the stories she heard and of the language they were told in, where "men sat around the store on boxes and benches and passed this world and the next one through their mouths" (Hurston, *Dust Tracks* 45). More importantly, Hurston felt she had been chosen to give voice to this rich vernacular tradition. In the description of watching her dying mother in *Dust Tracks* she hints at this sense of calling: "She looked at me or so I felt, to speak for her. She depended on me for a voice" (63). Hurston also tells us she had dreams and visions early in her life that foreshadowed her self-appointed, lifelong mission and that "the weight of the commandment laid heavy and made me moody at times" (43).

This mission, in part, was fulfilled when she began studying anthropology under the direction of Franz Boas at Columbia, where she had the opportunity to record the vernacular speech she had heard as a child and, in the words of Robert Hemenway, "to show that Afro-American folk expression was not subordinate to Anglo-American high art" (206). Indeed, what Hurston discovered, if she hadn't already known it, was, according to Claudia Roth Pierpoint, "a record of the unique explosion that occurred when African people with an intensely musical and oral culture came up hard against the King James Bible and the sweet-talking American South" (80). Moreover, Hurston was aware that such language was a means of power. In her first novel, what Rita Dove has called a "glorious paen to the power of the word" (xv), *Jonah's Gourd Vine* (1934), the protagonist, John Pearson, discovers his strength through his smooth talking and mesmerizing sermons. The power of language is also a major theme in *Their Eyes*, first introduced by Nanny, who had "wanted to preach a great sermon about colored women sittin' on high, but they wasn't no pulpit for me" (16). Later, of course, Janie fulfills Nanny's wishes by learning to "have de nerve tuh say what you mean" (109) and then telling Pheobe her story so she can pass it on to the other women in the community.

In *Moses, Man of the Mountain*, Hurston further explores this theme. The very beginning of the novel establishes the importance of having a voice; without it one is powerless. Unlike the mighty Pharaoh, who delivers long speeches and is entitled to say whatever he likes, the Hebrew women must literally stifle their voices during childbirth so their newborn sons won't be discovered and killed. In the King James' version of the story, Moses, of course, is one of these sons, left among the bulrushes and then found by the royal family who raise him as their own. In Hurston's version, however, Moses is Egyptian, the son of an Egyptian princess and an Abyssinian prince. But the Hebrew community believes Moses to be one of their own because Miriam, told to watch her baby brother, who had been placed in a basket in order to be saved, falls asleep, then wakes up to discover the baby is gone. In order to escape punishment, she makes up a story in which she claims that the widowed Egyptian princess had found the baby and taken him to the palace. Thus, in Hurston's version Moses is African, establishing the novel as an allegory of the struggle for African American liberation from slavery, which as, Timothy P. Caron and others have pointed out, had been a trope of African American folklore since before the Civil War (57). However, Miriam's lies spread throughout the community and are embellished to such an extent that even Moses, when he grows to manhood, is himself not quite sure who he is. Later, when he kills the Egyptian overseer whom he has seen brutally whipping one of the Hebrew slaves (91), he becomes aligned with the Israelites and seriously considers that he might, in fact, be a Hebrew (92).

This question of identity, I would like to suggest, can be seen as a paradigm for Hurston's own infamous struggle with her identity as an artist and also with the very act of writing itself. Refusing to stay within safe borders, crossing and re-crossing both artistic as well as geographical lines, Hurston changed identities as often as she changed residences. Writer, anthropologist, folklorist, playwright, performer, and teacher, she struggled with what Hemenway in his biography calls her "vocational schizophrenia" (63). She even crossed borders within genres. As Wendy Dutton suggests in her article on Hurston and voodoo, she was ahead of her time in merging literature with anthropology, something she was criticized for at the time, but which, significantly, anticipated the post-Modernist penchant for collapsing generic boundaries. Or in the words of Paola Boi, Hurston "refused to deal with reality in terms of a narrow, black-white binary opposition" (108). In fact, she can be seen as a kind of trickster, just as Moses, who recognizes that "[e]verybody is two-sided" (*Moses* 82), literally and figuratively crosses and re-crosses his own borders. Hurston, too, crossed boundaries of discourse, of language, mediating between black and white registers. Her strategy, revolutionary in its execution, was, unfortunately, misunderstood by most readers.

This "border jumping" is best illustrated in the novel through Moses' apprenticeship with the two figures who are responsible for his development as a leader and as a conjure man: first Mentu (in Egypt) and then later with Jethro (in Midian). A precocious and inquisitive boy who is always reading books and asking questions, reminiscent of Hurston's own compulsive childhood curiosity as described in *Dust Tracks*, Moses is attracted to Mentu, the illiterate old man who tends the Pharaoh's horses, because he teaches him the language of animals and plants, what he refers to as "lizard talk" (60). This compels Moses to "sneak into the temples of the priests where he learn[s] to feed the sacred snakes and handle the altar fires [...] and beg[s] to be taught the mysteries of signs and omens" (60). Moses' education under Mentu, like Hurston's own field work as an anthropologist under Franz Boas in the thirties in the American South, in Haiti, and in Jamaica, results in his becoming at times more participant than observer and eventually the "finest hoodoo man in the world" (147). Likewise, Hurston discovered the participatory nature of African-based folklore when she worked as an anthropologist, according to Franz Boas, "enter[ing] into the homely life of the southern Negro as one of them" and also "gaining the confidence of the voodoo doctors" (xiii). In her introduction to the novel she identifies Moses as Damballa, "the highest god in the Haitian pantheon" (xxii). He is also mentioned in both *Mules and Men* (184) and *Tell My Horse* (257). Hurston had even written a short story in 1934, "Fire and Cloud," in which Moses, rod in hand, conjures up flies and talks to a lizard.

Mentu is also important to Moses' education because he tells Moses about the Book of Thoth that will give him power to "know the secrets of the deep" (73) and then encourages him to find it. This mission, in addition to having provoked the Pharaoh's anger for killing the overseer, prompts Moses to leave Egypt. In one of the most compelling passages of the novel, reverberating with the rhythms of a Baptist sermon, Moses crosses over the Red Sea because "You have to go to life to know life" (105), echoing not only Janie's pronouncement to Pheobe in *Their Eyes* but more importantly underscoring Hurston's own crossing of artistic and geographical borders and her emphasis on lived experience in her own work.

Before Moses finds the Book of Thoth, however, he meets Jethro, "the stern patriarch" (264) of Midian, who teaches him more magic and also encourages him to use the language of the people because "[i]ts [sic] no use of talking unless people understand what you say" (121), a philosophy Hurston herself subscribed to. But as Susan Edwards Meisenhelder points out in *Hitting a Straight Lick with a Crooked Stick*, Jethro's teachings are primarily in order to procure power for his student, so that Moses can lead his people. Where Mentu's stories foster Moses' Africanist and spiritual education, Jethro's tutelage represents Hurston's Western academic education (Meisenhelder 119), a way into the Modernist literary canon, which she needed in order to be recognized as a serious writer. Although Hurston recognized both the Africanist and the Western traditions as vital to her development as an artist, such a strategy opened up her work to the criticism of many of her fellow writers, who either thought she was pandering to a white audience, or, like Ralph Ellison, misunderstood her work, claiming it was "artistically irrelevant" (qtd. in Boi 108) because it strayed from the tenants of Modernism. Recent re-examinations of Modernism, however, would suggest that Hurston's interest in dialect and in lively language, her "rich use of metaphor" (Scott 14), were an integral part of the Modernist tradition. Bonnie Kime Scott has noted in *The Gender of Modernism*, for example, that Hurston's "interest in language other than standard English [...] can be related to the prodigious word play of Joyce and Stein" (14), both paradigms of Modernism. And, as Paola Boi points out, Ellison's criticism of Hurston is not very convincing as "he himself delved too deeply into the realm of black folklore and manifested too similar a taste for puns, jives, and the dozens" (108).

Eager for Moses to carry on with his mission, Jethro, a possible stand-in for Franz Boas, Hurston's mentor at Columbia, reminds Moses that he must find the Book of Thoth at Koptos. So Moses again crosses over, finds the Book, and then "was able to command the heavens and the earth, the abyss and the mountain, and the sea. He knew the language of the birds of the air, the creatures that people the deep" (154). Significantly, so as not to forget what he has learned, he internalizes the text by copying the words onto papyrus, washing the papyrus with beer, and then drinking the beer. When he returns after a year, Jethro tells Moses he's now ready "for the big job" (155) of saving the Israelites, of fulfilling his mission as the chosen one to speak to God on the mountain (137). Like Hurston, who early on had dreams that indicated she was on a mission, Moses recognizes "this was the place that had called him in his unfinished dreams since childhood" (120).

However, Moses is reluctant to wield his power and to take on the role of leader. For one thing, he had already been accused by the Hebrews of trying to be their "bossman" (94). He also feels they won't understand his mission, something Hurston, of course, often felt was true about her own literary projects. As John Lowe points out, Hurston "saw herself as a leader and spokesperson and was all too aware of the resentment that her education and pronouncements frequently created in the community she wished to serve" (228). Moreover, Moses would rather sit on the mountain and ask God questions; he doesn't want to be a preacher, just as Hurston rejected overt racial politics in her writing, a reticence that stirred up the wrath of writers like Richard Wright, Alain Locke, Arna Bontemps, Ralph Ellison and other members of the Harlem Renaissance who felt it was her duty to lead her people by writing socially conscious books and by focusing on race. Ralph Ellison, for instance, said her work was "socially unconscious" (qtd. in Boi 108). Richard Wright attacked Hurston's *Mules and Men* as a "minstrel technique that makes the white folks laugh" (qtd. in Delbanco 105) and *Their Eyes* as "having no theme, no message, no thought" (qtd. in Hurston, *Their Eyes* x). Sterling Brown wanted her to be more bitter, and Roy Wilkins said she was a peddler of nostalgia for the Jim Crow South (Delbanco 105). The first black writer to be openly attacked by her fellow black writers, according to Paola Boi (107), Hurston "seem[ed] loath," as Deborah McDowell puts it in her introduction to the 1991 edition of Moses, "to use her fiction to 'lead' her readers toward any pat solution to the continuing problem of racism and oppression" (x).

Hurston not only felt such criticism keenly; she also tried to defend herself. In her famous and controversial essay "How It Feels to Be Colored Me," written in 1928, for example, she announces that she is

> not tragically colored. There is no great sorrow dammed up in my soul, nor lurking behind my eyes. I do not mind at all. I do not belong to the sobbing school of Negrohood who hold that nature somehow has given them a lowdown dirty deal and whose feelings are all hurt about it. (*I Love Myself* 152)

Given the many roles Hurston played in her literary and artistic life, it's difficult to assess just how seriously we should take such a claim in the essay. But it is clear that she is railing against her critics' insistence that, because she was black, she should only write novels that dealt directly with American racism. Hurston simply did not like labels and insisted on the freedom to express herself in any way she wanted.

In *Moses* Hurston gets her revenge on her critics through the portrayals of Aaron and Miriam who, as John Lowe points out, are "stand-ins for Du Bois's 'talented tenth,'" the "emerging black bourgeoisie" (228). After Moses liberates the Hebrews from Egypt, both Aaron and Miriam, jealous of Moses, try to usurp power from him by spreading rumors and causing unrest among the people. "I know exactly what's the matter with you two," Moses says to them.

> You want to stand in my shoes which they are much too big for your feet [...]. Aaron, you got ambition to be a leader without having anything else to go with it [...]. You are much too sensitive to the wishes of the people

but you are too unconscious of their needs. And then again, you got a big idea of your own importance. (299-300)

Compare this to what Hurston wrote of Alain Locke in 1938: "I will send my toe-nails to debate him on what he knows about Negroes and Negro life, and I will come personally to debate him on what he knows about literature on the subject. This one who lives by quotations trying to criticize people who live by life" (qtd. in Hemenway 242). And in response to Locke's calling *Their Eyes* an "oversimplification," she wrote to James Weldon Johnson that Locke was "a malicious, spiteful little snot that thinks he ought to be the leading Negro because of his degrees" (Kaplan 413). One wonders if Hurston was fulfilling a secret wish to get rid of Locke when she has Moses kill Aaron at the end of the novel, telling him, "You didn't think about service half as much as you did about getting served" (33). As for Miriam, who is "one of those people who learn nothing in the long turnings and twistings of experience" (300), Moses turns her into a leper after she refuses to keep quiet by calling, ironically, on God, the Voice. Eventually, Miriam is healed, but for the rest of her days she "was very silent" (301), a condition one can only assume Hurston wished on her critics.

However, despite his reluctance to lead his people, Moses is finally compelled to follow God's commandments when God appears to him in the form of a burning bush, hands him a rod, and offers him the power of the word, perhaps signifying God as a stand-in for Hurston's artistic muse. After a series of voodoo magic tricks and a long time spent on the mountain because "it takes a long time to learn God's secret words that have the power in them to make and to do" (281), Moses leads the Israelites out of Egypt and delivers God, the Voice, to them through the Ten Commandments. As Hurston writes: "[H]e had given Israel back the notes to songs [...]. He had called to their memories the forgotten word" (346), just as Hurston translated an authentic vernacular voice for the African American community despite all the criticism and setbacks in her life.

Both Moses and Hurston had been to the mountain. Though Hurston herself was not entirely happy with the results and though many critics pointed out its flaws – among them her own biographer, Robert Hemenway, who called the novel a "noble failure" because Hurston could not maintain the fusion of black creative style, biblical tone, ethnic humor, and legendary reference (270-71) – in telling the story of her people's exodus to find their authentic vernacular voice and, more importantly, in documenting the story of her own journey towards what she considered to be her life's work, the book reshaped the Moses legend. It also redefined and broadened Modernism to include not only an acknowledgment of the traditional Western canon (in the story of Moses) but also a recognition that her Africanist roots and her gender could and should be given a voice.

We know Moses fails to cross the River Jordan with his people. Content to ask God and Nature questions but more importantly to maintain his freedom, "the biggest thing that God ever made to me" (252), Moses "end[s] in the mystery as he had come [...]. [H]e could spend those last years away from conniving politicians, stupid, but stubborn pushers and suspicions and avarice. He could dwell forever in the mountain without having to descend and struggle with the sordid" (349), just as Hurston was often alone and isolated in her struggle to maintain her artistic freedom.

But in her isolation and her struggle, Zora Neale Hurston reshaped our understanding of Modernism. Her exodus, her journey, was unique among her fellow writers: crossing and re-crossing boundaries of genre and gender as well as race, Hurston could never have been the Formalist artist Joyce's Stephen Dedalus envisioned, "like the God of creation [...] refined out of existence, indifferent, paring his fingernails" (233). She was too much the participant in her own projects. Like Janie in *Their Eyes*, who "done been tuh de horizon and back" (182), Hurston knew she had "tuh go there tuh know there" (183). Nor could she be content as a spokesperson for the burgeoning social movement with which Richard Wright and Ralph Ellison aligned themselves. If her work sometimes disappointed her readers for its refusal to be one thing and not the other, more and more we are grateful for her courage to scale the mountain, to refuse to be anything other than Zora.

Works Cited

Boas, Franz. Preface. *Mules and Men*. 1935. By Zora Neale Hurston. New York: Harper Perennial, 1990. xiii-xiv.

Boi, Paola. "Moses, Man of Power, Man of Knowledge: A 'Signifying" Reading of Zora Neale Hurston (Between a Laugh and a Song)." *Women and War: The Changing Status of American Women from the 1930s to the 1950s*. Ed. Maria Diedrich and Dorothea Fischer-Hornung. New York: Berg, 1990. 107-25.

Boyd, Valerie. *Wrapped in Rainbows: The Life of Zora Neale Hurston*. New York: Scribner, 2003.

Caron, Timothy P. "'Tell Ole Pharaoh to Let My People Go': Communal Deliverance in Zora Neale Hurston's *Moses, Man of the Mountain*." *The Southern Quarterly* 36.3 (1998): 47-60.

Delbanco, Andrew. "The Political Incorrectness of Zora Neal Hurston." *The Journal of Blacks in Higher Education* 18 (Winter 1997-98): 103-08.

Dove, Rita. Foreward. *Jonah's Gourd Vine*. 1934. By Zora Neale Hurston. New York, Harper Perennial, 1990. vii-xv.

Dutton, Wendy. "The Problem of Invisibility: Voodoo and Zora Neale Hurston." *Frontiers: A Journal of Women Studies* 13.2 (1993): 131-52.

Gates, Henry Louis, Jr. "Zora Neale Hurston: 'A Negro Way of Saying.'" *Their Eyes Were Watching God*. By Zora Neale Hurston. 1937. New York: Harper and Row, 1965. 287-97.

Hemenway, Robert E. *Zora Neale Hurston: A Literary Biography*. Chicago: U of Illinois P, 1980.

Hurston, Zora Neale. *Dust Tracks on a Road*. 1942. New York: Harper Perennial, 1991.

---. "How It Feels to Be Colored Me." *I Love Myself When I Am Laughing...*. By Zora Neale Hurston. New York: The Feminist P, 1979. 152-55.

---. *I Love Myself When I Am Laughing...* New York: The Feminist P, 1979.

---. *Jonah's Gourd Vine*. 1934. New York: Harper Perennial, 1990.

---. *Moses, Man of the Mountain*. 1934. Chicago: U of Illinois P, 1991.

---. *Mules and Men*. 1935. New York: Harper Perennial, 1990.

---. *The Complete Stories*. New York: Harper Collins, 1995.

---. *Their Eyes Were Watching God*. 1937. New York: Harper and Row, 1965.

---. *Tell My Horse: Voodoo and Life in Haiti and Jamaica*. 1938. New York: Harper and Row, 1990.

Joyce, James. *A Portrait of the Artist as a Young Man*. 1916. New York: Penguin, 1992.

Kaplan, Carla, ed. *Zora Neale Hurston: A Life in Letters*. New York: Anchor Books, 2002.

Lowe, John. *Jump at the Sun: Zora Neale Hurston's Cosmic Comedy*. Chicago: U of Illinois P, 1997.

McDowell, Deborah. "Foreward: Lines of Descent/Dissenting Lines." *Moses, Man of the Mountain*. By Zora Neale Hurston. New York: Harper Perennial, 1991. vii-xxii.

Meisenhelder, Susan Edwards. *Hitting a Straight Lick with a Crooked Stick: Race and Gender in the Work of Zora Neale Hurston*. Tuscaloosa: The U of Alabama P, 1999.

Pierpoint, Claudia Roth. "A Society of One: Zora Neale Hurston, American Contrarian." *New Yorker* 17 Feb.1997. 80-86+.

Posnock, Ross. *Color and Culture: Black Writers and the Making of the Modern Intellectual*. Cambridge: Harvard UP, 1998.

Scott, Bonnie Kime, ed. *The Gender of Modernism: A Critical Anthology*. Bloomington: Indiana UP, 1990.

Washington, Mary Helen. Foreword. *Their Eyes Were Watching God*. By Zora Neale Hurston. 1937. New York: Harper and Row, 1965. vii-xiv.

---. "Zora Neale Hurston: A Woman Half in Shadow." *I Love Myself When I Am Laughing...* By Zora Neale Hurston. New York: The Feminist P, 1979. 7-25.

Małgorzata Ziółek-Sowińska

African American Modernism and the Music of Duke Ellington

Introduction
Jazz emerged at about the time that African Americans became immersed in modern American life at the turn of the twentieth century, coalescing in the city of New Orleans, a cosmopolitan port city with a rich diversity and a vibrant music environment. Blacks were exposed to ragtime, jazz, and blues in the South and also when they migrated to northern states in the early part of the century. One of the reasons why these styles were prevalent in the North as well as the South is because musicians in urban cities catered to the tastes of blacks who migrated from the South in increasing numbers between World Wars I and II. Subsequently, the opportunities to perform and to hear various styles of music in the urban city were plentiful.

During the 1910s and 1920s, leaders of the Harlem Renaissance such as W. E. B. Du Bois, Alaine Locke, James Weldon Johnson resuscitated debates about the significance of black music in elevating the social standing of African Americans. Jazz and other forms of black music became subjects of heated discussions among black intellectuals on the role of music in African American life. This paper explores the aesthetic vision in the music of Edward Kennedy "Duke" Ellington, one of the most prolific composers of jazz music during this period, and its importance in defining early twentieth-century African American modernism in music. A gifted and innovative jazz pianist, bandleader, and composer, Ellington's body of work reflected an aesthetic sensitivity consistent with the goals of Harlem Renaissance intellectuals. Mark Tucker has discussed Ellington's education in Washington D. C. and pointed out that black professional musicians such as Oliver "Doc" Perry, Louis N. Brown and Henry Lee Grant shaped his artistic vision for black music as they taught him grace and professionalism in performing music and respect for black culture. From Grant Ellington learnt that "popular music could show seriousness of purpose and meet standards of excellence" (Tucker, "Renaissance Education" 116). Tucker has also observed that after the 1920s Ellington revealed his reverence for the African

American heritage and utilized vernacular sources as the basis for his musical compositions (Tucker, "Renaissance Education" 112). I will discuss some of these vernacular idioms such as ragtime, blues, work songs, and the Negro spirituals and the ways that Ellington integrated them into his own work.

I will also analyze selected music examples from *Black Symphony* and the suite *Black Brown and Beige*, in which Ellington's sense of pride in African American history and black musical traditions are put to music that is far-ranging in its scope, vision, and compositional innovation. I will argue that – much like other Harlem Renaissance leaders – Ellington perceived African American music as a tool for racial uplift, and this theme became one of the defining features of his more sophisticated work, particularly his long forms and suites, and contributed to the move towards modernism in African American aesthetic expressions in the early part of the twentieth century. While some writers such as Alfred Appel Jr. have reduced his modernism to the primitivism of his so-called Cotton Club era "Jungle Music," Ellington's compositional techniques made use of folk themes and the language of the vernacular taken from musical idioms such as the blues and spirituals, to which he brought a grand elegance. His orchestral and compositional strategies and the expansive scope of his aesthetic vision elevated the humble musical material of the black working class to the level of European art music. Through the reframing of this music, Ellington hoped to instill a sense of pride in black history and to correct the distorted stereotypes of black people that had persisted in the United States since minstrelsy.

Harlem Renaissance Aesthetics and the Education of Duke Ellington
The Harlem Renaissance was a literary and intellectual movement of the 1920s and 1930s in which prominent figures from a number of endeavors and backgrounds began to define the parameters of black cultural expression and show that art could be used as a means of promoting the social advancement of African Americans (Porter 5). The Harlem Renaissance was linked with modernism as "they both share[d] the important motif of alienation" and "modernism borrow[ed] from the Renaissance the themes of marginality and the use of folk or the so-called 'primitive' material" (Reuben).

Black intellectuals aimed to define black culture in terms of American modernism, which was an artistic movement that drew an inspiration from the European avant-garde art. Pablo Picasso's *Les Demoiselles d'Avignon* was a seminal painting in the creation of Cubism which also revealed that African art played a crucial role in the creation of twentieth-century modernism. The potential for the political use of black art and literature was perceived by black intellectuals such as W. E. B. Du Bois, educated in Europe and at Harvard, and Alain Locke, a Rhodes scholar at Oxford in 1906 and afterwards a student of aesthetics in Germany ("Modernism and Modernity").

In 1925, Alain Locke published his anthology *The New Negro*. In the introductory essay, also called "The New Negro," he stated that "the younger generation is vibrant with a new psychology; the new spirit is awake in the masses." (47). Locke's New Negroes embraced "self respect," "self-dependence" and, as the scholar noted, "the day of 'aunties,' 'uncles' and 'mammies' is equally gone" (49). Locke used the metaphor of movement of rural Southern blacks to northern cities to show that the black migration would give black Americans a chance for a better life in the city. As he put it: "The wash and rush of this human tide on the beach line of the northern city centers is to be explained primarily in terms of a new visions of opportunity, of social and economic freedom" (49). Locke claimed that the black migration, which brought thousands of African Americans from rural areas into the northern cities, gave them a chance for democracy in the North. As he noted: "a mass movement toward the larger and the more democratic chance – in the Negro's case a deliberate flight not only from the countryside to city, but from medieval America to modern"(49). In the essay Locke also identified the characteristics of African American modernism as in his view the black migration symbolized the change from the past to modern times. He also asserted that "folk-expression and self-determination are playing a creative role in the world today" (50) and thus believed that African American folk culture was the basis of modern African American art, music, and literature.

Significantly, Harlem Renaissance scholars raised questions pertaining to the role of vernacular music in elevating the social standing of African Americans. As musicologist Samuel Floyd Jr. comments, the "spirit of the Negro Renaissance had began to manifest itself, in the late 1890s and in the first and second decades of the twentieth century" (Floyd, *Power* 103) and was anticipated by the work of early twentieth century black composers such as Scott Joplin, Will Marion Cook, Harry T. Burleigh, J. Rosamond Johnson, and Ford Dabney, who created extended musical pieces from vernacular black forms using European methods of composition and theory (Floyd, *Power* 104). Harlem

Renaissance intellectuals emphasized the idea that black music greatly contributed to American and world culture and held the firm conviction that black musicians should draw on the raw materials of spirituals, blues, and ragtime in creating larger classical works such as symphonies or operas that would equal the work of white composers (Floyd, *Power* 107).

Initially, these intellectuals dismissed jazz as a basis for artistic creation as well as the blues, ragtime, and other musical folk forms which they perceived as decadent and conjuring images of the "old Negro" (Floyd, *Power* 108). Du Bois' idea of the "talented tenth," of an elite class of blacks educated in the Western ideal of aesthetics, largely disregarded the vernacular music and lifestyles of uneducated blacks. Only the black spiritual was held in high esteem, a point Du Bois emphasized in the section on spirituals in his 1903 seminal work *The Souls of Black Folk*. Eventually, in their attempt to describe black culture in terms of American modernism, Harlem Renaissance thinkers turned to black vernacular music to provide the basis for a defining aesthetic credo and as a key intellectual tool in reshaping white perceptions of black life and culture. This is not surprising since, as Floyd observes, music had always been part and parcel of the existence of African American people while literature had not (Floyd, "Music" 4-5). In black communities black music reached more people than literature and was more accessible for ordinary blacks because they did not need to be educated or literate to relate to jazz and blues. They could experience black music in all kinds of social settings including rent parties, nightclubs, and other gatherings as well as through phonograph recordings, the main way in which recorded music reached black audiences since few early "race records" were played on white-owned radio stations. Harlem Renaissance intellectuals aspired to create "the New Negro in music" that would convert the folk material of black vernacular culture into high art, and encouraged composers to master the rules of theory composition that was the foundation of European music. Scholars such as Mark Tucker, Albert Murray, Eric Porter and others have shown that Ellington, more than any other black composer of his time, embodied the ideals of "the New Negro" by passionately utilizing black vernacular sources to represent black history in music.

Ellington's artistic vision was formed in Washington D. C., where the young Ellington was taught impeccable manners, dignity, patriotism, the value of the black contribution to American culture and a deep respect for the African American heritage. Ellington was born into a respectable, upper-middle class family that encouraged him to develop his potential and become a successful black citizen. In his autobiography *Music Is My Mistress* Ellington remarks that Miss Boston, his eighth-grade teacher, promoted good speech and racial pride, writing that

> she taught us that proper speech and good manners were our first obligations, because as representatives of the Negro race we were to command respect for our people. This being an all-colored school, Negro history was crammed into the curriculum, so that we would know our people all the way back. They had pride there, the greatest race pride. (17)

Ellington often stressed the fact that he grew up in a place in which there were many people for whom "quality mattered, and who required your personal best no less as a general principle than as a natural reaction to the folklore on white supremacy" (Murray 87).

Washington also provided the basis for Ellington's musical education. The city, which was an important cultural milieu, exposed Ellington to professionally trained musicians who not only taught him to read music but also to highly appreciate the value of black music. Ellington studied harmony with Henry Lee Grant, a black musician who extolled the virtues of black music and firmly believed that popular music could meet high standards of excellence. Grant's musical background made a lasting impression on the young Ellington, who would later become a perfect embodiment of the New Negro in music (Tucker, "Renaissance Education" 116-17) by employing both classical and black vernacular musical idioms to create more positive, respectful, and authentic depictions of black life in the United States, depictions that reflected the Negro's deep humanity and spirituality, and also exposed his sufferings, longings and hopes; it was a more authentic rendering of black life in that was based in a realism which pushed back against the stereotypes of the Negro's inhumanity that had allowed for the institution of slavery and the persistence racial oppression in the United States over centuries. Ellington's goal was to present the real picture of the African American community in his compositions. Tucker has noted that:

> Ellington continued to celebrate Harlem in music. His compositions described its echoes and air shafts, boys and blue belles. His songs advised people to drop off there and slap their shoes on Seventh Avenue. His signature piece even told them which train to take. ("Renaissance Education" 111)

The Influence of Ragtime and Blues in Ellington's Music

Ragtime was a distinctive style of entertainment music that developed during the last half of the nineteenth century (Rattenbury 54). A precursor to jazz, it is a highly syncopated music idiom that stresses rhythmical excitement, and that arguably began the modernist turn in black musical development and in American modernism generally. Its greatest expression as a written piano form was perhaps given by black composers such as Scott Joplin and James Sylvester Scott. Ellington was exposed to this music in his youth at rent parties and concerts given by the well-known ragtime pianists of the day such as James P. Johnson, Willie "The Lion" Smith, Thomas "Fats" Waller and others. Ellington expressed his admiration for their accomplished technique and skill at improvisation. He yearned to play like the great ragtime pianists and listened carefully to other musicians, reproducing by trial and error their ragtime pieces on the piano (Hasse 36).

In 1913 at the age of fourteen, Ellington composed his first piano score, "Soda Fountain Rag." As he later remarked of the piece,

> I began by tinkering around with some old tunes I knew. Then, just to try something different, I set to putting some music to the rhythm that I used in jerking ice-cream sodas at the Poodle Dog. I fooled around with the tune more and more until at last, lo and behold, I had completed my first piece of finished music. It was an extremely fast tune, requiring very tricky finger work, and I called it "The Poodle Dog Rag." (qtd. in Hasse 37-38)

The subsequently renamed "Soda Fountain Rag" consists of Introduction, Part A, Part B, Part A, and Coda. The melodic line reveals that Ellington effectively again made use of repetition. Part A is written in d-minor. In contrast, Part B is written in F-major. The syncopated rhythm is repeated in the melodic line in Part B in particular. The significance of this work, as John Edward Hasse notes, lies in the fact that it became a theme for improvisation in Ellington's future compositions. Ellington changed the tempo and played this instrumental ragtime as a one-step, two-step, tango, fox trot or even waltz. He used the musical material of "Soda Fountain Rag" in "Oklahoma Stomp" (1929) and "Swing Session" (1937) (Hasse 39). As musicologist Mark Tucker points out "these recyclings typified one of Ellington's most fundamental principles of composition: reusing older material in new contexts" (qtd. in Hasse 39). Hasse notes that "Ellington's reworkings belong to the black tradition of signifying" (Hasse 39) by reusing and restating older musical material as a means of demonstrating respect, which is why Ellington made great use of vernacular musical devices such as shouts, riffs, call and response, and various rhythmical motifs.

Concurrently with Ellington's attraction to the syncopated rhythms of ragtime, his music reveals a preponderant blues influence (Rattenbury 38, 46-53). Ellington embraced country blues and sought to capture in his written compositions the melodic and harmonic nuances of this type of blues. He deployed the blues idiom to capture the broad range of black experience and emotions and render it in musical terms. One hears the constant presence of blues in the structure of melodies or the use of harmonies in pieces such as "Mood Indigo," "Solitude," " Frustration," or Melancholia" (Tucker, "Duke Ellington" 142).

The use of a variety of unorthodox compositional methods would make Ellington's musical vocabulary particularly modernist as he devised ingenuous ways in which to work around the Western well-tempered scale, which consists of twelve equal semitones and cannot truly represent the microtonal pitch play of "blue notes" encountered in country blues devices such as bends, vibratos, and slurs. The most common blue notes may be represented by using the minor third or the flatted fifth in the diatonic scale, but Ellington also made use of glissandos, atypical harmonic voicings or voicing across sections (pairing a melody to the cornet and flute, for instance) to produce dissonances that refined the sound of the country blues into a sophisticated language that became his unique musical signature.

Ellington's music is framed within a modernist sensitivity as his goal was to incorporate innovative devices into his art taken from black aesthetic productions in the same way that artists such as Picasso used African masks to create cubism or that literary figures such as the black poet Langston Hughes and later, white writers such as Jack Kerouac and Allen Ginsberg used the fractured rhythms of jazz to reinvigorate American letters. Musical features and innovations such as his technique of vocalization, resulting in the mimicking of the human voice on the trumpet or other instruments, or utilizing microtones characteristic of vocal blues are expressive of modernity. In order to employ these innovative musical devices Ellington carefully selected the musicians who worked in his band. He wrote solos and melodic themes for his musicians and often collaborated with them on pieces that took advantage of their individual musical voices. Ellington worked for example with a trumpeter Bubber Miley, who employed a technique of vocalization by humming in his throat while playing and simultaneously manipulating a plumber's rubber plunger mute over the bell of his horn. As a result, Miley reproduced speech-like sounds that mimicked the human voice (Rattenbury 46). Another important musician who played in Ellington's band was trombonist Joe "Tricky Sam" Nanton, who also incorporated the technique of vocalization into his playing. The alto saxophonist Johnny Hodges was a key player in Ellington's band as well, who played musical phrases in microtonal intervals characteristic of the vocal blues by employing glissandi, portamenti, and dynamic accenting. Ellington also wrote a number of expressive solo pieces for his cornetist Cootie Williams, including the richly textured "Concerto for Cootie," which begins with the riff from "Do Nothing Till You Hear From Me." Ellington gives Williams a broad canvas to paint different textural colors using a repertoire of techniques that included tongue twirls, growls, and various muted sounds.

In selecting such musicians and providing them with a uniquely colorful soundscape in which to improvise, Ellington allowed them to make their own contributions to the modernization of the language of vernacular blues. He made extensive use of the blues idiom in more sophisticated kinds of ways than they had been performed in Southern juke joints or urban bars, giving it a new dimension of expressive power without dismissing it altogether. In Ellington's view, "blues is the rage in popular music. And popular music is the good music of tomorrow" (Zunser 45). Here Ellington makes clear the connection he has established between black American blues and American contemporary popular music in the decades and years to come, pointing out that they are essentially the same.

Ellington not only made effective use of the blues scale and dissonances to refine the sound of the country blues but used them to paint tone poems that captured the sounds of urbanization and the city. Ellington utilized "the very beat of the ongoing, upbeat locomotive onomatopoeia" (Murray 94), conjuring up the sonic images of driving pistons, steam whistles and departure bells – in pieces such as "Choo Choo," "The Old Circus Train-Turn Around Blues," "Daybreak Express," "Happy-Go-Lucky Local," "Mainstem," or "Track 360." Ellington's use of locomotive onomatopoeia, Murray comments, can be perceived not only as a "metaphorical underground railroad but also the metaphysical gospel train" (Murray 94). The train also represents modernity, migration, and the increasing move towards urbanization as America's rural populations moved to the city for jobs and a better standard of living, and was the primary method of transportation for many blacks leaving the south during the migrations in the early and middle parts of the twentieth century. Other songs such as "Harlem Air Shaft" and "East St. Louis Toodle-Doo" painted images that represented the mechanized, fast-paced urban city in which blacks now found themselves and the array of new sounds they now incorporated into the rhythms of their daily lives.

In 1931 Ellington wrote an article for *Rhythm*, a British magazine aimed at dance-band musicians, in which he emphasized that rhythmic sequences not only govern human existence but also play a significant role in the success of the dance band. Ellington defined his music as a vehicle of representing his race in opposition to the banal harmonies and rhythms of the ballroom bands, commenting that

> I think that the music of my race is something which is going to live, something which posterity will honour in a higher sense than merely that of the music of the ballroom today. I put my best musical thoughts forward into my tunes, and not hackneyed harmonies and rhythms which are almost too banal to publish. ("Duke Steps Out" 48-49)

He also praised the work of black classical singers such Paul Robeson and Ronald Hayes who contributed to the musical accomplishments of blacks, saying "I am proud of that part my race is playing in the artistic life of the world." Ellington also maintained that "Jazz is going to play a considerable part in the serious music of the future" and "from the welter of Negro dance musicians now before the public will come something lasting and noble" ("Duke Steps Out" 48-49).

The Influence of the Negro Spiritual in Ellington's Music
Beyond the influence of ragtime and blues, Ellington's music was rooted in the tradition of the black sacred song, the African American spirituals, religious songs created by black slaves who fused African music practices such as syncopation, pitch bends, call and response, melodic drumming, and physical body motion within the system of European harmony. Spirituals reflected the artistic creativity of slaves who revealed not only a profound religious consciousness but also existential insights that spoke to the eschatological aspect of freedom, the question of memory, suffering, and mourning (West 463-86). In short, spirituals delineated the black experience in America during slavery.

Throughout his life Ellington realized the goals of the Harlem Renaissance intellectuals by incorporating musical themes of African American spirituals into his own music. In 1927 Ellington co-composed with his trumpeter Bubber Miley *Black and Tan Fantasy*. The opening theme played by Miley is said to be based on a Negro Spiritual, "Hosannah," that Miley's mother used to sing (Stowe 209). In 1929 *Black and Tan Fantasy* was made into a short film which, as David W. Stowe asserts, juxtaposed the Saturday night milieu of the nightclub with the sacred sphere of the black church represented in the film by the Hall Johnson Singers.

In 1947 Ellington wrote *The Deep South Suite*. The last section of this extended musical composition tells a story of a little train in the South that is never on schedule. The train's fireman is a black man who plays Negro spirituals and blues on the whistle (Ellington, *Music* 184-85). It becomes evident that Ellington stressed the importance of singing spirituals and black secular songs, which he perceived as an essential part of black life in America. His *Symphony in Black: A Rhapsody of Negro Life* also contained a quasi-like spiritual "Hymn of Sorrow," which expressed the musician's desire to delineate the representation of death.

In 1963 Ellington created *My People*, which was a musical revue for the centennial of the Emancipation Proclamation. In this work Ellington drew on the blues idiom and the Negro Spiritual. He also recycled three extracts from *Black, Brown and Beige* and revised "Come Sunday" which served as a piece for tap dancer Bunny Briggs (Lock 114-16). *My People* contained two political songs: "King Fit the Battle of Alabam," and "What Color Is Virtue." In "King Fit the Battle of Alabam," Ellington employed the melodic theme of the Negro Spiritual "Joshua Fit the Battle of Jericho." Ellington selected the Negro Spiritual depicting the exploits of the Old Testament hero Joshua in order to comment on the political turmoil in the United States in the 1960s and lend support to the fledgling Civil Rights Movement in the South. In Ellington's piece the biblical battle site of Jericho becomes Birmingham where sheriff Bull Connor ordered fire hoses and dogs to be set on peaceful demonstrators, a pivotal moment in the battle for black civil rights (Steed 107). In this song of protest Ellington expressed his respect for Martin Luther King Jr., the guiding light of the movement for black civil rights in the 1960s. *My People* is a significant link between *Black, Brown and Beige* and the first of the *Sacred Concerts*, which became Ellington's main musical goal during the last decade of his life (Lock 116). Significantly, Ellington remained faithful to his Harlem Renaissance aesthetics his whole life.

In 1965 Ellington was commissioned to write a liturgical work for the Episcopal Grace Cathedral in San Francisco. The *Concert of Sacred Music* was premiered on September 16, 1965. After the performance of Ellington's sacred music Raymond Horrics praised the work, which he perceived as "a most remarkable religious synthesis" of Western Christianity and African religious elements, gospel singing, Biblical stories, and "not least, the extra problems faced by mankind in our modern society" (qtd. in Hasse 358). It may have been the apotheosis of Ellington's modernism at that point, drawing as it did so many historical themes to speak of the contemporary state of man, particularly the Negro and his existential dilemma in American society. Ellington wrote two more *Sacred Concerts*. The *Second Sacred Concert* was performed at New York's Cathedral of St. John the Divine on January 19, 1968. The *Third Sacred Concert* was premiered at Westminster Abbey in London on October 24, 1973. These *Sacred Concerts* expressed Ellington's deep religious consciousness and spirituality. He was a voracious reader of religious literature. His estate includes many versions and translations of the Bible along with numerous church and newspaper articles written by religious leaders and that show Ellington's annotations (Stowe 211). Ellington referred to his *Sacred Concerts* as his most ambitious and important musical work: "Now I can say openly what I have been saying myself on my knees" (*Music* 161).

In his *Sacred Concerts*, Ellington articulated the goals of Harlem Renaissance thinkers as he laid bare the value of the Negro Spiritual for American culture. In many performances of his *Sacred Concerts* Ellington incorporated gospel choirs singing, his own religious music and traditional Negro Spirituals. By employing elements of dance in "David Danced Before the Lord," Ellington also emphasized the interrelation between dance and music in the black religious experience, which can be seen in all black popular music forms up to hip hop.

The Central Position of Race in Ellington's Music
Like the New Negro thinkers, Ellington's aesthetic vision embraced the idea of creating "authentic Negro music" as a means of securing the social standing of blacks in American society. Ellington articulated his musical goals more fully in a 1939 interview in the jazz magazine *Down Beat*, remarking that

our aim has always been the development of an authentic Negro music, of which swing is only one element. We are not interested primarily in the playing of jazz or swing music, but in producing musically a genuine contribution from our race. Our music is always intended to be definitely and purely racial. Our inspiration is derived from our lives, and the lives of those about us, and those that went before us. ("Duke Says" 135)

Ellington states here that African American musicians should not concentrate only on performing jazz or swing. In his view artists ought to create purely racial music and draw an inspiration from the African American experience in the past and the present time.

That Ellington's aesthetic vision carried with it some of the goals of the Negro Renaissance is also evident in his view of black music as a vehicle for exploring the past (Porter 38). Ellington was a lifelong reader of black history and possessed 800 books on black history in which he marked passages about leaders of slave rebellions such as Denmark Vesey and Nat Turner (Hasse 254). Like Harlem Renaissance writers such as Zora Neale Hurston and Langston Hughes who sought to use poetry and literature to advance black intellectual culture, the goal of black history authentically rendered would become the foundation of his artistic and aesthetic vision. As Graham Lock notes, Ellington looked askance at the false stereotypical representation of blackness in popular culture (88-102). Ellington particularly wanted to counter minstrel stereotypes from the previous century in which blacks were depicted as happy-go-lucky slaves living under bondage to their white masters in the South.

In 1941 Ellington collaborated on the musical show *Jump for Joy* which for him was "an attempt to correct the race situation in the U.S.A. through a form of a theatrical propaganda" (*Music* 175). The show, one of the first black musicals to offer non-stereotyped depictions of black life, was meant to "take Uncle Tom out of the theatre, eliminate the stereotyped image that had been exploited by Hollywood and Broadway, and say things that would make the audience think" (*Music* 175). In his autobiography, he stressed that *Jump for Joy* "was done on a highly intellectual level – no crying, no moaning, but entertaining, and with social demands as a potent spice" (*Music* 176). Ellington frequently expressed his dislike of blacking up, and emphasized that he "had stopped all the comedians from using cork on their faces" when they worked with him. As he recalled, some objected before the show opened, but removed it, and were shocked by their success. As the audience screamed and applauded, comedians came off stage smiling, and with tears running down their cheeks. I think a statement of social protest in the theatre should be made without saying it, and this calls for the real craftsman. (*Music* 180)

In the late 1920s Duke Ellington and his orchestra gained enormous popularity in New York when he began radio broadcasts from Harlem's Cotton Club. During these years Ellington's interest in representing the black experience through music was evident in pieces that brought to mind images of black city life and caught the rhythms of Harlem's cacophonous soundscape. While it may seem rather ironic that Ellington played into black stereotypes with his 'jungle music' floor shows at the Cotton Club, which was segregated and reserved for rich white elites from downtown Manhattan, his later work would stand as more profound monuments to his artistic vision and his commitment to racial pride.

One of Ellington's artistic goals was to create an extended musical composition that would depict a narrative history of the Negro in the United States. In 1934, he composed the soundtrack for the short film *Symphony in Black: A Rhapsody of Negro Life*, which affirmed his dedication and love for the cultural heritage of African Americans. The piece lasted nine minutes and was Ellington's longest composition to that point (Steed 85). *Symphony in Black* is a suite depicting themes of black life such as work, love, religion, and the urban city. Part One ("Laborers") employs the rhythms of a work song to signify the importance of music to work and also depicts the quiet dignity of blacks pulling themselves up through the hardships of manual labor. Part Two ("Triangle") draws from the blues idiom to portray the suffering of a woman who is abandoned by her man for another woman, and is sung by the young Billie Holiday making her screen debut. It is suggestive of the ways in which the temptations of the city and urban nightlife problemmatized the dynamics of black romantic love. The haunting Part Three ("Hymn of Sorrow") is a spiritual mourning the death of a child that dignifies black suffering and human mortality while showing reverence for every black life loved and lost. The last section ("Harlem Rhythm") is a joyous celebration of black nightlife and community that also speaks to the ritual power of music to raise up and affirm the human spirit again and again through the communion of dance and song. In *Symphony in Black*, Ellington showed how music was part and parcel of the fabric black existence as it accompanied black people in their everyday life, work, love, suffering, and religious experience. As Lock has observed, *Symphony in Black* would become the impetus for Ellington's later suite *Black Brown, and Beige* which would stand as his most profound and expansive musical statement about the history of black people (108).

In December of 1942 Ellington began work on his extended musical composition *Black, Brown and Beige*, a forty-four minute suite that he completed in six weeks and that would become the longest and the most ambitious work of his career, and one of his most enduring. By embracing the history of black Americans and addressing issues of race pride, patriotism, and the pursuit of education, *Black, Brown and Beige* would even more clearly articulate the aesthetic vision and goals of New Negro intellectuals. In the introduction to *Black, Brown and Beige* Ellington translated the suffering and hard labor endured by enslaved blacks into sound, creating a new model of African American modernist expression in music by using folk themes and the language of the vernacular. By converting the folk forms into a suite – viewed by Harlem Renaissance leaders as high art – Ellington framed his music within the aesthetic credo of the Harlem Renaissance.

Ellington premiered the suite on January 23, 1943 at Carnegie Hall. It was, as Tucker points out, "the first time a major black composer would present an evening of original music in New York's most prestigious concert hall" (qtd. in Lock 108). In his autobiography, Ellington wrote that *"Black, Brown and Beige* was planned as a tone parallel to the history of American Negro" (*Music* 181). The first section, *Black*,

> delved deeply into the Negro past. In it, I was concerned to show the close relationship between work songs and spirituals. 'Work Song' used in many forms, recognized that a work song was sung as you worked, so that there was a place for the song and a place where you grunt. (*Music* 181)

In the opening section to *Black* ("Work Song"), the bass introduces a short rhythmic four-bar phrase with the drums joining in the third bar. In Part A Ellington stresses a central theme, a common practice in work songs, and orchestrates it for saxophones and trombones. It is repeated three times in call and response form, another common practice in work song and other black musical idioms. Saxophones introduce the melody using a blues scale using C, E-flat, F, and G-flat to depict the physical burden of chattel slave labor, while ensemble plays dissonant chords, suggesting the spiritual disharmony of black existence under slavery and racial oppression. A saxophone break follows and then another dissonance can be heard. The main theme is again repeated three times. In Part B the baritone saxophone introduces a motif based on a blues scale using A-flat, B, F-sharp, G, and B. Afterwards the ensemble responds to the saxophone's call. You can hear a repetition of the main theme in E-flat major three times. In Part C the trumpet makes a melodic call and the ensemble responds. In Part D, the call and response occurs between the trombone and the ensemble. The trombone plays a bluesy motif (A-flat, B-flat, E-flat, E-flat, C) which sets up a reiteration of the work song theme by the ensemble. The main theme in E-flat is played in unison by the trumpets. The trombone introduces a new musical motif and the ensemble responds. In the Coda, unaccompanied saxophones close the piece in E-flat major. As we can see, Ellington frequently makes use of call and response, repetition, blues scales, and the rhythms of work songs combined with the textured voicing of trumpets, trombones, and saxophones to link the past to the present and update vernacular folk expressionism. By such devices Ellington reframed African American folk traditions into musical modernism using the language of black jazz and the techniques of European art music.

In the section "Come Sunday" Ellington employs the Negro Spiritual to cross from the secular into the realm of the sacred and affirm the humanity of black people by underscoring that the sacred is an essential fact of human existence and that blacks share this profound experience. The trombone plays the theme of the spiritual "Swing Low, Swing Chariot," a lament that makes further use of the black sacred song. In his autobiography, Ellington remarked that "Come Sunday" was meant to portray the desire of black worshippers who congregated under a tree to pray to have a church of their own. Ellington described black people as "good souls praying and singing faithfully, […] without a word of bitterness or revenge – 'I forgive my past suffering just let my people go'" (qtd. in Hasse 261). *Black* closes with a section called "Light" that affirms the power of black spiritual life and the ongoing struggle for black social and political freedom in the United States.

In the second movement, *Brown*, Ellington wanted to acknowledge "the contribution made by the Negro to this country in blood" (*Music* 181). The first section of *Brown* celebrates the deeds of seven hundred free Haitians who helped Americans at the siege of Savannah in 1778, while the second part, "Emancipation Celebration," refers to the jubilation that followed the Emancipation Proclamation signed by President Abraham Lincoln in 1863 that freed

Southern blacks from bondage. The third movement, *Beige*, is meant to paint vivid imageries of the black experience in Harlem in the twentieth century. Ellington remarked that at Carnegie Hall,

> I introduced the third section, 'Beige' by referring to the common view of the people of Harlem, and the little Harlems around the U.S.A., as just singing, dancing, and responding to the tom-toms. On closer inspection, it would be found that there were more churches than cabarets, that the people were trying to find a more stable way of living, and that the Negro was rich in experience and education. (*Music* 182)

Conclusion

In conclusion, Ellington was unique among jazz musicians of the time in that his artistic vision referenced the modernist aesthetics advocated by the Harlem Renaissance intellectuals. Like other Harlem Renaissance thinkers Ellington perceived black achievement in art as a vehicle to elevate the social standing of black people in the Unites States. His discomfort with stereotypical representations of black life in America became the inspiration for works of stunning originality and beauty that reflected his great reverence for black people and pride in black heritage. In one of his interviews with jazz critic Nat Hentoff, Ellington remarked that "for a long time, social protest and pride in the Negro have been the most significant themes in what we have done. In that music we have been talking for a long time about what it is to be a Negro in the country" (qtd. in Lock 118).

In his desire to represent an authentic portrait of the black American experience, Ellington turned to vernacular black music styles – ragtime, blues, work song, and the African American spiritual. Drawing on these forms he created more sophisticated and extended musical compositions such as suites and concertos. Ellington absorbed into his works salient black musical features such as blues scales, call and response, and syncopation without losing the spontaneity and authenticity of black folk music.

His great legacy to black culture resides in the fact that he helped to correct distorted representations of black life and break down racial stereotypes using the majestic sweep of his music, and that he did so not by abandoning folk vernacular idioms, but using them as the basis for creating innovative works of great depth, scope, and sophistication. In his suites Ellington presented blacks as heroic figures who fought for human dignity, social equality and political freedom while remaining strongly critical of romanticized representations of black suffering in literature and other forms of black artistic expression. Throughout his life, Ellington was his own wandering bluesman, telling the truth about his people and extolling virtues of human dignity, racial pride, and the enormous sustaining spiritual power of black music. The great jazz trumpeter Miles Davis, every bit Ellington's creative equal, once commented to the effect that all jazz musicians should pick one day every year and get down on their knees to thank Duke Ellington, who may well have been the most significant and singularly unique American composer of the twentieth century, and certainly one of the most beloved.

Works Cited

Appel, Alfred, Jr. *Jazz Modernism: From Ellington and Armstrong to Matisse and Joyce*. New York: Alfred A. Knopf, 2002.

Du Bois, W. E. B. *The Souls of Black Folk*. 1903. New York: Penguin, 1989.

Ellington, Duke. "Duke Says Swing is Stagnant." *The Duke Ellington Reader*. Ed. Mark Tucker. New York: Oxford UP, 1993. 132-35.

---. *Music Is My Mistress*. New York: Da Capo P, 1973.

---. "On Swing and Its Critics." *The Duke Ellington Reader*. Ed. Mark Tucker. New York: Oxford UP, 1993. 132-40.

---. *Second Sacred Concert*. Prestige, 1968.

---. "The Duke Steps Out." *The Duke Ellington Reader*. Ed. Mark Tucker. New York: Oxford UP, 1993. 46-50.

---. "Things Ain't What They Used To Be." (Mercer Ellington). Broadcast 10 January 1945 from the Cafe Zanzibar, New York City. Reissued on Duke Ellington. *Duke's Joint*. Buddha Records, 1999.

---. "Work Song." Columbia, 1958. Reissued on Duke Ellington. *Black, Brown And Beige*. Sony Music Entertainment Inc, 1999.

Floyd, Samuel A., Jr. "Music in the Harlem Renaissance: An Overview." *Black Music in the Harlem Renaissance: A Collection of Essays*. Ed. Samuel A. Floyd Jr. Knoxville: The U of Tennessee P, 1993. 1-28.

---. *The Power of Black Music*. New York: Oxford UP, 1995.

Hasse, John Edward. *Beyond Category: The Life and Genius of Duke Ellington.* New York: Da Capo P, 1995.

Lock, Graham. *Blutopia: Visions of the Future and Revisions of the Past in the Work of Sun Ra, Duke Ellington, and Anthony Braxton.* Durham: Duke UP, 1999.

Locke, Alain. "The New Negro." *Voices from the Harlem Renaissance.* Ed. Nathan Irving Huggins. New York: Oxford UP. 1995. 47-56.

"Modernism and Modernity." 10 Nov. 2010 <http://iniva.org/harlem/modern.html>.

Morrow, Edward."Duke Ellington on Gershwin's 'Porgy.'" *The Duke Ellington Reader.* Ed. Mark Tucker. New York: Oxford UP, 1993. 114-17.

Murray, Albert. *The Blue Devils of Nada: A Contemporary American Approach to Aesthetic Statement.* New York: Pantheon Books, 1996.

Porter, Eric. *What is This Thing Called Jazz: African American Musicians as Artists, Critics, and Activists.* Los Angeles: U of California P, 2002.

Rattenbury, Ken. *Duke Ellington: Jazz Composer.* New Haven: Yale UP, 1990.

Reuben, Paul P. "Chapter 7: Early Twentieth Century – American Modernism: A Brief Introduction." *Perspectives in American Literature – A Research and Reference Guide – An Ongoing Project.* 11 Nov. 2010 <http://www.csustan.edu/english/reuben/pal/chap7/7intro.html>.

Steed, Janna Tull. *Duke Ellington: A Spiritual Biography.* New York: The Crossroad Publishing Company, 1999.

Stowe, David W. *How Sweet the Sound: Music in the Spiritual Lives of Americans.* Cambridge: Harvard UP, 2004.

Tucker, Mark. "Duke Ellington." *The Oxford Companion to Jazz.* Ed. Bill Kirchner. New York: Oxford UP, 2000. 132-47.

---. "The Renaissance Education of Duke Ellington." *Black Music in the Harlem Renaissance: A Collection of Essays.* Ed. Samuel A. Floyd Jr. Knoxville: The U of Tennessee P, 1993. 111-28.

West, Cornel. "The Spirituals as Lyrical Poetry." *The Cornel West Reader.* Ed. Cornel West. New York: Basic Civitas Books, 1999. 463-70.

Zunser, Florence. "'Opera Must Die,' Says Galli-Curci! Long Live the Blues." *The Duke Ellington Reader.* Ed. Mark Tucker. New York: Oxford UP, 1993. 44-45.

Emil Sîrbulescu

Louis Armstrong's Unknown Addiction, or the (Un)Willing Autobiographer

> Autobiography is the simultaneously historical record and literary artifact, psychological case history and spiritual confession, didactic essay and ideological testament.
>
> Albert Stone

1. Introduction

The lyrics of Louis Armstrong's piece "Let's Call the Whole Thing Off" reveal surprising linguistic peculiarities which bring the famous singer's musical work much closer to a linguist's job. Here are some revealing excerpts:

> You like potato and I like potahto,
> You like tomato and I like tomahto
> Potato, potahto, Tomato, tomahto,
> Let's call the whole thing off
> [...]
> So if you like pyjamas and I like pyjahmas,
> I'll wear pyjamas and give up pyjahmas
> For we know we need each other so we,
> Better call the whole off off
> Let's call the whole thing off.

It looks as if the poet/singer plays with his words, discovering unexpected meanings, and thus offering himself to new interpretations. It is an invitation to a close reading of his writings, which reverberate with the sounds, vocabulary, and sentence structures of his native New Orleans. Indeed, it is quite unusual to consider Luis Armstrong as an author, and most of the European fans of his songs know little or nothing of Satchmo's published works. Actually, there are two books written: *Swing that Music* (1936), and *Satchmo: My Life in New Orleans* (1954), to which we should add *Louis Armstrong in His Own Words*

(1999), a collection of letters. A closer approach to his writings reveals a different person, a sharp observer of the world around him, of those people and events that eventually shaped his existence. This is what I have been trying to capture in this presentation: a different and almost unknown facet of Satchmo's not so simple personality. It is not our intention to retell the Satchmo story, but to place his memoirs in the much larger tradition of African American life writing. Undoubtedly, Louis Armstrong was not only one of the greatest jazzmen in the history of the genre. He was an American institution, a jazz ambassador to the world. His rich personality, his love of the music he played and the people with whom he played it, his joy of life, were engulfing.

2. On Autobiographies and Memoirs

The Concise Oxford Dictionary offers several definitions for the memoir and autobiography. Briefly, we are dealing with a historical account or biography written from personal knowledge or special sources, a personal account of one's own life, meant to be published, which *may* take literary form. The literary form is not compulsory.

Generally speaking, a memoir – or an autobiography, as the case may be – is a rather special category of diary, having certain sources and functions. Autobiographies are not written to remain unknown. Moreover, they have been written by artists or non-artistic personalities who use the word, sound, and their art to justify themselves to their contemporaries and posterity. Their importance resides in the events they describe and comment upon. It is very possible that they will later become literary works in themselves, and that the author will be later considered as their own character, but the initial function of a memoir or an autobiography is not an aesthetic one.

Autobiographies written by different celebrities are meaningful as far as the respective celebrities have behind themselves a richness of actions they accomplished, or events they witnessed or even set in motion. Thus, we have autobiographies of Saint-Simon, Churchill and De Gaulle, Chaplin and Louis Armstrong. The question is: Are they literary works? Maybe not, but they all have the chance to become so.

There are several causes that contribute to the alleged inaccuracy or even imposture that has been attributed to autobiography. As early as 1929, in his *Aspects of Biography*, André Maurois systematizes these causes into a number of categories. The first category Maurois mentions is "oblivion." According to the

French biographer, we are prone to forget many of the events of our existence. Further on, Maurois refers to what he calls "distortion" or "voluntary amnesia" justified by aesthetic reasons, mostly in the case of those authors who happen to be talented artists as well. Then, there is another kind of distortion due to a natural censorship exerted by the spirit upon everything disagreeable. Censorship may also be exerted by decency. Last but not least, there is voluntary censorship due to reason. Certain events in one's life are later explained by rationalization. He/She invents a system of causes for which the event would constitute the effect. Thus, an event is conferred with an exemplary value. Actually, the event is the work of chance.

One important aspect should not be ignored: in this particular case, the lack of authenticity is not a literary criterion. As a matter of fact, all authors declare that they are totally sincere, and we must take this at face value. The author's introduction, an always present component in the structure of any confession, usually resorts to a reversal of the conative function of language – that *captatio benevolentiae* supported by such elements as sincerity and uniqueness common to all authors, irrespective of time and place. In order to stand on our guard against any ambiguities, we should not forget that any individual in this world will only tell of him/herself stories that can be encoded. The same material – the word – is used for the most intense passions and for the most insignificant sensations. The word is used by the author to talk about him/herself or about his/her characters. Individuals with the most unusual experiences are not more favored than those exhibition visitors who can only utter the 'How beautiful!' stereotype in front of the paintings on display. The literature of confession is and continues to be a convention, just like all other literary conventions.

Finally, whatever an author presents about himself is a certain image that he/she might not recognize after a while. Kio Gisors, the protagonist of Malraux's *La condition humaine* records his own voice on discs. When listening to the recordings, he fails to recognize it. His father explains: "We hear the voice of the others with our ears, while our own voice we hear with our throat; even if you plug your ears, you will hear your own voice." This might be the mechanism we could imagine as characteristic of the author and his/her autobiography.

Philippe Lejeune, in his essay "The Autobiographical Pact," gives the following definition to the autobiography: "[autobiography] is a retrospective narrative produced by a real person concerning his own existence, focusing on his individual life, in particular on the development of his personality" (192).

Commenting on Lejeune's definition, Kenneth Mostern considers that it "would quickly take us into the referential problematic on the side of the necessity of reference to a thing called a 'personality,' probably [...] an already given and unconstructed reification" (Mostern 33). Later on, the French critic acknowledges the inadequacy of this definition when it comes to establish whether a text belongs or does not belong to the genre of autobiography, and he introduces the notion of the 'autobiographical pact,' the very word 'pact' being an explicitly metaphysical notion rather than a contractual metaphor.

Such an autobiographical pact comes in several forms which have in common "their intention to honor" the "signature" of the autobiographer. This intention is demonstrated with reference to the title page of any given book; it is here that "we make use of a general textual criterion, the identity ('identicalness') of the *name* (author-narrator-protagonist). The autobiographical pact is the affirmation in the text of this identity, referring back in the final analysis to the *name* of the author on the cover" (Lejeune 13, 14).

Further on, the same author offers a surprising addition to his definition:

> In spite of the fact that autobiography is impossible, this in no way prevents it from existing. Perhaps, in describing it, I in turn took my desire for reality; but what I had wanted to do, was to describe this reality in its reality, a reality shared by a great number of authors and readers. (131-32)

In *Autobiography and Black Identity Politics: Racialization in Twentieth-Century America*, Kenneth Mostern offers a pattern that allows readers to properly understand contemporary theories on autobiography. We are invited to position ourselves according to two distributive axes: an axis of referentiality, and an axis of subjectivity. In this case,

> "Referentiality" refers to the question of whether autobiography is to be understood as representing, or as nonrepresentational with regard to, a real world external to the text. "Subjectivity" refers to discussions of the position of the speaking subject, the "I" (or, in those few cases without "I," the point of view) which narrates the autobiographical text – its social positioning and construction, its number, its autonomy, its relationship to other subject-positions. No definition of autobiography is possible without some explicit or implicit position along each of these axes. (28)

In his seminal study, *The Black Atlantic: Modernity and Double Consciousness*, Paul Gilroy refers to the tradition of African American autobiography, and considers that autobiography "expresses in the most powerful way a tradition of writing in which autobiography becomes an act or process of simultaneous self-creation and self-emancipation" and

> the presentation of a public persona thus becomes a founding motif within the expressive culture of the African diaspora [...]. Eagerly received by the [abolition] movement to which they were addressed, these [autobiographies] helped to mark out a dissident space within the bourgeois public sphere which they aimed to suffuse with their utopian content. The autobiographical character of many [public] statements is thus absolutely crucial. (69)

Kenneth Mostern comments on Gilroy's statement only to conclude that "The tradition of African-American writing is thus one in which political commentary necessitates, invites, and assumes autobiography as its rhetorical form" (11). According to Mostern,

> Gilroy's claim that the autobiographical mode of political representation is, then, a culturally-based ethical pattern, is borne out by the extent to which *nearly all* African-American political leaders (regardless of politics; self-designated or appointed by one or another community) have chosen to write personal stories as a means of theorizing their political positions. (11-12)

In his *"Race," Writing and Difference* (1985) Henry Louis Gates Jr. contributed the following comment on Black autobiography:

> The narrated, descriptive "eye" was put into service as a literary form to posit both the individual "I" of the black author as well as the collective "I" of the race. Text created author; and black authors, it was hoped, would create, or re-create, the image of the race in European discourse. The very *face* of the race was contingent upon the recording of the black *voice*. Voice presupposed a face, but also seems to have been thought to determine the very contours of the black face. (11)

One interesting approach to the genre is that offered by William Spengemann who, in his *The Forms of Autobiography: Episodes in the History of a Li-*

terary Genre (1980), distinguishes between *historical autobiography*, *philosophical autobiography*, and *poetic autobiography*. Thus, *historical autobiography* "assumes a kind of self-knowledge based upon a true and stable account of the past," *philosophical autobiography* "reflects a changing self determined by a mixture of present and past circumstance," while *poetic autobiography* "occurs when the self can be represented only through the performance of symbolic action" (xiii).

But the authenticity of autobiography has been questioned and even doubted. The autobiographer is expected to tell the truth. This assumption, according to Shirley Neuman, is "the most fundamental article of good faith between autobiographer and his readers." On the other hand, the difficulty of being truthful to one's memories, to one's past, makes Neuman ask:

> If the autobiographer does scrupulously recount what he *believes* to be true about his self (or to have been true at the time about which he is writing), how do we know that the so-called truth is not what he *wishes* were the case (and therefore may have come to believe *is* the case) rather than a verifiable presentation of himself? (317, 336)

The answer is given by John Paul Eakin in his *How Our Lives Become Stories* (1999). Eakin seeks to isolate and define both the author and truth in life writing: "Autobiographical truth is not a fixed but an evolving content in an intricate process of self-discovery and self-creation, and [...] the self that is the center of all autobiographical narrative is necessarily a fictive structure" (3).

An interesting example is given by the abolitionist slave narratives who were meant to be testimonies of the time, something like the "true and stable account of the past" mentioned above. But their truthfulness was first questioned and denounced by the supporters of slavery, then the realities they presented and even the literacy of the accounts were doubted. As a result of their controversial content and aims, the narratives were subjected to scrutiny never applied before or since to a *class* of autobiographies. To tell the story of one's escape from slavery was to run a gauntlet of critics: the narrator's progress toward freedom, like the slave's, was hindered, if not obstructed, by the surveillance of both friend and foe.

Writing about memoir and autobiography, Caroline M. Calvillo considers that "[the self] brings to dialogue detailed, personal knowledge and understanding with regard to issues and problems of multicultural selfhood, and serves as links between cultures and generations" (51). She goes on citing Paul John Eakin who, in *How Our Lives Become Stories: Making Selves* discusses the "legitimate sense in which autobiographies testify to the individual's experience of selfhood, that testimony is necessarily mediated by available cultural models of identity and the discourses in which they are expressed." He then questions "How much of what autobiographers say they experience is equivalent to what they really experience, and how much of it is merely what they know how to say?" (4)

3. Louis Armstrong: Contested Literacy and the Use of the Typewriter

We have started this paper with an epigraph by Albert Stone who confers the genre of autobiography six different dimensions: historical record, literary artifact, psychological case history, spiritual confession, didactic essay, and ideological testament (2). In the following sections we will analyze Armstrong's writings and try to demonstrate how they fit into Stone's definition. We shall first deal with Armstrong's autobiographical writing as literary artifact, which accounts for the title of our presentation: Armstrong's unknown addiction.

Biographers have often considered the different reasons that made Armstrong write. Thomas Brothers lists several apparently different motivations. One motivation was simply to stay in touch with distant friends and admirers. It is believed that Armstrong wrote thousands of letters that await publication. Furthermore, Armstrong wrote to supply professional writers with material that they could use for publicity purposes. He learned to cultivate strategic relationships that were beneficial to both parties. One example is the autobiographical material he supplied Goffin for use in the biography *Horn of Plenty*. Some magazines were interested in presenting Armstrong's own words directly to their readers. Publicity was one motivation for these articles. Armstrong had a great urge to set the historical record straight, and cherished any opportunity to communicate with his fans, and in this sense publication provided him with another kind of public stage. Last but not least, according to Brothers, Armstrong wrote because he saw himself as a writer. His writing became a hobby. This hobby was well suited for passing time in a dressing room or hotel. His portable typewriter became his off-stage passion, though visitors sometimes made it difficult for him to find the time to write. Eventually, the hobby became part of his identity.

The same Thomas Brothers cites from a letter that Armstrong sent to Leonard Feather on December 5, 1946:

Man – I've been trying so hard to write you a letter – but owing to the fact that they have been bouncing us around so fast one would swear that we were a bunch of adagio dancers, etc. […] Haha. But I just wouldn't let it 'Bugme […]. I intend writing you at the Golden Gate Theater in San Francisco California […]. Huh […]. My dressing room was so crowded all the times, until every time I made an attempt to write a paragraph they'd look at me so wistful until I'd stop writing automatically […]. You know how my disciples are. […] Tee Hee. (xx-xxi).

According to a radio interview that was transcribed by Armstrong's management and entered into a publicity booklet from the late 1940s, Armstrong, the "two-fingered blip on the typewriter," who carried a dictionary and a book of synonyms and antonyms in his brief case, did write a book in which every word of it was his own, so he could read it and understand it:

ANNOUNCER: You are a writer, too, Louie?
LOUIS: Man, I'm a two-fingered blip on my portable typewriter.
ANNOUNCER: That reminds me, you did write a book once, didn't you Louie, without the assistance of a ghost writer or press agent, they tell me?
LOUIS: That's right! We called it "Swing That Music" and it might not have been a literary masterpiece, but every word of it was my own, so I can read it and understand it (qtd. in Brothers ix-x).

It is the candid confession of the autobiographer, who disregards his own value as a writer who wrote down his thoughts and memories – a text that he could read and understand.

Armstrong's two autobiographies – *Swing that Music* (1936) and *Satchmo: My Life in New Orleans* (1954) – first introduce readers to his highly individualized, idiosyncratic writing style. Like his music, this style combines disciplined craftsmanship with inspired, exuberant improvisation – with plenty of sheer prankishness and showmanship on the side. Remarkably, *Louis Armstrong, in his Own Words* is even more unconventional than its predecessors. This is because Brothers has made it a point not to sanitize Armstrong's language, correct his (sometimes bizarre) punctuation, or curtail his whimsical typographic escapades.

In *Louis Armstrong: An Extravagant Life*, Bergreen explores the larger cultural and historical context of the virtuoso jazz entertainer, filling out the life of the great 'Satchmo' with the help of prolific autobiographical writings Armstrong was constantly working on at home and on the road, including previously unpublished manuscripts about his extensive use of marijuana which his managers suppressed during his lifetime 'for his own sake.'

According to Laurence Bergreen,

> Louis wrote as he spoke, in torrents of phrases linked by ellipses, as if he were writing an endless gossip column, the gossip of his life. He preferred to write on his stationery, in green ink on yellow paper, and when that was not available, on hotel stationery, even on the back of an envelope containing a letter inside.

He distributed his confessional letters across the world to his correspondents, and some of them later appeared in popular magazines such as *True*, *Esquire*, and *Ebony*, which were willing to run his raw tales of his youth and sexual adventures pretty much as he wrote them. Many others have found their way into libraries and archives, and countless others languish in private hands. Eventually, in his early fifties, he summoned the confidence to write his autobiography, published under the title *Satchmo: My Life in New Orleans*. He wrote it by himself, without the aid of a ghostwriter, secretary, or amanuensis, and the book became a summation of all the letters he had ever written and stories he had ever told about the good old, bad old days in New Orleans.

The outcome of all this ceaseless literary activity, which neatly complemented his musical outpouring, was a kind of self-analysis, for his writing always returned to the same cluster of themes: how I became who I am; how my experiences, especially as a boy, have left indelible marks on me; and, implicitly, how I learned to turn adversity into happiness most of the time, and music all the time. Though confessional, his writing was never intended to be private. Except when he was intent on saving his energy for a performance, Louis was exceptionally gregarious – too gregarious to confine his writing to a diary, and too much of an exhibitionist not to tell everybody, if only for sheer shock value. Writing was for him a transactional process, a conversation with another person, and his conversation always came back to the same point: how the grim circumstances into which he had been born and raised in fact constituted a charmed life, the ideal childhood for a jazz musician.

Composing in syncopated riffs, treating the keyboard like a musical instrument, Armstrong produced his own distinctive word-jazz: a spicy gumbo of standard English, Black English, street slang, Bronzeville and Harlem jive, down-home colloquialisms, Southern regionalisms, Louisiana pidgin, Creole patois, and, most remarkably, his own outrageous coinages and shorthand terms (e.g., "somphn" for "something," "sommitch" for SOB, or "son of a bitch").

Among the now well-known slang expressions that Armstrong either introduced into general use or helped popularize are *gage* (for marijuana), *chops* (for lips, mouth, or a horn player's embouchure), and *chick* (young woman). Similarly, *to get ice* in Armstrong-speak means "to receive a cool reception"; *to wedge* means "to fit together or harmonize musically;" *to lush* is "to go on a liquor binge;" and *to get gassed* means to get a konk or hair-straightening job. Armstrong is also frequently cited as the main source or popularizer of words like *scat, gate* (a greeting among jazz musicians that became a popular WWII term for a buddy or pal) and the still current use of *chill*, as in "chill out."

Meanwhile a few choice Satchmo-isms remain downright obscure. For example, his favorite way of describing a dynamite musical performance was to call it "the Livin' Aspirin" – apparently because good jazz makes everybody feel good! Similarly, his pet name for an old patched tuxedo (to this day a standard apparel item among New Orleans street musicians) was a "roast beef," though exactly why is anybody's guess. Armstrong's love of unusual or custom-crafted language even carried over to the signature phrases that he used to conclude his letters: three of his favorites were "Swiss Krissly yours" (referring to his favorite herbal laxative), "Red beans and ricely" (his favorite Creole dish), and of course "trumpetly" (self-explanatory).

In the Da Capo edition of *Satchmo: My Life in New Orleans*, Dan Morgenstern mentions the doubts cast on the authorship of *Satchmo* by James Lincoln Collier. According to Collier, "the two books Armstrong signed – one of which he probably wrote, in the main – are unreliable" (viii). Nevertheless, the Louis Armstrong Archives, located in the Benjamin Rosenthal Library on the Queens College campus Louis Armstrong House in Corona, Queens, contains 12 linear feet of personal papers, correspondence, and autobiographical manuscripts. Also, a copy of *Satchmo* can be found in the archives of the Institute of Jazz Studies at Rutgers University.

Unlettered as he was, Armstrong could write and enjoyed writing. He wrote with pen, pencil, and the typewriter, addressing himself to a less than ordinary audience of whores, pimps, and hustlers. To cite Morgenstern,

> Writing was a natural expression of his gift for the spoken word, his love of storytelling, and his ceaseless fascination with the foibles of human be-

ings. Graceful, effortless, unselfconscious, but always at pains to make his meaning clear [...] Armstrong's prose style reflects structural and emotional aspects of his musical expression. It is, of course, much more down to earth, but after all, Armstrong wrote for relaxation. Music [...] was work. (qtd. in Armstrong, *Satchmo* x)

4. Satchmo the Observer
4.1. New Orleans

Considering Stone's assumption that autobiography is, among others, a historical record, let us look at Satchmo's writings as a record of life in New Orleans, spiced by the author's own comments. Written when he was fifty-four, *Satchmo: My Life in New Orleans* evolves in a crowded section of the city, Back o' Town – which by no means should be compared to Front o' Town, Uptown or Downtown – on James Alley, in the very heart of The Battlefield, inhabited by "churchpeople, gamblers, hustlers, cheap pimps, thieves, prostitutes and lots of children. There were bars, honky-tonks and saloons, and lots of women walking the streets for tricks to take to their 'pads,' as they called their rooms." (8)

Satchmo interweaves a first-hand account of early-twentieth-century New Orleans with a first person narrative of the first twenty-one years of Armstrong's life. It tells the rags-to-riches tale of Armstrong's early life and the social and musical forces that shaped him. The city and the musician are both extraordinary, their relationship unique, and their impact on American culture incalculable.

In the early twentieth century, New Orleans was a place of colliding identities and histories, and Louis Armstrong was a gifted young man of psychological nimbleness. A dark-skinned, impoverished child, he grew up under low expectations, Jim Crow legislation, and vigilante terrorism. Yet he also grew up at the center of African American vernacular traditions from the Deep South, learning the ecstatic music of the Sanctified Church, blues played by street musicians, and the plantation tradition of ragging a tune.

Storyville was the only legal red-light district in the country. And it flourished at the time that Louis was growing up there. He lived about a block or two away from it. And it flourished until 1917, when the U.S. government shut it down. This meant that he grew up in an environment populated by pimps and gangsters and prostitutes and gamblers and other assorted hangers-on. These were the people he knew and felt comfortable with, and basically loved, throughout his entire life.

Dan Morgenstern concludes his *Introduction* to the Da Capo Edition with a friendly piece of advice to the readers:

> Reading this little book without preconceptions, and above all without the blinding burden of modernistic sociological and psychological notions about class, race, "intellect," and high versus popular culture, will bring you a bit closer to the mysterious wellsprings of Louis Armstrong's art, and to one of nature's noblemen – in the truest sense of the poet's term" (xiii).

I had no preconceptions in reading this book, as I have never had any preconceptions in dealing with other aspects of African American literature. I have read Armstrong's autobiography as one reads a *Bildungsroman,* trying to identify those elements that had contributed to the shaping of an extraordinary character, coupled with Armstrong's minute observations of his life in New Orleans. They are the observations of an insider to whom "Jane Alley hung between night and day, beast and man, Africa and America: a short passageway from the Congo forests to the white man's house – and the cesspool in which he [Louis's father] would drown if he did not escape very soon" (Goffin 8).

Of course, this is not a singular case. Franklin's *Autobiography* relies on a larger cultural narrative, the *Bildungsroman*, which has widely accepted currency in the United States. The *Bildungsroman* follows a classic narrative trajectory of conversion in which the individual hero embarks on a long journey that ends with his resolution with the larger social community – in Franklin's case, the national community as represented by Philadelphia. The *Bildungsroman* provides narrative shape and truth-value to a wide range of mainstream and marginal autobiographies published in the United States, from Franklin's to Mary Antin's *The Promised Land* (1912), Jade Snow Wong's *Fifth Chinese Daughter* (1950), Malcolm X and Alex Haley's *The Autobiography of Malcolm X* (1965), and Rodriguez's *Hunger of Memory* (1981).

Several immigrant, ethnic, and women autobiographers have relied on the *Bildungsroman* to give their stories a recognizable trajectory and broad cultural currency. And this is no accident. Indeed many autobiographers have used this form deliberately and strategically in order to persuade their readers that they too deserve a place of privilege in the United States and that their achievement of the "American Dream" is a result of individual hard work and intelligence. Therefore many autobiographies that are shaped by the *Bildungsroman* narrative downplay structural inequities such as gender, ethnicity, race, class, sexuality, and ability. Wong and Rodriguez, for example, openly dispute the assumption that gender or ethnicity has served as a barrier in their lives, even when their autobiographies clearly show otherwise. The *Bildungsroman*, then, is a form that both enables and constrains the kinds of life stories that can be told by particular autobiographers. In this wider context, Armstrong's experience of his childhood in New Orleans may be regarded as a *rite of passage*, a ritual that open his way to an early adulthood and influenced his own way of understanding the society around him.

Louis's un-thought-of *Bildungsroman* – and autobiography as well – is a first-person narrative. It has a setting and characters. There is no definite plot, as it is given by the autobiographer's own experience. He is the storyteller who finds strength and inspiration in his surroundings and the people he knows. They are the women and men of New Orleans and not only, they are the people who give shape and meaning to his life and music.

Before proceeding, I am taking the risk of a final remark, however wrong it might sound: regardless of the possible brushing up done by his editors, the language of Satchmo's sentences when he refers to his native Storyville is obviously much more carefully chosen than that of his numerous letters. His addiction to words is in a state of restraint, as if the author was fully conscious of the chance to have his work read by others.

4.2. The Women

I should say 'women as characters,' or women as actors in the formation of the protagonist. Armstrong's is perhaps the most user friendly account of the life of the ordinary women – prostitutes included – in the New Orleans of his time. I am not going into the linguistic or grammatical details of his accounts – such as 'nobody ain't going to give you nothing' – but a detailed description of the main characters is worth the trouble.

There were many women who – in one way or another – surrounded him during his early years. They were not only his grandmother and mother, and other close relatives (sister Mama Lucy and cousins Flora and Louis Miles), but also the musicians' wives with their good cooking and friendly attitude, and last but not least, the prostitutes that had surrounded him since his coming into this world.

Louis's childhood and adolescence revolved mostly around the personalities of his grandmother and mother. "Ever since I was a baby I have had great love for my grandmother. She spent the best of her days raising me, and teaching me right from wrong" (10). The boy's farewell promises to Grandma Josephine reveal the simple basics of a child's education in the New Orleans black community: "I love you so much, grandma. You have been so kind and so nice to me, taught me everything I know: how to take care of myself, how to wash myself and brush my teeth, put my clothes away, mind the older folks" (13).

The same grandmother would take Louis to the white folks' houses where she had to do washing and housework. It was the time that little Louis first became race conscious: playing hide-and-seek with the clever little white kids, he was always 'It':

> While she was working I used to play games with the little white boys out in the yard. Hide-and-go-seek was one of the games we used to play, and every time we played I was It. And every time I would hide those clever little white kids always found me. That sure would get my goat. Even when I was at home or in kindergarten getting my lessons I kept wishing grand-ma would hurry up and go back to her washing job so I could find a place to hide where they could not find me. (9)

The other woman in Louis's life was his mother, Mayann. It was she who went away from home, leaving little Louis in his grandmother's care, while she spent her time in a red-light district, "filled with cheap prostitutes," keeping his mother's business away from the boy's sight, and managing to be treated with the greatest respect both by the church folks and the lowest roughneck. The same Mayann is deeply concerned the boy's health: "Always remember when you're sick nobody ain't going to give you nothing. So try to stay healthy" (16), while her views on education show in Louis's own remarks:

> As I grew up around Liberty and Perdido I observed everything and everybody. I loved all those people and they loved me. The good ones and the bad ones all thought that Little Louis (as they called me) was O.K. I stayed in my place, I respected everybody and I was never rude or sassy. Mayann and grandmother taught me that. (28)

One final remark is on the way Mayann taught Louis how to deal with his drinks, and how their drinking adventure finally turned into a genuine rite of passage for the young man. It is quite an unusual aspect of the many possible educational influences a mother might have on her son, and therefore worth citing: "Son," Mayann said, "I am convinced that you know how to hold your liquor. Judging by what happened last night you can take care of yourself. I feel that I have found out just what I wanted to know. You can look out for yourself if anything happens to me. I felt very proud of myself" (205).

The prostitutes form the background of female presence in Louis's childhood. Most of them are anonymous, just like the pimps and other tough guys who proudly watch Louis leading the band of the Colored Waifs' Home for Boys. One of them is the nameless woman for whom Louis acted as a pimp himself, because he wanted 'to be in the swim.'

Others have names, like pretty Deborah and Mary Jack the Bear who fight over a pimp they were sharing. There is also Irene, whom Louis helped financially "until she could get on her feet," and for whom he almost got killed; Lulu White, the owner of Mahogany Hall, who had "some of the biggest diamonds anyone would want to look at. Some of the finest furs. […] And some of the finest yellow gals working for her" (147). Daisy Parker, who was wearing artificial hips to give herself a good figure and whom he eventually married. To put it in the author's words,

> The gals in my neighborhood did not stand in cribs wearing their fine silk lingerie as they did in Storyville. They wore the silk lingerie just the same, but under their regular clothes. Our hustlers sat on their steps and called to the "Johns" as they passed by. They had to keep an eye on the cops all the time, because they weren't allowed to call the tricks like the girls in Storyville. That was strictly a business center. Music, food and everything else was good there. (95)

Armstrong often provides a firsthand account of the intimate life of a brothel:

> Those prosperous prostitutes who came to our joint would give us lots of tips to play different tunes for them and their "Johns." Sometimes the girls used to make their tricks give us money on general principles. The chicks liked to see their boys spend money since they could not get it for themselves all at once. Besides, the chicks liked us personally. (197)

4.3. The Men

Among the men that Armstrong got in touch with and who contributed to his formation as a man, his father seems to have had the least influence on him: "My father did not have time to teach me anything;" Louis writes, "he was too busy chasing chippies" (29). Having left his family when Louis was only one, he only spent one year with his son when Louis was fourteen. Nevertheless, the boy's perception of his father was admiring enough:

> My real dad was a sharp man, tall and handsome and well built. He made the chicks swoon when he marched by as the grand marshal in the Odd Fellows parade. I was very proud to see him in his uniform and his high hat with the beautiful streamer hanging down by his side. Yes, he was a fine figure of a man, my dad. Or at least that is the way he seemed to me as a kid when he strutted by like a peacock at the head of the Odd Fellows parade. (29)

Numerous, and not so different from one another, were the boy's 'stepfathers,' whose trousers he was wearing: "Mayann had enough 'stepfathers' to furnish me with plenty of trousers. All I had to do was turn my back and a new 'pappy' would appear. Some of them were fine guys, but others were low lives" (26).

Albert was the worst of all, Slim "was not a bad guy but he drank too much" (27), and stepfather Gabe – the best of all – whom the boy liked a lot. Stepfather Tom used to bring them leftovers from the restaurant he served. And all of them, together with the other gamblers and pimps and tough guys were part of the boy's human environment that he loved and learned to respect. One interesting segment of this society was made up of the working people – childhood friends, neighbors – who often mingled in the honky-tonks to listen to music and partake of the drinking, gambling and the prompt service of the prostitutes. Many of the tough guys – quick with their gun or knife, just like some of the prostitutes Louis mentions – were also pimps, gamblers, and musicians: "Other characters who had me spellbound in the third ward during those years were Black Benny, Cocaine Buddy, Nicodemus, Slippers, Red Cornelius, Aaron Harris and George Bo'hog. They were as tough as they come" (75). Watching all these people fighting, Louis had developed a deep respect for tough fighters. "Let the best man win, that was the rule" (78). It was a rule that Louis later translated to his playing.

It is a dizzying world, in which everyone seems to be playing one instrument or another, be it in a honky-tonk, a cabaret, or in a parade, in a night long musical session or at a funeral. Schools are proud of their bands, prisoners are released on parole only to be able to play their instruments, and the competition is fierce. Bands were always forming and breaking up, the musicians changing jobs. The list of musicians is too long to mention here, but Armstrong himself never forgets to mention his early admiration for people like Buddy Bolden and Bunk Johnson, Mr. Jones of the Colored Waifs' Home, Isaac Smooth, or Black Benny, Freddy Keppard and Bunk Johnson, Joe Oliver, and Kyd Ory, to mention just a few:

> There's lots of musicians I'll be mentioning, especially the ones I played with and had dealings with from time to time. All in all, I had a wonderful life playing with them. Lots of them were characters, and when I say "characters" I mean *characters*! I've played with some of the finest musicians in the world, jazz and classic. God bless them, all of them! (141)

And everything was marked by fighting and rivalry, and such personalities of the underground world as Joe Segretta and Henry Ponce.

4.4. Attitude towards Race

The Jim Crow attitudes were always present in Armstrong's early life. He had his first experience of racial segregation when riding a street car with a woman who had accompanied him to his grandmother, and could not understand what the sign FOR COLORED PASSANGERS ONLY meant. Here is the full excerpt:

> It was my first experience with Jim Crow. I was just five, and I had never ridden on a street car before. Since I was the first to get on, I walked right up to the front of the car without noticing the signs on the backs of the seats on both sides, which read: FOR COLORED PASSENGERS ONLY. Thinking the woman was following me, I sat down in one of the front seats. However, she did not join me, and when I turned to see what had happened, there was no lady. Looking all the way to the back of the car, I saw her waving to me frantically.
> "Come here, boy," she cried. "Sit where you belong."
> I thought she was kidding me so I stayed where I was, sort of acting cute. What did I care where she sat? Shucks, that woman came up to me and jerked me out of the seat. Quick as a flash she dragged me to the back of

> the car and pushed me into one of the rear seats. Then I saw the signs on the backs of the seats saying: FOR COLORED PASSENGERS ONLY.
> "What do those signs say?" I asked.
> "Don't ask so many questions! Shut your mouth, you little fool." (14-15)

This rather long citation sends the reader to different directions. Linguistically, the text may be read as a version of the 'talking book trope': just as the slave in Gate's account could not possibly read the scriptures, the five-year old boy could not read and understand the sign FOR COLORED PASSENGERS ONLY. The slave opened the Bible and got no answer, the boy simply walked to the front of the car. On the other hand the excerpt is a clear example of racism, segregation, and exclusion. That the matter of sitting wherever you like on a bus had not yet been solved by Rosa Park who, later on, refused to obey the bus driver's order that she give up her seat to make room for a white passenger. It is the autobiographer's first instance of exclusion which – later on in his career – he would comment upon as a practically inexistent matter.

The excerpt is also an example of racism which goes hand in hand with exclusion. The Southern Blacks were denied access to the simple, everyday facilities of the city, and the boy is violently dragged to the end of the car, to 'sit where he belongs.' The sign was a proof of the exclusion policy that was a marker of the Jim Crow politics, which Armstrong knew so well. This denial had almost universal dimensions, and the African Americans could do nothing but to suit themselves in a space which – though belonging to all – denied their presence.

Notably, later in his life, Armstrong managed to cross the line of adversity and played to the enthusiastic whites.

Other mentions of race are rather scarce; the only explanation for this is that the world he lived in was a colored people's world and the presence of whites only occasional, mostly as employers. It is worth mentioning Armstrong's comments on the cruise up and down the Mississippi, in Fate Marable's Band and the barriers it broke:

> Fate Marable's Band deserves credit for breaking down a few barriers on the Mississippi – barriers set up by Jim Crow. [...] At first we ran into some ugly experiences while we were on the bandstand, and we had to listen to plenty of nasty remarks. But most of us were from the South anyway. We were used to that kind of jive, and we would just keep on swinging as though nothing had happened. Before the evening was over they

loved us. We couldn't turn for them singing our praises and begging us to hurry back. (189)

His personal relationship to whites is also recorded. Armstrong is seen as able to handle racism as long as his music – or music, in general – is appreciated:

> We were colored, and we knew what that meant. We were not allowed to mingle with the white guests under any circumstances. We were there to play good music for them, and that was all. [...] I have always loved my white folks, and they have always proved that they loved me and my music. I have never had anything to be depressed about in that respect, only respect and appreciation. (194-95)

5. Conclusion

I am again referring to Albert Stone's definition of autobiography which is "the simultaneously historical record and literary artifact, psychological case history and spiritual confession, didactic essay and ideological testament." We have thus far considered his writings as literary artifact and historical record. It has not been our purpose to go into a deep linguistic analysis of his writing. Also, his autobiographies do not fit into the framework of the rest of the four dimensions Stone mentioned.

On the other hand, at the beginning of the theoretical section of this presentation, I referred to Maurois's *Aspects of Biography*. If we were to apply Maurois's principles to Armstrong's texts, we will definitely come to the following conclusions: regarding 'oblivion,' Louis Armstrong clearly demonstrates an amazing memory, offering a great range of facts and names. Then, there is any voluntary amnesia in the case of *Satchmo*. The only doubts regarding Armstrong's autobiography refer to his birthday. He was born on August 4, 1901, and not on July 4, 1900, as he declares. As regards personal censorship, he was simply offering his inner thoughts and feelings to his publishers. The disagreeable things in his life were just normal, natural, and even to be expected. Considering the special milieu Armstrong grew up in – an environment abounding in prostitutes, pimps, gamblers, hustlers, and thieves – he showed great restraint in avoiding coarse language – not to be confused with his use of Southern regionalisms, colloquialisms, and Harlem jive. Last but not least, his is the story of a 'boyhood dream come true,' and the particular events in his early life are by no means rationalized in this manner.

Armstrong's autobiographies reveal the multiplicity of his personality, its extremes and its interior struggles. The texts offer a vivid picture of New Orleans in the first decades of the twentieth century, an insider's view of the world of jazz, written in a surprisingly varied spoken language, rich in colloquialisms, Louisiana pidgin, Creole patois, and, most interesting, Armstrong's own slang. Paraphrasing him, it was impossible for Satchmo to speak of anyone he knew nothing about. His characters are real people, and we are witnessing an amazing outpouring of emotions, intimate thoughts and feelings, all expressed with humor, and an overwhelming love of his "wonderful world" with its "skies of blue and clouds of white / The bright blessed day, the dark sacred night."

Louis Armstrong's addiction to the typewriter and the written word did not need any cure.

Works Cited
Primary Sources
Armstrong, Louis. *Swing That Music*. Cambridge: Da Capo P, 1936.
---. *Satchmo: My Life in New Orleans*. New York: Prentice Hall, 1954.
Armstrong, Louis, and Thomas Brothers. *Louis Armstrong in His Own Words*.
    New York: Oxford UP, 1999.

Secondary Sources
Bergreen, Laurence. *Louis Armstrong: An Extravagant Life*. New York:
    Broadway Books, 1997. N.d. <http://www.laurencebergreen.com/armstrong-excerpt.html>.
Brothers, Thomas. *Louis Armstrong's New Orleans*. New York: W.W. Norton
    and Company, 2006.
Calvillo, Caroline M. "Memoir and Autobiography: Pathways to Examining the
    Multicultural Self." *Multicultural Education* 11.1 (2003): 51-54.
Collier, James Lincoln. *Louis Armstrong, An American Genius*. New York:
    Oxford UP, 1985.

Eakin, Paul John. *Fictions in Autobiography: Studies in the Art of Self-Invention*. Princeton: Princeton UP, 1985.

---. *How Our Lives Become Stories: Making Selves*. Indiana: Cornell UP, 1999.

Gates, Henry Louis, Jr. "Writing 'Race,' and the Difference It Makes." *"Race," Writing and Difference*. Ed. Henry Louis Gates Jr. Chicago: U of Chicago P, 1985. 1-20.

Gilroy, Paul. *The Black Atlantic: Modernity and Double Consciousness*. New York: Oxford UP, 1994.

Goffin, Robert. *Horn of Plenty: The Story of Louis Armstrong*. Trans. James F. Bezou. New York: Allen, Towne & Heath, Inc. 1947.

Maurois, André. *Aspects of Biography*. Trans. S. C. Roberts. Cambridge: Cambridge UP, 1929.

Mostern, Kenneth. *Autobiography and Black Identity Politics: Racialization in Twentieth-Century America*. Cambridge: Cambridge UP, 2004.

Neuman, Shirley. "The Observer Observed: Distancing the Self in Autobiography." *Prose Studies* 4.3 (1981): 317-36.

Lejeune, Philippe. "The Autobiographical Contract." *French Literary Theory Today*. Ed. Tzvetan Todorov. Cambridge: Cambridge UP, 1982. 192-222.

Spengemann, William. *The Forms of Autobiography: Episodes in the History of a Literary Genre*. New Haven: Yale UP, 1980.

Stone, Albert, ed. *The American Autobiography: A Collection of Critical Essays*. Englewood Cliffs: Prentice, 1981.

Simone A. James Alexander

Embodied Subjects: Policing and Politicking the Black Female Body[1]

From time immemorial, the black female body has been the target of securitization or regimental policing. Dorothy Roberts' *Killing the Black Body* chronicles one such form of policing. Biological or reproductive control of black women's bodies is, in her summation, an obvious practice of racial oppression that serves the interests of white supremacy. Evelynn Hammonds concurs, articulating that "African Americans continue to be used as the terrain upon which contested notions about race, gender, and sexuality are worked out" (170). Illuminating a rather slight shift in the discourse over the years, Audre Lorde in recounting her personal experience with breast cancer demonstrates how mandatory state- or institution-sanctioned medicalization and surgical transformation of the body serve as regulatory forces, imposing strategies of policing and profiling of individual bodies.[2] Addressing state regulation or surveillance of the black female body, Lorde inscribes her body as primary text, challenging the normalized white, healthy able-bodied, while at the same time invalidating the established order of the "dominant" national body. Patricia Hill Collins shares that in keeping with the value placed on whiteness that becomes manifest in the "preoccupation with reproducing the White middle class," American national identity (body) is constructed within the framework of a white middle-class ideal (120-21).[3] Furthering this line of reasoning Jael Silliman and Anannya Bhattacharjee argue that "particular communities and women within them are conceived and reproduced as threats to the national body, imagined as white and middle-class" (xii). Consequently, state involvement is much more prevalent in controlling the bodies of working-class and poor women, who undoubtedly experience markedly different state surveillance or control than their white middle-class female counterparts.

Addressing this disparity, Lorde articulates how the dis-eased is "circumscribed and fractionalized by the economics of disease in america" (Lorde, *Burst* 99).[4] Of primary importance is not the patient's well-being, but rather "how much is this going to cost" (Lorde, *Burst* 99)? Responding in kind to state regulation of the black female body, Lorde practices a corresponding militancy that seems to be the only available tool, or more pointedly the most effective tool, of disarmament to dismantle racist and sexist ideologies and to foil bodily intrusion.[5] Hence, she posits the diseased black body as a counter narrative that threatens the national body (politic).

As such, Lorde initiates body reconstruction by enacting a political and poetic intervention. Making no apologies for her scathing critique of the powers-that-be and her relentless campaign to identify proper care and cure of the disease that disproportionately stricken working-class and poor women, Lorde pontificates: "Of course cancer is political – look at how many of our comrades have died of it during the last ten years" (*Burst* 98)! In chronicling her fourteen-year battle with cancer, she stages an intervention against the crippling disease, an intervention against the dominant medical discourse that privileges certain able bodies while silencing others, and an intervention against the dismissal and/or separation of the private and personal for the political. Cataloguing her battle with breast cancer and her eventual mastectomy, Lorde is forced to confront questions of life and choice as she makes a case for implementing new approaches to breast cancer research and a policy that reflects the diversity of women. Accordingly, Lorde rejects outright monolithic representation and universal categorizing and treatment of female bodies, cautioning that the adoption of an undifferentiated and limited approach results in the essentializing and eventual silencing of certain bodies. To this end, she calls for the articulation and interaction of race, class, and gender as a corollary to understanding women's bodies and their health concerns.

Arising out of Lorde's apprehension, and her interrogation of specific medical practices, this essay examines how despite the many accomplishments made by feminist scholars in bringing attention to women's concerns, the discourse of the black female body is still raced, gendered, and classed, notably as a means of reinforcing stereotypes rather than obliterating them. Assessing Lorde's personal journey with breast cancer or her dis/ease; using it as a gateway to address the larger societal ills that affect a people who have been rendered disabled by history (South African Saartjie Baartman is a classic example. Despite her able-bodiedness, she was rendered anomalous, a freak of nature and labeled the Hottentot Venus, by her European captors because of her physical difference),[6] and to some extent, the medical establishment (one need only recall the Tuskegee Syphilis Study), I incorporate the borrowed term "gender intersectionality," first introduced by black feminist social scientists, in my analysis to interrogate how denial of black women's embodied experiences further renders them disabled. Drawing on the theoretical musings of disability scholars in the likes of Margrit Shildrick and Rosemarie Garland-Thomson, I read Lorde's disability within a literal and allegorical framework. Sharing the childhood struggles she encountered as a disabled female subject, Lorde writes: "Growing up Fat Black Female and almost blind in america requires so much surviving that you have to learn from it or die" (*Cancer* 40; america is not capitalized in original text). Further, addressing disability as a social category, Lorde articulates: "As an African-American woman, I feel the tragedy of being an oppressed hyphenated person in America, of having no land to be our primary teacher. And this distorts us in so many ways" (*Burst* 66). As follows, Lorde introduces race to the equation, a fact reiterated by Bonnie G. Smith and Beth Hutchison: "Lorde raises the issue of what has been done to the bodies of women, of women of color, of lesbians, of the disabled" (5). Further quoting Smith and Hutchison, the following declaration is illustrative of Lorde's activism, her unwavering commitment to the women's movement: "the body – disabled, black, lesbian, female – is a recuperative one as the powerful analysis of Lorde's work demonstrates" (5).

Nevertheless, unethical practices such as the Tuskegee Syphilis Study have left an indelible mark on successive generations; hence the continued suspicion by some blacks of the medical establishment.[7] By Lorde's account, the medical establishment is complicit in reinforcing and perpetuating some of the negative stereotypes in its goal to normalize or regularize bodies, whereby it contributes to the disability of certain individuals, specifically those bodies that do not fit the ideal and are therefore deemed abnormal. In such instances that establish preconditioned health prerequisites, the issue of health itself becomes a site of debate and interrogation. As such, some of the questions I raise concern the reasons for and consequences (and oversights) of reading a body in sexualized and gendered terms as unhealthy and diseased if it fails to conform to the category of normalizing bodies.

As will be demonstrated, the category of normalization works against black women on several fronts. How, then, does this reading complicate the black woman's subjectivity who analyzes her dis/ease not only in terms of biology but in close relation with and resulting from social ills engendered by a racist, heterosexist hegemonic society? And how do women, as in the likes of Audre Lorde, who take up arms and repossess their own bodies counter this (white) masculinist discourse? Further, how does Lorde negotiate and reinforce the politics of the black female body?

Very much aware of the (obligatory) politicization of women's health, Lorde unequivocally states that she visualizes her battle with breast cancer in "very political terms." In the film *A Litany for Survival: The Life and Work of Audre Lorde*, in which director Michelle Parkerson offers a snapshot of Lorde's life and work, Lorde confesses that battling cancer "feels very, very much to me like battling racism, battling sexism." While she visualizes the "cancer cells as white South African policemen," she envisions her battle with the disease as "a sea of black faces marching over P. W. Botha; stamping apartheid into the ground." Taking a cue from Lorde, I analyze the "apartheid-like" relation and dismissal of black bodies, bringing into focus the politicization and poeticization of black women's bodies. Drawing on Edouard Glissant's brilliant theory of the "poetics," I coin the term poeticization that parallels his dis/engagement with the colonial language. Glissant unequivocally establishes

> that he had no interest in rejecting the language he speaks (French); his purpose would be better served by actions within it, by interrogating it. By the passionate intensity of his way of being in this language, he would force the Other to know his difference. He repeatedly destabilizes "standard" French in order to decategorize understandings and establish new relations, so that the constant transformation always at work in any living symbolic system, passing into the particularity of Antillean experience can form the vibrant grounds for a full and productive participation among world cultures now and in the future. (xii)

Furthermore, Glissant pinpoints how culture (that promotes domination) operates as a corollary to language whereby culture is projected unto the world as a means to dominate it, and language, "presented as universal with the aim of providing legitimacy to the attempt at domination" (28). Hence, the domination-subjugation model becomes manifest in the "Centers," self-appointed as the site of production and control and the "Peripheries," the locus of the recipients (Glissant 28). Reversing the site of knowledge; now operating from the "Periphery" to the "Center," I argue that Lorde engages the master (medical) narrative (in the given situation, the pervasive white masculinist medical discourse is paradigmatic of the patriarchal institution) in order to disengage and destabilize it. She cautions that "when language becomes most similar, it becomes most dangerous, for then differences may pass unremarked" (Lorde, *Burst* 70). Thus, women's difference can easily become the source of their marginalization and disenfranchisement. She further adds,

> As women of good faith we can only become familiar with the language of difference within a determined commitment to its use within our lives. Because we share a common language which is not of our own making and which does not reflect our deeper knowledge as women, our words frequently sound the same. (Lorde, *Burst* 70)

Mindful not to become complicit in patriarchal undertakings, Lorde objects to blindly mimicking or reproducing the patriarchal language of the medical discourse; by this accord, language functions simultaneously as a site of identification and contestation. Furthermore, the medical language that scripts the black female body is one of estrangement instead of familiarity that necessitates Lorde disengaging it so as to recuperate the black female body from oblivion. This disengagement not only facilitates dialogue between the "Peripheries," but it also destabilizes, if not altogether eliminates, the hierarchal construct of "Center" and "Periphery."

Registering the birth of the intersectional tradition, Amy Schulz and Leith Mullings draw attention to the fact that intersectionality theory was developed most prominently by black feminist social scientists in direct response to the essentialism of early second-wave feminism (5). Positing the argument that race, class, and gender inequality is a simultaneous production, Schulz and Mullings reflect on the impracticability of measuring the unique contribution of a single factor (5). Along similar lines, operating within the framework of feminist scholars' model of intersectionality, Garland-Thomson renders additional specificity to the term by referring to it as "gender intersectionality" (74). Making a direct connection between gender intersectionality and disability and crediting the nuanced and sophisticated analyses of disability to scholars' conversant with feminist theory, Garland-Thomson points out that the compelling analyses of gender intersectionality take "into consideration the ability/disability system along with race, ethnicity, sexuality, and class" (74). Following in the footsteps of the aforementioned feminists, Lorde, herself a staunch activist of women's rights and woman-centered ideologies, examines the impact of race, class, sexuality, and gender on women's health. In her quest to find a cure for and answers to women's disease/disability, she exposes immense injustices in the medical establishment, alleging that it is engaged strategically in treating breast cancer rather than preventing it. In Lorde's estimation, this corruption that is carried out at the patient's expense bears the imprint of medical breach.

Operating from a feminist perspective, grounded within the framework of feminist ethics that counters misinformation and misrepresentations, even as it interrogates "questionable" practices and calls for the empowerment of female patients, Lorde challenges biomedical science and traditional medical ethics for biases and exclusionary practices. Furthermore, Lorde's vigilance garners unflinching support from Angela Davis who refers to her heightened sense of activism as a gift that speaks directly to and convincingly of women's reality ("Sick" 18). Davis writes: "The pursuit of health in body, mind and spirit weaves in and out of every major struggle women have ever waged in our quest for social, economic and political emancipation" ("Sick" 19). Furthermore, Lorde's linking woman's disease with social ills, namely racism, sexism, classism, and heterosexism qualifies her as one of many African-American women writers during the 1970s and '80s who insisted that "individual disease is inextricably bound up with broader social ills" (Stanford 28).[8] Although in Lorde's texts the medical profession is not absent or relegated to the margins, per se (it is in fact the profession's "undisclosed dealings" that caused it to become the object of Lorde's scathing criticism), she nonetheless demonstrates how the medical profession, obsessed with medicalization, relegates women and their health concerns to the margins in favor of commercial profit. In light of this fact, Lorde adopts what Stanford appropriately refers to as a "biopsychosocial" model that entails a shift from the biomedical, whereby she is able to shed light on the sexist assumptions and presumptions in health care institutions (29).[9]

Unwavering in her effort to expose the sexism and racism inherent in medical practices, Lorde insists that we read women's health or illness through the lens of (socially-constructed) context, a claim reiterated by Davis who elucidates the need to "place our battle for universally accessible health care in its larger social and political context" (25). At the same time, Lorde cautions women about silence, which in actuality is not an armor of protection, but rather sets them apart, thereby establishing a fractured and "unhealthy" relationship between women. In this analysis, women's bodies are afflicted further and contaminated by silence, which, Lorde cautions, carries malignant symptoms similar to cancer, if not more deadly. Her campaign to cure silence, perhaps the primary symptom of disease, is indicative of her need to implement social change as "a possible therapeutic option" (Stanford 30).

One can safely argue that one of the major concerns of Lorde in *The Cancer Journals* is to bring social awareness to black women's health concerns; to break the silence that permeates their dis/ease. While doing so, she reappropriates and reinserts the black female body into the dominant discourse as healthy and able-bodied: "Battling despair does not mean [being unable to effect] change. […] It means teaching, surviving and fighting […] reclaiming this earth and our power" (Lorde, *Cancer* 17). Therefore, the disabled individual is not divorced from her social environment; does not exist in abstraction, but rather is defined in the "context of political relations and experiences" (Sherwin 23). Davis expands this discourse making a plausible assessment that "politics do not stand in polar opposition to our lives. Whether we desire it or not, they permeate our existence, insinuating themselves in the most private spaces of our lives" ("Sick" 18).

Attempting to understand her dis/ability, or more fittingly her quest for wellness, within a broader context, Lorde who embarks on what Davis calls "a collective quest for wellness" ("Sick" 18), realizes the need to venture beyond her personal lived experiences: "How do I give voice to my quests so that other women can take what they need from my experiences? How do my experiences with cancer fit into the larger tapestry of my work as a Black woman, into the history of all women" (Lorde, *Cancer* 16-17). By offering all women exclusive rights to and insights into her personal struggle, Lorde endorses the notion of a "positive woman-identified identity," rendering effective Charlotte Bunch's critical statement that "lesbian-feminism is not a political analysis 'for lesbians only'" (57). By reconfiguring the black female body within the framework of the national body, which is imagined as white, middle-class and always heterosexual, and reconstructing the disabled as able-bodied, Lorde threatens the ideology of normalization.

Further addressing what I argue is a form of "body contagion"; Lorde's interpretation of cosmetic surgery as "cosmetic sham," or what she interchangeably refers to as plasticization of the body, substantiates this line of reasoning. Cosmetic surgery, she assertively argues, similar to the carcinogenic in food, can result in the contamination of the body. In denouncing the practice, Lorde engages the process of decontamination. Here, I problematize Lorde's refusal of cosmetic surgery wherein had she accepted prosthesis she would have dismissed the more serious concerns of health, thereby rendering the non-prosthesized body as unhealthy. Shedding light on this matter, she remarks:

> Socially sanctioned prosthesis is merely another way of keeping women with breast cancer silent and separate from each other. The emphasis upon wearing a prosthesis is a way of avoiding having women come to terms with their own pain and loss, and thereby, with their own strength. (*Cancer* 16, 49)

I would like to point out that Lorde is not against prostheses in general but is against the accompanying glamorization that bears the imprint of commodification and commercialization; she objects to the performative nature of a false breast that entails and encourages the masking and masquerading of women and their bodies. Treating breast cancer as a cosmetic problem that can be "solved by a prosthetic pretense," the medical institutions and the cosmetic industries that profit from surgeries are thus involved in enabling disability (Lorde, *Cancer* 55). In countering this politics of normalization, Susan Bordo reminds us that in light of the fact that the female body is a site of struggle, "we must work to keep our daily practices in the service of resistance to gender domination, not in the service of docility and gender normalization" (*Unbearable* 105).

The public display of Saartjie Baartman signals the most efficacious historical moment of the consumption and commodification of the black female body. Baartman had been showcased to European audiences as a freak of nature because of her protruding posterior (her body, of course, was read through Western eyes). Garland-Thomson demonstrates how reading Baartman's body through the lens of Western, hegemonic discourse allows the implementation of the ability/disability system to "pathologize and exoticize" her (78). Undoubtedly, Saartjie Baartman's public display attests to Euro- and androcentric bias. In addressing the (racially-motivated and -biased) criteria for labeling bodies healthy or unhealthy, Schultz and Mullings argue that "physician scientists have played key roles in producing race, class, and gender hierarchies by 'seeing' differences in the bodies of presumably inferior groups" (28). As Saartjie Baartman's "excess flesh" becomes the object of Western consumption, Audre Lorde's lack (the result of her mastectomy) is read in similar consumerist terms. Whereas Lorde's lack points to her desexualization, Baartman's "excess flesh" that was intended to underscore her dehumanization and desexualization calls attention to her over-sexualization. Additionally, Lorde's lack both manifests in and is complicated by age. As she readily remarks: "The greatest incidence of breast cancer in american women appears within the ages of 40 to 55. These are the very years when women are portrayed in the popular media as fading and desexualized figures" (*Cancer* 63; lower case "american" in original text).

Assessing her post-mastectomy visit by a representative of the American Cancer Society's Reach for Recovery Program, Lorde notices the dissonance between her own and the representative's interest. Rather than address possible recurring health-related concerns and the transition into society, the female representative addressed issues related to physical body-image after surgery; the body (sex) appeal; its re-insertion into society as a sexualized (able) body. Lorde is quick to point out this lack:

> As a 44 year old Black Lesbian Feminist, I knew there were very few role models around for me in this situation, but my primary concerns two days after mastectomy were hardly about what man I could capture in the future, whether or not my old boyfriend would still find me attractive enough, and even less about whether my two children would be embarrassed by me around their friends. (*Cancer* 56)

Hence, the so-called medical treatment that the representative presents to Lorde arguably reproduces while it maintains systems of oppression.

A clear example where we witness oppression being reproduced is by the omission, or more pointedly the dismissal, of Lorde's lesbian sexuality, an omission that reinforces Barbara Christian's articulation that "lesbianism is a complex subject" (184). Further, Christian intimates that this subject takes on additional complexity, especially in relation to black women. As follows, Lorde's "otherness" is quadrupled as a black, lesbian, diseased woman. In like manner, her lesbianism takes on additional meaning as it is constructed within the framework of pathology, and therefore configured as dis/ease. Refuting the pathological discourse within which black lesbians are encoded, Lorde reveals that the Black lesbian has come under increasing and unwarranted attack; even by members of her own community. Accordingly, she poignantly remarks: "And within the homes of our Black communities today, it is not the Black lesbian who is battering and raping our underage girl-children out of displaced and sickening frustration" (*Sister Outsider* 49). Dismissing the perceived threat that the Black lesbian poses, Lorde cautions Black women that "view[ing] each other with suspicion, as eternal competitors" is detrimental to the black woman's sense of self for it implies "self-rejection" (*Sister Outsider* 49). Alternatively, Lorde calls for a return to female allegiance and solidarity, citing the "Amazon warriors of ancient Dahomey" and the "West African Market Women Associations" (*Sister Outsider* 49).

In Lorde's summation, the impending death with which she grapples was somewhat predetermined – indeed, preceded by symbolic death. Addressing in no uncertain terms the plight of black women, particularly their enslaved bodies and the continued oppression with which they grapple in the wider society, Lorde writes candidly; I quote her at length:

> Within this country where racial difference creates a constant, if unspoken, distortion of vision, black women have on one hand always been highly visible, and so, on the other hand, have been rendered invisible through the depersonalization of racism. Even within the women's movement, we have had to fight and still do, for that very visibility which also renders us most vulnerable, our blackness. For to survive in the mouth of this dragon we call America, we have had to learn this first and most vital lesson – that we were never meant to survive. Not as human beings. (Lorde, *Cancer* 21)

Drawing attention to black women's resulting demands for visibility, Lorde stresses that it is that coveted visibility – their blackness – which renders them most vulnerable. Ironically, survival of the horrific conditions of the Middle Passage, a journey that Bibi Bakare-Yusuf alleges is characterized by "the economy of violence" (313), indicated a strong, "healthy," able-bodied individual. Able-bodiedness in the context of the black (slave) woman whose body is subject to the worst case of codification and commodification and is regarded principally as capital investment is itself a challenge. She is violated because of her able-bodied status. By the same token, this bodily violation disables her. Yet subversively, before and after mis/use and continued abuse, the black female body, in spite of its laboring, sexual and reproducing attributes, was rendered unhealthy and invisible. This fact serves to reinforce Bakare-Yusuf's observation about the racialization of the body "whose physical health will determine whether it will become the body of labour or the body of scientific knowledge" (313).

Furthermore, the (successful) auction of slave bodies was predicated on the health and able-bodiedness of the slave. In like manner, Baartman's healthy body is proverbially auctioned off as she is displayed as a freak of nature in Europe, even as she is consumed by the white gaze.[10] George Yancy likens the consumption of Baartman to "a violent act of reduction and mutilation" (92). In essence, Baartman served as fodder for European scientific fantasy and voyeurism alike. To echo Yancy, Baartman's body was read within the "specific context of colonial desire, power, and knowledge production"; as a result the "colonial gaze constructed her body against the backdrop of a racist discursive regime of 'truth'" (91). Locked within the racist colonial gaze that alludes to her assumed sexual abnormality, which intimates a clear dismissal of her able-bodiedness in the name of a "white epistemic orientation to the Black (female) body," Baartman experiences routinized racial profiling (Yancy 92). "Criminalization" of a healthy body, albeit unwarranted, renders Baartman a "marked woman," to borrow Hortense Spillers' coinage (65). She is visible yet invisible, named yet unnamed. Consequently, Lorde's line of reasoning forces us to consider what health is. Since health itself, in Davis' poignant evaluation, has been "callously transformed into a commodity," it then might be safe to analogize that the "unhealthy" body that is subject to medical interrogation and probing undergoes routine commodification.

The health, or lack thereof, of black women/bodies has strong racial and historical overtones, crucially embedded in race theory. Dissecting the theory of racial hierarchy, Spillers suggests that the labeling and possessing of black women's bodies was assigned by an historical order that based its foundation on the inscription of ethnicity (65-66). Yet the very history that inscribed black women into the master narrative performs a double take, so to speak, denying them proper representation. Of this lack of representation, or more pointedly, misrepresentation, Lorde writes: "The blood of Black women sloshes from coast to coast and [Mayor Richard M.] [Mary] Daly says race is of no concern to women. So that means we are either immortal or born to die and no note taken, un-women" (*Cancer* 12).[11] Hence, Lorde's challenge is not only directed at white masculinist ideology, but it also includes white feminists who are complicit with the patriarchy. Additionally, this challenge exemplifies black feminists objecting to white feminist theory that has contributed to further marginalization of black women.

Adding to Lorde's critical investigation, Stanford posits the question whether health "can exist in a world whose history is written with the blood of oppressed people" (40). Alternatively, Stanford makes the point that medicine "cannot escape from the consequences of social injustice and oppression" and further problematizes medicine's role asking whether it "reproduces injustice and oppression or works toward eliminating them" (40-41). Conclusively, she calls for medicine to see itself as "part of a broader network for social change and the common good," which entails "expand[ing] its notion of itself while at the same time encountering its limits in the healing enterprise" (41).

Following in Lorde's footsteps, I would like to argue that Lorde proposes an interesting link between present-day black women's struggle and their foremothers', in the sense that similar to their forbearers they initiate auctions of sorts, although not of their bodies, but of their voices, for a position to be seen and heard as subjects and producers of knowledge. All the same, in my invocation and reappropriation of historical and social context of dis/ease, I am mindful not to make a fragile analogy of the auctioning of slave women, as Bordo cautions against comparing actual bondage in slavery with the metaphorical bondage of privileged nineteenth-century women who donned corsets, and twentieth-century women's obsession (bondage) with slenderness and youth (*Body* 81). Another interesting correlation that could be made is that similar to enslaved people whose humanity was severely questioned and ultimately denied, the humanity of the disabled was subject to disbelief (Smith and Hutchison 3).[12]

Lorde situates women's battle with and survival of breast cancer in a militarized zone, laying claim to warrior status, a position that correspondingly calls for women's militancy and aggression in dealing with (and reclaiming) their health and their bodies. Despite the tragic fact (and statistics) that the "warrior marks" of women affected by breast cancer are honorable reminder that they may become casualty in "the cosmic war against radiation, animal fat, air pollution, McDonald's hamburgers and Red Dye No.2," the battle wages on (Lorde, *Cancer* 60). Waging a continuous personal and political battle of her own, Lorde's autobiographical narratives that literally span the globe are pregnant with modes of resistance and resilience. The following quote exemplifies this statement in great detail:

> I visualize daily winning the battles going on inside my body, and this is an important part of my life. In those visualizations, the cancer at times takes on the face and shape of my most implacable enemies, those I fight and resist most fiercely. Sometimes the wanton cells in my liver become Bull Connor and his police dogs completely smothered, rendered impotent in Birmingham, Alabama by a mighty avalanche of young, determined Black marchers moving across him toward their future. P. W. Botha's bloated face of apartheid squashed into the earth beneath an on-

slaught of the slow rhythmic advance of furious Blackness. Black South African women moving through my blood destroying passbooks. (*Burst* 132-33)

Thus, "living her battle in the flesh," Lorde's body becomes the battle field upon which she wages war not only on the invasive cancer cells, but also on the factions of society that promote and support the racist political agenda (*Burst* 133). The deliberate conflation of the United States and South Africa has serious political implication that sheds light on a shared racist politics. Likewise, Lorde identifying with Black South African Women calls attention to pervasive male oppression even as it registers female resistance to patriarchal definitions of women's rights and citizenship. Giving palpable meaning to the personal as the political, she declares: "Those of us who live our battles in the flesh must know ourselves as our strongest weapon in the most gallant struggle of our lives" (*Burst* 133). Stepping outside the boundaries of public and private, Lorde has consequently transformed pain and suffering from the private to the public sphere. Therefore, Lorde's personal disease is read correspondingly in parallel juxtaposition as global dis/ease, affecting all oppressed people, but more specifically, black women, across the globe. Furthermore, Lorde's selfless sharing of the stage with other oppressed black women in the United States and beyond its borders lends voice to collective female struggles and suffering. Similar to cancer, racism is a virus that has severe, and as Lorde has indicated, deadly consequences. This viral dis/ease is infectious, evidenced by the global phenomenon that has come to define women's struggle. Paraphrasing Lorde, women train themselves for triumph by knowing it is theirs, no matter what (Lorde, *Burst* 133).

Lorde's personal narrative responds directly to Evelynn Hammonds' call for the minimal theoretical analysis of black women's bodies to be remedied (170). Furthermore, rejecting the monolithic, patriarchal portrayals of blackness and womanness, Lorde not only disrupts the neat narrative of patriarchy, but she also "scripts" an alternative discourse that disarms the tool of patriarchy even as it dismantles racist and sexist ideologies. No longer the site of patriarchal conquest and competition, the black female body has been recuperated and reinserted into the dominant discourse as able-bodied. In this effort, Lorde's poignant memoir leads the way as it is the first of many recuperative narratives.[13] Likewise, the recent proliferation of works on Baartman that postdates her posthumous return to South Africa signals overdue repossession and recovery of the black female body.[14]

---

[1] This essay is revised, culled from my manuscript in progress, *Migrating Bodies: Politics of Survival, Resistance and Citizenship*.

[2] Lorde narrates her fears, her struggle with breast cancer in her phenomenal memoir, *The Cancer Journals* (49).

[3] Although Patricia Hill Collins specifically addresses female reproductive rights in her essay, I find her arguments relevant and useful in underscoring race and class inequities.

[4] The terms dis-ease, disease, dis-eased, diseased will be used interchangeably in this essay. The hyphenated dis-ease calls attention to the relationship between biological and social illness, stressing that often biological illness is occasioned by social and economic disparities and inequities. America is non-capitalized in the original text.

[5] I'm referring here not only to the invasive characteristics of breast cancer but also to the insidious nature of cosmetic surgery. Interestingly, Lorde narrates her experience with breast cancer alongside the narrative of the invasion of Grenada by the United States, citing that "the smallest nation in the western hemisphere occupied by the largest" (*Burst* 72).

[6] Baartman is of the Khoi people; Khoi women are known for their large buttocks, known as steatopygia, and elongated labia.

[7] 399 impoverished African-American men were tricked by the United States Public Health Service into believing that they were being treated for their illness (the general consensus is that they were never told that they had syphilis); in actuality they were used as experiment. Accordingly, treatment was withheld from them, resulting in many deaths, in wives contracting the disease and children being born with congenital syphilis. Harriet A. Washington details various "malpractices" performed in the United States against black subjects in her comprehensive *Medical Apartheid*.

[8] Other writers include Jamaica Kincaid, Paule Marshall, Toni Cade Bambara, Edwidge Danticat, and Erna Brodber. This trend of linking biological ills with social/societal ills continues today and is evidenced in the works of contemporary women writers. Jamaica Kincaid and Edwidge Danticat are two examples.

[9] This biopsychosocial model acknowledges not simply the natural forces that contribute to ill health but calls forth attention to the social and political context of illness.

[10] Baartman was coerced by the brother of her slave owner, Henrick Cezar to travel to London where she was first displayed. Later, bought by a French citizen, she was taken to Paris where she was placed under the gaze once again. Even death did not spare her the body violation;

her brains and genitals were publicly displayed (in a jar) at L'Musée de l'Homme, as was her skeleton.

[11] In an open letter Lorde challenges American radical feminist philosopher, Mary Daly about her homogenizing analysis and dismissal of black women's concern in *Gyn/Ecology*. Daly did not respond publicly. However, her reply letter to Lorde was found in Lorde's files after Lorde's death.

[12] Bonnie G. Smith writes that the incredulity of the humanity of the disabled was just cause for theorist Adrienne Asch to theorize that philosophers like Peter Singer made a plea for them to be aborted instead of born.

[13] In *Zami* Lorde also normalizes the lesbian body by saving it from obscurity. Of this self-possession, Christian writes that the "definition of a lesbian relationship is extended, since Lorde beautifully demonstrates how the heritage of her Grenadian mother is integrally connected to her development as a woman-identified woman" (184).

[14] These texts include Rachel Holmes' *African Queen;* Clifton Crais and Pamela Scully's *Sara Baartman and the Hottentot Venus*; and Deborah Willis' *Venus 2010*.

Works Cited

Alexander, Jacqui M. and Chandra Talpade Mohanty, ed. *Feminist Genealogies, Colonial Legacies, Democratic Futures,* New York: Routledge, 1997.

Bakare-Yusuf, Bibi. "The Economy of Violence: Black Bodies and the Unspeakable Terror." *Feminist Theory and the Body: A Reader*. Ed. Janet Price and Margrit Shildrick. New York: Routledge1999. 311-23.

Bennett, Michael, and Vanessa Dickerson, ed. *Recovering the Black Female Body: Self-Representations by African American Women*. New Jersey: Rutgers UP, 2000.

Bordo, Susan. "The Body and the Reproduction of Femininity." *Writing the Body: Female Embodiment and Feminist Theory*. Ed. Katie Conboy, Nadia Medina, and Sarah Stanbury. New York: Columbia UP, 1997. 80-89.

---. *Unbearable Weight: Feminism, Western Culture and the Body*. Los Angeles: U of California P, 1993.

Bunch, Charlotte. "Not For Lesbians Only." *Materialist Feminism: A Reader in Class Difference, and Women's Lives*. Ed. Rosemary Hennessy and Chrys Ingraham. New York: Routledge, 1997. 54-58.

Christian, Barbara. *Black Feminist Criticism: Perspectives on Black Women Writers*. New York: Pergamon P, 1985.
Collins, Patricia Hill. "Producing the Mothers of the Nation: Race, Class and Contemporary US Population Policies." *Women, Citizenship and Difference*. Ed. Nira Yuval-Davis and Pnina Werbner. New York: Zed Books, 1999. 118-29.
Crais, Clifton, and Pamela Scully. *Sara Baartman and the Hottentot Venus: A Ghost Story and a Biography*. Princeton: Princeton UP, 2009.
Davis, Angela Y. "Sick and Tired of Being Sick and Tired: The Politics of Black Women's Health." *The Black Women's Health Book: Speaking for Ourselves*. Ed. Evelyn C. White. Seattle: Seal P, 1994. 18-26.
---. *Women, Race & Class*. New York: Vintage Books, 1983.
Garland-Thomson, Rosemarie. "Integrating Disability, Transforming Feminist Theory." *Gendering Disability*. Ed. Bonnie G Smith and Beth Hutchison. New Brunswick: Rutgers UP, 2004. 73-103.
Glissant, Edouard. *Poetics of Relation*. Trans. Betsy Wing. Ann Arbor: U of Michigan P, 1997.
Halberstam, Judith. "F2M: The Making of Female Masculinity." *Feminist Theory and the Body: A Reader*. Ed. Janet Price and Margrit Shildrick. New York: Routledge1999. 125-33.
Hammonds, Evelynn M. "Toward a Genealogy of Black Female Sexuality: The Problematics of Silence." *Feminist Genealogies, Colonial Legacies, Democratic Futures*. Ed. M. Jacqui Alexander and Chandra Talpade Mohanty. New York: Routledge, 1997. 170-82.
Holmes, Rachel. *African Queen: The Real Life of the Hottentot Venus*. New York: Random House, 2007.
Lorde, Audre. *A Burst of Light: Essays by Audre Lorde*. Ithaca: Firebrand Books, 1988.
---. "Age, Race, Class, and Sex: Women Redefining Difference." *The Cancer Journals*. By Audre Lorde. San Francisco: Aunt Lute Books, 1980. 114-23.
---. *Sister Outsider: Essays & Speeches by Audre Lorde*. Freedom: The Crossing P, 1984.
---. *The Cancer Journals*. San Francisco: Aunt Lute Books, 1980.
---. *Zami: A New Spelling of My Name*. Freedom: The Crossing P, 1982.

Parkerson, Michelle, dir. *A Litany for Survival: The Life and Work of Audre Lorde*. Perf. Ada Gay Griffin. Third World Newsreel, 1998.

Roberts, Dorothy. *Killing the Black Body: Race, Reproduction, and the Meaning of Liberty*. New York: Vintage Books, 1997.

Schulz, Amy J., and Leith Mullings, eds. *Gender, Race, Class & Health: Intersectional Approaches*. San Francisco: Jossey-Bass, 2006.

Sherwin, Susan. "Feminist and Medical Ethics: Two Different Approaches to Contextual Ethics." *Feminist Perspectives in Medical Ethics*. Ed. Helen Bequaert Holmes and Laura M. Purdy. Bloomington: Indiana UP, 1992. 17-31.

Shildrick, Margrit, and Janet Price. "Breaking the Boundaries of the Broken Body." *Feminist Theory and the Body: A Reader*. Ed. Janet Price and Margrit Shildrick. New York: Routledge 1999. 432-44.

Silliman, Jael, and Anannya Bhattacharjee, eds. *Policing the National Body: Sex, Race, and Criminalization*. Cambridge: South End P, 2002.

Smith, Bonnie G., and Beth Hutchison, eds. *Gendering Disability*. New Brunswick: Rutgers UP, 2004.

Spillers, Hortense. "Mama's Baby, Papa's Maybe: An American Grammar Book." *Diacritics* 17.2 (1987): 65-80.

Stanford, Ann Folwell. "Mechanisms of Disease: African-American Women Writers, Social Pathologies and the Limits of Medicine." *NWSA Journal* 6.1 (1994): 28-47.

Washington, Harriet A. *Medical Apartheid: The Dark History of Medical Experimentation on Black Americans from Colonial Times to the Present*. New York: Doubleday, 2006.

White, Evelyn C. *The Black Women's Health Book: Speaking for Ourselves*. New York: Seal P, 1994.

Willis, Deborah, ed. *Venus 2010: They Called her 'Hottentot.'* Philadelphia: Temple UP, 2010.

Yancy, George. *Black Bodies, White Gazes: The Continuing Significance of Race*. New York: Rowan & Littlefield, 2008.

Georg Bauer

Challenging the Great White Hopes: Black Boxers in Film

1. A Very Brief History of Professional Heavyweight Boxing

It was the time of white boxers: the turn of the twentieth century marked the beginning of modern world heavyweight championship fights. Boxing had attained legitimacy; new rules rendered it a sanctioned sport. For over 16 years, the world had white champions. James J. Corbett, James J. Jeffries, and Tommy Burns were among the most accomplished. Then along came a tall black hellraiser from Galveston, Texas, and challenged reigning champion Burns to a fight. "Burns will have the big coloured man's scalp dangling from his belt," said the fight's promoter (qtd. in Ward 117). Burns himself was brave: "Come on and fight, nigger!" he exclaimed (qtd. in Ward 123). Strutting and smiling for a good portion of the fight, Jack Johnson won by technical knockout in the fourteenth round. The world was stunned. "I was for Burns all the way," wrote Jack London for the New York *Herald*, "He was a white man and so am I. Naturally, I wanted a white man to win" (qtd. in Ward 132).

Naturally: After all, it had not been long since the country was used to seeing enslaved black men fight each other in arenas controlled by the oppressor and for the entertainment of the same: In the decades before the Emancipation Proclamation, slave owners used to arrange so-called battle royals in which they would pit their slaves (sometimes a large number at once) against each other and bet on who would be the last one standing. "The onlookers, of course, were white; and male" (Oates 65; cf. Remnick 221). Battle royals recur in fiction: Perhaps the most famous instance is Ralph Ellison's *Invisible Man*, which begins with a description of such a battle royal as part of high society's evening entertainment. When the narrator and a very strong man are the last two in the ring, the narrator offers his opponent the money if the latter goes down: "'Fake like I knocked you out, you can have the prize.' 'I'll break your behind,' he whispered hoarsely. 'For them?' 'For me, sonofabitch!'" (Ellison 24). For his opponent, it is not the money which counts, but the honor, despite – or because of – the humiliating situation. Physical superiority is a concept with a high value attached, perhaps explaining why the narrator opts simply not to throw the fight.

Setting the possibility to retain a semblance of honor aside, battle royals were mainly for the entertainment of the white male crowd and an allegorical reminder of the subjugation of the black people involved in it. At the beginning of the twentieth century, however, Jack Johnson was not forced to fight by a white person and showed pride in his skill. It was, then, this sense of independence which displeased Jack London and a multitude of other viewers. What ensued was a desperate search for a fighter who would show Johnson his place and prevent him from celebrating his champion-status with black pride, fast cars and white girlfriends. The concept of the 'Great White Hope' was born: a white boxer who would regain the heavyweight title and thus regain the white race's then widely assumed superiority (cf. Ward 197ff.). The white American public seemed to have found their Great White Hope in James J. Jeffries (cf. Ward 133ff., 164-65). Johnson, however, did not give in to these fantasies: he beat Jeffries on July 4, 1910, which resulted in riots in a number of American cities and the deaths and injuries of many black people (cf. Ward 215ff.; Remnick 223). No matter that Johnson was dethroned by Jess Willard in 1915, the concept of white supremacy in boxing was severely damaged.

Many white boxers refused to fight African Americans, and so it took another 22 years – which Jack Dempsey and Gene Tunney spent mostly punching inside the heavyweight ring – for another black fighter to emerge on the canvas. His name: Joe Louis. His mission: to be black as little as possible. In order not to repeat the furor caused by Johnson, Louis was designed by his media advisers to live his blackness in secret, never to show pride in his abilities, and never to be seen with white women in public (cf. Bak 74-75; cf. Oates 89, 267-68). Along with his catering to the general social tastes of 1930s white America, Louis had another major advantage: Nazi Germany. Having lost a fight to the German Max Schmeling in 1936, the United States was eager to see a rematch. By 1938, the year of the Louis-Schmeling rematch, the American media at large had begun to present Nazi Germany as the pinnacle of evil and had rendered Schmeling a representative of Nazi Germany (cf. Bak 118ff., 164ff.). As Thomas Hauser describes in *The Black Lights*, this view intensified when Louis won the fight: "The Louis-Schmeling fight was deemed the clearest confrontation between good and evil in the history of sports. And on that night Joe Louis was the greatest fighter who ever lived" (64). During tumultuous times such as these and the Civil Rights era twenty-five years later, boxing may become more than a sport; it may become a channel for social issues and racial politics.

Two black heavyweight champions, Ezzard Charles and Joe Walcott, followed Louis's reign. In 1952, an Italian American climbed through the ropes to win the heavyweight title: Rocky Marciano was considered by many the Great White Hope white America had been waiting for. In his career he won 49 fights, 43 by knockout, and never lost a match.

In the mid-1960s Cassius Clay defeated Sonny Liston, changed his name to Muhammad Ali, and changed the face of professional boxing forever. Rejecting the oppressor's culture as much as possible (cf. Oates 195, 218), Ali showed appreciation for Jack Johnson and explained the creation of his public persona as follows: "I wanted to be rough, tough, arrogant, the nigger white folks didn't like" (Remnick 224). But the white-black racial binary which would have contributed to Ali's quest faced a dilemma concomitant with Ali's reign, according to Gerald Early: "[T]here were very few white fighters left in the game" ("Three Notes" 24). This could have posed a potential problem in terms of ratings: "If two black fighters are in the ring the white public generally ignores it and the black public [...] tends to feel a bit uneasy when the fight is for high stakes, obviously thinking that 'two brothers shouldn't be beating up each other for entertainment'" (Early, "Three Notes" 25). However, Ali knew how to keep the crowd interested: "Nearly every Ali opponent became a representative of the white establishment" (Early, "Three Notes" 24). After withdrawing Ali's boxing license for refusing to take arms against the Viet Cong, the American establishment had become a greater foe. Hence, rising star George Foreman's patriotism was an easy target for Ali, which he exploited to great effect during the preparations for the *Rumble in the Jungle*, the historic bout between a young Foreman and an older Ali, set in Zaire 1974 and, due to weeklong delays of the event, came to be about much more than boxing. Ali embraced the opportunity to be politically subversive: "[N]ow you are impressed with Foreman," Ali told the press, alluding to his opponent's devastating punches. "But I let you in on a secret. Colored folks scare more white folks than they scare colored folks. I am not afraid of Foreman, and that you will discover" (qtd. in Mailer, *The Fight* 68). And Ali kept talking: "The man's in trouble; he's scared. He's in our country to start with! He's in my country" (qtd. in Gast).

When Ali beat Foreman that night, he showed that the Great White Hope would never be successful – even an African American could not lay claim to this title. With Muhammad Ali, the old wounds that had healed since the day of Jack Johnson burst open again, and now, along with white audiences' fierce and barely contained resentment of black achievement, black fighters spilled out. There were black boxers everywhere: Joe Frazier, Ken Norton, Larry Holmes, Mike Weaver, John Tate, Pinklon Thomas, and Michael Spinks, to name but a few – and this was just the heavyweight division!

A quick attempt was made to construct a White Hope in the 1980s with Gerry Cooney, who was pushed by the media and greeted with an excitement bordering on hysteria:

> All managers hype their fighters. It's part of the game. But with Gerry Cooney the hype reached unprecedented proportions. Cooney was good. Cooney had charisma. Cooney was a devastating puncher. And Cooney was white. More precisely, suburban, middle-class, Irish Catholic white. Boxing, more than any other sport, thrives on ethnic confrontation, and there are relatively few quality white fighters around. The most common ethnic confrontation in boxing today is Hispanic versus black. Suddenly in Gerry Cooney, boxing had a "white hope" – the first white man since Rocky Marciano to hold out the promise of preeminence in the ring. (Hauser 38)

Cooney's fight with Larry Holmes was the best-paid and one of the most-watched at the time. But Holmes defeated Cooney in thirteenth round (cf. Hauser 50ff.).

Fights were increasingly determined by modern media. Promoters and television (now mostly pay-TV) decided which two boxers to pit against each other (cf. Hauser 84, 103ff., 260). The breaking up of the title-monopoly into four (with four major boxing associations) and the splitting up of weight classes into the current seventeen has rendered the boxing world obscure. In addition to this, there are no great personalities in professional boxing anymore – the result of a vicious circle, for "to be a great champion one must have great opponents" (Oates 162). The last of these was Mike Tyson, around whom was created an "image of the outsider, the psychic outlaw, the hungry young black contender for all that white America can give" (Oates 120). The youngest of all heavyweight champions, Tyson was nicknamed 'Iron Mike' and was constantly associated with danger and wildness. His personality and his machine-like qualities as a fighter have made him a role-model nonetheless. Gangsta rappers write him into their lyrics.[1] And Oates writes,

> Mike Tyson has become a model of success for "ghetto youth," though his personal code of conduct, his remarkably assured sense of himself, owes nothing at all to the ghetto. He is trained, managed, and surrounded, to an unusual degree, by white men, and though he cannot be said to be a white man's black man he is surely not a black man's black man in the style of, for instance, Muhammad Ali. [...] Indeed, it might be said that Mike Tyson will be the first heavyweight boxer in America to transcend issues of race – a feat laudable or troubling, depending on one's perspective. (136)

After Tyson, there was silence. A few Russians here and there, but no Great White Hopes and no Great Black Hopes. No Marciano, no Ali. What to do? The entertainment industry has long known how to remedy a situation: after numerous films about glorious white boxers in the 1930s to the 1950s, an aspiring young actor created a new on-screen White Hope and called him Rocky. Five sequels followed, and many more films about white boxers.

2. Black Boxers and Great White Hopes in Film

A white American audience starving for a white champion may not need a real white champion – can they make do with an imaginary one? Two of the most successful film projects about boxers feature elements of the Great White Hope – counterbalanced with black opponents. The *Rocky* films as a whole are a pop-cultural success because they tap into the American self-made-man myth and present a likable Italian American boxer. *Raging Bull* (1980) presents an unlikable Italian American fighter who, in contrast to Rocky, is closely modeled on a historical person. The subjective way in which the boxing scenes were shot even allowed audiences to identify with Jake LaMotta in their desire for a Great White Hope.

I would argue that *Rocky* (1976) did more to cater to the needs of white American audiences than a real boxing champion would have. Not only boxing fans enjoyed *Rocky*, film fans did also. Even for people who were not familiar with the concept of the Great White Hope, Rocky was arguably a hero in a time of no heroes. Clay Motley notes:

> The iconic rise of the underdog from south Philadelphia, serendipitously plucked out of obscurity to fight the heavyweight champion of the world, clearly *meant* something to the packed, electrified theatres cheering Rocky on as if he were a real fighter. [...] Critics curious over the surprise success of *Rocky* conjectured that it was simply a fairytale of the Ameri-

> can Dream or sentimental Bicentennial pap; or perhaps it was an important statement about the neglected American working class, or a sign of growing "ethnic" American pride; maybe it was a dangerously racist film, or a portend of a vigorous and violent "New Right." (62)

With *Rocky*, Stallone may have tapped into the unconscious of many Americans in the 1970s, as Motley further explains using a scene from the beginning of the film, in which the failed Rocky Balboa looks at a childhood photograph:

> The flat-topped, smiling youth in the picture represents America of the 1950s, a place of success, potential, and optimism. The modern, wounded fighter, declared past his prime, symbolizes the loss of that potential by the 1970s, the failing of America to live up to the promises of its past. We are also to see that although Rocky is now a "man," as opposed to the boy in the photograph, he has none of the traditional features of "manhood." He is a professional, economic, and romantic failure, with no obvious hope for redemption or success. He is no longer a virile "contender": he is merely an inert "meat bag" and a "tomato," fit for mocking. He is an emblem of the failed modern man in a failed society. (62)

The origin of Sylvester Stallone's idea for the movie, was a similarly unsuccessful white "tomato" or "bum" boxer named Chuck Wepner, who, in 1975, went fifteen rounds with Muhammad Ali and even knocked him down once. Although Wepner lost, he was one of the few to go the distance with Ali. Stallone must have read into him a certain incarnation of the American Dream and constructed the character of Rocky Balboa around this notion. In the Official Rocky Scrapbook, Stallone writes,

> The turning point came without a doubt at my twenty-ninth birthday party. It was in July and I was sitting across the table from my wife who was getting wider with pregnancy and my dog who was eating his own fleas because we were so broke. [...] I looked around and I wished I was out of this place so badly and I knew that the only way I was ever going to get out of this place was not through "physicalization" but actually through creative endeavor, dedication, discipline. [...] [I went] to my writing table [...]. What did *I* really enjoy seeing up on the screen? I enjoyed heroism. I enjoyed great love. I enjoyed stories of dignity, of courage, of man's ability to rise above his station and take life by the throat and not let go until he succeeded. Yet no one was making films like that. "They" would call that corny [...]. Well, not me. [...] Through fate or whatever, I ended up at the Muhammad Ali/Chuck Wepner fight. Chuck

> Wepner, a battling bruising type of club fighter who had never really made the big, big time, was now having his shot. But the fight was not regarded as a serious battle. It was called a public joke. He would barely go three rounds, most of the predictions said. Well, the history books will read that he went fifteen rounds [...] with Muhammad Ali and he can hold his head up high forever no matter what happens. [...] That night I went home and I had the beginning of my character. I had him now. I was going to make a creation called Rocky Balboa, a man from the streets, a walking cliché of sorts, the all-American tragedy, a man who didn't have much mentality but had incredible emotion and patriotism and spirituality and good nature even though nature had not been good to him. All he required from life was a warm bed and some food and maybe a laugh during the day. He was a man of simple tastes. [...] Rocky Balboa was different. He was America's child. He was to the seventies what Chaplin's Little Tramp was to the twenties. (18-19)

It is telling that it took a white boxer for such inspiration – after all, Archie Moore and other African American underdogs had similar stories to tell. But Wepner, with his whiteness, balding head and mustache, signified a myth in the making to Stallone; an urge deep within the white, American psyche – an urge which came to the fore most visibly in the late 1970s with Gerry Cooney, as Thomas Hauser elicits:

> All managers hype their fighters. It's part of the game. But with Gerry Cooney the hype reached unprecedented proportions. Cooney was good. Cooney had charisma. Cooney was a devastating puncher. And Cooney was white. More precisely, suburban, middle-class, Irish Catholic white. Boxing, more than any other sport, thrives on ethnic confrontation, and there are relatively few quality white fighters around. The most common ethnic confrontation in boxing today is Hispanic versus black. Suddenly in Gerry Cooney, boxing had a "white hope" – the first white man since Rocky Marciano to hold out the promise of preeminence in the ring. (38)

The frantic search for a Great White Hope after the era of Muhammad Ali may lead us to believe that the American folk myth of variable penis size (which still thrives in contemporary media)[2] is transposed in boxing to the demonstration of physical superiority. Numerous white males begrudge black boxers their ability to take action. Booker T. Washington's stance of an industrious black person (as opposed to intellectual advancements), therefore, appears to white boxing fans as a threat. It must be infuriating: blacks have bigger dicks and get things done better – a fledgling inferiority complex. Ali was the culmination of all things whites begrudged, as Spike Lee remarks: "Muhammad was beautiful [...], a specimen, a fighting machine. [...] He was handsome, he was articulate; he was funny, charismatic. He was whuppin' ass too!" (qtd. in Gast).

The movie industry, then, had to counteract: in films about (imaginary) white boxing heroes, black bodies are a canvas onto which a boxing match is brought. It is not a conventional boxing match, not one that lasts fifteen rounds, not one that features a referee, not one which has the boxers wear gloves, necessarily. As Dyer notes, "The white man has been the centre of attention for many centuries of Western culture, but there is a problem about the display of his body [...]. A naked body is a vulnerable body" (145). In this context, it is interesting to note that boxing films usually pay much attention to the development of the white contender's body – the veritable forging of his physical armor (Dyer again: "The built body is hard and contoured, often resembling armour" [152].) in order to protect himself against his opponents, who are often black. Black bodies in boxing movies always carry meaning – and they frequently carry it as a burden.

While, as I will explain later, boxing has few sexual connotations, the will to action and the art of physical accomplishment constitute a boxer's prowess. What could be more humiliating to oppressors than to show men of a race which had thought itself superior for centuries that they are physically and actively inferior? After Ali, jealous reactions were more overt than in Jack Johnson's times: the fostering and construction of the persona Cooney was a desperate attempt to resurrect the White Boxer, and in the entertainment world, *Rocky* and *Raging Bull*, albeit in very different fashions, reestablished the white boxer as an icon. That there should be a Great White Hope is a logical consequence of the mythology of hero-worship: "The USA is of course a highly multiracial society, but the idea of being an 'American' has long sat uneasily with ideas of being any other colour than white" (Dyer 149).

In order to reestablish the white boxer as an icon, filmmakers tend to use a character as a foil to represent what has generated the need for such iconography. In *Rocky*, it is Apollo Creed, a capitalistic version of Muhammad Ali, who is, paradoxically, ideologically closer to the flag-waving George Foreman (whom Ali's flamboyance had rendered the embodiment of the American establishment).

Joel W. Martin writes that although Apollo Creed presents the positive image of a role model as a well-to-do African American, "the film expresses and directs European American working-class anger toward African Americans. [...] The film's narrative structure exploits Creed's success as one of a series of signs that the United States is racially out of order" (129). Order is restored when Rocky goes the distance with Creed and although losing the fight, the film's editing declares Rocky the spiritual winner.

Martin argues that, in light of the racial situation in the United States of the 1970s, "*Rocky* is a film about the triumphant return of European Americans' power" (132); this veritable utopia being democratically created with *Rocky*. While it may exist in the minds of many working-class and middle-class Americans (and, perhaps, even upper-class Americans, although they already are in positions of power), I believe that Martin interprets the film with too global a perspective. At no point does the film adopt a deprecatory stance toward the Civil Rights Movement, much less its political leaders. Chris Motley even argues that Apollo Creed cannot be interpreted as African American and should rather be seen as a representative of capitalist, elitist America – the American Dream gone bad; Apollo Creed is not a representative of black America because we always see him rich (cf. Motley: 63ff.). This reading is problematic, since it suggests that for a black person on celluloid there has to be a visible struggle from rags to riches for the audience to deem it authentic (and give itself a self-congratulatory pat on the back). At the time the audience encounters Creed in the movie, he is therefore neither a symbol of belligerent African American ideology (as Martin suggests), nor exclusively a symbol of the corrupted American Dream (as Motley suggests).

We see Rocky, who in the first film lives the American Dream the way it is supposed to be lived – from rags to riches through hard work and humility –, walk down the same path as Apollo in subsequent movies, increasingly indulging in conspicuous consumption. And while Rocky is always allowed to regenerate himself and return to the basic values which made him strong – modesty and a strong, industrious focus on physical fitness –, Apollo Creed is doomed to die by repeating Rocky's mistake of arrogance and extravagance in *Rocky IV* (1987). Both Apollo and Rocky waste the opportunity given to them by committing the sin of pride – but Creed is punished for it, and Balboa is perpetually redeemed by taking on new challenges and, eventually, taking them seriously. All the while Balboa worships Creed, to whom he never shows any hatred; such sentiments are transferred instead to the audience that envies and resents (black) Creed for his wealth and cheers (white) Rocky on to greatness.

To judge that the first *Rocky* film is a denunciation of African American political accomplishments is, I would argue, too harsh. Why can we not stay in the world of boxing and acknowledge that Rocky gives a (Caucasian) face to a Caucasian audience's desire for physical effectiveness? A very modern concept indeed: What would have been solved collectively in more primitive times is now projected onto one character. "*Rocky*," Chris Motley writes, "attempts to define 'true' manhood, providing its audience with the confidence that, like Rocky, American men can fight back and succeed too, both personally and nationally" (60). At the beginning of the movie, Balboa loses the locker he has occupied for six years to a black fighter – Rocky's trainer accuses Rocky of not being able make the grade as a contender and calls him a "tomato." However, in the course of the film, Rocky proves that he has the right attributes to go the distance with the heavyweight champion – the audience's thirst for white action is thus quenched. Admittedly, the subsequent *Rocky* films give voice to this desire in a cruder fashion than the first. And so, as we enter the Reagan era, in which representations of the male body adhere to different parameters, Rocky's opponent in *Rocky III* (1983) is a sight to behold – literally. Clubber Lang has larger muscles and is more ferocious than Rocky. He is introduced as an audience member at one of Rocky's victorious bouts. The success-montage of Rocky expands into a concomitant training-montage of Clubber Lang, which differs from Rocky's in that it does not show a progression (i.e., an achievement) of the body. In Rocky's case there is a progression, in Lang's, the physical standard is merely upheld. Rocky's physical achievements follow an upwards trajectory, they are a success narrative, while Clubber's are a story of maintenance.

Clubber sports a grim look throughout the film. He is angry at Balboa. He is also a loner: at no point in the movie does he appear in the company of friends, and he declares that he needs neither trainer nor manager. His head is adorned with a Mohawk haircut and feather earrings. These decorations, coupled with his fierce stare and snorting grimaces connote primitivism – not coincidentally, the layperson's romantic perception of boxing.

Clubber Lang represents, much like Rocky in the first film, those Americans who are frustrated with the American Dream dreamt the wrong way (symbolized by Rocky's conspicuous consumption and marketing deals). However, while Rocky's rise to the top is constructed as being more or less accidental and apolitical, Clubber's is presented as willful and aggressive. He bears a grudge against the champion, whereas Rocky admired Apollo.

The boxing montage shows Clubber Lang's highly unorthodox fighting style as he punches in the face a kneeling opponent trying to get back up. In another scene, one can hear the roar of a wildcat on the soundtrack as Lang pushes aside a referee. Even the name 'Clubber' alludes to a primitive, deadly weapon. His muscles are a great deal larger than Rocky's (in the final fight, the weight difference is striking) but in contrast to Rocky's they are not portrayed as *constructs*. This is deliberate: according to Dyer, Rocky's muscles "look tortured into existence, with veins popping out and strained skin, his eyes and mouth express vulnerability, iconic images have him bruised [...]. [His body], like those of all muscle heroes, [carries] the signs of hard, planned labour, the spirit reigning over the flesh" (Dyer 155). Neither the muscles of Apollo Creed nor those of Clubber Lang (nor those of Mason Dixon in the sixth film) are constructed on screen[3] – it is as if the black fighters' muscles have always been there. In this sense, Rocky, the white hero (along with the predominantly white audience) invests a lot of time in the manufacture of his muscles, a feat which in the film's terms demands determination, intelligence and spirit. Dyer explains:

> The built white body is not the body that white men are born with; it is the body made possible by their natural mental superiority. The point after all is that it is built, a product of the application of thought and planning, an achievement. [...] This makes the white man better able to handle his body [...]; no matter how splendid the physiques of non-white bodybuilders, they are never granted this quality (and thus the fact that their bodies too were produced ones is forgotten). The hero's physique may be fabulous, but what made it, and makes it effective, is the spirit within. (164-65)[4]

The hero's body is contrasted with the antagonist's visually more imposing, but spiritually less valuable body. Additionally, Clubber Lang remains alone throughout the film. While his anger at Rocky may be, in a sociocultural sense, quite legitimate, nobody acknowledges its validity. Thus, the crowd boos him when he is introduced as the heavyweight champion of the world. The general public in all *Rocky* films is portrayed as desirers of, and adheres to, a Great White Hope. In the *Rocky* cycle, Rocky repeatedly develops his body from vulnerable to victorious since the white male needs to back up his claim to power with action (cf. Dyer 147). While this is hard for real life white boxers the fictional-mythological white male needs to develop his physicality. Vulnerable to the gaze of many, the white body needs to prove itself when pitted against other bodies, and when it fails the test – as in the case of boxing – heroes have to be created: in *Rocky V*, as if the audience did not know already, a black fight promoter modeled on the infamous Don King says to Rocky: "You're the Great White Hope!"

Rocky III pits its hero against an animalistic black opponent, who defeats Rocky effortlessly in their first match. References to the primitive abound in *Rocky III*: trainer Mickey tells Rocky that the worst thing that could happen to a fighter happened to Rocky: "you got civilized." To train for the rematch with Clubber, Rocky gets help from his old nemesis, Apollo Creed: in order to reconnect with his animal side, Rocky needs to make contact with the primitive. Creed takes the hero to his old all-black Californian gym, in which, upon entering, Rocky gazes at black men working out their black, oiled-up, dimly-lit, shadow-throwing muscles. The black boxers look at him with disdain and Apollo comments on them as if evaluating feline predators: "See that look in their eyes? […] Gotta get that look back, Rock. Eye of the tiger, man." This project is geared toward discovering Rocky's animalism.

All the while, Rocky's brother-in-law Paulie is quite frank about the discomfort the situation creates in him. His humorous comments sound like recitations from a collection of racial stereotypes: "Let's leave before they leave us for dead!" Paulie says to Apollo, "You can't train [Rocky] like a colored fighter. He ain't got no rhythm," and he says the "jungle junk music" playing in the background is ineffective. Paulie is proven wrong by the outcome of the rematch: Rocky wins by employing the tactics Creed and his crew have taught him. White muscles, constructed with spirit and intelligence (by acquiring the enemy's tactics), win again. To emphasize the overall jungle-atmosphere of the film, one sports commentator summarizes the ecstatic reaction of the crowd (is this accidental?): "The place has gone bananas!"

A triumphant spirit inhabits Rocky in his victory but also Jake LaMotta in his defeat. He, too, has worked hard on his body. Although screenwriter Martin Mardik assures us about *Raging Bull*, "This was the anti-*Rocky*," *Raging Bull* features another Great White Hope. LaMotta is an unlikable character who is rude, crude, and violent, and yet the movie is constructed in such a way that it allows audiences to identify with him. Elements of white heroism bustle under the vile surface of LaMotta/DeNiro's physique. Although LaMotta is shown losing a number of matches in the film, the way he handles defeat is striking: he walks off proudly erect with bully-like arrogance. And since the fight scenes in *Raging Bull* are stylized and highly subjective versions of the historical events presented from LaMotta's point of view, the tone is exactly right: LaMotta does not give up – he might lose physically, but he will be triumphant spiritually, as far as boxing is concerned. "The initial Hollywood outsider status," writes Mark Nicholls, "provides something of the desired difference and separateness" (121). This seems especially true for Scorsese's LaMotta. LaMotta was known to take a severe beating in the ring in stride; he occasionally describes the pounding as a punishment he accepted willingly because he considered himself a bad person (cf. Scorsese). Michael Peterson detects in *Raging Bull* a "sense of white masculinity constituted through stoic suffering" (87).

Stoic suffering in both *Raging Bull* and the *Rocky* films is frequently combined with Christian imagery. Peggy McCormack notes that in the final bout between Robinson and LaMotta, "Scorsese crucifies Jake in this match – with attendant religious solemnity and symbolism" (112). Editor Thelma Schoonmaker confirms that these religious connotations were deliberate and planned by Scorsese. In this regard, *Rocky* director John G. Avildsen lets the viewers in on a secret: When you introduce Christian imagery along with your film's protagonist, a "subliminal connection will be made [...] and I've already got a lot of people on my side" (*Rocky*).

While Rocky is reminiscent of the likeable champ of the 50s boxing movies, *Raging Bull*'s Jake LaMotta displays white superiority in a less apparent but equally striking fashion: the American literary tradition of the underdog lives on in the film's LaMotta because, although he does not win all his fights, he retains his dignity in defeat. He never goes down and in the ring displays boyish arrogance after the fights.

In the first fight of the film, after a weak round against black opponent Jimmy Reeves, Jake is reminded by his brother (Joe Pesci): "Why the fuck do we have to come to Cleveland for you to get beaten by a *moolanyan*? Come on, champ, do the fuckin' right thing here!" From now on, the camera shows us LaMotta dealing considerably more punches than his opponent. Nevertheless, LaMotta loses by the judges' decision. When the scores are announced, a riot ensues and chairs and other objects are hurled into the ring. A community deprived of a Great White Hope can be brutal, and anti-modern behavior comes to the fore. In the DVD commentary, the real Jake LaMotta tells us that these events are historically accurate and that the National Anthem had to be played to calm the crowd down. After this incident, LaMotta had a name! LaMotta is validated in his arrogance by the audience's reaction, however symbolic it may be (the movie does not show that the real-life Jimmy Reeves was escorted out of the arena unharmed).

His arrogance culminates in a somewhat uplifting moment after the brutal sixth fight with Sugar Ray Robinson. A bloodied and beaten LaMotta drags himself (supported by someone from his corner) over to Robinson's corner and says, "Hey Ray. Never got me down, Ray. Ya never got me down, Ray. Ya hear me?" LaMotta is dragged off, but he still permits himself the luxury of a taunting gesture with his arms. The audience is made to sympathize with LaMotta, especially after the preceding scenes: in the final round, Robinson demoniacally towers over LaMotta; the camera closes in on Robinson with his mouthpiece gleaming white against his backlit black face. A reverse shot shows LaMotta with his mouth half-open, head bloodied and half-bowed, with an air of boyish innocence. We cut back to Robinson's almost grotesque face, arm raised to a punch like a pirate about to strike with his saber. The result: LaMotta's blood spatters over some individuals occupying ringside seats.

From this scene reminiscent of a Passion Play, we get a sense of spiritual victory: after cruel punishment, LaMotta does not drop to the canvas but remains on his legs. Although he loses many of the fights in the film, LaMotta *never goes down*, asserting a defiant pride – a spiritual pride – via the body. His body is not fit enough to knock the opponent out, but it is strong enough not to succumb to his opponent's battering, invoking the notion of defiance of seemingly insurmountable odds that audiences longed for at the time of the movie's release. Given the fighters' skin colors and the visual language of the film, this scene may even cause audiences to suspect a racial political statement in favor of the white boxer.

Both Clubber Lang and the screen version of Sugar Ray Robinson are fighters who commit the sin of beating the Great White Hope and are thus reprimanded for it physically (Clubber Lang loses the final fight) and spiritually (a beaten La Motta defiantly taunts Robinson). The historical counterpart to these narratives is the fight between Archie Moore and Rocky Marciano.

3. Racial Dynamics in Boxing Films

Rocky Marciano only went down twice in his professional career – once against Walcott and once against one of the hardest-working heavyweights in history, Archie Moore. The match, Marciano's last, led sportswriter A. J. Liebling to draw parallels with Melville's captain and the Great White Whale in his article "Ahab and Nemesis." Marciano was just as unconquerable as Moby Dick. Moore's grandiose yet curiously lean style reminds us of Ahab's Shakespearean theatrics. And Moore was a complex, intellectual fighter, whereas Marciano was a brawler.

Liebling writes, "I thought of [Moore] as a lonely Ahab [...]. I didn't think he could bring it off [...]. What would *Moby Dick* be if Ahab had succeeded? Just another fish story. The thing that is eternally diverting is the struggle of man against history" (253). This is a valid argument in the overall context of the analogy: what would Marciano be if Moore had defeated him? Just another likeable white boxer with a mediocre record and a primitive fighting style. But with Moore going down in the ninth round, the bout confirmed Marciano as a legend and Moore as an old, tragic hero who showed great determination:

> Moore's strategic problem [...] offered [...] infinitely more chances for error. It was possible [...] that jabbing and defensive skill would carry him through fifteen rounds, even on those old legs, but I knew that the mere notion of such a *gambade* would revolt Moore. [...] Besides, would Ahab have been content merely to go the distance with the White Whale? I felt sure that Archie planned to knock the champion out. (Liebling 256)

Interpretations of Moby Dick abound. When we think about the narrator's chapter, "The Whiteness of the Whale," in which the whale's appearance evokes terror in the (interpretive) narrator of Ahab's quest, Liebling's analogy gains validity. In the chapter, the narrator philosophizes in a rather selective fashion about the dichotomy of whiteness: it has been a tool to portray ideal beauty, grandeur and augustness but also a symbol of sheer horror. Whenever whiteness comes in contact with ferocity, it conveys transcendent terror:

> Is it that by its indefiniteness it shadows forth the heartless voids and immensities of the universe, and thus stabs us from behind with the thought of annihilation, when beholding the white depths of the milky way? Or is it, that as in essence whiteness is not so much a color as the visible absence of color, and at the same time the concrete of all colors; is it for

> these reasons that there is such a dumb blankness, full of meaning, in a wide landscape of snows – a colorless, all-color of atheism from which we shrink? (Melville 282)

The Moore-Marciano fight and other boxing matches bear material for similar existential and, not least, racially charged contention. The same holds true for boxing films. One could read Moore, whose 'people' – the body- and action-oriented black boxers – are in danger of 'annihilation' by the embodiment of idealized (physical and active) whiteness, as the defender against an ideal. The black boxer's wounds lead us to interpret Moore as pursuing the white hope, personified in Rocky Marciano. No matter what the ideological interpretation of Moby Dick, with Ahab, the whale goes beyond being a commodity and becomes a metaphor. This can also be said of Great White Hopes. At a time when a Great White Hope actually existed, the opponent is particularly Ahabean in that for Ahab, "destruction, not creativity, is the universal ideal" (Bryant 74). Here, modern elements of boxing become apparent in its individualized representation of a collective principle. What, then, does the notion of White Whale Marciano surviving mean for idealized whiteness? Does it live on gloriously? At least in the collective mind of mainstream white audiences, it does.

Moore is a version of Ahab, for whom the battle against a quasi-mythical opponent has to be fought just right. If not, the consequences (interpreted or real) are terrifying: after the third round,

> Marciano had been hit and cut, so he felt acclimated, and Moore was so mad at himself for not having knocked Marciano out that he almost displayed animosity toward him. He may have thought that perhaps he had not hit Marciano *just* right; the true artist is always prone to self-reproach. He would try again. (Liebling 263)

Moore's self-reproach is pure speculation on Liebling's part, but in the overall narrative of facing the Great White Hope, it follows dramatic logic.

Boxing is not only destruction, but also drama. It is not 'acting' – much less than other sports, for, as Oates reminds us, "One *plays* football, one doesn't *play* boxing" (19). "Its violation of the taboo against violence ('Thou shalt not kill' in its primordial form) is open, explicit, ritualized, and […] *routine* – which gives boxing its uncanny air" (Oates 106). The boxing ring is not a stage; it is an arena in which rules apply that are contrary to our society's, and the fighters engage in a conflict between two forces boiled down to its physical essentials and rendered dramatic contest. When this drama is *acted*, i.e., in film, Daniel Kogler argues that Barthes's notion of wrestling as a demonstrative spectacle (as opposed to boxing as a demonstrative sport) may well be applicable:

> [T]he sport becomes a spectacle, the fight becomes scripted to achieve various effects – in the case of *Raging Bull*, to offer the audience access into La Motta's psyche at the event of the fight [...] and, in the case of the *Rocky* saga, to make the audience want the Italian Stallion to triumph. The audience is expected (and expects) to root for Stallone's character at all times. (10)

As there are more clearly defined roles in wrestling (good versus evil), the demonstrative spectacle provides the audience someone to root for. Already in Melville's times, to "'do drama' was to 'act out' race, region, and class tensions, to affirm or deny difference in the context of the nation's great Equality" (Bryant 80). Therefore, film is a potent medium for fulfilling an audience's potential desire for a Great White Hope. In the *Rocky* films, this is, by default, the protagonist. In the context of affirming difference, paired with the reconfigured ideal of capitalist power in Reagan's America, it is evident why the antagonist in *Rocky III* is presented as a solitary animal-like black mountain of muscles. That in boxing we are dealing with ideals is made clear by Richard Dyer's remark that the "built body presents itself not as typical but as ideal" (151). The Great White Hope is an ideal – and ideals are good ingredients of a demonstrative spectacle.

Ahab's Shakespearean theatricality elucidates an inner struggle, much as Clubber Lang's well-built body demonstrates his rage at seeing an idealized white heavyweight champion. Lang's promise to inflict "pain" is not so much directed at Rocky Balboa, the person, but at the ideals he represents. Lang asserts: "I don't hate the man, I pity the fool." In contrast to Moore, Clubber Lang is not portrayed as an intellectual fighter – he is a baroque brawler. Nevertheless, he, too, displays Ahabean qualities: he is angry at the great white thing that unfolds before his eyes every time he attends a Rocky Balboa fight. Lang never sits at ringside, signifying his financial situation; the Whale is far out of reach. But Lang works out alone in his murky basement the way Ahab strategizes in his cabin on the Pequod. Lang even defeats Rocky in the first bout. He commits hubris as does Ahab in thinking that he can destroy the Great White Whale.

A boxer's solitude in the ring is a requirement of the sport. He cannot help but act autocratically, and Moore and Clubber Lang, as well as other black boxers, are thus prone to comparisons with Ahab. Boxers are not 'sexuality' (Ahab is impotent), they are 'action.' Both are concepts which may generate, and have occasionally generated, jealousy. To Joyce Carol Oates, boxing

> seems to be rooted in its paradoxical nature – the savagery that so clearly underlies, yet is contained by, its myriad rules, regulations, traditions, and superstitions. It seems to make the quotidian that which is uncanny, dangerous, forbidden, and unclean: it ritualizes violence, primarily male violence, to the degree to which violence becomes an aesthetic principle. In this, men's bodies (or, rather, their highly trained employment of their bodies) are instruments and not mere flesh like our own. That a man as a boxer is an action, and no longer a man, or not significantly a "man," puzzles those of us who feel ourselves fully defined in any of our actions. [In boxing, t]he aim is not to kill one's opponent, for one's opponent is after all one's brother: the aim is to render him temporarily incapacitated, in a simulation of death. (166-67)

By black supremacy in the sport, it is not primarily white manhood which is attacked, but white action. And how devastating is it to be demonstrated that your (white) race is considerably less capable of action than another? Especially since whites have prided themselves on their superiority and have felt confident in their self-proclaimed role of oppressors for so long! "Like a dancer," Oates writes, "a boxer 'is' his body, and is totally identified with it" (5). In the world of boxing, "strength of a certain kind – matched of course with intelligence and tirelessly developed skills – determines masculinity. Just as a boxer is his body, a man's masculinity is the use of his body. But it is also his triumph over another's use of his body" (Oates 72). Physical superiority in boxing can therefore be perceived as an affront to one's capabilities. Muscle, machinery, bone structure, arsenal, tools, constructions for destruction – not penis – are the concepts which enrage seekers of the Great White Hope. Therefore, Rocky is mostly desexualized, and *Raging Bull*'s LaMotta pours ice down his pants. What it boils down to, ultimately, is the action. When in 2007 I asked Martin Wright, a trainer at Gleason's Gym, what the best thing about boxing is, he answers with a smile: "Winnin'!"

Ahab versus Moby Dick is a metaphor we can apply to some black boxers in film: in *Rocky III*, the begrudging, angry black fighter is generally punished for his hubris by being defeated by the Great White Hope. In *Raging Bull*, Sugar Ray Robinson does defeat Jake LaMotta, but LaMotta is defiant and thus victorious in spirit. Robinson did not go down, but neither did the whale: "I never went down, Ray."

In the constructed bodies of Rocky Balboa and the spiritual superiority of Jake LaMotta, idealized whiteness becomes manifest. Ahabs fail – more apparently in the *Rocky* films, but also in *Raging Bull*.

4. New Trends in Boxing Films
What is boxing? To what end do we invest so much race-motivated energy in this framework?

Many writers opine that boxing takes sports back to its essentials. In our result-oriented Western civilization, sports are about competition. Competition carries conflict and produces a winner: "Every sport is a combat between its participants, but boxing is combat distilled, purer even than combat with weapons" (Hoagland 62). The sport elevates a boxer above other human beings and above most other athletes: "To not only accept but to actively invite what most sane creatures avoid – pain, humiliation, loss, chaos – is to experience the present moment as already, in a sense, past" (Oates 27). With boxing as the zenith of athletics we can imagine that our already competitive society begins to look for racial qualities within. The search for a Great White Hope may well stem from a fear for the usefulness of white bodies: "In this world, strength of a certain kind – matched of course with intelligence and tirelessly developed skills – determines masculinity. Just as a boxer is his body, a man's masculinity is the use of his body. But it is also his triumph over another's use of his body" (Oates 72).

Given that physicality is cherished in our society, people may be intimidated by black boxers, especially if they vastly outnumber white boxers. The (ideal) aim of boxing is to knock out your opponent, to stand in the ring with fists raised in victory while the opponent is being dragged to his corner and helped to regain consciousness. No other sport is gauged toward the pain of your opponent in such a literal (i.e., physical) sense. Receiving pain in the ring takes courage, and courage adds to the fighter's nobility, which in boxing is almost an accolade: "Boxing is one of the few professions that give people from the underclass an opportunity to earn large sums of money and be heroes in their native land" (Hauser 17; cf. Oates 85). A poor person's rise to such excellence as boxing permits is the fulfillment of the rags-to-riches American Dream at its best – because fame, glory and money are achieved (and consequently demonstrated) physically. The idea of a successful black boxer is, therefore, fraught with socio-political connotations.

Self-responsibility and solitude echo Ahab's quest, but despite their physical superiority, fighters are generally not monomaniacal:

> Perhaps because of their origins, there is little pretense in fighters. Most professional athletes are spoiled. Fawned over in high school, heavily recruited by colleges, they've been stars at every turn. There are very few pampered fighters […]. Their creed is simple. In the ring, the best man wins. (Hauser 14)

American society cherishes simplicity and, therefore, boxers suggest themselves as heroes. When these heroes are not white in real life, white ones are constructed in mythology.

Since a large number of (formerly poor) fighters are black, this "[r]acial contrast awakens the still uglier need of racial identification, something which the ludicrous boxing film *Rocky* exploited in such an obvious, almost embarrassing way" (Early, "Three Notes" 29). White audiences grow jealous of black boxers' success and demand retribution – overtly in Jack Johnson's times and covertly in the era of Rocky Balboa.

A boxer often creates an illusion of hating his opponent before the fight. He 'psychs himself up' against the contender in order to endure in the ring and hurt the other boxer:

> The emotional incentive for this must be deeper than the mere quest for championship belts and big money […]. Boxers […] must have 'something to prove,' or they must 'hold a grudge' against their opponent for some imaginary or petty slight […]. In short, the bouts become quests for manhood. (Early, "I Only" 43)

For a white boxer such as Rocky, in the overall context of the Great White Hope, who would be better suited to psych oneself up against than a person whose skin color has so many negative cultural connotations?

Writers such as Liebling and, more prominently, Norman Mailer harbor latent racism in their texts. Early especially criticizes Mailer's 1975 book on the Ali-Foreman bout, *The Fight,* for its ponderings on race and explains that with Ali as a subject I suppose one is, perforce, confronted with the issue of race. Yet I think white writers like Mailer use Ali as an excuse to write about race, or more precisely, about blacks: what a wonderful opportunity to clear the chest and spleen of numerous phobias and neuroses! ("I Only" 48)

There is more:

> the reader is confronted with Mailer's [...] confessed inability to understand that mind which symbolizes for him the nonwhite other. [...] For Mailer, the black is always the id-dominated beast, the heart of the white man's darkness; and always, in Mailer's tone, there is that juvenile penis envy that might as well be hate because it amounts to such an insulting kind of love. [...] It is no wonder that Mailer loves boxing, or rather loves the symbolism of boxing. His engagement with the black experience has always been limited to the male side of all matters – when Mailer says "Blacks" he means male. ("I Only" 49)

Clubber Lang, the id-dominated beast, conforms formidably to Mailer's ponderings on blackness. The Great White Hope may be a desperate attempt at verifying white maleness and the id-dominated beast as maleness may well be part of the attraction of boxing for its viewers. I would argue that Mailer's views on race are shared by many boxing fans who, unlike Mailer, are searching for a Great White Hope and that they are longing for the affirmation that the white man, too, can be primal and yet sophisticated – a blend epitomized in the character of Rocky Balboa. Early goes on:

> Mailer expresses a very simple and very old idea [...], namely, that the black male is metaphorically the white man's unconsciousness personified. What is of deeper interest in that formulation is Mailer's homogenization of the black male personality; in effect any black male, from jazz musician to boxer to pimp to bank robber, any black male who is estranged from the bourgeois culture for whatever reason [...] is, for Mailer, the same outcast, the same uninhibited, uncivilized self, the same untraumatized noble savage. Ironically, if the black or Latin prizefighter within the code of his own world has absorbed the masculine rites and morality of the Anglo-Saxon West, then as symbol in the larger world he is simply a new type of minstrel, a black face hidden behind an even deeper blackface: the secret shadow-self of the white man's mind. ("I Only" 50)[5]

In his primitivism, Clubber Lang reflects all these characteristics, but also *Raging Bull*'s Sugar Ray Robinson, with his demon-like aura, suggests primal, subconscious qualities. It is quite telling that the American industry – especially the entertainment industry – constantly seems to find a way to market a successful black concept by sticking a white face on it: jazz was dragged out of 1920s Harlem and into rich white people's dinner parties; the blues was sung by Elvis Presley, the "white Negro" Sam Phillips had hoped for, and Eminem rapped his way into the hearts of millions at the turn of the twenty-first century – all financially more successful than their black counterparts. Rocky Marciano is still deified, and Gerry Cooney was a short-lived, but financially rather successful attempt. But records show that boxing is a discipline in which white people are not more successful. And so, alternate realities (Great White Fictions) have to be created.

New trends in boxing films paint a grim picture for African American pugilists. In 1992, Metro-Goldwyn-Mayer released *Diggstown*, an unsuccessful comedy about a white con-artist (James Woods) who bets a powerful white businessman that 'his' black boxer, Honey Ray Palmer (Louis Gossett Jr.), will defeat ten challengers in a row. Palmer is an ageing underdog and – needless to say – wins the fights. He thereby regains his fame and belief in himself and wins the con-artist the ownership of the town. References to the battle royal are rather obvious here; however, many of Palmer's opponents are white and, thus, his victory is a further humiliation for the antagonistic white businessman. In one fight which looks like a mismatch, the con-man gives Palmer a little pep-talk: "He's bigger than you are, he's tougher, he's faster, he's younger than you are. […] But remember this: you … are black." This, of course, alludes to the numbers of successful African Americans in professional heavyweight boxing.

Walter Hill's *Undisputed* (2002) fared equally badly at the box office. It is a film about a black heavyweight champion (Ving Rhames) who, while in prison, has to fight another convict. The fight takes place inside a cage with no referee and all other prisoners watching. It is a brutal fight – one is again reminded of a battle royal.

One of the few films about a black boxer that ends with the protagonist winning the final bout is Michael Mann's *Ali* (2001), which was neither a critical nor a financial success. It suffers from a number of issues: Ali is one of the most revered living icons and it is therefore difficult for any director to refrain from a heroic portrayal which does not drift off to the melodramatic. As Early noted, texts about Ali provide white people with the opportunity to "clear the chest" of racial inhibitions. Mann's use of electronic African music from the 1990s is inexplicable – and, overall, it seems as if reverence has blinded Mann and prevented him from making a successful movie.

Since *Ali*, there has been a wave of boxing movies which present Great White Hopes in a fashion reminiscent of the golden age of celluloid pugilism – the 1930s to 1950s, from *City Lights* (1931) to *Requiem for a Heavyweight* (1962), in which the ethnic background of the protagonist was a big issue, but never reflected the ethnicity of the majority of professional boxers. The highly successful *Million Dollar Baby* (2004) features a darker-skinned antagonist – curiously enough from East Berlin – who in terms of animalism could easily compete with Clubber Lang, and who paralyzes the white protagonist in the final match. The audience's sympathy is fully on the side of the film's heroine.

2005's *Cinderella Man* renders the historical James J. Braddock a veritable saint (regenerating the Christ-parallels popular in films about white boxers), and 2006's *Rocky Balboa* is business-as-usual for Rocky. *Resurrecting the Champ*, released in 2007 through Phoenix Pictures, is based on the true story of a homeless African American who turns out to be a former contender for the heavyweight title. Also well-received, the film focuses on the (white) reporter who found the boxer in the alley, rather than on the boxer himself.

With Paramount Pictures releasing a film about Irish American boxer Mickey Ward directed by David O. Russell – *The Fighter*, December 2010 – (Siegel and Fleming), white boxers continue to thrive on screen. Conversely, the Mike Tyson biopic, which Jamie Foxx talked about producing in 2005, is still in limbo (Dewey) and Robert Townsend's low-budget Sonny Liston biopic was a commercial and critical failure.

However, it seems that if we want to see a successful film about a successful black boxer in the near future, more black directors have to take on the subject. Otherwise, the future of black boxers in motion pictures looks rather grim. Much as real life boxing has produced role models, film can give us characters as iconic as Muhammad Ali. And if it were not for boxing, Muhammad Ali would never have produced the cultural, social, and political impact that he did.

If one has any reservations about the argument that boxing can make sociocultural waves in a manner significant enough to be written about and discussed, consider this: George Foreman was seen by many Africans – and certainly by the majority of Zairians at the time – as the embodiment of the white American establishment simply because he waved a tiny American flag at the Olympics. Pitted against Ali's favored anti-Americanism, Foreman committed a major transgression. The *Rumble in the Jungle* was an iconic fight, which many Zairians and Ali himself mythologized in the run-up. Foreman was rendered the representation of the American establishment and many experts believed him to win the bout.

Ali proved these experts wrong. Even though Ali defeated a black boxer that night in Kinshasa, he had taught the white world a lesson: the era of the Great White Hope, had it ever existed, was finally dead. The contender, whom the oppressors side with, can be defeated, and underdogs can become black kings. Loudmouthed, (un)pragmatic, and funky. There is hope that not even films can distort this image. The weeks before and after the *Rumble*, Ali was a politician, an emblem that showed the oppressors how robbing someone of opportunity, restricting their abilities, and thereby wounding them, does not shut them up. Wounds heal. Boxers show that – boxer kings use it to grander ends. Ali, Louis, Moore. Transcending color lines and highlighting them at the same time.

---

[1] Two examples: "Still fightin' the power like Tyson / When nothin' else works, start bitin'!" (Masta Killa). "Word to Mike Tyson, hit you quick like lightnin' / Swing my left jab first, and then come in with the right" (Gang Starr).

[2] "The primal fantasy of the big black penis projects the fear of a threat not only to white womanhood, but to civilization itself, as the anxiety of miscegenation, eugenic pollution and racial degeneration is acted out through white male rituals of racial aggression," writes Stuart Hall (290). For examples of the on-screen representations of the penis size myth, confer Oliver Stone's *Any Given Sunday* (1999) and season four of Larry David's *Curb Your Enthusiasm* (2005).

[3] Conversely, the Russian fighter Ivan Drago in *Rocky IV* is shown gradually to increase his already superhuman punching power.

[4] A conversation I overheard between two black boxers at Gleason's Gym in Brooklyn tackles the discussion on muscles from a humorous side: One of them flexes his right bicep and exclaims, "I box – that's why you see dem hard muscles right here!" The younger boxer sticks his tongue out and points at his open mouth half smiling: "Hard muscle right here!" Laughter ensues (and a short vindication by the addressee: "I don't do that.")

[5] This latent racism also occurs in Mailer's text "King of the Hill," about the first Ali-Frazier fight: "If black people are also beginning to speak our mixture of formal English and jargon-polluted American with real force, so white corporate America is getting more sexual and more athletic" (126). He goes on to write, "[Ali] had taken all the lessons of his curious life and the outrageously deep comprehension he had of the motivations of his own people – indeed, one could even approach the beginnings of a Psychology of the Blacks by studying his encounters with fighters who were black – and had elaborated that into a technique for boxing which was almost without compare. A most cultivated technique. For he was no child of the slums" (131).

Works Cited

Avildsen, John G. *Rocky*. 1976. Prod. Robert Chartoff and Irwin Winkler. *Rocky Anthology*. DVD. Santa Monica: MGM, 2005.

Bak, Richard. *Joe Louis: The Great Black Hope*. 1996. Cambridge: DaCapo, 1998.

Bryant, John. "*Moby-Dick* as Revolution." *The Cambridge Companion to Herman Melville*. 1998. Cambridge: Cambridge UP, 2006. 65-90.

Dewey, Todd. "Iron Mike Tries to Help Troubled Kids Steer Clear of Iron Bars." *Las Vegas Review Journal* 22 Feb. 2008. 1 Apr. 2008 <http://www.lvrj.com/sports/15870627.html>.

Dyer, Richard. *White*. New York: Routledge, 1997.

Early, Gerald. "I Only Like it Better When the Pain Comes." 1984. *Reading the Fights*. Ed. Joyce Carol Oates and Daniel Halpern. New York: Little, 1990. 39-60.

---. "Three Notes Toward a Cultural Definition of Prizefighting." 1981. *Reading the Fights*. Ed. Joyce Carol Oates and Daniel Halpern. New York: Little, 1990. 20-38.

Ellison, Ralph. *Invisible Man*. 1952. New York: Vintage, 1995.

Gang Starr. "F.A.L.A." *Hard to Earn*. Audio CD. New York: Virgin, 1994.

Gast, Leon. *When We Were Kings*. Prod. Leon Gast, et al. Polygram, 1997.

Hall, Stuart. "The Spectacle of the 'Other.'" *Representation: Cultural Representations and Signifying Practices*. Ed. Stuart Hall. London: Sage, 1997. 223-90.

Hauser, Thomas. *The Black Lights: Inside the World of Professional Boxing.* 1986. Fayetteville: Arkansas UP, 2000.

Hoagland, Edward. "Violence, Violence." 1986. *Reading the Fights.* Ed. Joyce Carol Oates and Daniel Halpern. New York: Little, 1990. 61-63.

Kogler, Daniel. "Going the Distance: Representations of Timelessness and Identity from *Rocky* to *Rocky Balboa.*" Master's Thesis. U of Graz, 2007.

Liebling, A. J. "Ahab and Nemesis." *The Sweet Science.* By A. J. Liebling. 1956. New York: North Point, 2004. 251-67.

Mailer, Norman. "King of the Hill." 1975. *Reading the Fights.* Ed. Joyce Carol Oates and Daniel Halpern. New York: Little, 1990. 121-49.

---. *The Fight.* 1975. New York: Vintage, 1997.

Martin, Joel W. "Redeeming America: *Rocky* as Ritual and Racial Drama." *Screening the Sacred: Religion Myth, and Ideology in Popular American Film.* Ed. Joel W. Martin and Conrad E. Ostwalt Jr. Boulder: Westview P, 1995. 125-33.

Masta Killa. "Secret Rivals." *No Said Date.* Audio CD. New York: Nature Sounds, 2004.

McCormack, Peggy. "Women in *Raging Bull*: Scorsese's Use of Determinist, Objective, and Subjective Techniques." *Martin Scorsese's* Raging Bull. Ed. Kevin J. Hayes. Cambridge: Cambridge UP, 2005. 92-115.

Melville, Herman. *Moby-Dick or, the Whale.* 1851. New York: Modern Library, 2000.

Motley, Clay. "Fighting for Manhood: Rocky and the Turn-of-the-Century Antimodernism." *Film & History: An Interdisciplinary Journal of Film and Television Studies* 35.2 (2005): 60-66.

Nicholls, Mark. "My Victims, My Melancholia: *Raging Bull* and Vincente Minelli's *The Bad and the Beautiful.*" *Martin Scorsese's* Raging Bull. Ed. Kevin J. Hayes. Cambridge: Cambridge UP, 2005. 116-34.

Oates, Joyce Carol. *On Boxing.* 1987. Updated and extended ed. New York: Ecco, 2006.

Parsley, Delen 'Blimp.' Personal interview with author. Brooklyn, NY, 9 Mar. 2007.

Peterson, Michael: "*Raging Bull* and the Idea of Performance." *Martin Scorsese's* Raging Bull. Ed. Kevin J. Hayes. Cambridge: Cambridge UP, 2005. 69-91.

Remnick, David. *King of the World*. New York: Vintage, 1999.
Stallone, Sylvester. *The Official Rocky Scrapbook*. New York: Grosset and Dunlap, 1977.
Ward, Geoffrey. *Unforgivable Blackness: The Rise and Fall of Jack Johnson*. 2004. New York: Vintage, 2006.
Wright, Martin. Personal interview with author. Brooklyn, NY, 9 Mar. 2007.

Screen Works Cited

Avildsen, John G. *Rocky*. 1976. Prod. Robert Chartoff and Irwin Winkler. *Rocky Anthology*. DVD. Santa Monica: MGM, 2005.
Chaplin, Charles. *City Lights*. 1931. Prod. Charles Chaplin. DVD. Burbank: Warner, 2004.
David, Larry, et al. *Curb Your Enthusiasm*. Prod. Larry David, et al. Hollywood: Warner, 2005.
Eastwood, Clint. *Million Dollar Baby*. Prod. Clint Eastwood, et al. Lakeshore, 2004.
Hill, Walter. *Undisputed*. 2000. Prod. David Giler, et al. DVD. n.p.: Buena Vista, n.d.
Howard, Ron. *Cinderella Man*. Prod. Brian Grazer. Hollywood: Touchstone, 2005.
Lurie, Rod. *Resurrecting the Champ*. Prod. Louis Phillips, et al. Hollywood: Phoenix, 2007.
Mann, Michael. *Ali*. 2001. Prod. Jon Peters, et al. Director's Cut DVD. Culver City: Columbia, 2004.
Ritchie, Michael. *Midnight Sting*. [*Diggstown*, 1992]. Prod. Robert Schaffel. DVD. Santa Monica: MGM, 2004.
Scorsese, Martin. *Raging Bull*. 1980. Prod. Robert Chartoff and Irwin Winkler. Special Ed. DVD. Santa Monica, CA: MGM, 2005.
Stallone, Sylvester. *Rocky III*. 1983]. Prod. Robert Chartoff and Irwin Winkler. *Rocky Anthology*. DVD. Santa Monica: MGM, 2005.
---. *Rocky IV*. 1987. Prod. Robert Chartoff and Irwin Winkler. *Rocky Anthology*. DVD. Santa Monica: MGM, 2005.
---. *Rocky Balboa*. Prod. Robert Chartoff, et al. Santa Monica: MGM, 2006.
Stone, Oliver. *Any Given Sunday*. Prod. Richard Donner, et al. DVD. Hollywood: Warner, 1999.

Yvonne Gutenberger

I Am Remembered as a Hairdo:
Angela Davis's *Autobiography* as a Revision of the Public Persona and Self-Reconstruction as Political Activist

> One woman introduced me to her brother, who at first responded to my name with a blank stare. The woman admonished him: "You don't know who Angela Davis is?! You should be ashamed." Suddenly a flicker of recognition flashed across his face: "Oh," he said, "Angela Davis – the Afro." Such responses are commonplace rather than exceptional, and it is both humiliating and humbling to discover that a generation following the events which constructed me as a public personality, I am remembered as a hairdo. (Davis, "Afro Images" 87)

This quote from an essay by Angela Davis illustrates the discrepancy between Angela Davis's self-image and the public persona as which she is remembered. In her autobiography Davis depicts herself as a political activist. This is what she wants to be seen as and remembered. But years after the events that made her a public persona – the encounter Davis recounts in her essay "Afro Images" took place in the mid-1990s – Davis is actually remembered as the personification of a hairstyle, as a fashion trend. But this is not the first time Davis felt misrepresented by public images of herself. One of the predominant characteristics of Angela Davis's 1974 *Autobiography* is the author's effort to correct what she considers a public misconception of herself. In her autobiography, Davis takes up a struggle against powerful media images, which include that of the black militant Communist and the criminal fugitive.

In an article on Angela Davis's *Autobiography* as a prison narrative, Nina Bosnicova argues that Davis's is a purely political autobiography and, quoting Perkins, "a pedagogical 'tool for advancing political struggle.'" She further declares that the autobiography is "clearly not a simple reflection of the autobiographers' [sic] 'true' self" (Bosnicova). While I would agree with Bosnicova that Angela Davis's autobiography is clearly not a simple narrative of personal development, I want to argue that while the text has obvious political goals, it is nevertheless more than a political manifesto and that its function exceeds that of a purely didactic tool. Angela Davis did not have to write an autobiography to make herself a symbol of the movement; she had already been (made) that symbol. Davis was at once "a symbol of free speech and open resistance" (National Committee 174) and a symbol of an "armed and dangerous" criminal (Moore 196). According to Howard Moore, Davis was used as a symbol; she was judged by both black and white Americans by "what they think she thought, or even worse, would think" (199). Her autobiography as well as other auto/biographical writings such as *The Morning Breaks* and *If They Come in the Morning* served to show readers what Angela Davis really thought. Those texts were supposed to clarify already existing media images. Writing about artists' memoirs, Helga Lénárt-Cheng maintains that "an autobiographer can manage, manipulate, or even correct his own public image through autobiographical writing" (117). On the basis of this assumption, this essay will show how Angela Davis uses her autobiography to not only mediate her political message but to also correct her public image.

Angela Davis was a public figure in the United States even before she wrote her autobiography. However, she was not known as a person, but as a type. And she set out to write her autobiography in order to change that type and reconstruct her identity. In the introduction to her autobiography, Davis claims that she is not going to write about herself but about the movement, that hers is a "political autobiography." This is true in part only. Davis tries to correct public misconceptions both of herself and of the Black Power movement. This is only logical, because both aspects are intertwined in her life. The public image of Angela Davis only came into being because of her political activism. By reviewing and correcting the public understanding of the Black Power movement, Davis also rewrites the public image of herself. Thus, via a detour, Angela Davis does *in fact* write about herself. This is typical of political autobiographies since "[i]n writing their lives, activists seek to *document* their experiences, to *correct* misinformation, to *educate* their readers, and to *encourage* the continuation of the struggle" (Perkins 70; emphasis added). As a typical activist autobiography, Angela Davis's autobiography displays all of the above features. Davis writes the autobiography as a historical document of the 1960s and 70s (*Autobiography* vii). In addition, she writes to correct a public image that she considers distorted. She wants to correct public images both of herself and of the Black Power movement, and to educate people about the movement. And eventually, Davis wants to motivate others to join the movement (xvi). The "desire to persuade" is not only a main feature of Davis's autobiography but has also been a distinguishing element of American slave narratives (Bland 33). Thus, Davis's political autobiography seems to stand in the rhetorical tradition of slave narratives.

Autobiography has been claimed as a typical American genre of writing (cf. Karl 120; Spengemann and Lundquist 501). But it is also, and maybe even more so, a typical African-American literary genre. For Selwyn Cudjoe, African-American autobiography is "the most Afro-American of all Afro-American literary pursuits" (6). From the writing of the first slave narratives onwards, autobiography has held a special place in African-American literature. It has been used as a literary means of expression and as a medium for the recording of historical events (Olney, "Autobiography" 15). Slave narratives, the first literary texts written by Americans of African descent, are a distinctly African-American variety of life writing. In addition, slave narratives were for a long time the most popular forms of African-American writing. These narratives were sites of historiography, autobiography, and literature.

The special feature of African-American autobiographies is the combination of the two perspectives of being American and of being of African descent. This is what W. E. B. Du Bois termed "double consciousness" (11). Claiming the authors' rights as American citizens and asserting the consciousness of their African heritage are central issues of African-American life writing (Andrews, Introduction 1). Houston Baker writes of autobiography that it was and is a genre expressing the American character because it depicts the writer as a seeker for the self, the salvation of the self, and the expression of the self ("Problem" 19). Autobiography lends itself especially to the disclosure of the American soul; it also points out the different social and cultural positions of white Americans and African-Americans. The white American writer of autobiography can reach back to literary traditions and cultural codes that were denied to the first African-American writers. Baker highlights the aspect of self-definition as crucial to African-American autobiography. As the African-American writers could not easily identify with white American tradition, it was the first duty of the autobiographer to forge a self and a cultural identity in writing (Baker, "Problem" 19-25). Angela Davis's effort to correct the public image of herself and to create an alternative identity in her life narrative thus fits perfectly into the tradition of African-American autobiographical expression.

Regina Blackburn distinguishes four types of African-American autobiography: Black Nationalist autobiographies, quests for integration, attacks on the system, and stories of success within the system (134). All of these types of African-American autobiography ultimately serve the goal of liberation. Disclosing the truth and writing history function as a means of expressing freedom in writing (Stone 174-75). It is in this context that Roger Rosenblatt identifies African-American life writing as "the death weapon" (169). He claims that the center of African-American autobiographies is constructed out of the wish to gain autonomy and equality in life. Writing autobiography is used as a weapon to enforce freedom of choice, to express criticism of present conditions and one's wish to live life independently (Rosenblatt 170). Another important element of African-American life writing is the aspect of coming to voice, finding a voice of one's own and maintaining this voice. This finding of one's voice expresses a movement toward sovereignty. The historical prevention of African-Americans' speaking themselves and their history is one reason why this autonomous voice plays such a crucial role in African-American writing (Stone 176). This historical background, especially as it relates to slavery and the tradition of slave narrative writing, helps us to understand why life writing has become such an important means of expression in African-American culture and cultural criticism.

Slave narratives represent the first, and for a long time the most popular, form of African-American life writing. The *Encyclopedia of Life Writing* identifies *The Narrative of the Uncommon Sufferings and Surprizing Deliverance of Briton Hammon, a Negro Man*, of 1760, as the first American slave narrative, and thus the beginning of African-American life writing. However, the most famous and best-known American slave narratives are Olaudah Equiano's (1789), Frederick Douglass's (1845), and Harriet Jacobs's (1861). The central themes of these narratives are slavery and its inhumanity. Another important theme is that of literacy, and learning how to read and write as a liberatory act. In many slave narratives, especially those of the nineteenth century, literacy represents the first step toward freedom. The author's literacy was also central to his or her status as an authentic slave narrator. For this reason, many slave narratives have an assertion in the form of "written by himself/herself" added to their title, indicating that the narrative was authentic and had not been altered through the interpretation of an editor or an amanuensis.

We can trace the tradition of African-American autobiography back to the time of the beginnings of slavery in the United States. Along with the institution of slavery, the tradition of slave narratives was being introduced. The slave narrative became a vital part of American literary tradition, and, therefore, a crucial influence on the formation of American cultural identity. The most widely read slave narrative to this day was written by Frederick Douglass, who carries the label of the "greatest of all slave narrators," the one who "set the standards for the genre" (*Encyclopedia of Life Writing* 23). His first autobiography, the *Narrative of the Life of Frederick Douglass, an American Slave* was published in 1845. Douglass's *Narrative* is a very typical American autobiography in that it employs the pattern of the conversion narrative and the trope of the self-made man (as established in Benjamin Franklin's *Autobiography*, for instance). It represents a progression from bondage to freedom, from darkness to light, and Douglass's personal success in attaining both freedom and manhood. He is a man who makes his own choices and who shows responsibility for these choices. Thus, the *Narrative* fits perfectly into the pattern of the pilgrimage and the American success story, representing personal success instead of economic success. Freedom is the central theme and the purpose of Douglass's autobiography, with which he wishes to hasten "the glad day of deliverance to the millions of my brethren in bonds" (Douglass 102). Analyzing the tradition of African-American life writing following the days of slave narratives, Andrews claims that freedom is "not just the theme but the *sign* of Afro-American autobiography" (Andrews, "Toward" 89). Freedom, he declares, is expressed both in the content and in the form of African-American autobiographies (Andrews, "Toward" 89).

Another central element of Douglass's autobiography is the significance of reading and writing for the development of Douglass's will to escape and his eventual emancipation. The acquisition of the skills of literacy was vital to the personal development of Frederick Douglass. Literacy becomes a necessary prerequisite to freedom and humanity for Douglass. "In modern western culture (the culture out of which autobiography emerged), literacy is indispensable to fully human survival" (Gunn 19), which is true for African-American autobiography, as well. But before he or she can achieve human survival in the narrative, the slave narrator encounters the need to prove his or her humanity, which he or she can achieve by learning how to read and write and demonstrating this skill. This proof of their status as a person was required before the former slave could even begin to claim his or her status as an autonomous subject (Gates 9-

10).

Reading leads to an awareness of one's situation. However, the liberating force lies in the act of writing, writing oneself into humanity and by that into freedom. Writing might even be a practical assistance to escape, as it enables Douglass "to write my own pass" (Douglass 44).[1] Another characteristic of Douglass's *Narrative,* in which he depicts himself with qualities of an intellectual and an activist fighting for the rights of African-Americans, is his teaching of other slaves with the purpose of "bettering the condition of my race" (72). Writing, especially the writing of autobiography, not only liberates the individual; it is also crucial to the liberation of other individuals, of a whole community in many cases (Werner 205). The act of writing has thus always been central to African-American autobiography, both as a device for claiming one's individuality and for asserting the autonomy of a whole cultural group.

We can find all of these typical features of the slave narrative in Davis's autobiography as well. Freedom – freedom from racism, freedom from imprisonment, and freedom from prejudice – is the central theme of Davis's *Autobiography.* Furthermore, another aspect of her life emphasized by Davis is her education. When we view this in light of the tradition of the slave narrative, we can see that this description of her education serves to legitimize Davis as an author of autobiography and a social critic. In the preface to the autobiography Davis explains why she decided to write down her life story and how such a book might help people:

> Such a book might serve a very important and practical purpose. There was the possibility that, having read it, more people would understand why so many of us have no alternative but to offer our lives – our bodies, our knowledge, our will – to the cause of our oppressed people. In this period when the covers camouflaging the corruption and racism of the highest political offices are rapidly falling away, when the bankruptcy of the global system of capitalism is becoming apparent, there was the possibility that more people – Black, Brown, Red, Yellow and white – might be inspired to join our growing community of struggle. Only if this happens will I consider this project to have been worthwhile. (xvi)

While freedom was the central theme of the slave narratives, modernist autobiography focused on theories of race and on racial pride. One of the central figures of "modernist" – in the traditional[2] sense of the word – African-American autobiography is W. E. B. Du Bois. Du Bois met with wide acclaim as a theorist of

African-American culture and of the implications of being black in the United States. Kwame Anthony Appiah, for example, writes about Du Bois's second autobiography *Dusk of Dawn*: "More often, more intelligently, and with more passion and purpose than anyone before or since, Du Bois strove to capture the meaning of race for Afro-Americans" (37). Du Bois wrote three autobiographies and a number of autobiographical essays, some of which are included in his famous *The Souls of Black Folk* (1903). In his first autobiography, *Darkwater: Voices from within the Veil* (1920), Du Bois analyzes major cultural and social issues of his time, combining prose and poetry. In *Dusk of Dawn: An Essay toward an Autobiography of a Race Concept* (1940) he concentrates on ideas and concepts of race, as the title suggests. His third autobiography, written toward the end of his life, is the most traditional and the most comprehensive of Du Bois's autobiographies. In *The Autobiography of W. E. B. Du Bois: A Soliloquy on Viewing My Life from the Last Decade of Its First Century* (1968) Du Bois is more personal than in the preceding volumes and concentrates on narrating episodes of his life. In all three autobiographies, Du Bois relates his own experiences and memories to theoretical concepts. Du Bois's autobiographies represent typical instances of critical life writing, because he combines personal experience with cultural theory and criticism. The particular strength of all three volumes of his autobiography is that the "personal and the universal are interwoven and given equal treatment" (*Encyclopedia of Life Writing* 288).

African-American autobiography, as we have seen, stands in a tradition of connecting the personal and the political. As such, these writings can also be read in relation to Paul Gilroy's concept of modernity and the "Black Atlantic." Modernity, according to Gilroy, is traditionally understood as "a distinct configuration with its own spatial and temporal characteristics defined above all through the consciousness of novelty that surrounds the emergence of civil society, the modern state, and industrial capitalism" (49). Gilroy criticizes that this traditional understanding of modernity does not account for issues of racial difference. His concept of the "Black Atlantic" is marked by transgression, of national as well as ethnic and cultural boundaries:

> The specificity of the modern political and cultural formation I want to call the Black Atlantic can be defined, on one level, through [a] desire to transcend both the structures of the nation state and the constraints of ethnicity and national particularity. These desires are relevant to understanding political organizing and cultural criticism. They have always sat unea-

sily alongside the strategic choices forced on black movements and individuals embedded in national and political cultures and nation-states in America, the Caribbean, and Europe. (19)

For African-American autobiographical writing, correspondingly, I want to add that as a modern genre of writing it also transgresses boundaries of the personal and the political, structures which we tend to separate in life narratives or at least try to ascribe them unequal significance. We like to read an autobiography as either (predominantly) political or (predominantly) individual narrative. But even though Angela Davis's *Autobiography* might at first glance appear to be a purely political book, it is just as much the story of an individual character. Therefore, for a full understanding of the autobiography, we have to read both aspects of the story in conjunction.

Racial pride, of course, was a central element of Black Power. This feature of the Black Power era clearly functions as a legacy of black modernism.[3] So do the theorization of race and the social criticism which were central elements of Black Power writings.[4] The issue of black pride is also central to the revolutionary, black nationalist autobiographies of the 1960s, the most famous of which are Eldridge Cleaver's *Soul on Ice* (1968) and *The Autobiography of Malcolm X* (1965). Malcolm X's autobiography, written with the assistance of Alex Haley, contains elements of spiritual autobiography and the conversion narrative. His concept of black identity – as not only distinct from but even superior to the white identity that dominated American culture – represents the move toward black nationalism that dominated African-American politics in the 1960s (Andrews, "African-American" 196). This new sense of black identity promoted not only the recognition of difference but even encouraged pride in this difference. Pride in black identity and anger at social and political injustices are, along with the author's conversion into a leader of the Black Revolution, the main themes of Malcolm X's *Autobiography*. The structuring of life as a journey makes Malcolm X's *Autobiography* a typically American autobiography, while African-American autobiography employs a special variety of this motif, the journey from oppression toward new prospects (Stone 176).

In contrast to Malcolm X's autobiography, Davis highlights that she and her experiences are not different or exceptional. She depicts herself as a typical black woman who shares the typical experience of black people living in the United States. She writes that "the most essential fact" she wants to express through her autobiography is that "the forces that have made my life what it is are the very same forces that have shaped and misshaped the lives of millions of my people" (*Autobiography* xv). Here Davis already starts to deconstruct her public image as a member of the black elite who sees herself as something special, different from the masses of ordinary black people. But this is only one of the public images Davis wants to correct.

In the United States, Angela Davis was a public figure during the 1970s, and pictures of her were widely circulated. Thus, visual media in particular had a strong influence in the shaping of the author's public image. In her autobiography Davis discusses and writes against these public images at the same time. She uses the book to present an alternative self-depiction to her readership. The contrast between the public image and Davis's self-portrait in the autobiography is particularly intriguing in this context. The bias of media presentations of Angela Davis becomes apparent in a magazine article on her arrest in 1970 ("The Angela Davis Case"). In the pictures accompanying an October 1970 *Newsweek* article on her arrest, Davis is depicted as a somewhat misguided but essentially good American girl. The first picture shows her as a young girl scout, the epitome of the good American child. The next pictures show her with her family and as a young student at Brandeis. In these pictures, she still appears as the typical, assimilated black girl and young woman, with the straightened hair as a symbol of her political innocence. In the next picture we see Davis with Professor Marcuse at the University of California in San Diego. In this picture Davis already wears an Afro. This hair style fits into the publicly promoted image of Davis as the radical black communist and in the article it functions as an indication that she is beginning to move toward radicalism. While in this picture Davis is still only "talking" revolution, the next picture shows her in full action, demonstrating on behalf of the Soledad Brothers. The picture also seems to show us who led this good American girl astray – the Black Power Movement and its black men with their negative influence on the young girl. In the picture they are personified by Jonathan Jackson, standing next to Davis, and by the Soledad Brothers, signified by the poster she is holding up. These pictures sequentially present Davis's life as a course of events which inevitably led to the arrest of a beautiful young woman who had decided to take the wrong path in life. The change of hairstyle from straight hair to the Afro is used as a marker for the step from white America to black America, from good American to bad Communist and radical criminal.

This visual transformation underwrites the depiction of Angela Davis as one of the FBI's ten most wanted criminals. Indeed, the FBI's "Wanted" poster, showing Davis with a huge Afro, can be seen as a culmination of this media construction of Davis as a menacing criminal or, in Kenneth Mostern's words, as the "perfect Black Power monster" (174). The public image created by the FBI campaign and related to her Afro hairstyle is nicely summed up in Ayana Byrd and Lori Tharps's list of "Ten Memorable Moments in Black Hair History." One of these memorable moments is "1969: The year Angela Davis's image – massive Afro on display – is disseminated to the masses by the FBI. Warning: Afroed and dangerous" (183). Davis analyzes this development in her autobiography when she recounts her arrest by the FBI. She describes the arrest as a scenario staged to make her look threatening. The scene of the arrest as described by Davis illustrates the strategies the FBI used in its media presentation of Davis as a threatening black Communist and a menacing outlaw. She describes how her image was broadcast on TV in association with a fictional crime program. She was put on the list of the FBI's ten most wanted criminals and this alone would have made her appear threatening to the average American. The large number of agents and the crowd of photographers who were present in the motel lobby during Davis's arrest also add to this picture. Davis describes this scene in order to reveal the way the media are capable of distorting reality. She writes:

> As I passed the open door facing my room, the frail man reached out and grabbed my arm. He said nothing. More agents were pouring out behind him and others were streaming out of a room across the hall. "Angela Davis?" "Are you Angela Davis?" [...] During the ten or twelve seconds between the elevator and the point of confrontation, all kinds of thoughts tore through my mind. I remembered the television program I had watched in the Miami apartment: the FBI – a typical, inane TV melodrama of agents pursuing fugitives, complete with the final violent encounter which left the pursued with bullets in their skulls and the FBI agents shown as heroes. Just as I moved to turn off the set, a photograph of me flashed on the screen as if it were a part of the fictionalized FBI pursuit. "Angela Davis," a deep voice said, "is one of the FBI's ten most wanted criminals. She is wanted for the crimes of murder, kidnapping and conspiracy. She is very likely armed, so if you see her, do not try to do anything. Contact your local FBI immediately." In other words, let your "very likely armed" FBI have the honor of shooting her down. (*Autobiography* 15)

As she continues with her account of the arrest, we can see that even though Angela Davis was commonly associated with the Afro hairstyle, she was by far not the only black woman wearing her hair in a natural at that time. Davis herself claims that rather than setting a new trend, she was only emulating other black women who already wore their hair that way. She continues her account as follows:

> They forced David into a room on the right side of the corridor and shoved me into one on the left. There they ripped the wig off my head, cuffed my hands behind me and fingerprinted me on the spot. All the while pelting me with the same question: "Are you Angela Davis?" [...] Obviously they had gone through similar scenes many times before. They had rehearsed this moment with the false arrests of scores, perhaps hundreds of tall, light-skinned Black women with large naturals. Only the fingerprints would tell them whether they had caught the real one this time. (*Autobiography* 15)

The above quote shows how quickly the Afro – once a revolutionary statement – had become a widely spread fashion hairstyle in the 1970s. When the Afro became popular in the 1960s it was a radical political statement of black pride. However, during the following decade this radical hairstyle was transformed into a fashion trend (Walker 178, 183). Davis herself understood her Afro as a symbol which identified her with the Black Power movement, but for her opponents the Afro did not stand for the movement but for Davis herself as the most famous wearer of this hairstyle. In this context, Angela Davis is transformed from a political activist into a fashion trend-setter.

In Angela Davis's life, hair has become an important factor when it comes to group association. Early on she realizes that hair texture and hair styles are important markers of membership in a community. She recounts that as a child she wanted to have kinky hair, not to wear an Afro, as she does later in life, but in order to have it straightened like all of her friends:

> Sometimes I used to secretly resent my parents for giving me light skin instead of dark, and wavy instead of kinky hair. I pleaded with my mother to let me get it straightened, like my friends. But she continued to brush it with water and rub Vaseline in it to make it lie down so she could fix the two big wavy plaits which always hung down my back. On special occasions, she rolled it up in curlers made out of brown paper to make my Shirley Temple Curls. (*Autobiography* 96)

Being told that she has "good hair" is an insult to young Angela Davis, not because of the oppressive, racist nature of the categories of "good" and "bad" hair, but because this seemingly positive feature turns her into an outsider. Her hair excludes her from the group. Later, when Davis becomes active in the Black Power movement as a student, she decides to wear her hair in a natural style because this identifies her as a sympathizer with the movement (*Autobiography* 150). In the 1960s hair had become a political expression. Ayana Byrd and Lori Tharps sum up the political significance of the Afro in their book *Hair Story* as follows:

> Afros were not just a simple Black statement that 'we are not straightening our hair in conformity to a Eurocentric ideal.' They were an over-the-top expression – the higher the hair and the more it didn't look like anything that could be considered White, the better. And for many Whites, Afros – and all that they seemed to represent – inspired fear. (60)

One of Davis's strategies in reinterpreting her public image is that of relating her own experiences to those of fugitive slaves. Her participation in and affinity with the African-American life writing tradition, which encompasses the slave narratives, has already been noted. Yet her affinity goes beyond mere rhetoric or questions of form. Being a fugitive herself, Davis reinterprets her experiences from a new perspective. The familiar now appears unfamiliar and threatening. Davis's description of her experiences and feelings during her flight from the police and the FBI approximate us imaginatively to what fugitive slaves must have felt when escaping their cruel master:

> The route from Echo Park down to the Black neighborhood around West Adams was very familiar to me. I had driven it many times. But tonight the way seemed strange, full of the unknown perils of being a fugitive. And there was no getting around it – my life was now that of a fugitive, and fugitives are caressed every hour by paranoia. Every strange person I saw might be an agent in disguise, with bloodhounds waiting in the shrubbery for their master's command. Living as a fugitive means resisting hysteria, distinguishing between the creations of a frightened imagination and the real signs that the enemy is near. I had to learn how to elude him, outsmart him. It would be difficult, but not impossible. (*Autobiography* 5)

In the next paragraph Davis interprets this experience and her own motivation in relation to the history of American slavery when she writes, "Thousands of my ancestors had waited, as I had done, for nightfall to cover their steps, had leaned on one true friend to help them, had felt, as I did, the very teeth of the dogs at their heels. It was simple. I had to be worthy of them" (5-6). Here, she explicitly relates her own experience to the experiences of her ancestors. Thus, she lends her actions historical significance. She places herself in a historical continuum and thus ascribes a kind of universal value to her own experiences. Analogously to the experience of the fugitive slave, she interprets her own experiences in mid-twentieth-century America as those of a rebel against injustice.

By invoking the tradition of the slave narrative, Angela Davis establishes a connection to literary ancestors as well as to a shared history of enslavement and emancipation in the black diaspora. The genre of the slave narrative is most famously represented by Frederick Douglass, who" personifies the imperative of struggle itself" (Martin 271). For Davis, Frederick Douglass furthermore was representative of violent resistance (Moore 191-92). Douglass and Davis are thus both representatives of political movements and of activists-turned-symbols. Interestingly, Douglass who was a major black icon of the 1960s and 70s was known as "emblematic of the Afro-American search for race pride, full acceptance as American citizens, and *manhood*" (Martin 274; emphasis added). This black manhood is defined by "self-respect, strong moral character, aggressiveness, and a deep-seated sense of racial pride and responsibility" (Martin 274-75), all of them characteristics of Angela Davis's autobiographical self-representation.

As we have seen, many of the media-images of Angela Davis served to criminalize her, while Davis's own reinterpretation of events serves as a counter-narrative to these images. This counter-narrative, in turn, is intended to de-criminalize her in the public eye. Davis's central strategy of de-criminalizing herself is her self-depiction not as a criminal fugitive but as a political prisoner. One instance where Davis very obviously directs the reader's attention away from herself and toward the movement is in her analysis of the public dramatization of herself as a criminal. The morning after her arrest, Davis is led to her first court appearance. Contemplating the situation, she concludes that she is not chosen as the center of media attention for her personal opinions and actions, but because she is used as a symbol for the movement:

> A glimpse of the morning paper's bold-lettered headlines, peeping out from under some man's arm, stunned me: ANGELA DAVIS CAPTURED IN NEW YORK. It suddenly struck me that the huge crowd of press people summoned by the FBI the evening before had probably written similar headline stories throughout the country. Knowing that my name was now familiar to millions of people, I felt overwhelmed. Yet I knew that all this publicity was not really aimed at me as an individual. Using me as an example, they wanted to discredit the Black Liberation Movement, the Left in general and obviously also the Communist Party. I was only the occasion for their manipulations. (*Autobiography* 24-25)

We typically think of an autobiographer as someone who thinks of him- or herself as someone who is special, and whose life is worth the reader's attention. While the conventional autobiographer puts herself into the center of interest, Angela Davis tends to divert attention away from herself as an individual. In the text, Davis claims that her newly achieved publicity is a cause of discomfort to her, and in a somewhat martyr-like move, she claims to accept this unwelcome publicity only for the benefit of the movement. She writes about the burden of publicity as follows:

> If the need for constant security made life unwieldy for me, it was only one facet of the larger problem of getting used to the fact that I had been transformed into a public figure overnight. I hated being the center of such excessive attention. The snooping, often parasitic news reporters jarred my nerves. And I loathed being stared at like a curiosity object. I had never aspired to be a "public revolutionary"; my concept of my revolutionary vocation had been vastly different. Still, I had accepted the challenge which the state initiated and if that meant I had to become a public personality, then I would have to be that personality – despite my own discomfort. (*Autobiography* 220-21)

This attitude is in line with what Selwyn Cudjoe writes about African-American autobiography. According to Cudjoe, the opposition between the public and the private – between "me-ism" and "our-ism" – is an integral characteristic of African-American autobiography (9-10). This special feature of African-American autobiography highlights the importance of the group over the individual autobiographer. Cudjoe argues that African-American autobiographers write as a member of group, as a sort of collective subject. James Olney called this kind of life writing, which associates identity with community, "autophylography" – the typical form of African life writing, favoring group identity over personal identity ("Autobiography" 19). This focus on the group and on collective experience is in line with the tradition of African-American slave narratives, which "describe a reality that is simultaneously individual and collective" (Bland 30). The opposite of African or African-American autobiography in this context would be the typically individualistic, self-centered, and solipsistic type of Western autobiography, which puts the development of the self to the center of autobiography. For this type of life writing Olney suggests the term "autoautography" ("Value" 213). The autobiographer's dilemma is that even though she may put herself into the background of her narrative she can never erase herself from the text. Even though Davis claims she does not want to be the center of attention, she puts herself right there by writing an autobiography, a text about the author herself.

In order to decrease this tendency toward individuation, Davis emphasizes the connections of her personal struggle to a general fight against discrimination. She connects the black liberation movement to working-class movements all over world. Since she wants to use her own life story as an example to motivate others to join the movement, Davis tries to position herself and her struggle within the larger context of the struggle against injustice. The following is an example of how she depicts herself as someone who sacrifices her own life story for the welfare of oppressed people:

> The more the movement for my freedom increased in numbers, strength and confidence, the more imperative it became for everyone to see it not as something exceptional but as a small part of a great fight against injustice, one bough in a solidly rooted tree of resistance. It was not only political repression, but racism, poverty, police brutality, drugs, and all the myriad ways Black, Brown, Yellow and white working people are kept chained to misery and despair. (*Autobiography* 382)

Today, Angela Davis is indeed known by many because of her notable Afro hairstyle. In the 1960s the Afro was both a political statement and a fashion trend. But today we usually remember it as only one aspect of Sixties fashion. The political connotation is often shifted to the background. The emblematic quality of Angela Davis's Afro becomes most visible in art that uses the characteristic hairstyle as an identifier. These drawings and paintings usually depict Angela Davis in an expressionistic rather than a naturalistic style. However, we still can easily recognize her by her huge Afro. Davis is still widely known today. Some know her for her political activism, others for her public speeches, and still others might know her for her looks only. Angela Davis can be seen as emblematic of the fragmentation and double consciousness characteristic of modernity. On the one hand, her symbolic qualities – both now and in the past – help her to get across her politic messages. On the other hand, her autobiography shows that she longs to be known as person, too, not just as a symbol.

---

[1] The written pass and writing as a practical means to attain freedom are also central motifs in other slave narratives, such as William and Ellen Craft's *Running a Thousand Miles for Freedom*.

[2] Modernism is here understood as an introspective and self-conscious cultural movement of the late nineteenth and early twentieth century.

[3] Black modernism can be understood as unifying high art and folk art, or as Houston A. Baker Jr. defines it: "The blending [...] of class and mass – *poetic* mastery discovered as a function of deformative *folk* sound – constitutes the essence of black discursive modernism" (*Modernism* 93). Black modernist discourse, in Baker's definition, follows a period that was dominated by the discourse of slavery; thus, black modernism becomes a movement away from slavery, toward freedom, liberation, and "authenticity" (*Modernism* 101-02). This move toward liberation is followed by the achievement of what Baker calls "a life-enhancing and empowering public sphere mobility and the economic solvency of the black majority" (*Turning South* 33).

[4] Angela Davis's autobiography is a point in case here, as it theorizes subjects such as racism, capitalism, communism, the American judicial system, and the various black liberation movements.

Works Cited

Andrews, William L. "African-American Autobiography Criticism: Retrospect and Prospect." *American Autobiography: Retrospect and Prospect*. Ed. Paul John Eakin. Madison: U of Wisconsin P, 1991. 195-215.

---. Introduction. *African American Autobiography: A Collection of Critical Essays*. Ed. William L. Andrews. Englewood Cliffs: Prentice Hall, 1993. 1-7.

---. "Toward a Poetics of Afro-American Autobiography." *Afro-American Literary Study in the 1990s*. Ed. Houston A. Baker Jr. and Patricia Redmond. Chicago: U of Chicago P, 1989. 78-91.

"The Angela Davis Case." *Newsweek* 26 Oct. 1970: 18-24.

Appiah, Kwame Anthony. "The Conservation of 'Race.'" *Black American Literature Forum* 23.1 (1989): 37-60.

Aptheker, Bettina. *The Morning Breaks: The Trial of Angela Davis*. Ithaca: Cornell UP, 1975.

Baker, Houston A., Jr. *Modernism and the Harlem Renaissance*. Chicago: U of Chicago P, 1987.

---. "The Problem of Being: Some Reflections on Black Autobiography." *Obsidian: Black Literature in Review* 1.1 (1975): 18-30.

---. *Turning South Again: Re-Thinking Modernism / Re-Reading Booker T.* Durham: Duke UP, 2001.

Blackburn, Regina. "In Search of the Black Female Self: African-American Women's Autobiographies and Ethnicity." *Women's Autobiography: Essays in Criticism*. Ed. Estelle C. Jelinek. Bloomington: Indianan UP, 1980. 133-48.

Bland, Sterling Lecater, Jr. *Voices of the Fugitives: Runaway Stories and Their Fictions of Self-Creation*. Westport: Praeger, 2000.

Bosnicova, Nina. "'Revolution Is a Serious Thing': Angela Davis's *Autobiography* as a Prison Narrative." *Americana: E-Journal of American Studies in Hungary* 2.2 (2006): n. pag.

Byrd, Ayana D., and Lori Tharps. *Hair Story: Untangling the Roots of Black Hair in America*. New York: St. Martin's, 2001.

Cudjoe, Selwyn R. "Maya Angelou and the Autobiographical Statement." *Black Women Writers (1950-1980): A Critical Evaluation*. Ed. Mari Evans. Garden City: Anchor 1984. 6-24.

Davis, Angela. "Afro Images: Politics, Fashion, and Nostalgia." *Names We Call Home: Autobiography on Racial Identity*. Ed. Becky Thompson and Sangeeta Tyagi. New York: Routledge, 1996. 86-91.

---. *An Autobiography*. 1974. New York: International Publishers, 1988.

Douglass, Frederick. *Autobiographies: Narrative of the Life of Frederick Douglass, an American Slave; My Bondage and My Freedom; Life and Times of Frederick Douglass*. New York: Library of America, 1996.

Du Bois, W. E. B. *The Souls of Black Folk*. 1903. Ed. Henry Louis Gates Jr. New York: Norton, 1999.

Eakin, Paul John. "Malcolm X and the Limits of Autobiography." *African American Autobiography: A Collection of Critical Essays*. Ed. William L. Andrews. Englewood Cliffs: Prentice Hall, 1993. 151-61.

Encyclopedia of Life Writing: Autobiographical and Biographical Forms, 2 vols. Ed. Margaret Jolly. London: Fitzroy Dearborn, 2001.

Fox-Genovese, Elizabeth. "My Statue, My Self: Autobiographical Writings of Afro-American Women." *The Private Self: Theory and Practice of Women's Autobiographical Writings*. Ed. Shari Benstock. London: Routledge, 1988. 63-89.

Gates, Henry Louis, Jr. "James Gronniosaw and the Trope of the Talking Book." *African American Autobiography: A Collection of Critical Essays*. Ed. William L. Andrews. Englewood Cliffs: Prentice Hall, 1993. 8-25.

Gilroy, Paul. *The Black Atlantic: Modernity and Double Consciousness*. London: Verso, 1993.

Gunn, Janet Varner. *Autobiography: Toward a Poetics of Experience*. Philadelphia: U of Pennsylvania P, 1982.

Karl, Frederick R. "Memoirs: A Mutant of Biography/Autobiography/Fiction." *Biography and Source Studies 7*. Ed. Frederick R. Karl. New York: AMS, 2003. 117-63.

Lénárt-Cheng, Helga. "Autobiography As Advertisement: Why Do Gertrude Stein's Sentences Get Under Our Skin?" *New Literary History* 34.1 (2003): 117-31.

Lionnet, Françoise. "Autoethnography: The An-Archic Style of Dust Tracks on a Road." *African American Autobiography: A Collection of Critical Essays*. Ed. William L. Andrews. Englewood Cliffs: Prentice Hall, 1993. 113-37.

Martin, Waldo E., Jr. "Images of Frederick Douglass in the Afro-American Mind: The Recent Black Freedom Struggle." *Frederick Douglass: New Literary and Historical Essays.* Ed. Eric J. Sundquist. Cambridge: Cambridge UP, 1990. 271-85.

Moore, Howard, Jr. "Angela – Symbol of Resistance." *If They Come in the Morning: Voices of Resistance.* Ed. Angela Y. Davis, et al. New Rochelle: Third P, 1971. 191-200.

Mostern, Kenneth. *Autobiography and Black Identity Politics: Racialization in Twentieth-Century America.* Cambridge: CUP, 1999.

The National Committee to Free Angela Davis. "A Political Biography." *If They Come in the Morning: Voices of Resistance.* Ed. Angela Y. Davis, et al. New Rochelle: Third P, 1971. 171-76.

Olney, James. "Autobiography and the Cultural Moment: A Thematic, Historical, and Bibliographical Introduction." *Autobiography: Essays Theoretical and Critical.* Ed. James Olney. Princeton: Princeton UP, 1980. 3-27.

---. "The Value of Autobiography for Comparative Studies: African vs. Western Autobiography." *African American Autobiography: A Collection of Critical Essays.* Ed. William L. Andrews. Englewood Cliffs: Prentice Hall, 1993. 212-23.

Perkins, Margo V. *Autobiography as Activism: Three Black Women of the Sixties.* Jackson: U of Mississippi P, 2000.

Rosenblatt, Roger. "Black Autobiography: Life as the Death Weapon." *Autobiography: Essays Theoretical and Critical.* Ed. James Olney. Princeton: Princeton UP, 1980. 169-80.

Spengemann, William C., and L. R. Lundquist. "Autobiography and the American Myth." *American Quarterly* 17.2 (1965): 501-19.

Stone, Albert E. "After *Black Boy* and *Dusk of Dawn*: Patterns in Recent Black Autobiography." *Phylon* 39.1 (1978): 18-34. Rpt. in *African-American Autobiography: A Collection of Critical Essays.* Ed. William L. Andrews. Englewood Cliffs: Prentice-Hall, 1993. 171-75.

Walker, Susannah. *Style and Status: Selling Beauty to African American Women, 1920-1975.* Lexington: UP of Kentucky, 2007.

Werner, Craig. "On the Ends of Afro-American 'Modernist' Autobiography." *Black American Literature Forum* 24.2 (1990): 203-20.

Notes on the Contributors

David Abulafia is Professor of Mediterranean History at Gonville and Caius College, University of Cambridge. His research interests include the history of the Mediterranean as well as of the eastern and western Atlantic in the early modern period. Professor Abulafia's publications comprise several books on the Mediterranean, including the forthcoming *The Great Sea: A Human History of the Mediterranean* (2011). He is the editor of volume 5 of the *New Cambridge Medieval History* (1999) and *The Mediterranean in History* (2003), translated into several languages. His latest book-length publication, *The Discovery of Mankind: Atlantic Encounters in the Age of Columbus*, appeared in 2008 (Spanish edition, 2009).

Simone A. James Alexander is Associate Professor of English and immediate past Chair of the Department of Africana Studies at Seton Hall University, New Jersey, where she also teaches courses in African American literature, African literature, Caribbean literature, Russian literature, American literature, and women writers. Her book *Mother Imagery in the Novels of Afro-Caribbean Women* was published by the University of Missouri Press, 2001. In addition, she has authored articles and book chapters on Edwidge Danticat, Nawal el Saadawi, Grace Nichols, Audre Lorde, and Kamau Braithwaite. She has also published a book chapter on race and racial issues in the classroom in *The Teacher's Body: Embodiment, Identity, and Authority in the Academy* (SUNY Press, 2003). Her recent book chapter "En/gendering Home, En/gendering Difference: Performing and Representing Blackness in (Communist) Russia" appeared in *Russian-American Ties: African-Americans and Russia* (St. Petersburg Nauka Publishers, 2009). Her article on gender and citizenship is forthcoming in the spring 2011 issue *of African American Review*. Professor Alexander's current manuscript is titled *Migrating Bodies: Politics of Resistance, Survival and Citizenship*.

Georg Bauer received his Ph.D. from the Department of American Studies at the University of Graz in Austria. He has been working on topics related to violence in contemporary culture, literature, and film.

Alexander Beissenhirtz earned his M.A. in American Studies at the Ludwig-Maximilians-Universität, Munich, Germany in 2005. He is a Ph.D. candidate at the Berlin Free University. His Ph.D. thesis, *Affirmation and Resistance: The Politics of the Jazz Life in the Self-Narratives of Louis Armstrong, Art Pepper, and Oscar Peterson*, deals with the political significance of jazz music as inscribed in autobiographical texts by American jazz musicians. Since 2009, he works for a publishing house in Hamburg, Germany.

Paul Delaney, veteran print journalist, spent twenty three years with the *New York Times* as an editor and correspondent. He served as a reporter in *Times* bureaus in Washington, Chicago, and Madrid, where he was Bureau Chief; he was also an editor on the National Desk and Senior Editor for newsroom administration in New York. He is currently living in Washington and completing a memoir on his career at the paper. A graduate of Ohio State University, where he majored in journalism, Delaney was a founding member of two organizations, the National Association of Black Journalists and the National Association of Minority Media Executives. Delaney was also an editorial writer for the *Baltimore Sun*, editorial page editor of *Our World News*, director of the *Center for the Study of Race and Media* at Howard University, chair of the Journalism Department at the University of Alabama, and director of the *Initiative on Racial Mythology* at the Gene Media Forum of Syracuse University.

Simon Dickel is Junior Professor of Ethnic and Postcolonial Studies at Ruhr-University Bochum. Among his fields of research are African American Studies, queer theory, graphic narratives, and film studies. He is the author of *Black/Gay: The Harlem Renaissance, the Protest Era, and Constructions of Black Gay Identity in the 1980s and 90s*.

Mar Gallego-Durán has taught American and African American Literatures at the University of Huelva (Spain) since 1996. She obtained her Ph.D. degree from the University of Seville in 1997, and was awarded fellowships at the

Universities of Cornell (academic year 1991-92), Northwestern (1995, 2003, and 2007), and Harvard (1999). Her major research interests are African American Studies and the African diaspora, with a special focus on women writers and gender issues. She has published a monograph entitled *Passing Novels in the Harlem Renaissance* (Hamburg: LIT Verlag, 2003) and has co-edited several essay collections: *Myth and Ritual in African American and Native American Literatures* (2001), *Contemporary Views on American Culture and Literature in the Great 60's* (2002), *Razón de mujer: Género y discurso en el ensayo femenino* (2003), *El legado plural de las mujeres* (2005), *Espacios de género* (2005), *Relatos de viajes, miradas de mujeres* (2007), *Género, Ciudadanía y Globalización* (2009), and *The Dialectics of Diasporic Identification* (2009). Currently, she is completing a monograph on women writers of the African diaspora that will be published in 2011.

Alison D. Goeller holds a Ph.D. in American Literature from Temple University, Philadelphia and has published articles on Walter Mosley, Alvin Ailey, and Eudora Welty, as well as Italian American women writers. She is the co-editor of *Embodying Liberation: The Black Body in American Dance*, a FORECAAST publication (2001). She teaches literature and creative writing for The University of Maryland/European Division in Heidelberg, Germany.

Yvonne Gutenberger is a Ph.D. candidate in American Studies at Johannes Gutenberg University in Mainz, where she teaches and conducts research on her dissertation on "Contemporary African American Life Writing as Cultural Practice" as a fellow of the doctoral college on Life Writing. She was a visiting scholar at Columbia University, New York (2006) and an exchange lecturer at the University of Michigan, Ann Arbor, where she taught in the English Department (2008-09). Her article on "Anne Moody's *Coming of Age in Mississippi*: The Mediation of Cultural Criticism in Life Writing" was recently published in *Auto/Biography and Mediation* (Winter Verlag, 2010).

Clarence Sholé Johnson is Professor of Philosophy at Middle Tennessee State University (MTSU) in Murfreesboro, Tennessee. He earned his doctorate from McGill University in Canada, concentrating in Early Modern Philosophy and specializing in the philosophy of David Hume. Johnson is author of *Cornel West and Philosophy* (Routledge, 2002), and has also published articles in a variety of major scholarly journals such as *The Journal of Social Philosophy*, *Social Philosophy Today*, *The Journal of Philosophical Research*, *DIALOGUE: Canadian Philosophical Review*, *Metaphilosophy*, *The Southern Journal of Philosophy*, *The Southwest Philosophy Review*, and *The Journal of Thought*, to name a few. He has also contributed chapters to a number of books as well as entries in a forthcoming *Encyclopedia of African Religions and Philosophy*, ed. V. Y. Mudimbe (Kluwer Academic Publishing).

Violet M. Showers Johnson is Professor of History at Agnes Scott College, a women's liberal arts college in metro Atlanta, Georgia, USA. She teaches courses on US immigration history, African American history, African history, and the history of the African Diaspora. A scholar of the history of race, ethnicity, and immigration in the United States, she studies the experiences of immigrants of African descent. Her publications include *The Other Black Bostonians: West Indians in Boston, 1900-1950* (Indiana University Press, 2006), "'What, Then, is the African American?' African and Afro-Caribbean Identities in Black America," *Journal of American Ethnic History* (fall 2008), "Recreating Sustainable Communities in Exile: Leadership Roles of Sierra Leonean Refugee and Internally Displaced Women in Freetown, London, and Atlanta," *The International Journal of Environmental, Cultural, Economic, and Social Sustainability* (2009), and, with Marilyn B. Halter, "Young, Gifted and West African: Transnational Migrants Growing up in America," in *Helping Young Refugees and Immigrants Succeed: Public Policy, Aid, and Education*, Gerhard Sonnert and Gerald Holton, eds. (Palgrave, 2010). Currently, with Halter, she is completing a book entitled "African and American: Post-Colonial West Africans and the Remaking of the Atlantic World in the U.S."

Claude Julien (emeritus professor, Université de Tours, France) started research on African-American fiction as a social discourse with his doctoral dissertation (University of Paris VIII): "Childhood and adolescence in the African American novel, 1853-1969." He has taught American and African-American studies at the Universities of Le Mans and Tours in France, as well as at several American universities as an exchange professor where he also taught French studies. He has contributed articles to a number of journals, and edited or co-edited collections of essays on Jean Toomer (*Ellipses*), John Edgar Wideman (guest editor for *Callaloo* Vol. 22 n°3) and African-American detective fiction

(*CRAFT-2*). His most recent contribution is the editing of a collection "Reading Percival Everett: European Perspectives" (*CRAFT-4*). He served two terms of office as a member of the board of CAAR.

Ime A. S. Kerlee has a Ph.D. in Women's Studies from Emory University. She recently completed a dissertation fellowship at Middlebury College and a post-doctoral appointment at the University of New Mexico. Currently she is finishing additional funded research in the Dominican Republic that expands on her funded dissertation research on Dominican women transmigrants' negotiations of race, class, gender, and sexuality across transnational social spaces. She is also the Executive Director of the Women of Color Activist and Academic Collective that serves as a support and networking agency for women of color working on feminist research and/or activism inside and outside of academe.

María M. García Lorenzo (B.A. Universidad de Deusto, Ph. D. Universidad de Alcalá de Henares) has been a professor of American literature for over fifteen years at several Spanish universities. She currently teaches at the Universidad Nacional de Educación a Distancia. She specializes in modern American literature and cultural studies, and has published numerous articles on gender-related issues, popular forms, media culture and, more recently, the influence of science on US fiction.

Christopher Mulvey is Emeritus Professor of English at the University of Winchester. He taught in the United States from 1963 to 1978. He was President of the Collegium for African American Research from 2003 to 2007, and he was appointed a Fellow of the Royal Society for the Arts in 2008. His articles are numerous, and his books include *Anglo-American Landscapes* (1983), *Transatlantic Manners* (1990), *New York: City as Text* (1990), *Black Liberation in the Americas* (2001), *Dominic St John Mulvey: London Irishman* (2005), and *CLOTEL by William Wells Brown: An Electronic Scholarly Edition* (2006). He is presently working on a history of American transportation and culture.

Emil Sîrbulescu is Professor in English and American literature at the University of Craiova, Romania. His main research interests include: the African American novel, Shakespeare and the Renaissance, Literatures in English. He is the author of a number of books and articles published both in Romania and abroad (India, Poland, France, South Africa, Italy), such as: "The Talking Book: an Introduction to the African American Novel" (1999), and "Culture and National Identity in Mediaeval and Renaissance England" (2009). He is also a literary translator, having published translations from a number of British and American authors, such as William Makepeace Thackeray, Rudyard Kipling, Ursula LeGuin, and Kim Stanley Robinson.

Isabel Soto holds a Ph.D. from King's College and an M.A. from Queen Mary (both University of London), and a B.A. from the London School of Economics. She is an Associate Professor in English Studies in the Modern Languages Department of Spain's Universidad Nacional de Educación a Distancia. She was Visiting Scholar at Vassar College and an Honorary Fellow in the Scholars-in-Residence Program of the Schomburg Center for Black Research and Culture (1995-1997). In 2000 she co-founded the independent scholarly press *The Gateway Press*, devoted to publishing work on liminality and text. From 2008-2010 she was an Associate Fellow of the Rothermere American Institute, University of Oxford. Her research interests lie in liminality theory, African American studies, and diaspora and transatlantic studies. Her most recent book is a co-edition, *The Dialectics of Diasporas: Memory, Location, Gender* (2009). She is preparing a monograph on non-Anglophone constructions of the Black Atlantic, focusing on the work of Langston Hughes.

Małgorzata Ziółek-Sowińska graduated in 1997 from the Institute of Art, Music Department at Maria Curie-Skłodowska University, Lublin. She obtained her M.A. in music education for her thesis *The Polish Festival of Religious Song "Żakeria" 1990-1996*. In 2005 she graduated from the American Studies Center in the Institute of Americas and Europe at Warsaw University. Her M.A. Thesis was entitled *Emancipation and Redemption – Gender, Race, and Religion in American Cultural Debates and Selected Works by American Women Writers*. In 2005 she graduated from the Institute of English Studies, in the Neophilology Department of Warsaw University, after completing her M.A. Thesis on *Jazz and the Blues in the Harlem Renaissance and its Influence on American Culture in the 1920s and 1930s*. Since 2005 she has been a doctoral candidate at the Institute of English Studies, Warsaw University and is at work on her doctoral dissertation. Since 2006 she has been on the adjunct faculty at the Institute of English Studies, Warsaw School of Social Psychology where she teaches courses in cultural and literary studies and English. Małgorzata Ziółek-Sowińska has published articles on African American music and has taken part in Polish and international conferences which addressed the issue of American literature and culture. Her scholarly interests include African American literature and culture, spirituality and religiousness in African American music, American literature inspired by blues and jazz, history of African American music, black female vocalists, women in jazz, blues, soul and other African American music genres.